American Law

Lawrence M. Friedman

STANFORD UNIVERSITY

W·W·Norton & Company

New York · London

The text of this book is composed in Caledonia, with display type set in
Bulmer Italic. Composition and manufacturing by The Maple-Vail Book
Manufacturing Group
Book design by Jacques Chazaud

Library of Congress Cataloging in Publication Data

Friedman, Lawrence Meir, 1930–
American law.

Includes index.
1. Law—United States—Popular works.   I. Title.
KF387.F74   1984   349.73   83-42662

ISBN 0-393-01890-3

ISBN 0-393-95251-7 (pbk.)

W. W. Norton & Company, Inc., 500 Fifth Avenue, New York, N.Y. 10110
W. W. Norton & Company Ltd., 37 Great Russell Street, London WC1B 3NU

2 3 4 5 6 7 8 9 0

For Leah, Jane, Amy and Sarah

Contents

Acknowledgments

I would like to thank the staff of the Stanford Law Library, and especially Myron Jacobstein and Iris Wildman, for their help at so many points. I also want to thank my secretary, Joy St. John, who patiently worked on draft after draft during the period I was working on this book. Special thanks, too, to Leah for her strong and consistent social support.

Preface

This book is a general introduction to the law—and the legal system—of the United States. In a way, writing another book about American law is bringing another coal to Newcastle. There is certainly no shortage of books about our legal system. The Harvard Law School library, which is just about the biggest in the country (outside of the Library of Congress), has about a million and a quarter volumes. Perhaps three hundred thousand of these are books about American law. Every year, Harvard adds thousands more to its collection. Of the making of law books, there seems to be no end. Do we really need one more?

Perhaps we do. Almost all of those thousands and thousands of books are meant for the specialized eyes of the lawyers. Very few are written for the layman. True, in recent years, flocks of "how to do it" books have appeared: how to get your own divorce, how to avoid probate, how to deal with your landlord. There are also some popular handbooks about peoples' rights, how to "win big" in small-claims courts, and so on. Books of this kind are no novelty. In the nineteenth century, too, there were "how to do it" books, with names like *Every Man His Own Lawyer*. Some were extremely popular. One such book, published in 1867, claimed it would be valuable for just about everybody: the "city wholesale merchant," the retailer, the country merchant, attorneys, justices of the peace, farmers, mechanics—even the "discharged soldier or sailor" of the Civil War, who would find "all the instructions and forms necessary" to get back pay or pensions, in language "so plain as to make the whole matter perfectly clear and simple."[1]

Out of this vast literature, for lawyers and laymen, only a handful of books are designed to explain the system to general readers without having some immediate, practical goal. Most of these few books are somewhat specialized (constitutional law is a common subject; business law is another). There is room, then, for another book, written specifically for the general reader, giving an *overall* picture of the American legal system as it was and as it is, in operation.

Defining the legal system presents us with some tough questions. Exactly what is the legal system made of? What is its historical origin? What are its parts? Where does it begin, and where does it end? There are no simple answers—especially when we think of the hundreds of legal systems in the world and all the systems that existed in the past. Do we want answers broad enough to cover law in small tribes of nomads as well as in giant industrial societies; in societies ranging from those of the ancient Hittites and Chinese, through those of the Middle Ages, into the world of today? This would be a tall order indeed. Some scholars have tried to solve the problem. They have tried to define and describe law in a way that bridges all societies and all time periods. There is no general agreement on whether their results are worthwhile.

The goal of this book is more modest. It is an introduction to *American* law, and it is entitled, then, to focus on the United States and neglect radically different societies. After all, "law," "legal system," and "legal process" are all mental constructs. They are not things that exist in the real world. You cannot touch, taste, smell, or measure law. Any definition, then, has to be more or less conventional, or artificial. This does not mean that these definitions are wrong; it simply means that a definition is good if it is useful, and if we make clear to ourselves and to others exactly what we are about.

Our first job, then, is to lay out a kind of map of the American legal system—to catalog the subject of this book. Roughly, the criterion for including and excluding will be based on popular understanding: what scholars and laymen would agree is inside the circle of law. The starting point can be governmental rules; these are obviously part of what is understood as law. Clearly, too, whatever is concerned with making and carrying out these rules is inside the legal system. This means the courts, of course, and the legislatures, city halls, and county boards; also administrative agencies—the Internal Revenue Service, the Interstate Commerce Commission; state agencies that license doctors, teachers, and plumbers; and even the rather lowly zoning boards and sewer districts. They all make rules and regulations.

A legal system cannot enforce or carry out these rules and regulations without the work of a lot of men and women who carry out orders from above—policemen, for example, or elevator inspectors, or auditors who work for the tax bureau. We also include as part of the system our huge corps of lawyers. Their work—even their private dealings in the snug confines of a Wall Street office—is directly relevant to the legal system. Law is, after all, the lawyer's stock in trade. The lawyer advises his clients and tells them how to use law or how to pick a path among legal minefields. He works in the shadow of the law, and thus forms part of the legal system—indeed, a vital part.

But the activities of official agents of the law are not the whole story. Ordinary citizens participate in the legal system, not just by their actions, which may be law-abiding or not, but also by their attitudes and beliefs. The American legal system in operation is, thus, a very complex organism. It has many parts, many actors, and many aspects. The actors range from judges of the Supreme Court to hoboes sleeping in railroad yards; the institutions include courts, prisons, zoning boards, police departments, and countless others. As in all legal systems, what gives the organism life is the way rules, people, and institutions interact. How they do so is our general theme.

American Law

1

What Is a
Legal System?

*I*N MODERN AMERICAN SOCIETY, the legal system is everywhere
with us and around us. To be sure, most of us do not have much
contact with courts and lawyers except in emergencies. But not a day
goes by, and hardly a waking hour, without contact with law in its
broader sense—or with people whose behavior is modified or influenced by law. Law is a vast, though sometimes invisible, presence.

For example, when we go to the grocery and buy bread, milk,
soup, and potato chips, and when we make out a check for the food
and take the packages out to our car, we invoke or assume many facets
of legal order. To be sure, we do not feel that the legal system, like
some sort of Big Brother, is staring at us over our shoulder. But in a
sense it is: at us, and at the shopkeeper and his workers. Some branch
of law touches every aspect of this ordinary little piece of behavior.

To get to the store, we drove a car or walked, crossing several
streets. Traffic law walked or drove with us. Dozens of rules and regulations applied to conditions at the factory where the car was assembled—rules about the work force, and about the car itself, body and
engine. Inside the grocery store, there were labels on the cans and
packages—more rules and regulations; in the life history of every jar
of jam, every tube of toothpaste, rules and regulations are lurking.
And of course, workers in the store, like workers in the auto plant,
are covered by federal, state, and local labor regulations.

Indeed, most things we buy—TV sets, mattresses, shoes, whatever—are covered by some body of law, some rules about safety or

quality or other aspects of manufacture or use. Most buildings and places of business, including the grocery store itself, have to conform to building codes and to fire and safety regulations. Rules about standard weights and measures, employee comfort and safety, time and a half for overtime work, Sunday closing laws—the list is endless.

But there is more. When I buy a loaf of bread or a can of soup, I have entered into a contract, whether I realize it or not. If something goes wrong with the deal, the rules of contract law, of the Uniform Commercial Code, or of some branch of commercial law come into play, at least theoretically. The Commercial Code governs the rules that relate to checks; and a vast body of banking law is relevant to the way these pieces of paper provide credit and payment. If the can of soup is tainted and I get sick, I may have the right to sue the soup company; this will switch me onto still another legal track—the law of products liability, a branch of the law of torts.

This is not to say that we feel law lying on us like a suit of lead. Law is in the atmosphere, as light as air to the normal touch. (Manufacturers and storekeepers, of course, may see things differently.) Moreover, it is wrong to think of law as a tissue of don'ts, that is, as a kind of nagging or dictatorial parent. Much of the law is intended to make life easier, safer, happier, or better. When the norms do forbid something (or require something from somebody), it is usually for the specific benefit of somebody else. The law insists that soup companies put labels on their soup. They must tell us exactly what they put inside. This is a burden on the company, but is a benefit (or is supposed to be) for buyers of soup. There are also many ways in which the legal system *facilitates*, rather than forbids or harasses. It subsidizes; it promotes; it provides easy ways to reach desirable goals. The law about wills or contracts, for example, is basically about ways to do what you want to do, safely and efficiently; it is much less concerned with what not to do—with the price for disobeying rules. A great deal of law is facilitative in this way. It provides standard ways—routines—for reaching goals. It builds roads for the traffic of society.

Legal process is so important that it certainly behooves us to know as much as we can about it. But what is that "it"? What do people have in mind when they speak about "the law" or "legal process"? Much as we might want to avoid tricky problems of definition, we may in the end have to say exactly what we mean by the terms *law*, *legal system*, and *legal process*.

To define them is a tricky job. *Law* is an everyday word, part of the basic vocabulary. But it is a word of many meanings, as slippery as glass, as elusive as a soap bubble. It is impossible to talk sensibly about *the* meaning of law, as if law were some concrete object in the world around us—something we could feel or smell, like a chair or a dog. But we can try to get at some sort of working definition.

One way to start is to listen to the way people use words like *law*, and ask what they are referring to. To begin with, people seem to have in mind the network of rules and regulations that surrounds us. This is clear from such expressions as "breaking the law" or "obeying the law." It is also what the word *law* means in sentences like "It's against the law to drive ninety miles an hour." There may be, and certainly are, other shades of meaning; but the idea of rules and regulations is usually at the core. In ordinary speech, then, the word *law* is connected with "laws," that is, with rules and regulations.

Donald Black, in *The Behavior of Law*,[1] puts forward a concise, deceptively simple definition. Law, according to Black, is "governmental social control." By "social control" he means social rules and processes which try to encourage good or useful conduct or discourage bad conduct. There is a law against burglary; and police, judges, and criminal courts try to put teeth into it. All together, they form a pretty obvious example of social control (or at least attempted social control). The whole criminal justice system plainly aims in this direction. For the person in the street, it is perhaps the most familiar, obvious part of the legal system.

But law is more than criminal justice. The rest of the law (what lawyers call civil justice) is actually larger in size, however you measure it, and almost certainly more important. To make Black's definition work, we have to understand "social control" in a broader sense. It must mean the whole network of rules and processes which attach legal consequences to particular bits of behavior.

Take, for example, the ordinary rules of the law of torts. If I drive carelessly or too fast in a parking lot and smash somebody else's fender, there will be definite legal consequences. What I did is no crime; I will not go to jail; but I (or my insurance company) may have to pay for the damage. Directly or indirectly, this depends on rules of tort law—rules about what happens when one person injures another or damages his property.

These rules may change the way I behave. They certainly affect my pocketbook and the rates of insurance I pay. Hence these rules, too, are part of the system of social control. The rules reward some behavior and punish other behavior (or try to), just as surely as the criminal justice system. They distribute costs and benefits among people depending on how they behave. Careless drivers have to pay; victims get money.

Law, according to Black, is social control, but it is social control of one particular kind. Law is *governmental* social control. There are other kinds as well. Teachers use rules (and rewards and punishments) to make children behave; parents use rules (and rewards and punishments) at home. Both teachers and parents also hope to mold behavior for the future. Organized religions, too, are concerned with behavior—with social control. They aim to induce their members to live a godly or proper life, as the religion defines it.

But these forms of social control are not governmental: they are not official, not part of the state apparatus. Under Black's definition, then, they are not law. At least we can say that in a country like the United States they are not part of the *official* law. But there are, in fact, two distinct ways to look at law: one insists that law is made up exclusively of official, governmental acts; the other takes a broader approach.

The main focus of this book is not on "law" so much as on what can be called the *legal system*. The word *law* often refers only to rules and regulations; but a line can be drawn between the rules and regulations themselves and those structures, institutions, and processes which breathe life into them. This expanded domain is the "legal system."

It is plain that the legal system has more in it than simply rules. There are, to begin with, rules *about* rules. There are rules of procedure, and rules that tell us how to tell a rule from a nonrule. To be more concrete, these are rules about jurisdiction, pleadings, judges, courts, voting in legislatures, and the like. A rule that says that no bill becomes a law in New Mexico unless both houses pass it and the governor signs it is a rule about rules. It explains one way to make a legal rule in New Mexico. In a famous book, H.L.A. Hart called these rules about rules "secondary rules;" he called rules about actual behavior "primary rules." The rules against burglarizing the grocery store or against driving at ninety miles an hour to get there would be examples of primary rules. Law, according to Hart, is the union of primary and secondary rules.[2]

Both primary and secondary rules are, however, rules; in a sense, all rules are directives about how to behave. Our example of a secondary rule, for example, is after all a rule about how lawmakers should behave in New Mexico. Rules are important; but a legal system cannot consist of rules alone. We could read all the rules in a book and still know very little about the legal system in operation. Law is only words on paper if we do not consider the way people in society actually think, feel, and behave in regard to law. Orders, commands, and rules are blank and empty unless something happens—unless they make something *move*.

This, of course, is not a fresh idea. It is something that everybody knows. People say that a certain law is a "dead letter," while another rule is "in force." Or we use the term *living law*. Dead letters are not living law, just as a dead language like Sanskrit or Latin is unlike a language that comes tumbling from the mouths of real people, here and now. Living law is law that is alive in a legal system.

For example, the national speed limit right now is fifty-five miles per hour. This is a legal rule. But the living law—the actual practice—is much more complicated. The rule itself does not tell us, for one thing, that people can actually drive at sixty, or maybe even sixty-five, without any risk of arrest. Police do not take the speed limit literally. If, on the other hand, somebody barrels down the road at seventy or eighty, and a police car is around, its siren will scream and the police will come after the speeder. Each situation calls forth a particular interaction of the legal system's many elements, not only rules and institutions, but also people and their behavior.

Elements of a Legal System

We now have a preliminary, rough idea of what we mean when we talk about our legal system. There are other ways to analyze this complicated and important set of institutions. To begin with, the legal system has *structure*. The system is constantly changing; but parts of it change at different speeds, and not every part changes as fast as certain other parts. There are persistent, long-term patterns—aspects of the system that were here yesterday (or even in the last century) and will be around for a long time to come. This is the structure of the legal system—its skeleton or framework, the durable part, which gives a kind of shape and definition to the whole.

There is a Supreme Court in this country, made up of nine justices; the Court has been around since the late eighteenth century; it is likely to be around in the twenty-first century; and its work habits change very slowly. The structure of a legal system consists of elements of this kind: the number and size of courts; their jurisdiction (that is, what kind of cases they hear, and how and why); and modes of appeal from one court to another. Structure also means how the legislature is organized, how many members sit on the Federal Trade Commission, what a president can (legally) do or not do, what procedures the police department follows, and so on. Structure, in a way, is a kind of cross section of the legal system—a kind of still photograph, which freezes the action.

Another aspect of the legal system is its *substance*. By this is meant the actual rules, norms, and behavior patterns of people inside the system. This is, first of all, "the law" in the popular sense of the term—the fact that the speed limit is fifty-five miles an hour, that burglars can be sent to prison, that "by law" a pickle maker has to list his ingredients on the label of the jar.

But it is also, in a way, "substance" that the police arrest only drivers doing seventy instead of sixty; or that a burglar without a criminal record gets probation; or that the Food and Drug Administration is easy (or tough) on the pickle industry. These are working patterns of the living law. Substance also means the "product" that people within the legal system manufacture—the decisions they turn out, the new rules they contrive. We know something about the substance of the legal system when we know how many people are arrested for arson in any given year; how many deeds are registered in Alameda County, California; how many sex discrimination cases are filed in federal court; how many times a year the Environmental Protection Agency complains that a company dumped toxic wastes.

The last paragraph makes it plain that the ideas of substance in this book are not the same as those that, let us say, some lawyers put forward. The stress here is on living law, not just rules in law books. And this brings us to the third component of a legal system, which is, in some ways, the least obvious: the *legal culture*. By this we mean people's attitudes toward law and the legal system—their beliefs, values, ideas, and expectations. In other words, it is that part of the general culture which concerns the legal system. These ideas and opinions are, in a sense, what sets the legal process going. When people say that Americans are litigious (whether this is true or not)—that is, that Americans go to court at the drop of a hat—people are saying something about legal culture. We talk about legal culture all the time, without knowing it. If we point out that Catholics tend to avoid divorce (because of religion), that people who live in slums distrust policemen, that middle-class people make complaints to government agencies more often than people on welfare, or that the Supreme Court enjoys high prestige, all these are statements about legal culture.

The legal culture, in other words, is the climate of social thought and social force which determines how law is used, avoided, or abused. Without legal culture, the legal system is inert—a dead fish lying in a basket, not a living fish swimming in its sea.

Another way to visualize the three elements of law is to imagine legal "structure" as a kind of machine. "Substance" is what the machine manufactures or does. The "legal culture" is whatever or whoever decides to turn the machine on and off, and determines how it will be used.

Every society, every country, every community has a legal culture. There are always attitudes and opinions about law. This does not mean, of course, that everybody shares the same ideas. There are many subcultures: white and black, young and old, Catholic, Protestant, Jew, rich and poor, easterners and westerners, gangsters and policemen, lawyers, doctors, shoe salesmen, bankers. One particularly important subculture is the legal culture of "insiders," that is, the judges and lawyers who work inside the legal system itself. Since law is their business, their values and attitudes make a good deal of difference to the system. At least this is a plausible suggestion; the exact extent of this influence is a matter of some dispute among scholars.

These three elements, in American law—structure, substance, and culture—are the subjects of this book. It will take a look at the way the American legal system is organized, at what it does, and how it does it; and it will be especially conscious of legal culture—ideas and forces outside the law machine that make it stop and go. The three elements can be used to analyze anything the legal system does. Take, for example, the famous death penalty case, *Furman* v. *Georgia* (1972).[3] In this case, a bare majority of the United States Supreme Court—five judges out of nine—struck down death penalty laws in all of the states which had them, on constitutional grounds. (Later on, the Court backtracked somewhat; this subject will be dealt with in another chapter.)

To understand what happened in *Furman* we must first grasp the structure of the legal system. Otherwise, we will have no idea how the case worked its way up from court to court, nor why the case was in the end decided in Washington, D. C., and not in Georgia, where it started. We will have to know something about federalism, the Constitution, the relationship between courts and legislatures, and many other long-run, long-lasting features of American law.

But this is only the beginning. The case itself takes up no less than

230 pages of print in the official reports. (There are seven separate opinions.) As we plow through these pages, we are enmeshed in the substance of constitutional law. The case, to begin with, turns in part on whether the death penalty is "cruel and unusual" punishment; if it is, the Eight Amendment to the Constitution specifically forbids it. There are long discussions in the opinions about what "cruel and unusual" means, what earlier cases have said, what doctrines and rulings have been woven about this phrase.

But structure and substance together do not explain why the case came up and why it came out as it did. We have to know something about social context—the movement to get rid of capital punishment, who and what was behind the case, what organizations were fighting for and against the death penalty, and why the issue came up when it did—that is, the attitudes, values, and beliefs about the death penalty, law, courts, and so on, which explain how the case got started in the first place.

We might be interested, too, in a fourth element: *impact*, that is, what difference the decision made. The Supreme Court spoke; who listened? We know some obvious facts about immediate consequences. For one thing, the men and women on death row never kept their dates with the gas chamber or the electric chair. Their sentences were automatically commuted to long-term imprisonment. There were other impacts, as well, in substance, structure, and legal culture. *Furman* set off a storm of discussion, furious activity in state legislatures, and ultimately a flock of new lawsuits. It may have had more remote (but important) consequences, too: on the prestige of the Supreme Court, on the crime rate, on national morality. The more remote the consequences, the harder to know and measure them.

We know surprisingly little, in general, about the impact of decisions, even their immediate impact. It is not the job of courts to find out what happens to their litigants once they leave the courtroom, or what happens to the larger society. But impact is the subject of a small, growing body of research; from time to time the evidence from these studies will be noted or mentioned in this book.

The Functions of the Legal System

But why have a legal system at all? What does it do for society? In other words, what functions does it perform?

One kind of answer has already been given. The legal system is part of the system of *social control.* In the broadest sense, this may be *the* function of the legal system; everything else is, in a way, secondary or subordinate. To put it another way: the legal system is concerned with controlling behavior. It is a kind of official traffic cop. It tells people what to do and not to do; and it backs up its directives with force.

The legal system can do this in a very direct, very literal way. There *are* traffic cops, after all, who stand on busy corners, waving traffic this way or that, and they are certainly a part of the legal system as we have defined it. The criminal justice system is probably the most familiar example of law as social control. Here we find some of society's heavy artillery: judges, juries, jails, wardens, police, criminal lawyers. People who break the law, and other "deviants," are chased, caught, and sometimes punished; this is control in the most raw and basic sense.

A second broad function of law is what we can call *dispute settlement*. A dispute, according to Richard L. Abel, is the public assertion of inconsistent claims over something of value.[4] Two people both insist they own the same piece of land. Or a VW Rabbit rear-ends a 1978 Chevrolet, and the driver of the Chevrolet threatens to sue the driver of the Rabbit. Or the marriage of Mark and Linda Jones breaks up, and they squabble over who gets the house, the child, or the money. These are all disputes in Abel's sense: inconsistent claims to something of value.

Many times, there literally *is* some concrete thing (or person) that the parties are arguing about, something you can touch or squeeze or hug—a child, a bundle of money, a house. At other times, the "thing" is more abstract or nebulous: the right to citizenship, a reputation that has been dragged in the mud, damages for pain and suffering, somebody's goodwill or peace of mind. Disputes can be big or little, raucous or moderate. The phrase *dispute settlement* is usually reserved for fairly small-scale, local disagreements between individuals or private businesses. There are, of course, bigger, more basic disagreements in society—disagreements between classes or groups. There are, for example, clashes between labor and capital; or between regions of the country; between black and white, North and South; between the young and the old; between people who want to protect the beaches and people who prefer offshore oil.

It might be a good idea to give these macrodisagreements a name of their own, and call them conflicts rather than disputes. In any event, the legal system is as concerned with conflicts as it is with disputes, if not more so. The legal system, in other words, is an agency of conflict resolution as well as an agency of dispute settlement. Courts come immediately to mind in this connection, that is, as the institutions that help most notably to bring conflicts to an end. This they indeed do. But the work of the legislatures is probably, on the whole, more important. It is Congress and the state legislatures that iron out (if anyone does) most of the bitter battles between employers and labor unions, between businessmen and the Sierra Club, between retired people and the people who pay social security taxes. It is in the city council of Chicago, say, that boosters who want new stores and factories and highways bump up against people who want to preserve old mansions and fight for their neighborhoods. In the suburbs, it is councils and zoning boards that deal with conflict between those who want light industry and shopping centers, and "residentialists" who want nothing but one-family houses, green lawns, and rose-bushes.

The various functions of law overlap, of course. No single function has a clear and perfect boundary. The line between a dispute and a conflict is woefully indistinct. Other functions of law are even less clear-cut. One of these functions is the redistributive or *social engineering* function. This refers to the fact that law is sometimes used to bring about planned social change—change imposed from on top, that is, by the government. Social engineering is a very prominent aspect of modern welfare states. The United States—as do all other Western countries—levies taxes on people who have money and uses this money to give cash, food stamps, medical benefits, and sometimes cheap housing to the poor and to others who are felt to deserve it.

Law, then, embodies the planned or "engineered" aspect of social policy—whatever is done deliberately through public choice. It stands opposed to the unplanned market. In the market, the law of supply and demand sets prices. The market decides which products and businesses grow fat and rich and which ones shrivel and die. The market distributes goods and services, benefits and burdens, through a system of prices. It is a kind of auction in which buyers bid for goods; scarce, desirable goods go up in price, while common, less wanted goods go down.

The legal system is in a way a rival scheme for distributing goods and services. It, too, rations scarce commodities. To raise an army during times of war, we could literally *buy* soldiers; and in the past some countries did exactly that. Today we would never use this system. Instead, we would get soldiers through a draft. Congress would pass a law and make rules about who would or must serve in the army. There would be rules and regulations about deferments, city and state quotas, how to handle conscientious objectors, and how to deal with recruits with flat feet or poor eyesight. The market would have little or nothing to do with these rules. If we change the rules, we change the allocation system. In other words, whether we realize it or not, our legal system is a kind of giant rationing system, a giant planning system, a giant system of social engineering.

We should not push the term social engineering too far. This gives the legal system too much of an active, reforming flavor. Most of the time, legal allocations do exactly the opposite: rather than change things, they tend to keep the status quo intact. This function can be called *social maintenance.* The legal system keeps the machinery going more or less as it was in the past. After all, even the "free market"— even the "invisible hand"—needs law to guarantee the rules of fair play. Even in the most laissez-faire system, the law enforces bargains, creates a money system, and tries to maintain a framework of order and respect for property.

Every society has its own structure; and this structure does not stay put by magic or accident, or even by inertia or the laws of gravity. What makes the structure persist over the years is, first of all, social behavior and social attitudes—customs, culture, traditions, and informal norms. But these, in modern society, do not seem to be enough. Contemporary society needs the muscle and bone of law to stay healthy, or even to stay alive. If somebody breaks into my house and refuses to get out, I can call "the law" and get him driven out. If my neighbor owes me $300, I can go to court and collect my money. The law defends my rights, including my property rights. This is the social maintenance function. The criminal law is part of it. After all, the crimes most commonly prosecuted are property crimes—theft, burglary, embezzlement. These are offenses against people who own property. If we punish people who steal things we are at the same time protecting people who own the things that are stolen; hence we are preserving the economic (and social) structure of society.

It is clear, then, that the law protects the status quo in a very direct and obvious way. The phrase *status quo* is not a happy one. It is usually spoken with a sneer; it sounds static, even reactionary. It suggests that law (and society) are fat and hidebound, upholding the privileged against the poor and the helpless. This may or may not be true. Every society—even revolutionary societies—tries to preserve some parts of its status quo. The revolutionary society tries to preserve and strengthen the revolution. The traditional society tries to preserve and strengthen tradition. Any society would immediately collapse unless it took steps to preserve itself. There is no such thing as a total revolutionary—somebody who wants to change everything. Whether it is good or bad to keep up old ways depends on what the old ways are and which old ways we are talking about.

The central fact of human life is that nobody lives forever. People serve out their little terms of life and die. But societies and institutions go on. A social structure is much more durable than the people who fill its roles. Structure is like a play—*Hamlet*, for example—in which the text carries on from generation to generation, but with different actors to play the parts and with new versions, new sets, new costumes every once in a while. We know that norms, morals, and customs help bridge generations. We realize that each generation teaches its language and culture to its children, so that the next generation carries on pretty much as its parents did. If we speak English, so will our children, and their childrens' children, too, even though a newborn baby speaks no language at all and would learn Hausa or Portuguese if that was what was spoken all around it.

Of course, we do have to remember that social roles are not exactly like the role of Hamlet in Shakespeare's play; they are much more subject to change. And social change is taking place today at a fast and furious pace, faster than ever before. But even so, not everything changes at once and in every sphere of life. A man or woman of a century ago who fell asleep like Rip Van Winkle and came to life again today would be amazed by many things: cars, computers, the "sexual revolution." He might have trouble adjusting to our world. Yet many other things—clothes, customs, buildings, ways of thought—would be at least vaguely familiar; some aspects of life would strike him as exactly the same.

Continuity—and yet change. These are the constants of social life. And the legal system plays a crucial role in promoting both continuity and change. It helps bridge generations, but it also helps direct social change into smooth and constructive channels. For example, there are laws about the inheritance of wealth—about ways to make out a will, about death taxes, about the rights of widows and widowers. We talk about the "dead hand," somewhat ruefully. But without the "dead hand"—without a person's right to determine, more or less, what will happen to his money when he dies—each generation might have to rebuild its structure from scratch; each generation would have to make up who is rich and who is poor all over again. That might be either good or bad; it would certainly be different.

All our legal institutions—courts, legislatures, and agencies alike—are designed, at least in part, for both continuity and change. They are designed to permit change to take place, but in a regular, orderly, patterned way. After all, every time Congress sits, every time the Delaware legislature meets in Dover, every time the city council of Omaha goes into session, volumes and volumes of laws are spewed out. Every new law changes *something;* every law tries to attack some social problem, big or small. Happily, it is an orderly process (most of the time) in this country. Like the rest of the world, America is trying to ride the wild horse of change instead of letting it gallop off in all directions. The legal system is one process for preventing too much change and changes that are too fast; it is a process for limiting volcanic bursts of change. It does not always succeed. Nor should it.

Claims of Right. When we think about social control, we usually have in mind a picture of law and government in control of their "subjects"—the people underneath them. Social control is a policeman giving out a ticket for speeding, for example. But we need controls over policemen, too. In our society, there is no horse without a bridle. Nobody—not the mayor of Memphis, not the governor of New York, not the president, not the Supreme Court itself—is supposed to be truly, absolutely supreme. Only law is supreme.

This, to be sure, is theory. Practice is more complicated and considerably less than perfect. Everybody knows that some people in authority abuse their positions. We know about bribery; we know about the petty tyranny of bureaucrats. To correct these evils, there are controls built into the system. Law, in other words, has the further job of keeping an eye on the rulers themselves. This is, in a way, a process of turning social control upside down. (In another way, it is simply another form of social control, but over a selected subgroup in society.) Control over controllers is of course a basic theme in American government; it is the idea behind "judicial review" (the power of courts to decide when other branches of government have overstepped the mark). Courts regularly, and sometimes fearlessly, rebuke or override Congress, administrative agencies, the police, and even the president himself, when they have gone beyond what the court feels are the limits of legitimate authority. This is especially true of those limits written into the Constitution or put there by courts in the process of "interpreting" the text.

We also sometimes speak of "claims of right." By this we mean claims of private citizens or of companies against the government. Claims of right help control abuse of power; but most of the time what the claimant wants is relief from some particular mistake of government. There are innumerable examples: pension claims, benefit claims, grievances and complaints about the million and one ways a civil servant in twentieth century America can bungle his job. To take one example out of thousands: a man named James T. Blanks, living in Alabama, who said he was sixty-two years old, applied in 1967 for old-age benefits. The Department of Health, Education, and Welfare turned him down. According to their notion, he was only sixty, two years short of eligibility. They got this idea from a school census record of Marshall County, Alabama. Blanks countered with a family Bible, federal census records, insurance policies, and affidavits from neighbors and relatives. The HEW people were not impressed; they stuck by their original decision. Blanks went to court. He sued HEW and won his case.[5]

Citizens do not, of course, always win these cases. Probably more often than not, the government comes out ahead. In a Pennsylvania case, a state policeman, Joseph McIlvaine, was forced out of his job because (according to the rules) he was too old to serve. This seemed grossly unfair to McIlvaine, and he sued to get back on the force. The Pennsylvania courts turned him down.[6] He tried to get the Supreme Court of the United States to take his case; but this, too, failed.[7]

As we leaf through reported cases, federal and state, we find countless claims of right. They are, perhaps, the tip of an iceberg. Such claims seem to be getting more common. Why this should be so, and whether they bring about effective control of government, are questions that will be taken up later in this book.

The Common Law and Its Competitors

There is a bewildering variety of legal systems in the world. Every country has its own; and in the United States, each state has a legal system for dealing with its internal affairs, with the national (federal) system on top of it. A law student usually studies the law of a single country—the one he or she plans to practice in. This is true of the United States too; legal education sticks largely to American law. Our legal education, though, is fairly national-minded; it tends to ignore differences between the law of the various states. The curriculum and the materials are much the same in Oregon and in Alabama. Except in this regard, the study of law is quite parochial. Medicine is more or less the same all over the world; and this is generally true of all the natural and applied sciences: electrical engineering in Uganda is no different, in essence, from electrical engineering as understood in China or the United States. But law is strictly defined by nationality: it stops at the border. Outside its home base, it has no validity at all.

No two legal systems, then, are exactly alike. Each is specific to its country or its jurisdiction. This does not mean, of course, that every legal system is entirely different from every other legal system. Not at all. When two countries are similar in culture and tradition, their legal systems are likely to be similar as well. No doubt the law of El Salvador is very much like the law of Honduras. The laws of Australia and New Zealand are not that far apart.

We can also clump legal systems together into clusters, or "families"—groups of legal systems that have important traits of structure, substance, or culture in common. The word *family* is used deliberately: in most cases, members of a legal family are related, that is, they have a common parent or ancestor, or else have borrowed their laws from a common source. English settlers carried English law with them to the American colonies, to Canada, Australia, New Zealand, Jamaica, Barbados, the Bahamas. Many countries in the world once were part of the British Empire. These countries are now independent and have distinct legal systems of their own; but they have kept their basic traditions. The legal systems of the English-speaking world have a definite family resemblance. The Spanish brought *their* law to Latin America. Spanish-speaking countries in that part of the world share many traits and traditions.

The largest, most important family is the so-called *civil-law* family. Members of this family owe a common debt to Roman law. The ancient Romans were great lawmakers. Their tradition never completely died out in Europe, even after the barbarians overran what was left of the Roman Empire. In the Middle Ages, Roman law, in its classic form, was rediscovered and revived; even today, codes of law in Europe reflect "the influence of Roman law and its medieval revival."[8] Western Europe—France, Germany, Italy, Spain, Portugal, and the Low Countries, among others—is definitely civil-law country. Through Spain and Portugal, the civil law traveled to Latin America. The French brought it to their colonies in Africa. In Canada, the civil law is dominant in the French-speaking province of Quebec. It strongly colors the legal systems of two unlikely outposts, Scotland and Louisiana. It plays a major role, too, in countries like Japan and Turkey, which stand completely outside the historical tradition but which borrowed chunks of Roman law in recent times, in hopes of getting modern in a hurry.

Civil-law systems are, generally speaking, "codified" systems: the basic law is set out in *codes*. These are statutes, or rather superstatutes, enacted by the national parliament, which arrange whole fields of law in an orderly, logical, and comprehensive way. Historically, the most important of the codes was the civil code of France, the so-called Code Napoleon, which appeared in 1804. It has had a tremendous influence on the form and substance of most later codes. Another influential code was Germany's, which dates from the late nineteenth century.

During the Renaissance, European legal scholarship was dazzled by the power and beauty of the rediscovered Roman law. One country, however, managed to resist the so-called "reception," that is, the acceptance of Roman law. England alone was not seduced. It held fast to its native traditions. Many ideas and terms from Roman and European law did, to be sure, creep into English law; but the core legal system of this island held firm. This tenacious local system was the so-called *common law*. It differed and continues to differ in many ways from the legal order in its neighboring countries. For one thing, the common law resisted codification. There never was an English equivalent of the Napoleonic Code. The basic principles of law were not found primarily in acts of Parliament, but in the *case law*—the body of opinions written by judges, and developed by judges in the course of deciding particular cases. The doctrine of "precedent"—the maxim that a judge is bound in some way by what has already been decided—is strictly a common-law doctrine. The common law also has its own peculiar features of substance, structure, and culture. The jury, for example, is a common-law institution. So is the "trust," an arrangement in which a person (or bank) as trustee receives money or property to invest and manage for the benefit of certain beneficiaries.

The common law is no longer confined to a single small country. The English brought it to their colonies, and in most cases it took root and thrived. All common-law countries were once colonies of Great Britain, or, in some cases, colonies of colonies. Roughly speaking, the common law reigns wherever the English language is spoken. This means our own country, for one, plus Canada (outside Quebec), Australia, New Zealand, and new nations such as Jamaica and Trinidad. Other systems contributed bits and pieces here and there—remnants of Spanish-Mexican law poke through the surface in California and

Texas—but English law is by far the strongest historical element in our own legal system (Louisiana stands off in a corner by itself). England and the United States have been drifting apart, legally speaking, for more than 200 years, and there are now big chasms between them.

The civil-law system was described as the dominant system in Western Europe. No mention was made of Eastern Europe, which is a rather difficult area for purposes of classification. Some scholars feel that the socialist countries are distinctive enough to make up a separate family of legal systems. Other scholars are not so sure. Russia and its satellites once had close ties with the civil-law systems. Socialist revolutions have transformed these countries; but legal resemblances to Western Europe are still fairly close. This is why some scholars treat these systems as still part of that family—black sheep, perhaps, or oddball deviants, but family members nonetheless.

The controversy is perhaps nothing but a matter of definition—of words, if you will. Obviously, Russian, Polish, and Hungarian law have a lot in common, and many of their common traits set them sharply apart from, say, Dutch law. There are no collective farms in Holland, for example, and hence no rules about collective farms. In Holland, too, most lawyers work in the private sector and are not employees of the government, as are lawyers in Russia; the economy is not centrally planned; there is no censorship. Marx—and the Russian bear—have laid heavy hands on the law of the "people's democracies" in Eastern Europe. They are deeply influenced by Russian law and by the functional requirements of their socialist economies.

In general, it is a fairly crude business to assign legal systems to this or that family. There are always troublesome cases at the margin. The Scandinavian countries, for example, do not fit in very well with their European neighbors; some scholars assign them a family of their own. Besides, a legal system is not an exercise in history; it is a problem-solving machine, and the problems that face it are the problems of today, not yesterday. Legal tradition may explain some aspects of the shape and style of a system; but it is probably not as decisive a factor as most lawyers—and laymen—think.

For example, Haiti and France are supposed to have very similar legal systems; they are close relatives inside a single family. The Haitian system is derived from that of France. This is certainly true on paper. But is it true when we look at the living law? Haiti is a dictatorship and is desperately poor, almost entirely rural and illiterate. France is rich; has a parliamentary system; and is urban, and highly industrialized. The two countries may have codes of law in common (on the books), but it is possible that the "living law" of France has more in common with the law of England than with the law of Haiti, even though English law belongs to a different family.

This is a guess, because we know surprisingly little about how legal systems actually work. But it is certainly plausible to assume that the level of development in a country has an enormous influence on that country's law. If you ever traveled by car in England and France, you noticed (or took for granted) that the traffic rules in the two countries are basically the same, even though the English insist on driving on the "wrong" side of the road. Traffic rules are similar in every country touched by the automotive revolution. Technology is a great lawmaker—and a great leveler. The railroad, the problems it brought, and the opportunities it created practically rewrote the law books of the United States in the nineteenth century. In this century, the automobile has had almost as big an influence on law. Neither the railroad nor the automobile shows much respect for what family a legal system belongs to.

It is hard to exaggerate the importance of technology in explaining the history of laws. The pages of our own history virtually shout this out. Tort law (basically the law of accidents) was practically speaking the child of the railroad; it is now the adopted child of the automobile. The automobile is responsible for a vast body of rules about roads, traffic, auto safety, buying cars on the installment plan, and so on. Its invention has changed society (and thus the law) in absolutely fundamental ways. We take many of these changes for granted. Could either urban or suburban life survive without cars? Yet the automobile is not something that separates civil-law and common-law countries. It poses the same problems for all of them. It does indeed separate modern systems from older or more primitive systems. And it has a deep impact on the way we live and on the structure of freedom.

Only two or three main groups—families—of legal systems have been mentioned thus far. But the civil-law and common-law systems are not the only families. Every society has a legal system; thus, many countries have clearly been left out. No mention has been made, for example, of the legal systems of the Far East, or the sacred-law systems of classical India, Israel, and the Islamic countries. Islamic law, in particular, is a living force in the world today. In Saudi Arabia, for example, it has official status; and it has made a dramatic comeback in other Moslem countries, most notably in Iran under the Ayatollah Khomeini. Africa is the home of dozens and dozens of tribal systems of law. Many of them are extremely interesting; some have been carefully studied; all are under great pressure from Western codes and rules in this age of modernization.

This book is about American law, and it is impossible to go into the details of these various systems. But comparisons and contrasts are always interesting and sometimes enlightening. It is not fashionable any more to talk about "primitive law"; but it is as plain as day that the law of a tribe of hunters and gatherers, or the law of the nomad empire of Attila or Genghis Khan, has got to be different from the law of modern America. Does it make sense to talk about evolutionary patterns in the history of law—progressions moving inexorably from stage to stage? In other words, do legal systems evolve in some definite, patterned way, starting from stage A and passing through B and C on the road to D? Are there natural stages and a fixed order of progression?

This is a classic question of legal scholarship. There is no definite answer; some people even deny that the question makes sense. A small band of people with spears and knives has legal needs very different from ours; a feudal system generates one kind of law, big-city America quite another. Changes in social systems and technology necessarily push a legal system toward new burdens and new habits. The railroad and the automobile almost literally *made* the modern law of torts, to repeat one example. Legal systems are never static. They change with changing times. In a country like ours, constantly moving, squirming, changing, the law is especially dynamic. Whether we call the main lines of growth "evolution" is only a question of words.

Whatever one might think of legal evolution, legal dynamics are a fact. The rate of change, the kind of change, the effects of change—these are all matters of vital interest at the very core of the questions discussed in this book.

2

Law: Formal
and Informal

*W*HEN PEOPLE THINK about law or talk about law, what they usually have in mind is the *official* legal system, that is, the system run by the government—the one we pay taxes to support. Many definitions of law make this concept explicit: Donald Black, for example, has defined law as governmental social control.

But there are other ways to define law; and some of these are broader than Black's definition. The legal scholar Lon Fuller once defined law as "the enterprise of subjecting human conduct to the governance of rules."[1] Of course, the government is very much in the business of subjecting behavior to rules (or trying to); but it is not the only entity playing this game. Fuller deliberately framed his definition in such a way that it was not limited to official rules—rules put out by the government. He said simply: rules. If we take his definition at face value, the government has no monopoly on law, in this or any society.

Fuller's definition, in fact, points to quite another way of looking at law. He asks us to look not only at the source of legal process—that is, whether it comes from the government and wears an official badge, so to speak—but also at the process itself. Any organization of any size has rules and tries to enforce them. The bigger the organization, the more rules it is likely to have. Students at university or college do not have to be told that schools make rules and regulations and try to enforce them. These rules and regulations are part of the life all around them. Just as obviously, any business bigger than a mom-and-pop store—and any hospital, prison, or factory—must work with rules: rules about the jobs of employees, about buying equipment, about handling customers and patients, about income and outgo, about bosses and underlings, and so on.

How does a company enforce these rules? It has no official policemen or courts. But it certainly has sanctions—ways of delivering rewards and punishments. A company cannot hang a worker, whip him, or deport him to a desert island; but it can fire somebody who comes in late all the time, or is drunk on the job, or refuses to follow the rules. At one time, the boss had unlimited power to hire and fire. He was rule maker, judge, and jury. But in large companies, at least, this is no longer the case. The process tends to be highly "legalized" today. There are complicated procedures for handling discipline on the job and for settling grievances. Where the work force is unionized, the labor contract may give details on how each "case" should be handled. Often, both sides agree to let a neutral third person—an arbitrator—make final decisions. Today, even nonunion companies tend to have some kind of grievance and discipline procedures.

This is not the only way in which a big company resembles a kind of private government, with a private legal system. Not only will a big company have private "courts"; it will also have private police. General Motors, for example, had 4,200 plant guards in 1978; this meant that the police force of this company was bigger than the police departments in any except the five largest cities in this country.[2] Security guards wear uniforms and often look like the police who are paid by the state. They often walk regular beats, and they can and do make arrests.

The private police business is growing very fast. But it is not a new phenomenon. The famous Pinkerton National Detective Agency ("the eye that never sleeps") guarded Abraham Lincoln, spied on crooked railroad employees, and supplied scabs to companies whose workers were on strike.[3] Other detective agencies sprang up in the late nineteenth and early twentieth centuries. Companies stung by losses from crime, inside and outside, have turned more and more to private police and detectives for help.

In a sense, then, every institution has a legal system of sorts. It would not stretch Fuller's definition very much to claim that even families make law and enforce it. Mother and father lay down rules and make decisions all the time: who does the dishes, when the children can stay out past ten, how much TV they can watch. There are rules, big and small—that nobody gets more than one slice of cake at a birthday party; or that chores and toys must be shared. These rules are, in a sense, part of the "law" inside the family.

There is nothing wrong in defining law to include these rules, and the way fathers and mothers run families; but to do so makes the subject unwieldy. To use the word *law* in this sense swallows up all of human life and reclassifies all patterns of behavior as legal. Nonetheless, it is good to remember that the name "law" can be applied to processes of many kinds—even those that are very informal, very far from the official legal system. What makes them like official law is what Fuller pointed out: they subject behavior to rules.

There are some processes which are both formal and official (in the sense of governmental). This is true, for example, of any law that Congress passes. Other norms are part of the law, but are unwritten, informal—more "custom" than hard law. Here the speed limit provides us with a good everyday example. The formal, official rule sets the limit at fifty-five miles an hour. But everybody knows that the "real" rule—the one actually enforced—is closer to sixty-five; in other words, a policeman will not stop you if you are driving fifty-eight miles an hour, even though you are technically breaking the law.

If we turn to *private* law, we also find examples of both formality and informality. Grievance procedure committees in industry sometimes look a lot like courts, may be quite elaborate procedurally, and may even behave like courts. Formal procedures abound in other big institutions. A student will not be expelled from a university without (if he chooses it) some sort of hearing or "trial." In some schools or universities, a student may even have the right to "appeal" from a C grade in organic chemistry, and get the grade reviewed at a higher level. In case of serious infractions—for example, if a student is accused of cheating on an exam—he will certainly have the right to some sort of formal process. He may even have the right to bring a lawyer to his hearing. If he is found "guilty," he can probably appeal to a dean or the president of the university. Yet all of this, thus far, is strictly private. The government plays no part in it.

This does not mean, of course, that the formal, official legal system had nothing to do with the development of these procedures. Quite the contrary is true. These inside procedures came about historically partly because of outside pressure—from court decisions, for example. Indeed, the support of the courts has been a crucial factor in the rise of "due process" in schools. For example, in *Goss* v. *Lopez*[4] the United States Supreme Court, the highest court in the land, decided that a high school student could not be suspended from school without some sort of hearing, if he wanted one.

There are also unofficial courts of various sorts scattered all through the country. Some of these are run by organized religious bodies; Orthodox Jews, for example, can bring disputes to a rabbinical court for settlement. The Catholic church presides over an elaborate system of canon law. Church courts decide whether a marriage can be annulled, for example. This does not bind the regular secular courts, but it is most important to a devout Catholic, whose religion forbids divorce and who might want to get married again and yet stay within the church's good graces.

Leigh-Wai Doo has described in some detail a quite different kind of court: the Chinese Consolidated Benevolent Association in New England, which handled disputes within the Chinese community. Let us look at one example of this "court" in operation. One busy day in a Chinese restaurant, the chef asked the owner for a raise of $25 a week. The owner said no. The chef then walked off the job. Later, he sent a bill for back wages, plus $25; the owner, for his part, demanded $500 in damages. Neither one paid the other's claim.

Two months went by. The restaurant could not get a good chef, and its business began to suffer. Meanwhile, the chef's "family association" appealed to the Benevolent Association, demanding the back wages and denying that the restaurant for its part had any right to claim damages. The Benevolent Association consulted with the restaurant association and with the family groups; it turned out that the restaurant wanted the chef back at work, and was willing to give him a raise (of $10), if he would change his "unreliable ways." The Benevolent Association then had the "task" of discovering "whether the chef wanted the job back," and, if he did, whether he could be talked into making amends. They "studied the man's character and the best ways of approaching him." After a week of "patient persuasion and stressing that he would not find work if he continued his erratic behavior," the chef agreed.

The Association now knew that both sides were willing to settle. It called on them to meet before the Association's board. The reconciliation took about two hours. The chef apologized; the owner rehired him at a $10 raise. They "finalized the settlement by drinking tea together."[5]

Neither the rabbinic courts nor the Chinese Consolidated Benevolent Association, for that matter, have the power to back up their decisions with force. They have no way to throw a "litigant" in jail or to squeeze money out of a loser. But they do have moral force, and this may be no small matter. They can bind those people who voluntarily submit to them. By inclination, and also because they are unable to crack the whip, these "courts" lean heavily toward compromise, toward restoring harmony, toward reconciliation and voluntary agreement. In this sense, they are less lawlike than ordinary courts. They are not so very different from the way some judges work "in chambers." And they much resemble courts in simple societies, as anthropologists and others have described them.

They may also be fairly prone to decay in a society like ours, which is very fragmented and very pluralistic. The old traditions may die hard, but they do eventually die. Apparently, the dispute-settlement models described by Leigh-Wai Doo have lost much of their strength in Chinese communities in the last ten years. New waves of immigration might conceivably strengthen them once more.

There are countless other ways in which Americans use law that is unofficial (nonstate) and yet quite formal. Every trade association or occupational group—every big institution of any kind—will make rules and will have some way to enforce them or to settle disputes. Businesses often handle differences through the use of arbitration. Very often, when two businessmen enter into a contract, they write into it an arbitration provision. This means that if some dispute or problem comes up, the two sides will take it to arbitration and keep it out of the courts. Labor contracts (collective bargains) also typically provide for arbitration. In other words, arguments over what the contract means, or over work rules and the like, will be decided by a third-party—someone on whom both management and the union can agree. In some companies and industries, there is a permanent arbitrator; this is true of U.S. Steel and the Ford Motor Company, for example. It is also true of the contract between the Major League Baseball Players' Association and the owners of major league baseball teams. Under other industry contracts, the arbitrator may be chosen case by case.

Arbitration is in some ways a kind of halfway house between official and unofficial law. The arbitrator is, after all, not a professional judge. But his word is usually final, just like a judge's. If a soap company and one of its suppliers agree to arbitrate their disputes, they are going to have to abide by this agreement. The courts will, if pushed, force the losing side to carry out what the arbitrator decided. It is in this sense that arbitration is a kind of mixture of the public and the private.

Just as every institution, down to the family, has the habit and need to make rules, so too is there a general habit and need to enforce them and to clear up ambiguities. Hence it is no surprise that arbitration or processes like it are so pervasive in society. There is a hunger for ways to settle disputes that the regular courts cannot satisfy, or can satisfy only at too high a price: we can think of the formal courts as fancy French restaurants in a society that also needs pizza joints and McDonald's, for fast, cheap food.

In California, one rather curious system, a hybrid between public and private dispute-settlement, has been given the nickname "rent-a-judge." The "rent-a-judge" system is based on an old, rather murky state law, which was rediscovered and put to modern use. In the rent-a-judge system, parties to a dispute sidestep the regular courts; they hire their own judges (actual judges who have retired from the bench). These judges resolve the dispute—privately, but with all the trappings and procedures of a regular trial. The results are treated as binding on both sides.[6]

Public and private spheres of law thus interact. They are not totally independent of each other. Students have hearings in universities not because universities decided to grant hearings out of the goodness of their corporate hearts, but in part because they were pressured by court cases on student rights. Arbitration awards, too, can be enforced in court. The private sphere is also influenced by the public sphere in other ways. Most claims for damages (in automobile accidents, for example) are settled out of court; but the parties bargain "in the shadow of the law."[7] That is, both sides know that there is an operating legal system in the country—that there are rules and doctrines about damage cases—and they or their lawyers have some idea what is likely to happen if they go to court. These ideas enter into their bargaining and influence it, even though the bargaining and dickering is strictly private.

The discussion so far has isolated four types of law. There is law which is both formal and public (an act of Congress, for example); law that is public (or governmental) but informal (the "real" rules about the speed limit); law that is formal but private (grievance procedures); and law that is both private and informal (rules inside a family). We can also draw a line between *legitimate* and *illegitimate* processes. Usually, a system is not illegitimate just because it is informal or private; nor is there anything illegitimate about the formal private systems (like the work of the Chinese Consolidated Benevolent Association or a cheating hearing at the university).

The informal part of the *public* system is a more complicated story.

Some aspects of it are illegitimate, or downright illegal. It is a basic fact about the American legal system—and the legal systems in other modern countries—that we cannot tell from the way the system is described on paper how it actually operates in life. Sometimes we are perfectly willing to accept the gap between form and reality. The speed laws can serve as our example once more: it does not seem to trouble us that the speed limit is officially fifty-five, but really somewhat more.

Other situations are not so benign or so readily accepted. Some hover in a kind of twilight zone between the legal and the illegal. Prostitution, for example is against the law everywhere, except for some counties in Nevada. Yet police and city officials have often closed their eyes to the "social evil," provided certain conditions were met. In many cities, in the past, police would not raid a house of prostitution so long as the house was inside an area of vice, the so-called "red-light district." The police sometimes even issued rules to regulate prostitution despite the fact that the business, strictly speaking, was completely illegal. In Chicago, for example, the superintendent of police in 1910 issued a whole sheaf of rules: "No house of ill-fame shall be permitted outside of certain restricted districts, or . . . within two blocks of any school, church, hospital, or public institution, or upon any streetcar line." Prostitutes in Chicago were not supposed to wear transparent dresses, and "houses of ill fame" had to have double doors, not "swinging doors that permit . . . a view of the interior from the street."[8]

Prostitution, in other words, was half inside, half outside the law. It was officially illegal, yet at the same time it was regulated—and by the same legal system which condemned it to illegality. This was not and is not a unique situation. The "real" law about gambling, divorce, abortion, immigration, and many other subjects is quite different from what it is supposed to be; and many aspects of social behavior, like prostitution, are both inside and outside the law at the same time.

There are other forms of "justice" that stand completely outside legality. The justice of underworld gangs, or of organized crime, is of this nature. Gangland justice stays hidden, operating only in certain dark corners of society. But our history is also full of open outbursts of unofficial law, or "popular justice," as it is sometimes called. Perhaps the most famous examples are the so-called vigilante movements.

Vigilantism goes far back in American history. There were examples even in the colonial period—the so-called Regulators of South

Carolina appeared on the scene in 1767. But the golden age of the vigilantes was in the West, in the period after 1850. The two San Francisco "Vigilance Committees," both active in the 1850s, were particularly famous in their day; but there were many other vigilante groups, in Montana, Colorado, Nevada, Oregon, and Texas. One scholar counted at least 326 vigilante movements; and if records were more complete, the count would probably rise to about 500. The vigilantes dispensed quick, often bloody "justice" against horse thieves, rustlers, desperadoes, and ne'er-do-wells of one stamp or another. One estimate is that they shot or hanged some 729 men.[9]

In their day, the vigilantes were often controversial. They were criticized by defenders of orthodox law and order. Still, many people—perhaps a majority—felt that the vigilantes performed a public service; that in the raw, lawless towns of the West, there was no real alternative to vigilante justice. The chief justice of Montana Territory—who might be expected to stick up for law if not order—praised them in 1864 as genuine "tribunals of the people." They were, he felt, an absolute "necessity."

"Popular tribunals"—private systems that rival the official system—come up (we often hear) out of a "vacuum" of power. This usually means that there is some group which feels official law is too weak, or has fallen into the wrong hands. For example, the merchants of Dodge City, Kansas, in 1872, were so concerned about lawlessness that they hired an unofficial marshall, gave him a badge, and set him loose. In 1873, the business men formed a vigilance committee, which started its work by killing two men in a dance hall and ordering five more to get out of town. The committee itself later became such a disorderly nuisance that it had to be put down with force.[10]

The vigilantes of history have died out; but even today there are neighborhood associations that call themselves vigilantes (or "neovigilantes"). These groups patrol city streets and keep watch in their neighborhoods, because they feel the "real" police are not doing the job. Richard Maxwell Brown mentions some examples from the 1960s: the Deacons for Defense and Justice (a black organization); the Maccabees of Crown Heights, Brooklyn (largely Jewish); and the North Ward Citizens' Comittee of Newark, New Jersey (largely Italian).[11]

In the old West, the vigilantes explained and justified themselves in various ways. The job of justification was easiest where "the law" itself was corrupt: where the sheriff, for example, was part of a gang of horse thieves. Another aspect of the vigilantes is illustrated by the so-called White Caps. The White Cap movement started in southern

Indiana in 1887; it spread to Ohio, New York, and other states as far off as Texas. It was a "movement of violent moral regulation by local masked bands." The White Caps usually "punished by whipping"; their victims were "wife beaters, drunkards, poor providers, immoral couples and individuals, lazy and shiftless men, and petty neighborhood thieves."[12]

Most of these offenses were not crimes at all, or if they were, the law punished them quite weakly. Throughout the nineteenth century there were outbursts of rioting directed against immorality: in Detroit, for example, between 1855 and 1859, "one bordello after another felt the fury of an angry mob." Seventeen brothels were damaged or destroyed.[13] Similar incidents took place in other cities, too.

"Popular justice," then, took many forms. At one end of the scale, there were self-appointed judges and juries who took some care to imitate regular legal process, even to the extent of holding "trials." At the other end of the scale, popular justice degenerated into blind fury, rioting, lynch law. Some of the most sinister episodes came about where communities (or parts of communities) felt they could not trust "the law," because it was too squeamish, or (from our standpoint) too moral.

The notorious Ku Klux Klan arose in the South, after the Civil War; federal troops occupied the southern states, and state governments could not or would not allow whites to terrorize black people openly. The Klan took over the job. In the 1870s, when the federal troops left, white supremacy came to power in most of the southern states. These governments developed other ways to keep down their black populations. Some methods were more legalistic. For example, poll taxes and literacy tests kept blacks from voting. Other methods, however, were even more savage and violent than the Klan—for example, the outbreak of "lynch law" in the 1890s. Hundreds of blacks in the south were hung for breaking the southern "code"—dragged from prison cells or from their homes and killed by jeering mobs. The Klan cropped up again in the 1920s; and still a third outburst followed in the wake of *Brown* v. *Board of Education* (1954), when local white custom once again conflicted with firm orders from outside to dismantle segregation in schools and public institutions. This time, however, there was no federal retreat; and the Klan today is a much weaker group, on the fringes of society.

The main line of vigilante history is less bloody and less one-sided than its bastard brother, lynch law. The leaders of the western vigilante groups were by no means thugs. The leaders, indeed, were often solid citizens. It was the business community that organized the group in Dodge City. Vigilante leaders themselves were, or became, bank presidents, leaders—in a couple of cases, even United States senators. Few people today would defend lynch law; but there is a certain yearning for the simplicity and swiftness of "popular justice." There are situations of frustration and rage—mostly over street crime— which lead people to feel that do-it-yourself law and order is justified. A number of popular movies and books have as their hero a man who "takes the law into his own hands." The phrase is worth thinking about. It asserts—as the vigilantes did—that the private avenger comes not to deny the law, but to fulfill it. Whether or not this is the result, or ever was, is another question.

Yet in the long run one of the most important trends in criminal justice has been running in the opposite direction: away from the layman, toward the professional lawman. Criminal justice is becoming more and more professionalized. In the eighteenth century, there was no organized police force, certainly no FBI, no detectives, no police science. The role and power of the jury (a band of twelve laymen) was greater than it is today. The activity of the mob was a fact of life. The word *mob* has a lawless sound; but there was often only a fine line between mob action and legitimate public action. The community in general rose up to catch thieves when the hue and cry was sounded. A magistrate could form a "posse"—that is, a group of able-bodied men, private citizens—to help out the sheriff.[14] This system survived into the American West; the sheriff's posse is familiar to every fan of Western movies. The West is, of course, the same terrain where the vigilantes flourished. By the late nineteenth century, eastern cities all had police forces and criminal justice was rapidly professionalizing.

Sometimes there are whole governments that technically speaking have no legal basis and are, from a certain standpoint, illegal. History or war is often the ultimate judge. When Grant crushed the armies of the South, he swept away the government and legal system of the Confederacy. Other "governments" have been formed to fill a vacuum in power and law. This often happened in the West—among the Mormons in Uthah, for example, before the organization of territorial government. From the standpoint of the United States, there was no law in Utah; in fact, the leaders of the Mormon church exercised tight and effective control. The "government" in Utah was no different from a legitimate government, in any practical way.

Other examples are closer to the borderline. On the American frontier, settlers often formed "claim clubs" to protect their interests against "claim jumpers" (and against each other). In other parts of the country, there were groups of miners who drew up their own codes of "customs." The claim clubs were often necessary because, strictly speaking, none of the claims were legal. The settlers were squatters on public lands. Acts of Congress starting in 1796 provided for an orderly way of disposing of public land. First the land had to be surveyed; when this was done, the president could announce that the land was ready for sale. The sale of tracts of land would then take place at local land offices. Before the auction date, nobody but the government owned the land, and nobody was supposed to settle on it.

This was "the law," but it was almost universally disobeyed. Hundreds of thousands of people crowded onto the public domain. They built houses and farms long before the land was officially sold to them. As far as the settlers were concerned, they had a perfect right to the land, which they had earned by their time and their sweat. But legally speaking, they lived in a vacuum. For this reason, they banded together, drew up constitutions and codes to govern their rights, and formed little governments of their own. Their methods were not always sweet and gentle; and their treatment of outsiders was sometimes harsh. But the squatter organizations were yet another example of makeshift law, springing up in the cracks and crevices of the larger society.[15]

The Birth of Formal Law

No legal system in a developed country can be purely formal or informal. It is invariably a mixture of both. State law is generally (though not always) formal: patterned, structured, leaning on the written word and on regular institutions and processes. Nonstate law is usually much less formal; but both the official and the unofficial codes are mixtures of the two. Why is it that some parts of a system of order are highly formal, some parts much less so, and some completely loose and formless?

We can start to answer with a point that may be obvious: historically speaking, the informal comes first. The simplest societies, which probably resemble older human societies more than the urbanized societies, have highly informal legal systems. Formality seems to take over when an informal system no longer works, for one reason or another. In small societies—societies where most relationships are face-to-face—a formal legal system may not be needed at all. Not many people break the rules. Custom is king. Public opinion—what friends, kinfolk, neighbors think—is a powerful force, a powerful pressure. People do what social norms say they should do, not because they are angels but because their relatives and neighbors can inflict such terrible "punishment." In fact, these societies even dispense with any organized method for applying public force to somebody who breaks the rules. Many simple societies, in other words, do not have courts, judges, or police. They make do without them.

An extreme case is the community on Tristan da Cunha, a lonely, isolated, barren spot of land in the middle of the South Atlantic Ocean. A few hundred people live here, growing potatoes and catching fish. A team of scholars visited the island in the 1930s to study animals, birds—and social life. The social scientists on the team were amazed to see how law-abiding the people were—if we can apply the word "law-abiding" to people living in a place where there is nothing that even looks like law as we know it. Nobody could remember a time when a serious crime was committed on the island. There were none of the trappings of criminal justice—no police, courts, judges, or jails. Nobody needed them.

What made the people of this island such models of behavior? One idea leaps immediately to mind: the islanders had no choice. They were trapped on their island, with no hope of escape; they were absolutely dependent on each other for social life and support. Life on the island was totally "transparent"; everyone on the island was exposed, inexorably, to the "Argus-eyed vigilance of the community." Under circumstances like these, informal norms are just too powerful to be disobeyed.[16]

Of course, in a broad sense, there was law on the island, and lots of it. There were norms of behavior, and people followed them; these norms were enforced by real sanctions. Prisons, fines, whippings, and the gallows are not the only ways in which societies punish people. Teasing, shaming, and open disapproval are also methods of punishment. They can be terribly severe, in their own way. It is because they were so strong on Tristan da Cunha that the community never needed courts, policemen, and jails.

There are similar forms of punishment in other small, face-to-face communities. Some are quite familiar from our own legal history. In the American colonial period, Massachusetts Bay and other colonies forced certain offenders to sit in the stocks, where everybody who passed by could see them. Sitting in the stocks was not physically painful, but it exposed a person to public scorn and shame. Whipping was another common form of punishment. It was painful to the body, to be sure; but there was also psychic pain. Whipping was always done in public, before the eyes of the whole community.

But we do not have to go to far-off islands or to the long ago for examples of the process we are describing. It happens every day in our times, too. We see it in schools, in family life, in clubs, in small groups everywhere. The drill sergeant in the army punishes by yelling at the clumsy recruit, exposing him to ridicule. The law school professor in the movie *The Paper Chase* used ridicule and sarcasm to punish a student who was unprepared or did not understand the work. Schoolteachers and parents have a whole repertoire of tricks to invoke shame, guilt, and derision.

It is equally clear that the bigger, the more complex, the more "advanced" the society, the less it can rely completely on informal sanctions. The United States is about as far as one can get from Tristan da Cunha, socially speaking. We live in face-to-face contact with friends and relatives; but at the same time, we are in daily contact with people who are strangers to us; we use products and processes made and presented by strangers. We constantly have to deal with people we do not know—on the streets, in the workplace, in banks and hospitals and government offices. The food we eat is packaged in faraway factories; the clothes we wear are woven in distant mills. People we never see manufacture the necessities of our lives, using procedures we do not understand. When we ride in a plane, a train, a taxi, or a bus, we put our lives in the hands of strangers.

These are the facts of life. They have tremendous consequences. As individuals, we have little control over these vital strangers. We open a can of soup and eat it. How can we be sure the soup is wholesome? The wholesomeness is beyond our control, and certainly beyond our knowledge. Nor can we rely on informal norms or public pressure to guarantee that the soup is not poisonous, that it is nourishing and good. We want something stronger and more reliable than custom, something with independent force. In short, we want law. Hence in societies like ours—complex, interdependent—there arises an enormous demand—a need—for formal controls which have to come from some sort of organized government.

We are not dependent exclusively on strangers. Even in a big, impersonal society like this one, we have families, we have friends, we have strong personal ties to people and places. Even in this mega-society, we spend much of lives in tiny groups. The big society is made up of these little molecules of people. Each one of us has some personal zone or sphere, his own island of Tristan da Cunha. Inside our little group, informal norms still rule. But for most of us, there is this vital difference: there is escape from the island. On Tristan da Cunha, the boat comes only once a year. For us the boat comes every day, every hour, every minute. To a large extent, we have chances to change jobs, change cities, change families, if we wish—even, in a sense, to change lives. We may be prisoners to our characters, to our conditions of life, to traditions. But compared to most people in most societies, for us there are many doors of escape.

This means that informal norms stay powerful only when we let them—when we agree, in a sense, that they should remain in full force. Of course, psychological bonds can be, and often are, tremendously powerful. But, in a way, if we stay bound to the world of informality, it is because of *agreement*—that is, because of consensus— either about the norms themselves or about the authority to set standards and make up the rules. The Chinese-Americans did not have to abide by the rules of their Benevolent Association. They could escape from that island, so to speak. Increasingly they do tend to escape—particularly the younger generation. If they stay on their island, it is because at some level they want to, or feel compelled to for inner reasons. But more and more the agreement to abide by old norms and to submit to (informal) authority breaks down, in American society. At this point, formal law steps in, even in face-to-face settings.

We can illustrate this point by looking at the way law has entered the life of the American schoolhouse. In the past, schools were places where children learned to read and write, to do math—and also learned to obey the rules. The rules were for the most part informal; the teacher was in charge of the classroom, the principal in charge of the school, the school board in charge of the district. In a few rare instances, some parent or student challenged the way schools were run; but these rare cases were for the most part failures. Until deep into the twentieth century, nobody heard about such things as "dress codes." Everybody knew more or less what children were supposed to wear, how they were supposed to be groomed, and so on. In any event, parents (and children) understood that the teacher ran the classroom; on such matters the teacher's word, or the principal's, was final. There were no written norms, no procedures, no structure of appeals.

This cozy system broke down in the late 1960s. Styles of dress and behavior were changing rapidly. Long hair, for boys, had become a fashion—and a symbol of rebellion besides. At least, this is the way some boys regarded long hair, and teachers and principals tended to agree with them. Since informal norms were not working, the schools turned to formality—to "dress codes." According to the rules in the Williams Bay High School (Wisconsin)—rules which ended up in court—hair had to be "worn so it does not hang below the collar line in the back, over the ears on the side and must be above the eyebrows." In this school, beards, mustaches, and "long sideburns" were also forbidden.[17]

Many other schools had similar rules. But they were not necessarily obeyed. In any number of school districts, high-school boys refused to cut their hair and were sent home, disciplined, even expelled from school. There was no longer a consensus about the norms, nor was there any real consensus about authority itself. Most parents and students accepted the rules; but an important minority of parents and students did not. They refused to accept the idea that schools had the right to lay down rules about hairstyle. In a few aggravated instances, parents and students felt deeply enough about the matter to go to court; and schools like the Williams Bay High School found themselves, perhaps to their surprise, forced to defend their dress and hair codes in front of a federal judge. In the federal courts, there were no less than eighty-seven reported cases on hair length alone. The schools faced a dilemma. Agreement was unraveling, and the result was controversy, unpleasantness, disruption.

One way out was to submit; another was the path of formality. The dress codes themselves had been a step in this latter direction. Parents and students would at least know what was expected of them. Schools also developed formal procedures for dealing with disputes about student rights. A whole new field of law developed. Nobody in the nineteenth century had ever heard of "student rights" as a category of litigation or as a problem for the law and for society. The new procedures spread to other institutions—universities, for example. The general pattern of development was much the same. Once upon a time the professor's word was law in the college classroom. By the 1970s this was no longer quite so absolute. Now *law* was law. In many universities and colleges, a student had some right to challenge the professor, even with regard to the professor's most personal, most sacrosanct act: the grade given out in the course. Not that many students ever took up this opportunity. But the chance and the procedures were there, if anybody chose to use them.

We can draw a rather obvious general principle out of this story:

informal norms break down in a situation of conflict. Indeed, this proposition is almost tautological—almost like saying A equals A. In a conflict situation, any society (or subsociety) is likely to give up on informal norms—they simply don't work—and turn to a more complicated, more formal system of handling the problems presented. New procedures will spring up. More law will be generated, and law will turn its heavy guns toward higher formality. The innocent days of consensus are over. The teacher in the one-room schoolhouse, ruling the roost, is a ghost out of the past. He has been replaced by professionals, by a massive school bureaucracy, by a dense thicket of regulations and procedures. To a degree, this is absolutely inevitable. Sheer size, and diversity of opinion, make it so.

This gives us at least a preliminary answer to a puzzle that runs through this book: how come there is so much "law" in this country, so much "procedure," so much "due process," so much "legalization"? Society, like nature, hates a vacuum; and the breakdown of consensus—the decay of authority—which is certain to occur in a big, sprawling, diverse, and open society, *creates* a vacuum. At this point, the law (in its formal sense) moves in. It gives us, too, a clue to another puzzle: whether the trends we see will continue in the future, slow down and vanish, or get faster and stronger. We do not know the answer for sure, but at least we know what to look for in daily life, what barometers to watch, what gauges to read.

3

The Background of
American Law

*T*HIS BOOK IS about American law today. But legal systems have a past, a history, a tradition. To understand American law as it is, it is helpful to know where it came from and how it grew to its present shape. This chapter briefly sketches the historical background of our law.

Beginnings: The Colonial Period

The territory which is now the United States was first settled by English-speaking people in the early seventeenth century. Their settlements were scattered along the east coast of the country. The Puritans sank their roots into the soil of New England; the Quakers settled in Pennsylvania; English Catholics colonized Maryland. There were also early settlements in what is now Virginia and the Carolinas.

The English were of course not alone in the race to plant colonies in the New World. The Spanish and Portuguese dominated what is now Latin America, and many of the Caribbean islands. The Spanish flag once flew over what is now Florida. Spain also owned territory in the far western deserts and along the west coast. The Dutch settled in New York, only to be pushed out by the British before 1700. The Dutch language and some bits and pieces of Dutch law lingered on in New York for a considerable period.

A few traces of Dutch law perhaps spread beyond the borders of New York. The office of district attorney may have originated in the

Dutch-speaking areas. The matter is in some dispute. But no one disputes the survival of rather big chunks of Spanish law, and civil law generally, in the vast territories once under Spanish rule. Another survivor, too, must be mentioned: the indigenous law of the native tribes. Laws and customs of Native Americans are sometimes still significant on their scattered reservations.

All these are exceptions. The main historical element in American law comes from a single source: that source is England. No other body of law really had a chance, just as no language other than English could have hoped to establish itself. Through the English, the common-law system—its habits, its traditions, its ways of thinking—crossed the Atlantic and took root in this country.

Books on legal history often talk about "the" colonial period; but this can be somewhat misleading. After all, more than 150 years went by between the landing of settlers on Plymouth Rock and the outbreak of the Revolution. This is as long a stretch as the span of time between 1834 and 1984—an interval full of tremendous social change. The colonial period was not quite so turbulent and fast-moving, but it was long and structurally quite complex. For one thing, there were many different colonies—colonies whose identities were as distinct as those of New Hampshire and Georgia. The settlements were strung out like beads along the narrow coastline. Communication among them was poor. Communication with the mother country was even poorer; an immense and turbulent sea separated the colonies from England.

This was a fact of vital importance. In theory, the British were in full control of the colonies; their people were subjects of the king. In fact, the British had only a feeble hold over their distant children. The British were too far away to be effective tyrants, even when they wanted to be. Also (at least in the beginning) they had no consistent policy of empire, no idea how to govern far-off lands. For much of their history, then, the colonies (or most of them) were virtually independent.

The colonies can be divided into three more or less well defined groups. The northern colonies—Massachusetts, New Hampshire, Connecticut—were, in terms of English law, the most deviant. The middle group of colonies—New York, New Jersey, Pennsylvania, Delaware—stood halfway between north and south, legally as well as geographically. The southern colonies were the most conservative, in law and legal culture; they stuck more closely to English models.

These differences among colonies were not, of course, accidental. Puritan New England or Quaker Pennsylvania struck out deliberately on new paths, in ways that were not true of Virginia or the Carolinas. Climate and land conditions were also influential. In the South, mild winters allowed a different kind of agriculture, organized on the plantation system. Black slavery was another striking aspect of southern life. The first African slaves arrived in Virginia and other southern colonies before the middle of the seventeenth century. By the time of the Revolution, slaves made up as much as 40 percent of Virginia's population.

There were no blacks in England, and there was no such thing as slavery under English law. The law of slavery was an American invention, stitched together out of various sources, powerfully influenced by strong feelings of race, and mixed together with the labor customs of the West Indies and the southern colonies. There was slavery in the northern colonies, too; in New York, over 10 percent of the population was made up of slaves. There were slaves even in Massachusetts and New Hampshire. But slavery never dominated the northern labor system, as it did that of the South. New York slaves, for example, mostly "worked not in gangs but as domestic servants."[1]

Instead, the North had thousands of "indentured servants." Indentured servitude was a kind of temporary slavery. Indentures were written documents—contracts of labor, in a way—which spelled out the terms and conditions of work. An indentured servant signed on to serve his master for some definite period: seven years was common. The servant earned no salary. During the term, the master had the right to sell the servant, or (to be more precise) he could sell the right to the servant's labor for whatever was left of the term. The servant could not control this process, although some of the colonies tried to prevent abuse. When his time was up, the servant, unlike a slave, became completely free. Under custom and law, the servant was not supposed to leave the master empty-handed; he had the right to "freedom dues." In early Maryland, for example, these consisted of clothes, a hat, an ax, a hoe, three barrels of corn, and (until 1663), fifty acres of land. Later, clothing, food, and money were more typical dues ("Corne, Cloaths and Tolls").[2]

A good deal of research has been done on the colonial legal system. Most of it has concerned the northern colonies, especially Massachusetts. In truth, the legal system of Massachusetts Bay (as the colony was called) is uncommonly interesting. It deviated tremendously from English law, or at least from the English law practiced in the royal courts in London. Massachusetts law, in fact, looks so different from English law that at one point scholars argued among themselves whether it ought to be considered part of the common-law family at all.

By now, this idea seems a bit foolish. Despite some strange habits and language, the law of the colony was firmly rooted in English law and English practice. Some of its peculiarities disappear when we remember that the early colonists were not lawyers and were not members of the English landed gentry. The law they first brought with them was not the law of the great royal courts, but local law— the customs of their communities.³ We might call this element "remembered folk-law." Naturally, it was different from strict, official law. The key elements in it were English: after all, what else did the settlers know? Their law, in other words, was a kind of Creole or pidgin dialect of common law.

The details of colonial law are complicated and confusing, but its essential nature is easy to grasp. Imagine a group of American college students shipwrecked and marooned on a desert island, forced to build a new society. They will organize some crude sort of government, and they will create something that can be called a legal system. It will be very different from the one they left behind. For one thing, most of the old legal system will be irrelevant. Traffic laws, for example, will not be needed. On the other hand, the "colonists" will have to make up many new laws—rules about posting sentries on a hill, to try to signal passing ships; rules about how to divide fish and clams caught in local waters; and so on. People on the island will reproduce those parts of American law that they remember and that fit their new life and their new community. Ideology will also play a role. It will make a good deal of difference to know who the students were— whether it was a shipload of Young Libertarians that landed on the island, or a shipload of Young Socialists; what part of the country the students came from; what their religion was.

Colonial law was a little like a legal system built up by ship-wrecked, stranded people. It, too, was made of three elements: remembered folk-law, new law created because of the brute needs of life in the new country, and legal elements shaped by the settlers' ideologies (Puritanism in Massachusetts, for example). If we look at the *Law and Liberties of Massachusetts*, one of the earliest colonial law books (1648), we find dozens of examples of all three elements. We find, to begin with, all sorts of references to juries and judges, to documents like wills, to a system of private property—all of these brought over from England as part of the baggage of memory and custom and taken almost for granted.

On the other hand, life in a raging wilderness demanded arrangements far different from those of Stuart England. There were rules, for example, against selling or giving "to any Indian . . . any . . . gun, or any gun-powder, shot or lead . . . or any militarie weapons or armour"—a rule that of course had no counterpart in England. Ideology mattered, too: this was a community dominated by stern men of religion. There were rules against Jesuits, Anabaptists, witches ("any man or woman . . . that . . . hath or consulteth with a familiar spirit" was to be severely punished). There were also laws against heretics (those that "go about to subvert and destroy the christian Faith and Religion, by broaching or mainteining any damnable heresie").

Massachusetts law, inevitably, was simpler than the general law of England. It was stripped bare of old technicalities, for the most part; it was streamlined and altered so as to make it much easier to handle. English law in the 1600s was a trackless labyrinth of technicality. Its slow evolution allowed it to take the form of a dense texture of irrational, overlapping segments—a crazy patchwork that had developed over centuries of time. Only a handful of lawyers even pretended to understand it completely. Even had the settlers wanted to, they had no way to duplicate this kind of system exactly. A colony is always, in a sense, a fresh start.

In form and substance, then, Massachusetts and other colonies struck out on their own. To take one example, the king's law in England called for primogeniture. That is, if a landowner died without making out a will, his land went to his eldest son. Massachusetts, from the word go, discarded this rule. *All* children shared in the inheritance, though the eldest son got a double share. Most of the other northern colonies (Rhode Island and New York were exceptions) simply abandoned primogeniture, and quite early. It lasted much longer in the southern colonies: in Georgia it was abolished in 1777, in North Carolina in 1784, in Virginia in 1785. It is hard to resist the idea that differences in land tenure had a good deal to do with the fate of primogeniture. Only in the South were there large estates or plantations; in New England, "the topography and soil conditioned the small freehold and the compact settlement," and this favored dividing the land among all the children.[4]

The court system in England was as complicated as the rest of the law, if not more so. Lord Coke, who described the court system as it was in the seventeenth century, needed a whole volume just to list and explain the dozens of separate courts—royal, local, customary, special courts in mind-numbing numbers—a maze of jurisdictions that litigants (and their lawyers) somehow had to thread. Irrational as this system was in England, it would have been totally ludicrous in the small, poor, struggling settlements along the American coastline. Massachusetts set up a clean, simple structure of courts; so did the other colonies. Court structures tended to be similar, though never identical, in the various groups of colonies. Differences, too, were often striking. Massachusetts, for example, lacked separate courts of "equity," which were so prominent (and baffling) a feature of law in the mother country. South Carolina, on the other hand, had well-developed courts of this type.

In the eighteenth century, legal systems, both North and South, seemed to converge somewhat with English law; that is, they began to look more like their English model. This took place naturally and, for the most part, automatically. Partly it was because the British forced themselves on their colonies: they came to realize, with a bit of surprise, that they were in charge of an empire and that they might as well run it accordingly. As we all know, these attempts ended in disaster. The British began too late, in a sense. The colonists were used to running their own affairs; and when the English imposed new taxes, set up new courts, and in general behaved as imperialists, they touched off a revolution. As a result, they lost the crown jewel of their empire.

But pressure to conform to English models also came from more natural sources. First of all, whatever their political differences, the colonies had close commercial ties with the mother country. In the middle of the eighteenth century, America was a more sophisticated place than it had been a century before. The population was larger; cities had grown up; and the colonists needed areas of law which had been beside the point in the days of small, struggling little villages, living hand-to-mouth. This was particularly true of commercial law: the merchants, whose ships sailed to England, Jamaica, and ports all over the world, were eager users of up-to-date mercantile law as it was practiced in England and the rest of the European world.

There were also strong cultural ties with England. Lawyers who practiced in the colonies were Englishmen; some had actually gotten their training in England. The legal materials they used were English. Aside from collections of local statutes, the colonies published no native law books to speak of. All the treatises were English. All the published case reports were English. Anybody who wanted to learn about law had to read English books; and these books of course told about the English way of law, not the American.[5]

In 1756, William Blackstone's book *Commentaries on the Laws of England* first saw the light of day in England. It became a best-seller there; but it was an even greater success on this side of the ocean. Blackstone had a clear, concise style. He wrote his book for English gentlemen—laymen who wanted to know something about their law. Americans—laymen and lawyers alike—seized eagerly on the book, because it was a handy key to the law of the mother country. An American edition was published in Philadelphia in 1771–72. Blackstone would never have become so popular in this country if there had been an American treatise which was even roughly equivalent.

The colonial period has been dwelt on in some detail here, first, because it is interesting in itself, and second, because it illustrates one of the major themes of this book: how social conditions mold the legal system of a country. This principle operates today; it is also the key to understanding the legal past.

A Free Nation: American Law After 1776

In 1776, war broke out and the fragile ties between England and its colonies snapped. The war for independence was successful; but it left the colonies with the problem of finding the right way to glue themselves together. They wanted to form some kind of federation— a body with a central nervous system, so to speak—but the individual colonies also wished to keep a good deal of autonomy for themselves. After one false start (the Articles of Confederation) the colonies drew up a charter—the Constitution of 1787—which is still the highest law of the land. The Constitution gave the central government much more power than it had under the Articles of Confederation; but the government was still one of limited powers, in a federal system. Each state stayed sovereign in its own sphere. The United States—the national entity—soon elected a president and went into business. Later it built itself a capital (Washington, D.C.). The national government ran the capital, foreign affairs, the army and navy, and the post office. The states continued to run most other public affairs.

The new government faced one early and fundamental question: what should be done with the western lands? The United States owned a huge tract of wilderness. The public domain consisted of hundreds of miles of forest, stretching all the way to the Mississippi and including what are now the Middle Western and border states, and down through Alabama and Mississippi. The individual colonies had claims to most of this land, especially Virginia; but these claims were ceded to the federal government between 1781 and 1802.[6]

It was still the case in the 1790s that most of the population lived in settlements strung along the eastern coast. The western lands were almost empty; but to people of vision, it seemed clear that they were lands of the future—lands that would fill up with settlers someday. The basic policy decisions were embodied in the famous Northwest Ordinance (1787). The United States, itself recently part of an empire, decided not to run its lands like a colonial power. The dependent lands were its children, and like children, they would someday be adults. "Territories" would be carved out of the wilderness. When its population reached the right size ("five thousand free male inhabitants, of full age"), the territory would elect a "general assembly" to help the appointed governor govern it. And when the population reached "sixty thousand free inhabitants," Congress was to admit the territory as a new state, "on an equal footing with the original States, in all respects whatever."

And so it was. The original states ultimately grew into fifty. In almost every case, the new state passed through a period of territorial government—its childhood, so to speak—before emerging into state-hood. In only a few instances—Texas, for example, which began as an independent country—did the states avoid this period of pupilage. And it was not for a full century that the United States acquired possessions that were not organized on a territorial basis. The booty wrenched away from Spain after the Spanish-American war (1898), included Puerto Rico and the Philippines. These were the first important instances in which the Constitution did not "follow the flag" and in which the United States held colonies in the true imperial sense.

The law of the United States spread east to west, not by conquest so much as by natural infection from the original states. New states borrowed heavily from the law of older states. After all, settlers always came *from* somewhere; except for foreign immigrants, the older states were the "somewhere." Very often we can explain peculiarities in the law of a new state simply by looking to see where its settlers came from. In the old Northwest, the new arrivals—Americans all—swamped the handful of trappers and villagers who lived in Illinois and elsewhere, spoke French, and carried on their lives in accordance with French legal customs. The old Northwest Territory borrowed pieces and chunks out of the statute books of Pennsylvania, Virginia, and other states. As the population of the northwest grew, new states were admitted to the Union from the Northwest Territory, starting

with Ohio shortly after 1800. When fresh territories were organized—Indiana, Illinois, Wisconsin—the old Northwest Territory split
like an amoeba; and its legal system divided like the rest of it.

Everywhere, the wave of American settlers was strong enough to
crowd out whatever body of settlers lived under different languages
and law. Only in Louisiana was a "foreign" population big enough to
make a difference. In Louisiana, Spanish and French tradition were
too firmly entrenched to give way without a struggle: the common
law never succeeded in overthrowing the old legal system. It was a
decisive step when Louisiana adopted its Digest of 1808, modeled
after France's Napoleonic Code. Scholars still quarrel over whether
French or Spanish law provided more raw material for the Digest. In
any event, both of these systems were alien to the common law; they
were civil law to the bone.[7]

English did, in time, overwhelm the French language in Louisiana, except in remote bayous; but the French legal tradition had
more staying power. In theory at least, Louisiana is to this day not a
common-law state; and in some ways its law sticks out like a sore
thumb. The state is rather proud of its "codes" and its peculiarities of
law and procedure. Whether by now the living law of Louisiana is all
that different from the living law of other states is a more difficult
question. Louisiana enjoys (or suffers) the same federal tax law as
other states, and the same federal regulations. It is protected by the
same Bill of Rights. Its lawyers speak English, and the legal culture
is open on all sides to massive influence from forty-nine stepbrothers
and stepsisters.

Spanish or Mexican tradition strongly colored the law of California, Texas, New Mexico, and other western states wrested from Mexico. The civil law was never strong enough to survive as a system in
these states, but big chunks were left behind. One famous example is
the so-called community property system (totally unknown to New
York or Iowa). In a community property state, whatever a husband
earns and whatever property he acquires belong automatically one-
half to his wife; and the same is true the other way around. In other
words, in these states a married couple is, generally speaking, treated
as a unit—a "community"—unless they specifically make some other
arrangement. But in the days before women's liberation, the unit was
not a community of equals. The husband ran the show: he had the
exclusive right to manage and control the community property.

We must be careful not to make too much of survivals—old anom-
alies, pieces of law left over from dead or submerged traditions. Social,
geographic, and economic conditions were always much stronger

influences on law in these western states than the traditions that pre-dated American settlement. Community property did not survive in California because of nostalgia or historical accident; it survived because it was a useful and powerful system which seemed to suit the population well. The community property system has lived on to this day because it was able to compete with the common law and win a place for itself. It carried on despite, not because of, its Mexican roots.

A striking example of law generated by local conditions was the law of slavery—an enormous body of rules, statutes, and doctrines built up primarily in the southern states. Black slavery had existed in the North as well; but every northern state abolished slavery after the Revolution. The Vermont Constitution of 1777 began the trend; by 1800 the other states in the North had either gotten rid of slavery completely or had "provided for its gradual extinction."[8] From this point on, the line was sharply drawn: there were slave states in the South and "free" states in the North. A state was either one or the other, not both or in-between.

Ultimately the slavery issue poisoned relations between North and South to the point where the country fought what was then the bloodiest war in human history (1860–65). There were other issues behind the Civil War, of course; but the slave question was at the emotional heart of the conflict. Slavery was also at the core of the southern social system. Slaves were capital assets of enormous value to their owners. In the days before farm machines, black bodies were the motor force that made plantations productive. Slaves cleaned southern (white) houses, raised southern babies, worked in southern factories. In many parts of the South, most of the population was black and enslaved: there was a white layer of rulers on top of a large black mass.

Slavery was a vital part of southern society; naturally, then, it was a vital subject of law. Each slave state had an elaborate code of laws to govern slavery and slaves. These codes set out the rather paltry rights of the slaves, and provided for the rights and duties of masters. Masters, of course, had almost complete control over the lives of their servants. The slave was a piece of property. He had to obey his master; and, indeed, it was an offense for a slave to be "insolent" to a "free white person." Slaves could not legally marry. They could not own property. They could not come and go as they pleased: a slave was not to "go from off the plantation . . . without a certificate of leave in writing from his master." These provisions come from the North Carolina code of 1854; they are typical of the codes of slave states in general.

Even a freed slave was shackled with many disabilities. The slave code was also a race code. No black man, slave or free, had the right to vote or hold office in the South—or in most northern states, either. If a slave owner set a slave free in North Carolina, as in many other southern states, the freedman had ninety days to get out of the state. An ex-slave who stayed on without permission (it was sometimes granted) was liable to be arrested and sold into slavery once more.

Southern slave law had to concern itself with the massive fact that slaves were pieces of property. Black people were bought and sold on the open market, mortgaged by slave owners who were in debt, leased out by slave owners who had "extra" slaves, left as legacies in the wills of dying slave-owners, seized by a slave owner's creditors when the owner could not pay his bills. States from Maryland to Arkansas to Florida built up an elaborate structure of rules and cases—all of it now extinct—to cope with the business problems of men and women who owned and dealt in slaves.

In one case, for example, decided in Georgia in 1853, a man named Latimer had an extra slave; he auctioned off the slave's services. A certain Dr. Thompson, who ran a hotel in Atlanta, was the winning bidder; he paid ninety-one dollars to get this slave for a one-year term, and put him to work as a waiter in his hotel. One of the guests came down with smallpox; the slave was "put to wait on him" and came down with smallpox himself. A doctor was called who treated the slave and presented his bill. The question was, Who pays the doctor? Is it the original owner, because the slave belongs to him; or is it Dr. Thompson, who bought a year's worth of work and should perhaps bear the risk? In the end, the Georgia Supreme Court put the burden on Dr. Thompson.[9]

This case is only one of many in which slaves figure as part of the property system. This vast body of law was, of course, unknown in the North. The North was concerned with slavery, but as a political and moral issue and an issue of federal relations. There was bitter controversy, for example, over the duty of northern states to return runaway slaves to their masters. The various fugitive-slave laws were deeply resented, and at times defied, by the northern states.

Northern states had their own set of economic issues. These were by no means uniform. Farm states had one set; commercial states on the seacoast, quite another. In New York at the beginning of the nineteenth century the courts handled dozens of cases about marine insurance. Kentucky, quite naturally, had very little of this. The states of the old Northwest were much more concerned with public-land law than was Rhode Island. And so it went.

These differences are still very important. Some states are crowded and industrial. (New Jersey is as densely packed with people as Holland.) Farmers, growers, or miners dominate the politics of other states. In the dry western states, the population is light; and grazing rights on public land, or restrictions on strip mining, may be major issues. Southern states still have large black populations, memories of a lost war, and a tradition of conservatism. The Sun Belt, however, is growing and changing fast, while the old industrial states (as of this writing) are in deep economic stagnation. One state (Nevada) is dominated by an unusual industry, gambling.[10] One (Hawaii) is tropical, was once a Polynesian kingdom, has a largely oriental population, and lives off the tourist trade. The core of the law in all states (Louisiana is something of an exception) is the American version of the English common law. But the pressure of events, the rush of social forces, the needs and demands that come from people and places, from businesses and workers, are the basic forces molding the law at any given time.

In many ways, American law is distinctly and uniquely American. This is a natural and obvious fact. Every country has something unique about its law. By our law, the Fourth of July is a national holiday: on this day we celebrate our independence. Other countries celebrate their independence on other days. Every country has a unique place in space, its own birds and animals, its own history and products. Every aspect of a society colors its law. Thus no two systems of law are ever the same.

But American law also has features common to the laws of whole groups of countries. It shares many traits with the law of England. Yet the American and English systems are as different as the German language and the Dutch, or as Spanish and Italian. An American lawyer would have trouble if he tried to practice law in England without special training, even if he tried to read and understand the decisions of high British courts. Still, he could probably learn English law pretty quickly; French law, even in translation, would take more doing. The legal differences among American states, big as they are, are of a much lower order.

It is not surprising that the substance of American law has a lot in common with that of the law of other modern Western industrial countries. For example, it has an income tax; so does Sweden. Colonial Georgia did not have one, nor did medieval England or France.

America: A Middle-Class Civilization

In the eyes of many nineteenth century visitors, America was an amazing place. Some of its characteristics which we take for granted struck outsiders as remarkable in the extreme. Compared to European countries, America seemed exceedingly classless. Even before the Revolution, there was more equality of condition in the United States than in European countries, including England. It is important to put this "equality" into perspective. We had rich and poor, of course; and we had a large population of black slaves. Free blacks could not vote or hold office. Neither could women. Indeed, married women could not really own property or enter into contracts. When a woman married, her property automatically fell into her husband's clutches. He had total dominion and control. A married woman, legally speaking, was on a par with idiots and babies. These rules were not changed until the middle of the nineteenth century. The pioneer law was passed in Mississippi in 1839; New York enacted important reforms in 1848 and 1860. But bits and pieces of these old "disabilities" (legal inequalities) lingered on in the law much longer.[11] Women did not get the vote until the twentieth century.

On the other hand, it was never the case that a few great families owned all of the land in America, or even most of it. There were large landowners, to be sure, but nothing like the vast estates of Europe. There were no real peasants or serfs in this country. Especially in the North, men owned their land; tenancy (renting or sharecropping) was the exception, not the rule. Only in the South after the slaves were freed was there a large body of farm workers who lived more like peons or serfs than the free farmers of Iowa or Illinois.[12]

The wide ownership of land was no accident. It was a matter of deliberate policy. The national government, as we noted, came into possession of millions and millions of acres after the Revolution. The Louisiana Purchase (1804) brought millions and millions more. Yet no one ever intended to keep this land under federal ownership. On the contrary, it was national policy and national destiny to sell the land to the public—to people who would clear away boulders, cut down trees, settle on the land, and grow crops.

This was the basic spirit of public-land law. This body of rules, before the Civil War, was in philosophy completely unlike public-land law today. Today a strong central theme is conservation, preservation—holding on to the land, working it or using it (if at all) in the public interest, for the good of the population as a whole. Land law before the Civil War was mostly concerned, not with keeping, but with getting rid of the land—selling it or giving it away. Even when land was sold, it was sold at low prices—a dollar or two an acre, at most.

Public-land law was a maze of rules, and in practice there was a wide gap between theory and reality. There were endless scandals and corruptions at the level of local land offices. Yet, on the whole, the policy worked. True, speculators sometimes got hold of huge tracts of land, but even these people never intended to hold onto it. They were wholesalers, not land barons. Their aim was to sell out at a profit. In any case and by whatever path, the land passed out of government hands and wound up in the hands of small holders—hundreds of thousands of settlers, farmers, and tradesmen. The year 1836 was probably the peak year for land sales. The federal government sold over 20 million acres of land and took in about $25 million. Between 1820 and 1842, some 74 million acres were sold—about as much land as there is in Michigan and Wisconsin combined.[13]

These were sales. At the same time, the government gave away millions of acres. Some of this land went to state governments; they in turn sold the land, using the money for schools, roads, railways, and so on. In the Revolutionary period, soldiers were given, as part of their pay, pieces of paper that entitled them to bits of the public domain—100 acres for a private, 500 for a colonel. Many of the states, too, granted such military bounties.[14] The so-called Morrill Act (1862) gave every state a gift of public land, to be used to endow higher education. Out of this came such "land grant" schools as the University of Illinois.

Symbolically, at least, the famous Homestead Act of 1862 was a fitting climax to the policies that came out of pressure for easy land terms. This law offered 160 acres of public land, absolutely free, to actual settlers. In fact, most good farmland was already gone by 1862; what was left was mostly in the West—dry, rocky, or otherwise unsuitable. Still, the law restated, in an especially vivid way, what had always been one goal of land policy.

One theme stands out, then, in the tangled history of American land law: private ownership, and not by a small elite, but by millions of people. There is no General Motors or IBM of American land. Large landowners—even the largest—own only a trivial portion of an enormous continent. Legal policy insisted on, and reinforced, the pressure for mass ownership of land. Mass ownership, in turn, had incalculable consequences for the legal system. English land law had been a maze of technicalities. Generations of law students broke their heads over land law; no layman could wander into the maze without getting hopelessly lost. The law was so technical that it could work only in a society where landowners were few, rich, and leisured—a class that could afford skilled lawyers to disentangle legal knots.

American law never had this luxury. To get by at all in a country with millions of landowners, land law had to be revised—stripped clean of its worst technicalities. It had to function for ordinary people who owned small amounts of land, people who could read and write, but were not rich and not legally sophisticated, and who did not and could not know the small details of land law. The law also had to fit the needs of a fast-moving, active land market—a market where tracts of land changed hands almost like shares of stock on a stock exchange.

In England, a single great family might live in one place for centuries, developing deep, sentimental ties to its house, its land, its "estate." The very meaning of land was different in America. Only in the South, with its great plantations, were there estates in the English sense: the "Tara" of *Gone With the Wind* had no analog in Vermont or Illinois. In the North and in the West, men started farms, built them to the point where they could be sold at a profit, and then (very often) sold out and moved on, to start a new farm somewhere else. Even when the owner stayed put, his sons were likely to move on rather than stay on ancestral soil. After all, there was plenty of land—and plenty of opportunity. From the start, Americans were a restless bunch.

Land law was not the only branch of law that needed to sing a fresh tune in the New World. Law never lost all its maddening complexity; but the various fields were at least streamlined and refined to the level where they worked. This was certainly true of commercial law; it was also true of family law and the law of wills and succession at death.

The rise of divorce law is a good illustration of the process. Divorce was rare and expensive in England (until 1857, practically speaking, divorce was available only through an act of Parliament). Divorce was also extremely rare in colonial America. Here, too, divorce was mainly "legislative"; that is, each divorce was a separate law passed by the colonial assembly. In the nineteenth century, divorce began to become more common and also easier to get, especially in the northern states. Many states passed laws that allowed "judicial" divorce—divorce as we know it, divorce in court.

How do we explain this change in divorce law? Were American families less happy than families in Great Britain? Did they break up more often? Possibly: the rising divorce rate certainly says something about changes in the structure of the American family. But it is also clear that people wanted—demanded—a quick, cheap way to "legalize" their status, that is, an authoritative ruling on whether they were married or unmarried. Why? Because legal status makes a difference to people who have money or who own a farm or a house. For people like this (and this included millions of Americans) it was important to be sure of their legal status. This was the best way to keep titles and claims of ownership clean and distinct: it made sure that one's children were legally legitimate, that the right wife inherited a husband's property, and so on. A society of landless peasants or paupers can do without formal divorce. Americans could not.

There was also a shortage of legal skill. True, there were plenty of lawyers in the country; but they were not well trained, as English lawyers were, in the old common-law technicalities. American lawyers were known more for cunning and business sense than for legal learning; in any event, the kind of fancy legal work that the English gentry could afford was far too expensive for the ordinary American. And even the great hordes of lawyers in this country would not have been enough to meet the demand if every little land sale, every last will and testament, every promissory note, and so on, were to take large chunks of a lawyer's time. Hence, the constant simplification of the laws and the constant selling of how-to-do-it books—books like *Every Man His Own Lawyer*, which was mentioned in the preface.

A typical example of this literature, if we can call it literature, was *The American Lawyer and Business-Man's Form-Book*, published by Delos W. Beadle in the 1850s and frequently reprinted. It had "forms and instructions" for making out contracts, chattel mortgages, bills of sale, bills of lading, bonds, drafts, promissory notes, deeds, mortgages, landlord-and-tenant agreements, charters of vessels, letters of credit, marriage contracts, trust forms, articles of partnership, and wills; plus interest tables, digests of the laws of the states on various subjects, and all sorts of other material. The book claimed to be "a manual for the guidance of any and every man in business transactions." Its popularity is another sign of the way legal process percolated into the public mind and public needs, in this middle-class society.

Law and the Economy

A second aspect of the American legal system, in the period after the Revolution and up to the Civil War, follows closely from the one just described: the dominant goal of legal policy was to increase the wealth of the country. We were a nation of economic boosters. Law

Law was a tool to develop the country—to foster growth, to make people rich. J. Willard Hurst has used the term "the release of energy" to describe the basic function of law in this period. We often hear people say, somewhat loosely, that law is conservative. In the first century of our independence, it would be more accurate to say, along with Professor Hurst, that law was dynamic: people "put law in action fast and boldly where they saw tangible stakes in improving physical productivity."[15]

What this means, roughly, is that influential people in this country—voters, property owners—consciously and deliberately used law in all its forms to push for economic growth. They (and the law) respected property rights, of course, but chiefly because property was an agent of dynamic movement. They valued not the fat, old, encrusted "estates" of an aristocracy, but the swift, lean, moving assets of a young country on the make. The legal system was probusiness, proenterprise. People were willing—even eager—to throw away old rules of law, if they stood in the way of "progress."

This was, for example, the message of the *Charles River Bridge* case.[16] This great case, decided by the Supreme Court in 1837, turned technically on a narrow issue. The Massachusetts legislature had in 1785 granted a charter to a group of men who undertook to build a toll bridge over the Charles River in Boston. They built the bridge, successfully, and collected tolls for many years. Then in 1828 the legislature chartered a rival bridge, the so-called Warren Bridge; this bridge, after it recovered its costs, would be a free bridge, not a toll bridge. The two bridges were extremely close to each other; and it was clear that the free bridge would drive the toll bridge out of business. The owners of the old bridge fought back in court. They claimed the second charter "impaired" the first charter, and was beyond the legislature's lawful power.

The case found its way eventually to the Supreme Court. The issue was hotly debated; but the majority, speaking through the mouth of the chief justice, Roger Brooke Taney, decided in favor of the Massachusetts legislature and the second, free bridge. The first charter did not say in so many words that the legislature promised not to charter any bridge that would compete. Taney refused to read such a promise into the legislative act. That disposed of the Charles River Bridge claim.

There were close technical issues in the case, but it was also a kind of inkblot test, measuring attitudes toward property and enterprise. To Taney, the real issue was the conflict between old vested rights and the demands of new enterprise—demands of "progress." Faced with such a choice, American law and American judges tended to choose the direction of change—the direction they viewed as progress. This meant the second bridge and not the first.[17]

We often assume that the nineteenth century was the age of laissez faire, that is, that public policy and public opinion as a whole were dead set against government regulation and against any meddling in business. By modern standards, it is true that governments of the time were incredibly weak. The annual budget of a state like Massachusetts, toward the end of the eighteenth century, was less than a city might spend in a day in our times. The state government of Massachusetts spent $215,000 in 1794; and more than half of this was interest on state debt.[18] Millions of people today are on the government payroll; in the early years of the republic, there were the merest handful. Salaries cost Massachusetts $54,000 in 1794.

But it would be wrong to think that government was completely inert, or that the public by and large was made up of people who would be called libertarians today. Ordinary people were, on the contrary, quite anxious to get government help so long as it benefited them (this should surprise nobody); in particular, they wanted government action that would boost the national economy. Government (federal and state) did its best to promote roads, canals, turnpikes, bridges, and ferries. Later on, there was a positive orgy of boosterism in aid of railroads. Pennsylvania spent more than $100 million—an astronomical amount in those days—on its main canal and railroad system.[19]

Pennsylvania was no exception. Some states used their resources to set up or to strengthen banks; all of them (and the federal government) used land grants to encourage enterprise, especially transportation. After 1850, the federal government gave out huge tracts of land to help get the railroads built. This giveaway was very popular at the time, whatever later generations thought of it. The farmer could not prosper, could not sell his crops, without some way to get them to market. What the typical landowner wanted, in Iowa or Kansas, was simple: good times, good prices for his wheat or corn, and rising land values. Farmers knew that the only way to get rich was to link their farms with markets back east. Only the iron horse could accomplish this. The same middle-class mass that brought about simpler deed forms and easier divorce lay behind the great policy of land grants.

The Civil War and Beyond

The Civil War (1860–65), bloody and disruptive, was a cataclysmic shock to American society. It is also a convenient dividing point between periods in American legal history. It is a useful marker of the end of the age of "release of energy"—the boom period of building and settlement, the period of western expansion and early railroads, when agriculture ruled the economy. After the war, a new age began: an age of factories and big cities and floods of immigrants from eastern Europe; an age of technology and industry; an age that marked the slow decline of rural America.

In one regard, of course, the war was a real watershed. It ended slavery, though it certainly did not bring about any golden age for black men and women who used to be slaves. As soon as the war ended, the southern states passed harsh laws—the so-called Black Codes—to preserve as much of the old way of life as they could, to keep blacks in their place, and to grant them as few rights as possible. But the North would have none of this; northern armies moved in, the Codes were repealed, and three new amendments to the Constitution (the Thirteenth, Fourteenth, and Fifteenth) were rammed down the throats of the South. The Thirteenth Amendment abolished, once and for all, slavery and "involuntary servitude." The Fifteenth Amendment gave blacks the vote: no state could abridge voting rights "on account of race, color, or previous condition of servitude." The Fourteenth Amendment made "all persons" born in the United States (including blacks, of course) full citizens—state and national. Its other provisions (especially the "due process" and "equal protection" clauses) were destined to have a rich, complicated, and ultimately glorious history.

The tale of blacks and the Constitution was less benign in the nineteenth century. During Reconstruction (the late 1860s and the 1870s), blacks gained some political power in the South. But this was ended when "white supremacy" governments took over. By 1900, few blacks voted in the South. The federal government did little or nothing to prevent this disenfranchisement. Only when a strong voting rights law was enacted, in 1965, did real change come about.

The years after the Civil War were years in which government, in one form or another, played more and more of a role in the economy, especially in the northern states. This development was almost inevitable in the new industrial age. Big business confronted a growing labor movement. What could not be resolved around the bargaining table (sometimes because employers refused to bargain), or through strikes on the streets, spilled over into courts and legislatures. State legislatures passed hundreds of new laws on issues of industrial society: wages and hours, company stores, union labels, sweatshops, the work of women and children, and so on.

In this period, too, regulation of business expanded mightily and (for the first time) on a national scale. This was the age of the Interstate Commerce Act (1887), which set up the Interstate Commerce Commission, the first of the great national agencies to regulate business. In 1890, Congress passed the Sherman Act. This law, practically speaking, created a new field of law: antitrust law. This is the branch of law which deals with monopolies and other business practices that "restrain trade" and (in theory) harm competition. The administrative state has grown steadily since the late nineteenth century; its huge bulk outweighs all the rest of the law today.

The New Deal of Franklin D. Roosevelt, in the 1930s, was the next great watershed in legal life. The Great Depression wrecked the economy; in one sense the New Deal was simply a response to this desperate crisis. In another sense, the New Deal merely speeded up what was already in the works: an ongoing process in which the scope and extent of government intervention increased steadily and consistently. Law invaded more and more areas of life. During the New Deal, the federal system changed course dramatically; and the modern welfare state arose from the ruins left behind by depression and war.

Freedom and Law

In any brief sketch of the way American law has developed, it is easy to ignore (or take for granted) something that struck nineteenth century visitors to this country with hammerlike force: our amazing level of personal freedom. During most of our history, Americans tended to congratulate themselves on this point. They may have overdone it. Every nationality has a tendency to pat itself on the back; America was no exception.

In the 1960s, there was a revulsion and a reaction, especially in scholarly writing, against this rose-colored view of American history. Historians pointed out, quite properly, that the story of race relations in this country was bloody and dismal. They rubbed our faces in some facts many people wanted to forget. They reminded us that in the nineteenth century freedom and justice were most decidedly *not* for all, legally or socially speaking. The black population did not share equitably in America's freedom and wealth. Women, too—half the population—were legally and socially subordinate.

There are other skeletons in the American closet. The treatment of the native tribes is a sordid and disgraceful story. At best, they were cheated and dispossessed; at worst, slaughtered in cold blood. The Bureau of Indian Affairs never really understood or tried to understand the culture of these "savages," and it pursued a mindless policy of assimilation. The Chinese on the West Coast were subject to legal and social harassment in the late nineteenth century. During the Second World War, Japanese-Americans were shipped off to camps in the desert on trumped-up, hysterical charges. In the first half of the twentieth century, immigration law was racist to the core; Asians were not allowed to enter the country or become citizens; in California they could not even own land. Toleration stopped short, too, when it confronted (in the nineteenth century) the Mormon minority (the Church of the Latter-Day Saints). The Saints were clannish people with strange and offensive beliefs—in polygamy, most notoriously— and they enraged the "moral majority" of their day. The federal government passed harsh laws against the church and followed an active program of persecution. Leaders of the church were thrown into jail; some went underground. The persecution died down only after the church gave up polygamy (1890).

It is a fairly daunting list. And yet, despite it all, there is a strong balance in the accounts on the side of liberty. For much of our history, we were indeed one of the freest, most democratic, most "equal" countries in the world. Where we were bad, other countries were (and are) much worse. America was never utopia; it has always been a mix of good and bad, plus and minus. It began as an experiment in letting people run their own country. Not *all* the people, but more than were allowed to have power in England or France or anywhere else. This experiment worked. But it also meant that law reflected, and had to reflect great waves of popular sentiment. It could never stray too far from the mean. It could express ideals, it could express "enlightened" opinion, but it could never be dramatically better or worse than the values of articulate people. That was its weakness, and also its strength.

4

The Structure of
American Law:
The Courts

*I*N MANY WAYS, the courts are the most familiar part of the American legal system. When people think about "the law," they usually have the courts in mind. This is so even though most people do not have much experience with courts and the way they work. A fair number of people every year serve on juries; a fair number have dealings in traffic court. Others may go through a divorce or come in contact with probate court. Very few (except for jurors) have seen or been part of a trial in the flesh. As for the higher courts, only lawyers and judges confront them directly. On the other hand, everyone, almost without exception, has watched a trial on TV or in the movies or on stage.

The American court system is complex, partly because of our federal system. Each state runs its own separate system of courts; no two are exactly alike. The details of court structure can be quite technical, and confusing even to a lawyer. What makes matters even more mixed up is the double system of courts in this country. There is a chain of national (federal) courts, on top of (or besides) the courts of individual states. In every state, from Alabama to Wyoming, there is at least one sitting federal court. A person who lives in Philadelphia falls under the jurisdiction of two very different courts—the local Pennsylvania court and the local federal court—and can sue or get sued in either one, depending mostly, but not entirely, on what the case is about.

An Outline of Court Structure

The *state court system* is a logical place to begin, since the overwhelming majority of lawsuits begin and end in these courts. Despite
many local complications and technicalities, it is easy to describe the
essential shape of the typical court system. We can think of it more
or less as a kind of pyramid.

At the bottom, the broadest part of the pyramid, there are the
lower courts, dotted all over the state and sprinkled about municipal,
areas. These courts handle the least serious offenses and the least
serious claims. They have various names: justice courts, small-claims
courts, traffic courts, police courts, municipal courts, mayors' courts.
Many of them are somewhat specialized: traffic courts stick to traffic
cases; police courts deal only with petty offenses (you cannot sue your
landlord or get a divorce in police court); small-claims courts never
touch traffic offenses or cases of drunkenness.

These courts are the bargain basement of justice, in a way; their
goods are popular and cheap. They tend to be rather informal. Some
of them refuse to let lawyers take part. Some permit a jury if one of
the parties insists. Others do not allow a jury; and if a litigant insists
on his right to a jury, the case is transferred to a higher court. On the
other hand, the judges in these basement courts are usually quite
professional. They are trained in law, which was by no means always
the case in the past. The "justice of the peace" in England was usually
not a lawyer at all; he was a member of the local gentry who served
as a judge. Some states still have laymen as "JP"s—men and women
who have never gone to law school and never taken the bar exam.

There has been a good deal of debate about the quality of justice
in these lower courts. We hear about slapdash procedures, assembly-
line justice, and the like. Maureen Mileski studied a lower criminal
court in a "middle-sized eastern city" around 1970. In this court, 72
percent of the cases were handled in one minute or less. In other
words, "routine police encounters with citizens in the field last on the
average far longer than court encounters."[1] It is not hard to see why
this kind of "rough justice" is open to criticism.

Small-claims courts have also taken their lumps. The first such
court was established in Cleveland in 1913, as a branch of the municipal court. The idea spread quickly. It was argued that these institutions would serve as the poor man's court—cheap, easy to use, with
no lawyers and no legal tricks. In many ways, these courts have been

a spectacular success; hundreds of thousands of claims are processed through small-claims courts every year.

Whether they have really supplied justice for the poor is quite a different question. In the 1960s, some scholars levied serious charges against them. These courts had become only one more example of the way the scales of justice were tilted against the poor. These were not courts *for*, but *against*, the workingman. They were in essence collection mills for businessmen—"courts of the poor" only in the sense that the poor person was dragged before the court and, in an "intimidating atmosphere," forced "to confront a powerful creditor," or a landlord, or the government.[2]

Since the 1960s, there have been many exposés of these courts. The bad publicity has led to reform efforts in some cities and states in recent years. The aim is to restore the courts to what was supposed to be their original function. New York, for example, does not allow collection agencies, corporations, or insurance companies to use small-claims courts. In many places, the clerk will help a litigant fill out forms; some courts even give legal advice to bewildered litigants.[3]

The next level of the pyramid is made up of *courts of general jurisdiction*—the basic trial courts of the community. These are the courts that hear civil cases "worth" more than the ones the basement courts try (that is, more money is at stake). These courts also handle cases of serious crime—not drunkenness or walking on the grass, but burglary, rape, manslaughter, and murder. There are fewer of these courts, but they tend to be more professional. The judges are always lawyers. The atmosphere is more dignified, more solemn. There is much more of a full-time staff.

These trial courts usually have jurisdiction over more people and more area than the municipal or police courts. In many states, the basic trial courts come one to a county. (In counties with big populations, the court may be divided into "departments.") There is no uniform name for the basic trial courts of the United States. In some states, they are called circuit courts; in others, district courts. The California name is superior court. In New York, through an odd quirk of naming, the basic trial court is called the supreme court; the highest court of the state is the court of appeals.

Only a small percentage of the cases that get filed in court ever go to full trial; the vast majority are settled out of court, dropped, compromised, or handled summarily. Still, every year thousands of cases do go the whole route—either to trial by jury or to trial in front of the judge alone (the so-called bench trial). In California, for example, in the fiscal year 1980–81, the superior courts disposed of 584,300 cases. Only 11.1 percent of these were contested; the majority of these contests were bench trials. A mere 1.3 percent went to a jury; still, this comes to a bit more than 7,500 trials.[4]

In the contested cases there are, of course, winners and losers. The loser can throw in the towel; and most do. Or he can continue the struggle and "appeal." The term *appeal,* in ordinary language, means taking a case to a higher court—an *appeal court,* higher up in the pyramid of courts. Typically, the appeal court does not review every aspect of the trial (it does not try the case de novo—that is, all over again). But trial de novo is not completely unknown. The loser in a petty court—a justice of the peace court, for example—can take his case to the next court up; here the trial is usually de novo. But beyond these petty courts, the party who appeals will get only limited review. The higher court looks at certain features of the case, certain parts of the record, checking for errors.

Suppose, for example, someone is tried for murder and the jury brings in a guilty verdict. The defendent is almost certain to appeal— but on what basis? The appeal court will not convene a jury, will not hear new evidence, will not even go over the old evidence. Rather, the defendant (actually, his lawyers) will have to find some "error" to complain about—something done wrong at the trial. He might claim that the judge let the jury hear improper or irrelevant evidence, or that the judge gave the wrong instructions to the jury, or that the judge showed prejudice, and so on. The appeal court will consider these questions carefully. But it will not try to second-guess the jury. It will not rehash the facts. In a civil case, too, findings of fact (generally speaking) will not be reviewed.

In states with small populations, like Idaho or Rhode Island, the loser in the trial court can appeal directly to the state's top court, usually called the supreme court. In other words, if you count the trial court as the first tier, these states have "two-tier" systems. In these little states, the supreme court will generally hear everybody who wants to appeal; the court does not screen its cases, or pick and choose the best or the most important. It takes them all. In these states, appeal is "as of right."

This works well enough in Idaho, but it would hardly do in a state like California, which has over 20 million people and an enormous network of trial courts, all of them churning out decisions. If we let everybody who lost at trial in California appeal "as of right," the supreme court would be totally swamped. It is no surprise, then, that California, like other states with big or middle-sized populations, has developed a "three-tier" system. A layer of intermediate courts stands between the trial courts and the supreme court. Most appeals go to the middle level; and there they end.

In three-tier systems, the top court has tremendous discretion; it can usually decide which cases to hear and which to reject. A trial loser has the right to appeal at least once within the system; he gets one bite of the apple. He has, ordinarily, no right to demand a hearing from the *highest* court. That privilege is reserved to those who convince the court their case is important. There are exceptions written into the law in many states. For example, a man or woman sentenced to death may get automatic review in the highest court. That is true in California.[5] In Ohio, constitutional cases also go right to the top.[6] But generally speaking, the high court in three-tier states has control over its work load, and this has important consequences for judicial policymaking.[7]

How does the high court, with this freedom and power, decide which cases to take? Obviously, the judges choose what they consider important cases. (Tastes in what is and what is not important tend to change over the years.) As population grows, more people clamor to be heard; courts have to be tough and selective or they will drown in an ocean of paper. In 1950, there were 130 petitions for leave to appeal to the supreme court of Illinois; in 1978, there were 989—an enormous jump. The court actually decided fewer cases with full opinion in 1978 than in 1950 (195 as against 253). Illinois is a three-tier state. Most people who appealed in 1978 had to be content with the middle tier of courts.[8] The supreme court dealt with a select group of cases, chosen for their legal or social significance.

Federal courts are also organized on a three-tier system. They lack the "bargain basement" tier, however. There are no federal small-claims courts or federal justices of the peace (although the District of Columbia has a Small Claims and Conciliation Branch in its superior court). In the states, the bottom federal level is the *district court:* this is the basic federal *trial* court. The other two tiers—the *circuit courts* and the *United States Supreme Court*—confine themselves to appeals, by and large.

This was not always true. We take for granted today a strict separation between trial courts and appeal courts. The distinction was not

so firm in the early nineteenth century. High court judges, state and
federal, often did trial work as well. Even the justices of the United
States Supreme Court had "circuit duty." Each justice was assigned
to a region of the country. Every year the judge traveled to his circuit
and tried cases there. This burden was not lifted until the end of the
nineteenth century. In 1891 Congress made this traveling show
optional; circuit work then became quite rare. It was totally abolished
in the twentieth century.

There are roughly a hundred federal district courts. Every state
has at least one. In the smaller states, the whole state makes up the
district; in the larger states, there will be more than one district in
the state. San Francisco, for example, is in the Northern District of
California; Los Angeles is in the Southern District. There may, of
course, be more than one judge to a district (imagine having only one
district judge for the whole Los Angeles area!); each case, however,
is tried by a single judge, sitting alone.

The next step up is the level of the United States Courts of Appeals,
the federal *circuit courts*. For many years, there were ten of these.
Congress recently set up an eleventh, by splitting in two the old Fifth
Circuit, which stretched from Florida through Texas and had been
growing very fast in population. Circuit courts, unlike district courts,
are not one-judge courts. The judges sit in panels made up of three
judges each. The total number of judges varies from four in the First
Circuit (this circuit handles Massachusetts, New Hampshire, Maine,
and Puerto Rico), to twenty-three in the Ninth Circuit—a giant circuit that includes California and eight other states of the West, plus
Guam and the northern Marianas. If a case is important enough, it
will be heard not by a panel, but "en banc," that is, by all the judges
of the circuit. (In the Ninth Circuit, by way of exception, "en banc"
does not mean all the judges, but a sizeable number; the full bench
here would be unbearably cumbersome.)

For most cases—indeed, the overwhelming majority—the circuit
courts are the end of the line. Above them looms the *United States
Supreme Court*, in all its majesty; getting a hearing in that court is a
rare privilege indeed. The Supreme Court sits at the top of the pyramid of federal courts; it can also hear cases which come out of high
state courts, if they raise important federal issues—usually issues under
the federal Constitution. The Court has only nine justices; and its
work load is heavy. It has to be jealous of its time and effort, and it
is. Few of the cases that knock at its door actually get inside. In 1974,
3,661 cases were filed with the Court (the figure for 1880 was 417).

The court heard only a small percentage of these; the rest were turned down. There were 2,520 petitions to the court for certiorari from the United States Courts of Appeal alone. Certiorari is a writ the Supreme Court issues to a lower court, pulling up the case for hearing. The court granted 158 of these requests, or a bit over 6 percent.[9] The other applicants went away empty-handed.

The Supreme Court has enormous control of its docket. But like the top state courts, it was not always in such a privileged position. A century ago, its work load included many rather prosaic cases—ordinary contract or property cases appealed from the territories or from the District of Columbia or from lower federal courts. This is no longer true. Yet even today the Court is not a simon-pure appeal court. The Court hears a few "original" cases—cases which come to the Supreme Court first, without any stops along the way. The Constitution so provides. Cases "affecting Ambassadors, other public Ministers and Consuls, and those in which a State shall be a Party" are part of the original jurisdiction of the Court.[10] Under this provision, the Court might hear (for instance) a boundary dispute between two states. An example of an original case before the Supreme Court was the long-drawn-out wrangle among Arizona, California, and other states over how much water each state could draw from the Colorado River and its tributaries.[11]

Some states give their high courts "original" jurisdiction over cases of various types. In Nebraska, for example, the Supreme Court has authority to issue certain extraordinary writs and to take original charge of "cases relating to the revenue, civil cases in which the state shall be a party . . . [and] election contests involving state officers other than members of the Legislature."[12]

The structure of courts, state and federal, has been described here in a simple, rather idealized way. In many states, there are oddities or extra wrinkles. Court structure can be very complicated; the farther back in history one goes, the more confused the situation gets. A number of states have tried to reform their court systems—make them more streamlined, more rational. Arthur T. Vanderbilt (1888–1957), chief justice of New Jersey after 1947, led a notable and successful fight to reform the judicial system in his state, which was woefully out-of-date. But many states have preserved a flock of specialized courts, hangovers from the past.

These courts come in various shapes and forms. Georgia, for example, has separate probate courts which administer affairs relating to wills and estates of the dead. (These same matters, in California, are dealt with by branches of the superior court, that is, the ordinary, general court.) Delaware has the distinction of preserving a very ancient tradition: separate courts of chancery, which decide cases of "equity." This was once a common pattern, but the other states have long since merged "law" and "equity" into a single system of courts: New York joined the two together in 1848. In some states, there are separate juvenile or family courts, distinct from the regular courts. Massachusetts has a Land Court, to hear cases of foreclosure, eviction, land titles, and other matters of housing and real estate. Boston has its own special housing court. Michigan has a "court of claims," for claims against the state. A few states separate criminal cases from civil cases (there is a St. Louis Court of Criminal Correction, in Missouri). We have already mentioned municipal, traffic, and small-claims courts. Even in the federal system, there is a special court for custom and patent appeals, a court of claims, and a tax court (not technically a court at all, but in practical terms exactly that).[13] In the planning of court systems, there is a tension between simplicity and flexibility on the one hand and functional specialization (which has its points, too) on the other.

The Judges

Judges in America are overwhelmingly lawyers; the only exceptions are a few justices of the peace and the like, in a handful of states. They are the last survivors of what was once a mighty tribe of lay judges. Basically, then, all judges are lawyers; but only a tiny percentage of lawyers are, or ever become, judges. Who are they, and where do they come from?

In civil-law countries like Italy or France, judging is a career of its own. Judges are civil servants, separated by training and experience at an early stage from the practicing bar. A person who wants to be a judge will typically take some competitive examination right out of law school (or after some period of practical training). Those who pass the exams become judges. They will probably stay judges for the rest of their careers. Beginners start out as beginner judges; successful judges rise to higher and better courts. Usually the sitting judge has never practiced law and never will.[14]

The situation in the United States could hardly be more different. American judges are lawyers, plain and simple. Usually, they are lawyers who are, or have been, politicians. One survey of judges in the

United States Courts of Appeal, for example, found that about four out of five had been "political activists" at some point in their careers.[15] The situation is the same on state courts—perhaps more so. Judges are usually faithful party members; a seat on the bench is their reward for political service. They are also supposed to be good lawyers and to have the stuff of good judges; whether this is actually taken into account depends on where they are, who does the choosing, and so on.

The political nature of judgeships is underscored by the fact that in most states judges are elected, not appointed. They run for office on a regular slate, and in many states they have to attach party labels to themselves—that is, they run as Democrats or Republicans. This idea of electing judges strikes Europeans as very peculiar—as odd as if we elected doctors or policemen or government chemists. But the elective principle goes back rather far in United States history. It was of course unknown in the colonial period; it began to take hold soon after Independence and became a marked trend in the first half of the nineteenth century. Lower court judges were elected in Vermont from 1777 on; in Georgia from 1812. Mississippi decided in 1832 to elect all its judges; New York followed in 1846.

Why elect judges? Essentially, the election of judges is based on the same theory that justifies electing governors or congressmen: making judges responsive to the public. Precisely because judges come from political backgrounds—because they do *not* resemble the cold civil servants of France or Italy—some kind of public control seemed necessary. But the election system did not work out quite as expected. For one thing, few elections were actually contested in most of the states. Elections tended to be bland and colorless. Sitting judges did not often lose, regardless of party. There were, to be sure, some notable exceptions. The chief justice of Illinois, Charles B. Lawrence, went down to defeat in 1873.

The elective principle was never universal. There have always been a few states in which the governor appoints the judges (sometimes with legislative approval). Massachusetts never adopted the elective system, for example. But the main exception is and has been the federal system. The president, under the Constitution, appoints the justices of the United States Supreme Court "by and with the Advice and Consent of the Senate."[16] The president appoints all other federal judges, also with senatorial consent. This has been the system since 1789. In practice, the senators play an influential role. The custom of "senatorial courtesy" gives senators a loud voice in choosing those

federal judges who will sit in their states. Once appointed and confirmed, a federal judge has no time limit—no term of office. He serves
"during good Behavior," as the Constitution puts it.

In practice, this means federal judges have their jobs for life, or
at least until they step down voluntarily. The only way under the
Constitution to get rid of a sitting federal judge is to impeach him for
"Treason, Bribery, or other high Crimes and Misdemeanors." This is
rare and difficult. A senile or a drunken judge—or an outright luna-
tic—has, in theory, the right to stay on the bench until they carry
him off feet first. Obviously, this system has its drawbacks; but it is
supposed to guarantee that judges will be independent, nonpartisan,
free from pressures of politics. This is worth the price of an occasional
dodderer or misfit. Most observers of court history seem to agree.

Of course, the power to name the judges in the first place is no
small power; the president will try to appoint men and women who
agree with his policies. This is especially true for appointments to the
Supreme Court. Still, once in office, a judge can thumb his nose at
the president and the president's program; there is no recourse, no
way to fire him, no effective sanction. Dwight Eisenhower came to
regret that he appointed Earl Warren as chief justice; he thereby
joined a long line of presidents who felt betrayed by men they put on
the bench. And, of course, judges who live long serve years and years
after the president who appointed them is gone.

A growing number of states have begun to back off from the pure
elective principle. In the twentieth century, some states have adopted
the so-called Missouri plan. Under this scheme the governor appoints
judges, but his choice is restricted. A commission made up of lawyers
and citizens draws up a list of names and gives it to the governor. The
governor must choose from the list. The judge serves until the next
election; then he runs for reelection on his record. That is, he does
not run *against* anybody; the public is simply asked to vote yes or no.
Since you cannot fight somebody with nobody, the sitting judges almost
never lose. The very controversial chief justice of California, Rose
Bird, came fairly close to doing so in 1978; other California justices,
appointed by Governor Edmund Brown, Jr., had narrow victories in
November 1982; but this California ferment is quite exceptional.

Why do sitting judges so rarely lose, even in states that do not
have a plan like the Missouri plan? Judicial elections are low-key affairs.
It is hard to campaign against a sitting judge. An upstart who tries to
defeat a judge already in office has to walk a narrow line. The candidate, unlike candidates for Congress or the statehouse, really cannot

make any promises. It is not cricket, after all, to express an opinion about situations that might come before the court. The sitting judge will sanctimoniously hide under the mantle of the law; he will not defend his decisions, but claim that he was just doing his duty—just deciding "the law." About all a frustrated candidate can say is that he can do it all better. Meanwhile, voters on the whole neither know much about these elections, or the candidates, nor seem to care.

Yet there are signs the process is becoming a bit more political. Between 1916 and 1973, there had never been a real contest in New York for the office of chief judge of the court of appeals (the highest court in the state). Candidates had "always been anointed in amiable cross-endorsements by Republicans and Democrats."[17] In 1973, Jacob Fuchsberg contested the election of Charles Breitel—a brash move that offended the organized bar. Breitel, the logical candidate, was already sitting on the court of appeals. He beat Fuchsberg; but in 1974 Fuchsberg tried again. This time he won a seat on the court as an associate justice. Both campaigns were tough and bitter. They generated a lot of publicity. This brought the office more into the public eye, which may be a good thing in the long run. The recent California elections, too, and the storm over Chief Justice Bird, focused attention on judgeships; this made them more vulnerable, politically, than they had been before.

Still, judicial elections are not likely to become as political as elections for governor or assemblyman. There is a deep feeling that judges, somehow and in some sense, must stand outside partisan politics. Even elected judges are less beholden to voters and to political leaders than other elected officials. And nobody but the voters—not the governor, not the legislature—can get rid of them at all so long as they avoid gross misbehavior or incompetence. Judges are supposed to be independent, and to a surprising degree they are.

This does not mean that they operate outside public opinion, outside social forces, or free from the constraints of society. That would be impossible—and undesirable. It does mean that the *regime* does not dominate the bench, as it does, alas, in totalitarian countries. A Soviet judge who decided an important case against the wishes of the government, who acquitted a dissident, or who ordered the regime to grant more civil rights, would lose his job and find himself with a one-way ticket to Siberia. This simply does not happen in America. The government loses dozens of important cases each year; the regime swallows hard, but takes its medicine.

The Work of the Courts:
Procedure and Substance

Trial Courts. The organization of court systems has now been briefly sketched. But what do trial courts actually do, and how do they do it? It is, of course, not easy to generalize. Each state has its own codes of procedure—its own rules on how to start lawsuits, how to run them, and how to finish. Each state is free in theory to think up its own special procedures. In fact, state procedural systems have a lot in common. For one thing, the Federal Rules of Civil Procedure have been an alluring model. The federal rules were adopted in 1938. Something on the order of thirty-five states have adopted these rules for local use. Moreover, all states (except Louisiana) are part of the common-law tradition; and they are all part of the same society (this time including Louisiana).

The common-law tradition puts heavy stress on "orality." Common-law courts prefer the spoken word to the written document. Not that courts are averse to pieces of paper. Indeed, they are swimming in it: in many cases, boxes and boxes of "exhibits," depositions, and documents of all sorts are introduced into evidence. (A deposition, essentially, is the statement of a witness, reduced to writing; it is used, for example, to get testimony from people who are too feeble, too sick, or too far away to come to the courtroom in person.) Documents are indispensable, but still the spoken word is the heart of the common-law trial—testimony fresh from the mouths of living, breathing witnesses, who stand or sit in plain view in the courtroom, examined and cross-examined by the lawyers. The system is so familiar— so ingrained—that we take it completely for granted; Americans find it astonishing to learn that there are other ways of running trials— that there are systems in which, basically, judges proceed by shuffling papers and documents.

Then, too, ours is a so-called *adversary* system. This means that the parties (and their lawyers) control the case. They plan the strategy; they dig up the evidence; they present it in court. The two sides battle it out mainly by putting witnesses on the stand and asking questions. Lawyers (or teams of lawyers) are the chief actors in the courtroom drama. The judge sits on the bench, more or less in the role of an umpire. He sees to it that both sides obey the rules of the game. He goes no further. If there is a jury, the judge does not usually decide the big question of who wins and who loses. That is the jury's job. The judge keeps the trial going; and he "instructs" the jury—that is, he tells them what rules of law have a bearing on the case. Unless the case is so lopsided that there is nothing for a jury to decide, the decision is left to the jury; the judge has to accept it, whether or not he likes it or agrees with it. Harry Kalven and Hans Zeisel, who carried out a major study of jury trials in criminal cases, claimed that the judge would have come out differently, had he decided, in about one case out of four.[18]

The adversary system is very familiar. Not everybody knows it by name or can describe it; but everybody recognizes it from books, movies, and TV. The adversary system is the system of courtroom drama, with lawyers parading their skills to an eager jury. It is Perry Mason and other detectives of fiction. It is Paul Newman in *The Verdict*. We take this method for granted.

But of course it is not the only way to run a trial. Civil-law countries, for example, do not use the adversary system. Their systems are *inquisitorial*. In France or Germany or Brazil, judges play a much greater role in building and deciding a case; they investigate the facts, they put the evidence together, they try to get to the bottom of the affair. Historically, civil-law systems have not used juries, and lawyers are not the dominant presence in the courtroom, as they are in common-law countries.

The two systems—adversary and inquisitorial—seem as different as day and night. There has been endless debate about which one is better. It is no surprise that common-law lawyers prefer their own ways. The very word *inquisitorial* leaves a bad taste in the mouth of people who speak English. Our lawyers feel that the adversary system is the only fair way to run a trial—the only way to give each party a proper shake. Justice and truth will win out nearly all of the time if we let each side argue, compete, cross-examine.

European lawyers naturally take a different point of view. To them, the adversary system is primitive and often unfair. Adversary trials, they feel, degenerate into battles carried on by trickster lawyers and the truth gets smothered in the process. *Their* system emphasizes the work of honest professionals—judges, in short. It is more efficient, more impartial, more just.

In fact, the adversary system is much less adversary than most people think; and the inquisitorial system is less inquisitorial. An American judge is not always neutral and helpless. He *runs* the trial in both obvious and subtle ways. Some specialized courts (family courts, for example) have gotten far away from the adversary system: the judges have tremendous leeway, and lawyers rarely or never show their faces. In fact, the power of the judge in such courts has been subject to a good deal of criticism; and some courts (juvenile courts, for example) have gotten more "legal" (that is, adversarial) in recent years.

Still more important is the fact that most cases never go to trial at all: they are settled out of court. What counts, then, is what happens outside the courtroom—in the corridors, in the lawyers' offices, and in the chambers of the judge. This may be equally true of legal disputes in civil-law countries. For this and other reasons, some scholars feel the two systems are tending to converge.

A Note on Equity. A short detour is in order here to explain one of the curious features of our legal history—one which, surprisingly, still has meaning today. Medieval England, which incubated the common law, also produced another system, almost entirely different, with its own courts, its own rules, its own procedures. These were the courts of the chancellor—the courts of "chancery." The rules and procedures of chancery made up the system called *equity*.

The origins of equity are shadowy.[19] In the Middle Ages, the chancellor was one of the king's highest officers. He had important administrative duties; he was also a clergyman, could read and write, and was in charge of the "writs" that set lawsuits in motion. Sometimes he also heard complaints about this or that instance of injustice; and, as the king's representative, he occasionally exercised his power to bend the rules of law a bit, to right some wrong or prevent some injustice. By the sixteenth and seventeenth centuries, equity had developed into a kind of full-blown rival to the common law. It was not just a difference of rules; the whole flavor of the system was different. The chancellor had never been immersed in the common law; if anything, it was church law (canon law) that he knew and that influenced him. Canon law was continental—civil law, in other words. Hence, procedure in equity looked a lot more like European law than like common law. For example, proceedings were written, not oral, and courts of chancery had no juries.

In many ways, equity was less rigid than the common law. This was even true of some of its procedures. In other ways, the two systems dovetailed. Only equity, for example, ever granted an "injunction"—that is, an order to a defendant to stop doing something wrong (or start doing something right). Common-law courts had no way of issuing such an order. On the other hand, the common-law courts could award money damages; equity could not. The English system of justice was essentially made up of law *plus* equity. Each one was, in itself, somewhat defective; together they made up a more satisfactory whole.

An example might make this clear. Suppose my grievance is the behavior of my next-door neighbor. He is running a business on his property. From my standpoint, the business is a nuisance. Foul odors and smoke pour out onto my property; my garden is getting ruined; noise keeps me up at night; the value of my property is certainly impaired. If I go to a court of "law," I can get money damages to make up for the harm my neighbor has done to me. But the court of "law" will not and cannot order him to stop. If he persists, I will have to go into court over and over again, each time collecting damages for harm done in the past.

To put a stop to this nuisance once and for all, I will have to find my remedy in "equity." There the judge, usually called a chancellor, can issue an injuction ordering my neighbor to stop his unlawful practices or suffer the consequences. So far, so good; but if I had gone to equity first, and asked for an injunction *and* money damages for harm already done to me, the chancellor would have politely turned me down on my claim for damages. For that, one has to go to "law."

Obviously, as this example shows, there is something clumsy about a dual system of this sort. It is certainly not ideal to have two separate systems, run by two separate structures of courts. Often in past times a litigant needed both to get justice. Law and equity coexisted in the United States, somewhat uneasily, until the nineteenth century. In that period, most of the states reformed their systems of procedure and merged law and equity into one. From that time on, the same courts administered both systems, and many distinctions between the two were abolished. Nonetheless, the old double system left fossil traces behind. It can still be important to know if a case would have been "law" or "equity." For one thing, equity had no jury; if a litigant today demands a jury in a case that historically is on the equity side, the court will turn him down.

Settled Out of Court. Systems of procedure and ways of managing trials are important to the American legal system. But most cases filed never get to trial. They fall by the wayside far earlier. In the lowest courts, creditors file thousands and thousands of claims to collect small debts, to repossess cars, television sets, suites of furniture; landlords file for thousands of evictions; and so on. Ninety-nine percent of the time (or more), the defendant never shows up, never defends himself in any way. Plaintiff wins "by default." (If defendant owes the money and has no real excuse for not paying, why *should* he show up?) Most of us have paid for parking tickets by sending money to traffic court in the form of "bail." Since we never show up for the trial of this dastardly crime, we forfeit the bail. This is what everybody expects: the forfeiture of bail is just a way to collect a fine without a trial, disguised under a different name.

The examples in the last paragraph are all small cases—petty matters—in the eyes of the law, at any rate. The situation in regular trial courts is not much different. Thousands and thousands of couples file for divorce; all but a few suits are uncontested. Thousands and thousands of estates go smoothly through probate without a will contest or serious dispute. Most criminal trials, even for serious offenses, do not go to trial: the defendants "cop a plea"—that is, they plead guilty as part of a plea bargain. Thousands and thousands of accident cases are filed every year; only a tiny percentage go to trial. In San Mateo County, California, in the 1970s, about 5 percent of the personal injury cases filed got to the jury stage. Even in federal court, only 8.7 percent of all civil cases filed in 1974 went to trial.[20] In California, as noted, almost nine cases out of ten in superior court ended without any trial, in 1980–81.

Most issues, in fact, never even reach the stage of filing. An elaborate recent study of disputes and dispute-settlement points up this fact. The study surveyed selected households in South Carolina, Pennsylvania, Wisconsin, New Mexico, and California to see what legal "grievances" people had and what became of them. The authors found that for every 1,000 grievances in tort—mostly personal injury matters—only 201 "disputes" emerged; and only 38 of these disputes ever got to the stage where somebody filed a complaint in court.[21] Most of these 38, moreover, will not go to the jury: they will get filtered out or settled before reaching that point. Thus only a third or so of one percent of all grievances go the whole route.

Yet this is supposed to be a litigious society. The fact is that courts play the role of decision maker in only a tiny percentage of grievance situations. Few contentious situations actually hatch and grow into regular trials. The survival rate is like that of the thousands of eggs which fish, frogs, or insects lay: out of each batch only a few survive.

What happens then to the other grievances? Why do so few cases start? Why do so few reach the goal line? The general answer is simple: trials are risky and expensive. Usually, both sides would be better off settling—and so settle they do. In auto accident cases, it makes sense for an insurance company to pay off the claim if the dollars are less than what a court case would cost and what it would probably lose at the trial. Similarly, it makes sense for the victim to settle, even for less than he would probably win at a trial. First of all, there is always the risk of losing. And the trial itself and the lawyers will cost him money, win or lose.[22] For most smallish claims, it *always* makes sense to try to settle.

This means that the "real" law of auto accidents is not to be learned simply by studying trials and cases. The real law is the law of insurance adjusters, lawyers' negotiations, and the like as well as the law of the courtroom. Of course, when a woman hit by a car settles with the driver's company we cannot assume that the law did not influence the outcome. The insurance company and the woman's lawyer are well aware of the state of the law. Hanging over their heads as they dicker are their guesses about the law and about the way a trial will actually come out if they get that far. These guesses affect the terms of their agreement. The parties bargain and reach settlement on their own; but they bargain "in the shadow of the law," to use one current and pungent phrase.[23]

The Business of the Courts. Exactly what kinds of case do courts handle? What is the business of the courts? We know surprisingly little in any systematic way about this subject. Judicial statistics are a sorry mess, generally speaking. Each state handles its own statistics; some are better than others; in all cases, it is hard to compare across state lines. Legal scholars have not done much to fill in the gaps. There are only a handful of studies that have tried to get a grip on the flow of business through general trial courts; petty courts are even more obscure.

You may find this surprising. After all, courts hardly work in secret. They deal with the public every day; ordinary people come in contact with them. These people no doubt form impressions about what courts do. Judges, lawyers, and court clerks have their impressions, too. But it is one thing to have impressions; to have a sound, systematic grasp of the facts is another thing. After all, we see other people every day, we look at them, we talk and interact with them; but without a census, we would never know exactly how many people live in this country, where they live, who they are, and so on. We would have impressions, of course; but impressions can be very, very wrong.

Bad as they are, published statistics on the work of the courts are a good place to start. They give some idea of the work load of courts. The Ohio courts of common pleas are trial courts of general jurisdiction. In 1975, 296 judges, in eighty-eight counties, served on these courts. Plaintiffs filed 249,822 cases during the year. These broke down roughly as follows: About 20,000 were personal injury cases (almost all of them probably automobile accidents). There were 97,000 "family law" cases; these were primarily divorce cases (80,000)—marriage accidents, as it were. There were 81,000 cases under the general heading of probate: the court processed 65,000 estates of people who had died, and the rest of the probate cases were about guardianships, trusts, and estates of minors. Some 6,700 cases were labeled "mental illness." (Most likely these were petitions to have somebody committed to a mental institution.) There were about 870 workmen's compensation cases (industrial accidents). This leaves about 42,000 miscellaneous cases—property and contract matters and whatever did not fit into any of the other categories. All this was on the civil side. The Court of Common Pleas also handled 31,554 felony cases and dealt with 194 juvenile matters.[24]

The Ohio figures are probably fairly typical. Each state does have its own quirks of jurisdiction, as well as its own way of counting and classifying cases. In some states, for example, separate courts would deal with probate or juvenile matters. The published figures for Florida's circuit courts are essentially similar to those of the Ohio courts. The Florida circuit courts are also courts of general jurisdiction. In 1975 there were twenty circuits and 272 judges in the state. They handled about the same number of civil cases as the Ohio courts—roughly 254,000. Of these, 34,000 were listed as "contract"; and 24,000 involved property rights (including 17,000 mortgage foreclosures). In other regards, the breakdown of cases was much the same as that in Ohio. In sheer bulk, auto accidents, divorce, and probate loomed very large.

These numbers are impressive. The numbers filed in petty courts, however, are almost astronomical. In California, traffic courts are branches of the regular municipal courts, and they accounted for the lion's share of the 14,970,216 filings in those courts in 1976–77. Of the filings, 58.5 percent (8,763,280) were about parking; another 32 percent were also concerned with traffic in one way or another. Another 6 percent were civil cases, half of them "small claims."[25] These figures give at least some idea of the tremendous number of petty cases that come up every day in the lowest courts. They are the plankton in the ocean of law.

What the numbers do not tell us, for whatever level of courts, is how much time and effort cases of particular types take up. Often, the states count the number of cases filed, not the number that go to trial (which, as we know, is a much smaller figure). Uncontested divorces, for example, puff up the figures enormously, especially in these days of no-fault divorce. These cases are short, snappy, routine. One big trial may gobble up more energy and manpower in court than hundreds of these cut-and-dried affairs. The bare statistics do not give us much feel for the court as a living organism.

We get a better idea from the (rare) studies of courts in actual operation. These confirm that much of what courts do is utterly routine. The uncontested, no-fault divorce is the perfect example. Often there is—or was—a real dispute. A marriage is on the rocks. He and she might argue about property—who gets the house or the car, how should the bank accounts be divided—or about custody of the kids or visiting rights. For most people, these problems are ironed out long before any papers hit the courtroom—or, in any event, long before the case reaches His Honor, the judge. The parties themselves work these matters out, sometimes with the help of lawyers. They—the parties and the lawyers—are the ones who decide the case.

The studies all agree on this point. The courts do a lot of routine administrative work; they rubber-stamp uncontested judgments and out-of-court decisions in a high percentage of the cases. Wayne McIntosh's study of the St. Louis Circuit Court from 1820 to 1970 shows clearly the dominance of voluntary dismissals and uncontested judgments. Less than one case out of five in 1970 called for any real judging.[26] Thousands of cases are handled every day in court that a clerk could dispatch—or a well-made machine.

Have courts, then, abandoned their historic functions? Some scholars think they have; others find the evidence conflicting. What is clear is that at most it is the ordinary dispute which has dropped out of court. A minority of extraordinary cases are still there; indeed, these extraordinary cases are becoming more common. Balanced against those who think the courts are doing too little are those (more numerous, probably) who think they are doing too much.

Appellate Courts. The work of appellate courts is, in a way, less obscure than the work of trial courts. High courts publish their opinions; their output is thus an open book. Moreover, these opinions are what students study in law school; they are the raw materials that lawyers often work with in deciding the state of the law. Also, it is the high courts that make headlines (if any courts do). No court in the world sits in the spotlight as much as the Supreme Court of the United States.

Despite this, the general public has only the vaguest idea what the Supreme Court does, day in and day out. They know chiefly about a few sensational cases. They probably know that the Supreme Court struck down state abortion laws; educated people almost certainly know that the Court ordered schools to desegregate. Almost certainly, they have never read any Supreme Court opinions (they might be dismayed to find out how wordy the justices are). People know only a little bit about the Court, and many of them probably have as much wrong information as right. (They know even less about what *state* high courts do.) There is a certain hunger for information (or gossip), which is only natural. *The Brethren,* by Bob Woodward and Scott Armstrong (1979), promised a look "inside the Supreme Court"; it was a runaway best-seller.

So much for the layman. Lawyers, on the other hand, know a great deal about certain aspects of appellate courts; but for lawyers, too, there are great gaps. Not many lawyers ever appear in front of an appeal court. Even the lawyers that do have not systematically studied the work flow in appellate courts (why should they?); they have only vague impressions about the state of the docket.

One lawyerly impression is that over the years the United States Supreme Court has been hearing more and more big, important cases; has gotten enmeshed more and more in controversy; and has handled more and more hot potatoes. This impression may well correspond to the facts. The Supreme Court has gradually gotten almost total control over the cases it takes and rejects; it has used its power to get rid of ordinary cases. Not every Supreme Court case makes the headlines; but every case is by some standard important and is worth at least a paragraph or two in the *New York Times.*

This was not true a century ago. Most of the opinions in Volume 105 of the United States Reports (covering October Term, 1881), are from cases the Court of today would never deign to take. In one, the Court had to decide whether a method of packing cooked meats for transport was novel enough to deserve a patent. (The meat was to be cooked at 212 degrees Fahrenheit, and "while yet warm," pressed into a box or case "with sufficient force to remove the air and all superfluous moisture, and make the meat form a solid cake.") The Court said no.[27] There were cases about public lands; what the customs tax should be on snuff and on white linen laces; whether a railroad was liable to a passenger who committed suicide in a fit of despondency six months after a railroad accident; whether a commodore in the navy who traveled under government orders to Rio de Janeiro, but in a foreign ship, was entitled to mileage at eight cents a mile. Cases of these types have totally disappeared from the Supreme Court docket.

State supreme courts have traveled a somewhat similar road. Many of them now have almost as much control of their cases as the United States Supreme Court. A statistical study of the work load of sixteen state supreme courts by Robert A. Kagan and associates, covering the period between 1870 and 1970, reveals dramatic changes in court business over time. The typical case in 1870 in the Supreme Court of North Carolina or California would be either a property case (a dispute, say, over who owned some tract of land) or a commercial case (whether a buyer, for example, had a good excuse for refusing to accept a carload of lumber; or an action to collect on a promissory note). In the period 1870–1900, 33.6 percent of the cases in these sixteen courts fell under the heading "debt and contract"; 21.4 percent fell under the heading "real property."

A more recent period (1940–70) showed quite a different picture. Debt-and-contract cases had shrunk to 15 percent, property cases to 10.9 percent. One big winner was "public law," up from 12.4 percent to 19.4 percent. These were cases on taxation, on regulation of business, on government abuse of authority. Criminal cases had risen from 10.7 percent to 18.2 percent, torts cases from 9.6 percent to 22.3 percent. Some of these trends were clearly accelerating; by 1970, criminal appeals had grabbed an amazing 28 percent share of the business of state supreme courts. Free counsel in criminal cases helps explain this great bulge of cases. The rise in torts cases is also not wholly unexpected. It reflects the great boom (if that is the word) in industrial accidents, followed by an even greater harvest of auto accidents, products liability cases, and such newfangled fads as medical malpractice.[28] Of course, more accidents does not necessarily mean more accident cases; many people feel there has also been a rise in claims-consciousness, but this is a matter of some dispute.

We must remember that the Kagan study looked only at the top courts in the sixteen states it studied. Many of the big states—California, for example—now have three layers of courts, not two. Some of the cases disappearing at the top are common at the middle level. It seems clear though, that something is happening even in smaller, two-tier states, like Idaho and Rhode Island. They are following the same road, though a bit more slowly and with less control of their destinies. The study tells us, at least, what kinds of dispute top courts consider important enough to spend time on; to a certain extent, we also learn something about the demand for the top court's time.

The trends are not inconsistent with what seems to be happening at the trial court level. Here, too, it is the ordinary case that gets squeezed out. Everyday business cases (contracts, property), which have become less common at the high court level, and the simpler family cases (estates of the dead) are also dropping off at the trial court level, or else, as in divorce, filings may be high, but actual trials are uncommon. On the other hand, cases in which individuals or groups confront the government seem to be increasing in number. This category includes criminal cases. Most criminal cases get plea-bargained out, but of those that "stay the course," more will be hard-fought and more will get appealed than would have been true a century ago.

There seems also to be rapid growth in numbers for some cases of special and extraordinary types. This is certainly true in the federal courts; also, to a lesser extent, in state courts. These are cases about society's toughest problems and dirtiest linen—the deepest, most sensitive, most poignant issues of the day. Many people—from the Chief Justice on down—wonder why some of them are in court at all. They illustrate something mysterious and fundamental about American society and its legal system. In the United States, social issues often dress themselves up in legal costume and muscle their way into court. There are few countries in the world where abortion policy is decided, in the first instance, by judges. In few, if any, countries would courts draw the boundary lines of school districts or demand wholesale reform in state mental health facilities. Yet these things happen in the United States.

A movement is going on which is bringing these issues into court more and more—which expands the very idea of law and spreads it throughout society, into nooks and corners where it never penetrated before. Nobody has quite found the right name for this movement or trend. We can call aspects of it judicialization, legalization, constitutionalization, the due-process revolution, or something similar. Whatever its name, it is certainly a significant trend. Courtlike procedures and habits extend their tentacles throughout government, big institutions, and society in general. Courts themselves have become final arbiters of many social issues, not just individual disputes.

How Courts Decide Cases

We have looked at the kinds of cases courts hear, the way they are handled, and the numbers that get filtered out along the way.

What kinds of outcomes do the surviving cases produce? And how are they decided? What factors tilt verdicts and decisions one way or the other?

Lower courts take evidence, hear arguments. Then the jury, if there is one, retires, talks things over, votes, and brings in a verdict. The jury deliberates in secret and never gives out reasons for what it does. (Individual members sometimes talk to reporters after the verdict is in, when the case is newsworthy.) Generally speaking, the mind of the jury is a closed book. Research has lifted the curtain a little bit. We know, for example, that the thought processes of juries are not terribly different from those of judges (there is about an 80 percent overlap); that juries *do* pay attention to what the judge tells them; that they generally try to live up to their expected role.[29] Historically, there have been many examples of jury "lawlessness": refusals to convict bootleggers or drunken drivers or poachers or even rapists, and even when the defendants were clearly guilty. This happened because the jury reflected norms outside the official norms of the law. This sort of jury lawlessness still exists; but on a very modest scale.[30]

What about the higher courts? Appeals courts do not run trials; but they hear oral arguments, receive "briefs," confer, decide, and write opinions. (A brief is a lawyer's formal argument, putting before the judge one side's version of the law and facts. Many of them are anything but brief.) The opinions pour out of the presses every year, volume after volume. Every state publishes opinions from its highest court, and many states (New York, California, and others) publish opinions from middle-level courts as well. Pennsylvania even publishes some trial court opinions. A good law library has literally thousands of these volumes of reports, and more of them come out every year. There are over 450 bound volumes for the United States Supreme Court alone. Opinions of the lower federal courts fill over a thousand volumes; there are many times that number for state courts. Inside these volumes are millions of words—all, in a way, telling the world how the court decided its cases.

The typical written opinion follows a fairly standard format. The opinion sets out the facts, states what the issues are, looks at past cases (if any) on the same subject, looks at statutes (if any) which have a bearing, and discusses the relevance of these "authorities." The court will announce certain legal principles, which it (or courts in earlier cases) squeezed out of precedents or statutes. It matches these principles with the facts of the case and comes up with an answer to whatever question or riddle is posed. This, then, is the decision. It either agrees with the results of the lower court (in which case the decision below is "affirmed"), or it disagrees (in which case the decision below is "reversed").

Usually, the decision is unanimous—that is, all the judges agree with the outcome. Less often, one or more of the judges has a different view of the matter, and there will be a "dissent." Courts almost always have an odd number of judges (three in Idaho; nine in the United States Supreme Court). The majority wins. If there is no majority (if a judge is sick or absent or disqualifies himself and the rest split evenly), the lower court decision will stand. Once in a while, a judge who agrees with the majority as far as its result is concerned will nonetheless quibble about the reasons. Such a judge can write a special opinion, called a "concurrence."

In some courts, dissent is quite common; in others it is rare. Cases of some kinds are dissent-prone; others are not. The percentage of cases with dissents has been rising over time. In the study of sixteen state supreme courts, it was found that all but 8.7 percent of reported cases in 1870–1900 were unanimous. The nonunanimous cases rose to 15 percent by 1940–70. In the latest decade of the study, 1960–70, the rate had risen still more, to more than 16 percent.

These were the aggregate figures. Variations from court to court were striking. About 98 percent of the cases decided by the highest court of West Virginia were unanimous in the 1960s, but only about 56 percent of such cases in Michigan. In some courts, there seems to be a tradition of squelching dissent. Other courts place less value on presenting a united front. The overall trend, however, is clear. High courts take and decide fewer cases than they did a century ago; but the ones they take are more controversial and this generates more dissent, though the rate is rising rather slowly.[31]

Dissents are often more personal, less legalistic than majority opinions; but in essence they rehash the same sorts of legal arguments. They do make clear, at the very least, that in many cases there are no "right" legal answers—or at any rate the right answers are not self-evident, even to a judge. Most close scholars of the legal process also doubt that the law is clear and knowable, even in unanimous decisions. After all, few appeals are "frivolous" (that is, totally hopeless). There is *some* argument, at least, for either side.

In general, scholars who study courts are a fairly skeptical lot. They read the written opinions, but they take them with a grain of salt. They certainly do not think that written opinions give an accurate picture of what goes on in the minds of the judges. They are suspicious of the dry legal arguments. They find it hard to believe that these arguments really persuade the judges—really move them to choose one side over the other.

But if not, what does? And is the elaborate facade of legal reasoning nothing but window dressing? An immense effort has gone into the study of judicial decision-making, trying to smoke out the governing factors and paint a realistic picture of the process. It is not an easy job. Nobody can read minds; few papers, notes, or diaries of judges are available; and judges rarely tattle on themselves. They are shy creatures, who dislike public attention. They want obscurity, and they generally get it.

The United States Supreme Court is a special case. Its decisions can hardly avoid the limelight. Yet its actual work goes on behind a velvet curtain of secrecy. Some judges even destroy their legal papers. Enough remains to shed some light on the process, but there are many gaps. The air of mystery is probably one reason for the astounding success of *The Brethren*, the "exposé" of the court which was published in 1979. The book was based in part on gossip leaked from the justices' clerks. It titillated the public with its claim of tearing aside the veil of secrecy. In the introduction, the authors described the court as an institution working "in absolute secrecy." No other institution has "so completely controlled the way it is viewed by the public." The public was in general quite eager to read this collection of tidbits about the justices, their habits, their likes and dislikes, their internal bickering, their opinions about each other, the little inside dramas that led to this or that famous decision.

The Brethern was hardly systematic. Some scholars, however, have tried to study judicial behavior in a more rigorous way. Much of the effort has gone into dissecting the work of the United States Supreme Court; much less has been done on the work of state courts or lower federal courts. The overall questions are the same: Can we find some factors which explain why judges decide the way they do? Does it matter whether a judge is a Republican or a Democrat? Whether his family was rich or poor? Whether he is Protestant or Catholic? How much can we learn by exploring judges' attitudes or values? How much would we learn if we could give the judges personality tests?

The results are not terribly exciting. One study of the supreme court of Michigan found that Democrats were more likely than Republicans to favor "claims of the unemployed and the injured."[32] But on the whole the studies do not tell us much that is new or surprising or enlightening. The background or the personality of a judge apparently do not carry us very far in explaining why he votes the way he does. Perhaps the measures are too crude. In any event, the research has not reaped much of a harvest.[33] Much more sophisticated research and better theories are needed.[34]

Trial court research has been disappointing, too. Many scholars suspect that judges, consciously or not, are prejudiced against blacks or poor people; or that white-collar criminals are treated better (or worse) than street criminals; or that courts are more lenient (or harsher) toward women defendants. There have been many, many studies—well over a hundred—on such issues. What is surprising is how little has been proven one way or another. Do blacks charged with a crime in the United States today (yesterday may be different) get a worse shake than whites facing the same sort of charge? It turns out that this question is devilishly hard to answer, because of problems with data and because there are so many variables.[35] The jury is still out, so to speak, on this general subject.

The meager harvest from these lines of research led some scholars to try a different tack. Have we been too skeptical about the effect of the law itself on decisions? Perhaps judges honestly try to live up to what is expected of them. Perhaps they really try to play their part. Society has cast them in the role of judge, and they try to follow the script. In other words, the job description, the black robes, the tradition may be as important in explaining judicial behavior as are childhood background or training or social class. As far as appellate courts are concerned, there is also the doctrine of "precedent," that is, the idea that courts are supposed to follow past cases—indeed, they are "bound" by them. Despite our skepticism, is it possible that this is what judges are really trying to do? It at least sounds plausible. But the idea that the law itself is the decisive variable still waits for more rigorous tests.

The conceptual and methodological issues are quite complex. A recent article by Ilene H. Nagel analyzes decisions on whether to grant bail or not, in about 5,600 criminal cases from a borough of New York City, 1974–75. The study seemed to confirm that "formal law" was a significant factor in the "decision calculus" of the courts. It was not the only factor, but it was extremely significant. "Bias" on the part of judges played a lesser role. But Nagel also points out what many studies gloss over: the law itself often embodies a flexible, shifting standard. Judges are allowed by law to take many factors into account. Thus the distinction between legal and extralegal factors has been much overdrawn and overemphasized: "the complexities of law have often been ignored, and the extralegal category has been narrowly and selectively defined." Understanding how courts work will take continued study and greater sophistication in design.[36]

A few scholars have stressed what we might call the "structural" element in decisions.[37] High court cases are decided by groups of judges, not by one judge sitting alone. The Supreme Court, as we mentioned, is made up of nine justices. California's top court has seven. The middle-level federal courts usually deliberate in panels of three. Typically, there will be some sort of process for assigning cases to particular judges, who then draft an opinion. To build a majority, a judge may have to make some sort of "deal"—concessions to other judges who more or less agree with him. He may have to tone down certain language, or change the emphasis, and so on.

This process was one of the Supreme Court "secrets" that *The Brethern* so breathlessly revealed. No political scientist or court watcher was much surprised, of course. *This* inside dope was old hat. It does say something about structure: a single judge, sitting alone, does not have to shade his views to construct a majority. He is, however, concerned with the structure on top of him. He prefers not to be reversed on appeal. It is also obvious that upper courts need and want the cooperation of lower courts, which, after all, apply the doctrines and rules that upper courts lay down. Some high courts may make concessions or frame rules with the lower courts in mind.

There has been surprisingly little work on still another factor: the influence of outside social forces. One reason is that research tends to focus on differences among judges. The studies ask why Judge A seems to disagree with Judge B in his voting. This means concentrating on cases where at least one judge dissented. But it might be just as interesting and important to note the ways in which Judge A and Judge B think alike—to see how all judges change their tune in the course of time, under the pressure of social change.

For example, all judges (or almost all) today have attitudes about race relations, powers of government, civil liberties, and the like that are light years away from the attitudes of almost all the judges who worked and wrote a century ago. If you brought back to life a nineteenth-century judge, he would be dumbfounded to learn about the state of civil rights law today. He would even be amazed at what has happened in tort law—how far the courts have gone in making companies pay for damages caused by badly designed products, such as defective cold cream, soup, medicine, and automobiles. The wheels of doctrine have turned many times, in response to changes in the world outside the courtroom. True, some judges today stand on the right side of the political spectrum, while others stand on the left. But the point around which they revolve—the point *from* which they deviate, right or left—is determined by social forces; by the national agenda; in short, by the way things are today.

If we look at the long run—at major trends—the law seems like so much putty in the hands of the larger society. Probably there was not one judge in the nineteenth century who thought the death penalty was unconstitutional. Some were for it, some against it; nobody imagined that it violated the Eighth Amendment of the Constitution, or any other amendment, for that matter. Today, some judges think it does. The Supreme Court, as we will see, has gone around and around on this question. To be sure, most judges feel the death penalty should be upheld. But even they would agree that it poses a serious legal question. This was not true a hundred years ago.

Similarly, most nineteenth century judges saw nothing wrong, legally speaking, with segregation of the races. Today, not a single federal judge thinks it acceptable (or is willing to admit he does). If anybody suggested to John Marshall or his associates—or to Thomas Jefferson himself—that the First Amendment meant the right to sell picture books showing naked people making love, they would have thought that person crazy. The world has changed since then; judges' ideas have changed accordingly. And so has the law.

Social change drags doctrine along. Judges live in society; and their way of thinking shifts, unconsciously, as things happen in the world all around them. Often they are hardly aware of what is going on. If you ask judges what they do and how they decide cases, they are still likely to tell a rather old-fashioned tale. They will say that they search conscientiously for the law, and that they are guided by existing law. Most of them deny that they take social policy into account. Yes, they have values and beliefs; but they try to suppress them. This general pattern emerges from the few interview studies of judges. There is variation among judges (and courts); but on the whole, the typical judge is quite conservative in what he says about his job. In a study by Henry A. Glick, for example, Louisiana judges—almost to a man—expressed the opinion that "nonlegal factors" play no role in a judge's decision making.[38]

There is no reason to accuse the judges of Louisiana of hypocrisy. No doubt they meant what they said. Judges do try to play the "legal" role, though probably not in every case. Some cases seem minor or unimportant; they are interesting only to lawyers, or not even to them.

When a case of this kind comes up, the judge may have no strong feelings one way or the other. He (or a clerk) "looks up the law," figures out which way old cases point, and goes with the flow of past doctrine.

Even these cases, of course, may not be as cut-and-dried as one might think. As every law student comes to know, the law is often cloudy, ambiguous, uncertain. What the judge sees as the law is, in many cases, a little like a social inkblot test. He sees the case through his personal lenses. In these cases, the law is not in the books; it is inside the judge's head.

A small but important batch of cases falls into quite a different and distinctive group. These cases cut much closer to the bone. They have massive importance, massive consequences. Here social currents swirl all about, filling the courtroom with their sound and motion; and these currents affect the judge whether he knows it or not. In other words, we can think of decision making as a kind of two-stage process. The first stage is the judge's decision whether to play the law game or not. The second stage is the actual decision.

At both stages, attitudes, values, and social forces are crucial. After all, these are what determine whether the judge sees a question as boring or exciting, important or trivial, technical or nontechnical, socially and politically sensitive or only "legal." The judge, though, may not be aware at all of this two-stage process. He feels that he is strictly bound by the law; and nine times out of ten he is quite sure that "looking for the law" is exactly what he is doing. But the two-stage process explains a mystery—how is it that social forces seem to have a powerful influence on the way the cases come out; yet at the same time judges say (and feel) that they simply "follow the law."

Glick's study found that most high-court judges do not think of themselves as policymakers or as lawmakers. They are old-fashioned in their attitudes about judging. But not all of them: some have a more sophisticated notion. This was true, for example, of the judges in New Jersey. Their minds were much more open to policy issues, which frankly played a role (they felt) in decisions. There is some evidence—it is rather indirect—that high court judges in general are moving in this direction. We can call this attitude legal realism. "Legal realism" is the name of a school of legal thought which flourished most notably in the 1930s. The realists argued that judges were much more independent than they admitted; they sneered at the idea that the way to decide cases was by logical deduction from preexisting cases and rules. Judges in our system make law; they create new pol-

icy. In fact, they cannot help doing so, in certain cases. A realist judge
would be a judge who is aware of outside and inside pressures—aware
of the way they affect his work. He would be sensitive to the impact
of his decisions, that is, their social consequences; and he would be
willing to take these into account.

How do we know that legal realism is a genuine force—that judges
are gradually converting to this faith? Some crude measures can be
found by looking at the style of judicial opinions. This is definitely
changing over time. For one thing, opinions are getting longer; dissents have become more common. Interesting changes are taking place,
too, in citation patterns. When a court writes an opinion, it typically
sprinkles citations about in the text. These are the "authorities" that
justify its decision.

Mostly, the "authorities" are cases—prior decisions on the same
legal points. The court will also cite any laws (statutes) on the books
that have a bearing on the case, or cite the Constitution, if that is in
issue. In a small but growing percentage of cases, the court reaches
out a little bit further. In California, for example, the citation of law
reviews (scholarly journals, mostly published by university law schools)
doubled between 1950 and 1970. In 1960–70, about 35 percent of the
opinions written by New Jersey's highest court cited law reviews; the
California figure was about 26 percent. (In such states as Alabama and
Kansas, however, only 2 or 3 percent of the opinions cited law reviews.)
A few cases even cited newpapers or studies by social scientists.
Typhoon winds of social change rage about the courts; the problems
that high courts face become more and more massive and intractable.
As a result some judges reach, however gingerly and delicately, for
outside help.[39]

Most of the research has dealt with high courts, and especially the
United States Supreme Court. It is certainly no surprise that this is
the prime focus of study. The Supreme Court is unique in our system. The state high courts are also of obvious importance. After all,
they make and unmake common law. The lower courts suffer from
scholarly neglect.

This is a pity. The lower courts may be undramatic; but that does
not mean they are unimportant. The day-to-day work of lower courts—
even traffic courts and small-claims courts—has a tremendous effect
on the lives of ordinary people. In the long run, these courts have a
tremendous effect on the life of society, as well. It was in the lower
courts that the collusive or friendly divorce developed, long before
anybody thought of a no-fault system. In the lower courts, creditors

repossess thousands and thousands of pianos, automobiles, TV sets, suites of furniture. These courts foreclose mortagages, evict tenants, garnishee wages. In all these cases, they act as the agents of a bustling, growing, rampant economy—for better or for worse.

That is not all. They also process hundreds of thousands of wills, they naturalize foreigners, they let people change their names, they put their stamp on the adoption of children, they send someone's senile old uncle to a home, they approve accounts of guardians and trustees. They smooth over (or aggravate) unnumbered disputes among families or neighbors. They punish millions of drunks, millions of speeders, millions who disturb the peace. They register far-reaching changes in social and economic life. They take part, in other words, in a series of events, utterly trivial looked at one at a time, but of volcanic importance in the mass. Fresh research may someday clarify how much they have meant to this country.

5

The Structure of American Law: Statutes and Statute Makers

*C*OURTS ARE PROBABLY the best-known legal institution, except perhaps for the police. But they are not necessarily the most powerful. One classical and durable legal theory has always insisted that courts have no right or power to make new law. They can only "find" law, or at best apply old law to new situations. It is the legislatures that have the right to make law, boldly and openly. Indeed, this is their job: they "pass laws." Yet when students study legal process in this country, they focus almost entirely on the courts (including the way in which courts *do* make law, despite the theory). Legal education more or less neglects legislative bodies—Congress, state legislatures, city councils. It also neglects the administrative agencies.

Yet the legislative branch is a tremendous presence in society and in the legal system. It is part of the bulk and body of Leviathan. There are great numbers of lawmaking bodies, all up and down the land. As with the courts, we can imagine them arranged in a kind of pyramid. At the base of the pyramid, in the typical state, are the lawmaking organs of local government. In the 1960s, according to one authority, there were over 3,200 local legislative bodies in California alone.[1] These included city councils, county boards (boards of supervisors), and thousands of special purpose bodies. At the time there were fifty-seven counties in California (San Francisco was specially classified as a "city-county") and 394 cities. There were 1,575 school districts and 3,224 special districts (in charge of parks, sewers, bridges, mosquito abatement, and so on).

One could quibble about whether these were all really legislative bodies, but they all have one thing in common: it is part of their business to establish general rules. This is of course obvious for legislatures, which churn out "laws" or "statutes"; towns and cities produce "ordinances." Park districts, transit authorities, sewer districts, and so on, also make rules which are binding inside their own small orbits of power.

The state legislature sits at the top of the pyramid in California. It is made up of two houses—a senate and an assembly. Every state has a legislature; and in every state except Nebraska the legislature is bicameral, like California's—that is, there are two houses, an upper and a lower. California is divided into legislative "districts," which elect senators and assemblymen. At one time, senators were elected more or less on a county basis. One man represented the millions of people in Los Angeles County; at the same time, a few thousand voters in the high Sierra counties had a senator all to themselves. The United States Supreme Court put an end to this; it declared most forms of "malapportionment" illegal, in a series of cases that began with *Baker* v. *Carr*.[2] Today, all senatorial districts in California are more or less equal in population.

Legislative bodies in California have been described as forming a kind of pyramid, like the courts. The analogy is somewhat misleading. In some ways, the organization is very much looser: there is no such thing as an "appeal" from the city of Fresno, California, to the legislature; or from Yolo County to the legislature; or from the city of Hollister, California, to the county of San Benito. A citizen can, of course, complain that a city or town has overstepped its legal powers. But this complaint need not go to the legislature, and normally would not. It would most likely go to the courts.

But in another respect, legislative control over cities, counties, and towns goes far beyond the control which a high court exercises over lower courts. The legislature is in theory totally supreme. It can completely change the laws about towns and counties. It can shift boundary lines or add new counties. It can charter cities, amend charters, or take charters away. It could even abolish some local governments. In practice, the legislature stays out of most local affairs. But the state capital does have the last word; it is politics, not legal structure, that protects cities and counties from massive change from above.

We live, of course, in a federal system. There is a national legislature, too: the Congress. It, too, is divided into an upper house (the

Senate), and a lower house (the House of Representatives). The House is elected on a population basis; but every state is entitled to at least one representative, no matter how tiny its population. There are 435 members, or roughly one for every 500,000 people. There are 100 senators; each state has two, regardless of the size of the state or its population. California, with over 20 million people, has two senators; so do states with less than a million people, like Wyoming, Alaska, and Vermont. This scheme was written into the Constitution, and it is immune to *Baker* v. *Carr*.

The legislative system, like the rest of our legal structure, is influenced by federalism and, more significantly, by the American habit of decentralization. Voters take it for granted that the people they elect represent localities and local interests. We do not elect senators or congressmen "at large." The representatives in Congress must please the people in their districts, or they will find themselves out of a job. Also, in states and in most cities, each lawmaker is elected from a particular district, and must be a resident of that district.

This is not the case in England, for example; a member of Parliament from East London need not live there at all. The American system struck James Bryce (who wrote a classic description of American government in the late nineteenth century) as plainly deficient. It meant that "inferior" men would inevitably sit in Congress: "There are many parts of the country which do not grow statesmen, where nobody . . . is to be found above a moderate level of political capacity." It was his opinion that men of "marked ability and zeal" were "produced chiefly in the great cities of the older States."[3] This sounds snobbish and wrong to American ears; but clearly, our system tends to send men to Congress (and to state capitals like Albany and Sacramento and to city halls) who lack the "big picture"; they think first and last of the wants and needs of their own little districts.

It is easy to think of legislatures and courts as alternative, or even as rival, lawmakers. In some ways they are. But in our tradition, legislatures do many things which courts cannot do at all, or do only poorly. Legislatures can impose taxes and can spend money, which courts cannot really do, at least not directly. Courts respond to particular cases, in which John Smith sues Mary Jones, or the Acme Toothpick Company sues the city of Little Rock. In making a decision, an appeal court may lay down a general rule; but even so, the rule is supposed to be limited to the class of cases which *Smith* v. *Jones* represents.

Of course, it is anybody's guess how broad that category is. But in theory, anything that goes beyond the case is "dictum" (incidental talk) and is not binding on later courts. Whatever the theory, courts do act with caution most of the time. They do not presume to lay down minute, specific, detailed regulations. When a court hears a zoning case that turns on whether a gas station can be lawfully opened for business on the corner of Oak and Elm, the court may think the whole zoning ordinance or plan badly needs redoing; but it will not assume it has the right or the power to redo it on its own. Nor do courts change the speed limit or adjust parking fines; they do not generate systems of traffic rules or propose a list of chemical additives that can safely be used to make chicken soup yellow. Courts, in general, do not evolve quantitative measures. That is left to the legislature. In the opinion of some critics, courts have strayed far from their classic preserves, but the general line between courts and other bodies still holds.

The Legislative Output

The sheer volume of work done by legislatures, in the mass, is growing by leaps and bounds. This fact seems crystal-clear, though there are few systematic studies of legislative output and even fewer on the output of city councils and other similar bodies. In 1975, 4,331 bills were introduced in the California legislature.[4] The typical statute book of a typical state, in the mid-nineteenth century, consisted of one fat volume; in other words, all the statutes in force in, say, Michigan or Indiana were gathered together in a single book. Today, the collected statutes of the states, even small states, run ten or twenty times that size.

The reasons are not difficult to find. This is a complex society, and governing it calls for many detailed rules. (Consider, for example, how much law is on the books because of, or about, the automobile.) And, just as courts have occasionally fudged the borders between their work and that of legislatures, so too have legislatures encroached on what was historic turf of common-law courts. For example, there was a vast body of law (and litigation) on industrial accidents in the nineteenth century; the courts created and developed almost all of the rules. Around the time of the First World War, the states began to pass workmen's compensation laws, which covered most of this field and basically changed the rules of the game.[5]

The change was, of course, not just a matter of taste. The courts had developed rules which were for the most part vague and general.

The new statutes were precise and detailed. For example, in the Idaho statute (passed in 1917), a worker who lost his "great toe at the proximal joint" in a work accident would receive 55 percent of his average weekly wage (but not more than twelve dollars a week) for fifteen weeks. It is exactly this kind of precision which goes beyond the traditional power of courts. At any rate, though an immense body of case law on workmen's compensation has accumulated in the last sixty-five years or so, the basic scheme operates in a routine and administrative way, under ground rules and schedules set up by the legislature. Even court cases on the subject use the statute as their starting point.

Codes and Uniform Laws

The common-law system is inherently messy; to understand what the law is, one must (in theory) rummage about in volume after volume of published cases. Judge-made law, in the United States, with its fifty states, is especially ragged, nonuniform, inconsistent. A code setting out the rules of law is much neater and more concise. Perhaps it is fairer, too, since it makes clear what the law is in advance. As the English philosopher Jeremy Bentham pointed out in the early nineteenth century, common-law judges made law "as a man makes laws for his dog. When your dog does anything you want to break him of, you wait till he does it, and then you beat him for it."[6] Civil-law systems, with their clean, logical codes, at least *seemed* much more rational.

In the nineteenth century, some jurists in the United States, too, were intrigued by the idea of codifying the law—taking excess power away from judges and setting out the basic rules of law in modern codes. The idea is associated above all with David Dudley Field, a New York lawyer (1805–94). Field drafted or supervised a whole series of codes. The most successful was the Code of Civil Procedure. New York adopted this code in 1848. It merged law and equity into a single system; and in other ways, too, simplified and modernized pleading and process in court. But New York turned down Field's other codes, which dealt with substance. These codes, orphaned in New York, found homes in some of the western states—states like California and Montana. Even in these states, lawyers were not trained in habits of reverence for statutes; the attitude of judges and lawyers toward the civil code of California is far different from the attitude of French judges and lawyers toward *their* civil code.

At the end of the nineteenth century, another strong but quite different codification movement arose. This movement focused on commercial law. The United States had entered the age of railroads, telephones, telegraph, interstate business. Goods and labor moved freely across state lines; laws did not. A company that did business in many states, or that sold its goods in many states, had to try somehow to comply with a whole host of slightly different laws.

The "uniform laws" movement was the brainchild of law professors, jurists, and bar groups; but the reason for its success was almost certainly the fact that the business community felt a need for its products. In 1892, a Conference of Commissioners on Uniform State Laws was founded. The commissioners were appointed by the governors of the states. The first "uniform" law suggested by the Conference was the Negotiable Instruments Law (1896), dealing with checks, bills of exchange, and promissory notes. It was quite successful; every state eventually adopted it. The Uniform Sales Act (1906) won thirty-four adoptions. The commissioners continued their labors and drafted many other laws, some of which also proved popular. The Uniform Simultaneous Death Act is one example. This statute dealt with the mess that results when, for example, husband and wife die together in a common wreck and their estates are entangled with each other. Most states have adopted this uniform act.

But no state is forced to enact a "uniform" law; and in practice the laws may not be quite so uniform as they may look in print. Interpretations sometimes vary from state to state, and local amendments are always possible. Undaunted, scholars in the 1940s and 1950s proceeded with a complex task: drafting (and selling) a whole commercial code. The leader was Karl Llewellyn, one of the country's foremost legal scholars. The Uniform Commercial Code, divided into ten divisions ("Articles"), goes over ground covered by at least half a dozen older laws. It replaces the Negotiable Instruments Law, the Sales Act, and others of the older "uniform" laws.

The code got off to a rocky start, and met with considerable sales resistance. Massachusetts and Pennsylvania adopted it, however; and finally, after intensive efforts, it took off everywhere. Louisiana is now the main holdout. Still, each state is formally free (if it wishes) to repeal or change the code. The code is a good example of how it is possible to come close to legal unity in this enormous country, simply through state cooperation and parallelism. But obviously this sort of uniformity can never be as stable and complete as the uniformity that comes from a single central government.

Statutes: Form and Content

It is hard to generalize about the form or content of statutes. A statute can be about any subject that law touches on—which means, in practice, anything. The form, too, is infinitely various. Usually we think of statutes as being general directives, unlike decisions, which apply to particular cases. It is a statute that makes burglary a crime and fixes a range of punishment; but whether Joe Doakes, a particular burglar, goes to jail is a decision made by judges, juries, and others, not by a legislature.

But even this statement is only partly right. Not all statutes are general directives. Congress, for example, still passes many so-called private laws, which may apply to a single person. Private Law 95-19 of the 95th Congress (1977) authorized a visa and permanent residence for Kam Lin Cheung, "notwithstanding the provision of section 212(a)(25) of the Immigration and Nationality Act." A day later, a private law authorized the secretary of commerce to sell "two obsolete vessels, AOG-1 Patapsco and AOG-9 Kishwaukee" to Mid-Pacific Sea Harvesters, Inc., of Hawaii. Still another private act of 1977 excused a trucking company from the consequences of filing a bill too late and awarded the company $1,725.60 for carting a load of explosives to Fort Walters, Texas.[7]

Private laws were once common in state legislatures, too: they chartered corporations, settled minor property disputes, straightened out administrative messes, and even granted divorces. In 1850, for example, the Alabama legislature passed a law changing the name of Matthew Robinson McClung to Matthew McClung Robinson.[8] Another private law allowed a certain John B. Moore ("who has been engaged in practicing medicine nine years . . . and is considered skillful and useful") to continue as a doctor, even though he had no license.[9] But private acts came to demand too much legislative time, and were open to corruption besides. After the Civil War, state constitutions began to outlaw the practice. The Illinois Constitution of 1870 forbade "local or special laws," and provided that "in all . . . cases where a general law can be made applicable, no special law shall be enacted."[10]

The output of Congress or a state legislature, in any session, consists of dozens and dozens of statutes. Some are long, complicated, and important; others may change a comma or two or make some trivial amendment to an older law. Some statutes lay down broad principles which courts or agencies will have to flesh out and interpret; other laws contain detailed regulations, dotting almost every i and crossing every t.

The Internal Revenue Code (the federal tax law) is probably the most complicated law (or system of laws) in the United States. Some of its provisions are broad and general; other parts of the code go into incredible detail. It is also totally unreadable, a dark, impenetrable jungle which only specialists can tackle; and even they have plenty of trouble. Here is a sample of its prose. This is Section 71 of the code, and essentially it carries this message: if a divorced or legally separated woman gets alimony payments, she must report these payments as taxable income on her income tax return. This rule, however, does not apply to a lump-sum alimony payment.

(1) **Decree of divorce or separate maintenance.**—If a wife is divorced or legally separated from her husband under a decree of divorce or of separate maintenance, the wife's gross income includes periodic payments (whether or not made at regular intervals) received after such decree in discharge of (or attributable to property transferred, in trust or otherwise, in discharge of) a legal obligation which, because of the marital or family relationship, is imposed on or incurred by the husband under the decree or under a written instrument incident to such divorce or separation.

(2) **Written separation agreement.**—If a wife is separated from her husband and there is a written separation agreement executed after the date of the enactment of this title, the wife's gross income includes periodic payments (whether or not made at regular intervals) received after such agreement is executed which are made under such agreement and because of the marital or family relationship (or which are attributable to property transferred, in trust or otherwise, under such agreement and because of such relationship). This paragraph shall not apply if the husband and wife make a single return jointly.

(3) **Decree for support.**—If a wife is separated from her husband, the wife's gross income includes periodic payments (whether or not made at regular intervals) received by her after the date of the enactment of this title from her husband under a decree entered after March 1, 1954, requiring the husband to make the payments for her support or maintenance. This paragraph shall not apply if the husband and wife make a single return jointly.

(c) Principal sum paid in installments.—

(1) **General rule.**—For purposes of subsection (a), installment payments discharging a part of an obligation the principal sum of which is, either in terms of money or property, specified in the decree, instrument, or agreement shall not be treated as periodic payments.

(2) **Where period for payment is more than 10 years.**—If, by the
terms of the decree, instrument, or agreement, the principal sum referred
to in paragraph (1) is to be paid or may be paid over a period ending
more than 10 years from the date of such decree, instrument, or agreement, then (notwithstanding paragraph (1)) the installment payments shall
be treated as periodic payments for purposes of subsection (a), but (in
the case of any one taxable year of the wife) only to the extent of 10
percent of the principal sum. For purposes of the preceding sentence,
the part of any principal sum which is allocable to a period after the
taxable year of the wife in which it is received shall be treated as an
installment payment for the taxable year in which it is received.

At the other end of the spectrum are laws which delegate broad
authority to the president or some agency, or which speak in very
vague, general terms. The famous Sherman Act, passed by Congress
in 1890, is the fountainhead of federal antitrust law, the branch of law
that deals with monopoly and restraints on trade. The Sherman Act
is only a page or so long. One key provision simply outlaws "every
contract, combination . . . or conspiracy in restraint of trade"; another
provides that everyone who "shall monopolize or attempt to monopolize" any part of interstate commerce is guilty of a misdemeanor.
Obviously, this leaves many questions unanswered. What *is* a monopoly? What does it mean to "restrain" trade? If a company controls 56
percent of the market in lead pencils, is it "monopolizing" this market? Anyway, do pencils constitute a "market"?

The act is, to say the least, not very specific. Nor does it set up
any special agency or body to run the fight against "trusts" and to
decide how the law should be interpreted and enforced. In this regard,
the Sherman Act is quite different from other regulatory statutes,
particularly later ones. But the law which created a Federal Communications Commission is also marvelously vague. The commission
has power to license radio and television stations; the only standard
mentioned in the law is "public convenience and necessity." This means
nothing much in itself, but at least we know that the commission will
be in charge. They will put some flesh on the bare bones of the statute. It would have been nice if Congress had given the commission
some guidance; Congress chose not to.

As far as the Sherman Act is concerned, policy is set by the attorney general, the Justice Department, and the lower courts. They have
the job of deciding what to consider a violation, whom to prosecute,
whom to let alone. The attorney general and the Justice Department
make these decisions in the first instance; the federal courts accept or

reject the government's line. More than ninety years have gone by since the Sherman Act was passed; a huge body of law has accumulated. Without the statute, this body of law would not exist; yet its exact shape owes little to the *words* of the statute.

Why should Congress give away so much power? Why should it delegate its authority to other agencies? Much of the development makes sense simply in terms of the scope of government. Congress is made up of only so many men and women, and there are only so many hours in the day. Congress has neither the time nor the know-how to handle every detail that the modern law requires. For example, Congress decided, in the Pure Food Law of 1906, to forbid the manufacture and sale of adulterated food. This is the general principle. But it is the Food and Drug Administration which makes specific choices. The FDA, not Congress, will decide how much butterfat ice cream must contain to be called proper ice cream, and what chemicals can or cannot be used to make cucumbers green and shiny in the stores. It is the FDA which hires chemists and doctors and puts them to work on this problem. Deciding questions about butterfat and additives is the agency's job. Congress has other things to do.

This is not the only reason for delegation. Delegation is also a form of delay, a way of dodging or compromising an issue. In the background of the Sherman Act, there was a tremendous controversy over the issue of "trusts." Trusts were huge industrial combines; the biggest of all was the Standard Oil empire of John D. Rockefeller. Congress had to do something to calm the aroused public of the 1880s. But it did not quite know what to do; and big business, of course, was a powerful political force on the other side. Congress responded to conflicting pressures by passing a broad, sweeping act, marvelously vague. This served to calm the public down; at the same time, the act set up no real machinery for carrying out the policies so broadly expressed. In this way, Congress dodged the long-term issue, and passed the buck to the executive branch and the courts.[11]

Every important law or ordinance, whether passed by Congress or by a state legislature or city council, is its own special blend of specific detail and broad, vague principle. Some, of course, leave out the detail altogether; some leave out the big, broad brushstrokes. Still others mix them together. Ohio—to take one example out of thousands—has a food, drug, and cosmetic law which prohibits the sale of "adulterated" food. What does the word *adulterated* mean? There is a long chain of definitions. Some are quite general: food is adulterated if any "valuable constituent" has been "omitted." But the statute also gets down to minute detail: candy is adulterated if it has "any alcohol or nonnutritive article or substance except harmless coloring, harmless flavoring, harmless resinous glaze not in excess of four-tenths of one per cent," and so on.[12]

Why are statutes one way or the other? Who makes these decisions and why? The mixture of detail or nondetail depends in each case on the history and politics of the particular law. Beyond this, it is hard to say anything more definite, except to point out that "historical accident" has almost nothing to do with the matter, nor is it a mere question of the techniques of draftsmanship. Legislatures do not pass laws as academic exercises or out of whim, but because somebody is pushing them; the social forces that lie behind any particular statute explain its form as well as its substance.

Statutes and Their Interpretation

A statute is, of course, a kind of command. Legislatures pass them, but they are not in the business of enforcement or interpretation. These jobs are left for others to do. Every statute, then, has a double message. In the first place, the statute delivers to the public (or some part of it), a statement of dos or don'ts, or rights and privileges. In the second place, the statute also contains a message to some legal authority, giving instructions about carrying out the law. The second message may be, and often is, implicit; the statute does not necessarily say it in so many words.

For example, the Indiana Penal Code (Section 35-42-5-1) provides that if a person intentionally takes "property from another person" with force or threat of force, the crime called robbery has been committed. A convicted robber can be sent to prison. This section of the penal code is, first of all, a message to the general public, warning people (if they need the warning) that robbery is forbidden and can be punished. At the same time, the statute is a message to district attorneys, policemen, judges, jurors, prison wardens, and a whole host of other officials, authorizing them to do their job with regard to robbers. None of these officials are mentioned in this particular law. Other Indiana laws deal with the structure of the criminal justice system; and the code section on robbery implies and assumes these other provisions. If we want to know whether the robbery statute "works" or not, we have to examine the impact of both of its messages. Is it getting through to robbers and potential robbers? And is it also getting through to law enforcement officials? Are they doing their job of enforcement? These questions are, of course, not unrelated to each other.

This is a simple example, because the robbery statute is itself relatively simple. The wording is not particularly difficult. A street holdup is an obvious case of robbery. There may be borderline situations, but the main thrust of the law is clear to anyone who reads it. Moreover, the layman does not have to read it. People do not read the penal code, but they know that robbery is a crime nonetheless, because the law rests on a well-known, basic norm of American culture. The other branch of the message is also fairly clear. Dealing with robbers is part of the normal, ordinary work of police, judges, prison people, and so on.

Many statutes are much more problematic: they are ambiguous, or confused, or novel, or very complicated, or extremely vague. We have seen some examples: the Internal Revenue Code is an example of enormous complexity; the Sherman Act, an example of great vagueness. Even "clear" statutes run into problems of interpretation. Life is full of surprises; and situations often come up that do not quite fit the statute—but then again perhaps they do. In other words, there are constant problems about what a statute actually says, how to interpret it if there are two conflicting meanings, or what to do when we are not sure that it covers some special situation.

Who decides what a law really means? A lawyer would say, almost automatically: the courts. In a difficult case, it is true, courts have the last word in deciding on the meaning of a law. When Congress enacted Title VII of the Civil Rights Act of 1964, did the legislators mean only to get rid of discrimination against black people and other minorities, or was it their plan to sweep the law clean of *any* race discrimination, however "benign"? Could a white person claim the protection of the civil rights laws? The background was ambiguous; and the words of the statute were no help in the toughest cases. The Supreme Court had to decide, in the end, what to do about "reverse discrimination." In one notable case, for example, *United Steelworkers* v. *Weber*,[13] the court confronted the issue head-on. The union had entered into a collective bargain with Kaiser Aluminum to reserve for blacks half of all new openings in craft-training programs. A white worker complained. In a split decision, the Court upheld the plan and ruled that the Civil Rights Act did not forbid this arrangement.

In a real sense, courts make law in many cases because they are the ones that interpret the laws. Without authoritative interpretation, many laws lack meaning. Still, this point can distort our picture of legal process. Of the hundreds of laws and amendments to laws that pour out of legislative chambers every year, only a tiny (though important) minority ever goes to court for interpretation. The rest are interpreted by other people. Everybody who handles the law in any way, including policemen, officials of the Social Security Administration—yes, and members of the general public—interprets the law, whether he knows it or not. Lawyers play a key role in this process. Take, for example, the murky provision of the Internal Revenue Code which has been quoted. This message is much too complicated, much too "legal," for the general public. Somebody else has to receive the message, digest it, store it up, and feed it out in an easier form. This is the tax lawyer's job.

He does not do it alone. In his office, he gathers material from law-book companies, commercial tax services, trade associations, and so on, which help keep him current. Similarly, there are people working for any big company or any big institution (a university, a hospital) who have the job of sifting through the piles of matter that flow in to the institution—all the laws, rules, and regulations which affect what they do. These staff people, too, digest law and store it in a form that their organizations can use. They, too, interpret the law.

The statutes that courts interpret, of course, tend to raise the most hotly controverted issues. This is why they get to court in the first place. How does a court decide what a statute means? Courts have been working with statutes for centuries. They have built up a body of doctrine on "construction" (interpretation) of statutes. These are rules about rules—or, more realistically, guidelines, rules of thumb. Some of them are in the form of "maxims" or "canons of construction"—slogans or sayings that sum up guidelines of interpretation in a pithy sentence or two.

There is, for example, one maxim to the effect that penal laws should be "strictly construed." This means that when a law makes behavior criminal, courts should interpret the law quite narrowly. They should stick as close as they can to the literal meaning of the words. They should avoid any interpretation that would apply the law to conduct which is not clearly, unmistakably covered by the text of the law. Otherwise, we might punish people without giving them fair warning in advance that their behavior is a crime.

Put this way, the idea is just and sensible. In practice, the notion can easily be carried too far. In one famous case,[14] the United States Supreme Court had to construe the National Motor Vehicle Theft Act of 1919. The law defined a motor vehicle as an "automobile, automobile truck . . . motor cycle, or any other self-propelled vehicle not designed for running on rails." Congress made it a crime to cross state lines in such a vehicle "knowing the same to have been stolen." Defendant McBoyle flew a stolen airplane from Illinois to Oklahoma. Had McBoyle violated the law of 1919? An airplane is a motor vehicle, and it definitely does not run on rails. But the Supreme Court set McBoyle free. A penal law must give "fair warning," in "language that the common world will understand." The statute here was couched in words that would "evoke in the common mind only the picture of vehicles moving on land." It would not be fair for the court to extend this law to airplanes. McBoyle went free, and Congress amended the law in 1945 to include aircraft.[15]

According to another famous maxim, statutes in "derogation of the common law" must also be strictly construed. This does not have a very precise meaning, but it expresses an interesting bias. The bias is this: courts should look suspiciously at changes in law that come from legislatures instead of from the courts themselves. Historically, many courts have indeed taken a rather narrow, illiberal view of statutes. They have looked on them as (in a sense) alien intruders, disturbing the beauty and symmetry of common law. This general habit of courts helps explain the rather peculiar style of American (and English) statutes. Many of these statutes are incredibly verbose, piling synonym on top of synonym. Here is a typical example:

> All promises, agreements, notes, bills, bonds or other contracts, mortgages, or other securities, when the whole or part of the consideration thereof is for money or other valuable thing won or lost, laid, staked, or betted at or upon a game of any kind, or upon a horse race or cockfights, sport or pastime, or on a wager, or for the repayment of money lent or advanced at the time of a game, play, or wager, for the purpose of being laid, betted, staked or laid, betted, staked or wagered, are void.

This language comes from an Ohio statute; and all it means is that gambling contracts are void (that is, a court will not lift a finger to help either party collect or enforce them).[16] Its essential meaning can be expressed in four words; about a dozen more might help to explain it a bit further. The code uses more than eighty separate words, all part of a single very long and difficult sentence. The draftsman wrote as if he had to cover every possible crack or gap in meaning—as if the text were a small, leaky boat in a storm on a hostile sea. These precautions, these synonyms, these countless legalisms, were to prevent courts from punching holes in the statute or changing little holes into big ones.

There are many other maxims or canons of interpretation. Some states list them as official and make them part of the statute books. Even when this is done, it is questionable whether the maxims are very effective—whether they are anything other than convenient excuses for courts to do more or less what they want to in the way of interpretation. Karl Llewellyn, in a well-known essay, pointed out that most maxims have their countermaxims; these are escape hatches, so that a court can ignore whichever of the two it wishes and use its opposite instead. For example, according to one maxim, courts should interpret statutes in such a way as to give sense to every word or clause in the text. On the other hand, a court can (by another maxim) reject as "surplusage" words that are "inadvertently inserted" or "repugnant" to the rest of the statute. The two maxims are clearly inconsistent.[17]

Systematic information is lacking about the ways courts actually handle statutes. Probably a great deal depends on the attitudes of judges toward the substance of statutes. Even the maxims make distinctions—for example, disfavoring criminal statutes, as we saw. In any event, courts operate within certain limits. They can twist and pull a little; but they cannot construe black to mean white, or up to mean down. The words of a statute are not putty; they are more like a rubber sheet that gives a little here and there but cannot change shape totally. To "interpret" in such a way as to turn black into white or night into day would violate the boundaries of judicial tradition, and upset the judges' own sense of their legitimate role.

As was said, it is wrong to talk about interpreting statutes as if this was something a court decided on its own—as if there was no such thing as the meaning of a statute unless and until a court told us what it was. Yet, as we know, most statutes are not interpreted by courts at all, and still have definite meaning: they are understood in this or that way by the people who carry them out or who come under them. Beyond this, there is the question of what the role of courts should be, when a statute comes up for interpretation. Is there such a thing as the "true" or "real" meaning of a text?

There is often a literal meaning, but even this sometimes makes no sense or leads to absurd results. The meaning of a statute has something to do with its purpose—with what the members of the legislature had in mind, or the reason why the statute was passed in the first place. This actually carries us only a little bit further. Legislative intent is a slippery concept. First of all, no one can actually read the minds of the legislators; and second of all, there are too many minds to read—435 in the House of Representatives alone. Neither in theory nor in practice is it easy to find out the actual purpose or intention of a law.

Indeed, for most legislative minds there may be nothing to read, even if we could get somehow inside congressmen's heads. Many congressmen have never read the bills they vote on; others may have only a faint idea of what was in them. Some vote out of party loyalty; others, to do a favor to another legislator. Even those congressmen who take an active part in the drafting or passage of some particular law might have among them quite different, conflicting notions of the purpose and sense of the law.

Of course, in a doubtful case, the interpreter makes an honest search for the purpose and sense. He or she might begin by asking what prompted the legislature to act. There might be important clues in what is called "legislative history." This term refers essentially to the materials outside the actual text which shed light on its meaning. It includes the events or situations which led to the introduction or drafting of the bill, the various drafts and how they changed, committee reports and debates on and off the floor of the legislature, testimony from the public—everything, in short, till the president or the governor signed the bill into law.

In England, courts generally speaking refuse to pay attention to legislative history; they insist on looking only at the text. American doctrine is quite different. Some judges have argued that background is important only when the text is ambiguous: if the law has a "plain meaning" there is no reason to rummage around in the windy expanses of the Congressional Record, and so on. But the "plain meaning" rule was discarded a generation ago, and it is now standard practice to use legislative history to interpret statutes.[18] For example, in *United Steelworkers* v. *Weber*—the 1979 case in which a white worker challenged an affirmative action program for black workers as a form of race discrimination against whites—Justice Brennan quoted extensively from the Congressional Record to drive home his points about the meaning of Title VII of the 1964 Civil Rights Act. Not to be outdone, the dissent of Justice Rehnquist quoted even more extensively, to make the very opposite point. In this case, as in so many, legislative history hardly leads to a single right answer.

Though state legislative history tends to be skimpy, Congress spews forth reams and reams of paper. In many cases, the trouble is that there is entirely too much history. There may be so many versions, drafts, debates, reports, messages, and so on, that a judge can find some material to support *any* interpretive position. The *Weber* case is a good example. But this is no real argument against the use of legislative history. As Professor Kenneth Davis has put it, that would be "a little like saying that we should not drill for oil because much of the drilling ends with dry holes. The important fact is that some of the drilling yields oil."[19] In any event, legislative history is clearly here to stay.

Legislative Decision-Making

Just as there is a body of literature on decision-making in the courts, so there is a body of literature on the way legislatures make decisions. This literature is concerned, among other things, with the effect of public opinion (in general) on the legislative process, and (in particular) with the role of lobbyists and organized interest groups. The literature is rich and complex, and cannot be summed up in any single, simple formula. A few points stand out:

First, most scholars agree that legislators, at least to some degree, behave in response to their constituents. They tend to do what the voters in their districts want—or at least those voters who write letters, donate money, or otherwise try to exert some pull. Legislators do not simply follow their own inner values. Of course, ideals and convictions are important to legislators; but a congressman or state assemblyman knows that it is fatal to get *too much* out of touch with the voters' wishes; he can be thrown out of office at the next election.

Second, what legislatures do reflects the social force exerted—in other words, we can explain output (legislation), through input (social pressure). The man or woman in the House is a medium, a conduit, not an independent force. There is, however, a good deal of controversy about the source of the pressure. Who is it that exerts the force? Moderates (and conservatives) tend to stress the "pluralism" of American political life. They do not claim that everybody in the country has an equal say; but they stress how many groups and how many interests get some response from the lawmakers. There is a good deal of popular rule. Legislators listen to many voices, demanding many different ends and means. The groups have to deal with each other, inside and outside the legislature; they have to bargain and compromise; no single group ever gets its way entirely. The very form of the government reinforces this system: there is no "single center of sovereign power"; rather, there are "multiple centers of power, none of which is or can be wholly sovereign."[20]

Many scholars reject this image. They feel that it paints too rosy a picture. These critics argue that the rich and the powerful are the only serious influences on major decisions; they are the only ones who can afford lobbyists, the only ones who can mount a real campaign to get results in Congress or a state legislature. Besides, campaigns themselves have become very expensive. Candidates cannot survive without heaps of money to buy television time, to print leaflets, to hire managers and staff, and so on. Only big interests have the financial power to make important contributions; this gives them a say in elections and in the behavior of legislators which the average person can never hope to have. The poor, the minorities, the unpopular are shut out of the process. So are such "diffuse" interests as those of consumers and pedestrians.

The word *lobbyist* has, if not a sinister, at least a distasteful ring. Since 1946, Congress has required all professional lobbyists to register. The statute defines a lobbyist as anyone who "for pay" tries to "influence the passage or defeat of any legislation." The lobbyist must disclose who he or she represents, and what he or she gets paid.[21] Literally thousands of lobbyists have registered under this law.

Lobbyists claim, with some justice, that they do not deserve their shady reputation. Of course there have been corrupt lobbyists—lobbyists who used pressure or bribery to get their way. But in general lobbying is a vital part of the democratic process. Lobbyists mobilize public support or opposition to bills; they keep legislators informed of what is going on at the grass roots level (or other levels). The Sierra Club has lobbyists; so do the National Rifle Association, the Japanese government, and Harvard University. In fact, like so many facets of law and government, lobbying is a complex phenomenon, neither all good or all bad, and deeply ingrained in the American tradition.

Studies of the legislative process emphasize the fact that votes on bills are not isolated acts. A legislature is an institution, a system; its members know each other, and they must learn to live and work with their colleagues. Congress is not "an anonymous group of men and women who occasionally meet to pass legislation"; on the contrary, it is a continuing body, with "an elaborate formal and informal structure, traditions, norms, and agreed-upon practices."[22] The same is true of state legislatures.

This means, for example, that to understand the legislative process, we have to understand the committee structure, seniority, the party system, and so on. We must also realize that members do not deal with each single bill in isolation. Rather, they "deal" with each other; they trade votes, in subtle and not-so-subtle ways. There is a lot of open "logrolling," especially in regard to "pork barrel" bills— legislation about construction projects (irrigation works, dams, harbor improvement) in local districts. That is, legislator A agrees to vote for a dam in B's district, because B will vote for A's harbor. More subtle, and more important, is what has been called "implicit" logrolling; vote trading which is less blatant, less open, but still part of the process of "getting along."[23] A legislator is always aware of other legislators (and of the president or governor); he is generally willing to accommodate others in exchange for goodwill or a helping hand, or at least a friendly hearing, on *his* issues. There are, of course, limits to how far a legislator can "deal." He must be careful not to deal himself out of office.

One would expect, then, that any complex statute would turn out in the end to be some sort of compromise. It comes about after an intricate game of give-and-take in which legislators, nudged constantly at the elbow by constituents, play power poker with each other. Almost any big bill could serve as an example. Any important law regulating railroads will surely reflect in various ways the influence of shippers, consumers, and the railroads themselves. The Sherman Act reflected both the outcry of the public and the defensive maneuvers of big business. How much weight each interest has had is of course in each instance the important question. It is not always easy to tell.

There is a middle view, then, between the exaggerated pluralist position and the extremists on the other side. The legislative process is neither as good at accommodating everybody as some have thought, nor as elitist and undemocratic as the worst of the cynics has described it. Rather, it is rough, complex, and imperfect. It also changes over time. Blacks and consumers have, for example, a much greater chance to win the ear of legislators than was true some fifty years ago.

In general, legislative lawmaking needs a good deal more research. We particularly need to know a lot more about the bottom layers of decision making. Most of the research we have puts the searchlight on Congress, although a certain amount deals with state legislatures. We are much more in the dark about city councils, zoning boards, and school districts. The city council of Memphis, Tennessee, or the school board of Bangor, Maine, may not seem very important to the rest of the country; but the work of these local agencies, taken all together, is absolutely fundamental, and worthy of careful study.

6

The Structure of American Law: Executing Policy

*T*HE ADMINISTRATIVE SECTOR is the fastest-growing part of the legal system—the cutting edge. This is the domain whose body and bones are made up of hundreds of boards, agencies, authorities, committees, commissions, and the like, poking their fingers into every aspect of modern life. It is also a domain under attack: *deregulation* is one of the catchwords of the day; and the Reagan administration won power in 1980 as the sworn enemy of "bureaucrats." In fact, no one seriously thinks the end is near for administrative law. Even the most zealous cutter and chopper hopes at most to slice an inch or two off its tremendous bulk; miles and miles will remain.

It is easy to reel off examples of administrative agencies or administrative tribunals. But it is hard to come up with an exact definition of the administrative sector. Indeed, the best definition, sloppy as it seems, may be a negative one: the administrative sector is everything left over in law and government if we take away the courts and legislative bodies, the president, and all the governors, mayors, and county supervisors (along with their immediate staffs), the police, and agencies concerned with national defense. The residue—everything else in the legal system concerned with rules and policy and with making rules and policy stick—represents the administrative sector.

This residue comprises an enormous body of men and women and an enormous apparatus. Here we have the Interstate Commerce Commission, the Food and Drug Administration, the Securities and Exchange Commission, the Civil Aeronautics Board, the Federal Trade

Commission, the Federal Power Commission, and dozens of other important federal bodies. Many of these agencies have counterparts in the states; many do not.

On the other hand, the states have many agencies which have no real federal (national) equivalent. Among these are most occupational licensing boards. These obscure bodies (housed, perhaps, in small offices in the state capital) run exams, make rules, and give out licenses to doctors, nurses, plumbers, watchmakers, barbers, clinical psychologists, and midwives, among others.

These boards are by no means unimportant, if we take them all together. Every state has many licensing boards. Some trades and professions (that of doctors, for example) are universally subject to licensing rules. There is a common core of licensing functions in all states, along with some local variations and additions. Tennessee has a state board of accountancy, a state board of examiners for architects and engineers, and boards for barbers, cosmetologists, funeral directors and embalmers, general contractors, real estate brokers, "registered professional environmentalists," land surveyors, auctioneers, collection agencies, pest control operators, "rental location agents," private investigators, and "polygraph examiners," not to mention members of the healing and helping professions—doctors, nurses, veterinarians, psychologists, speech pathologists, dentists, chiropractors, hearing aid dispensers, optometrists, osteopaths, and pharmacists, as well as those who practice "the art of body massage, by hand or with a mechanical or vibrating device."[1]

Administrative bodies are found on the local level, too—for example, boards of zoning appeals. These decide such questions as whether Mr. and Mrs. Smith can open a restaurant on Elm Street, or whether Elm Street must stay residential. This is not a question of earthshaking importance; but it means a lot to the Smiths, and to their next-door neighbors. On the local level, there are also park commissioners, port authorities, bridge commissions, and tax assessors; there are sewer districts and agencies charged with mosquito control. And most important, perhaps, there are local boards that run the schools.

Do all these agencies and bodies, from the top to the bottom of the pyramid, have anything in common? They share, on the whole, a curious combination of dependence and independence. It takes an act of Congress, or a law of some state legislature, or a municipal ordinance, to bring them into life. Their parents can also put them to death, simply by repealing the law or ordinance. It is a well-known fact that this does not happen very often. Once born, they cling stubbornly to life and their "parents" oblige. Still, history is littered with fossils of extinct agencies. The Office of Price Administration, for example, had almost dictatorial power during the Second World War, fixing prices, wages, and rents. It is only history now.

In many agencies, there is a curious mixture of powers. On the one hand, they act like legislatures; that is, they make up rules and regulations. The Food and Drug Administration, for example, decides what chemicals can be added to food. It also has a staff and inspectors to enforce its rules. It also can act like a court. That is, if a food company complains about some ruling or decision of the FDA, the agency can hold a hearing, sift the evidence, and come to a reasoned decision. Thus, in 1981 the FDA decided after long proceedings that a sweetener called "aspartame" was safe and could be used in food, but that the makers of an aerosol nasal spray called "Alevaire" had not shown that this product was effective—its use was disapproved.[2] Many agencies even publish reports. Volume after volume of decisions of the National Labor Relations Board, for example, sit on the shelves of law libraries. These contain accounts of NLRB decisions, which are often as important as the decisions of courts.

Some scholars and politicians are dismayed by the rapid development of the administrative state. They look on it as a kind of cancerous growth. Yet the fact that the administrative state is massive and pervasive must mean some great social demand is at the root of it. And there obviously is: the demand for continuous, systematic, planned attention to social problems and concerns. The rest of government has a short, spasmodic attention span. Congress lurches from crisis to crisis, the courts from case to case. Only the Securities and Exchange Commission doggedly keeps after the stock exchange, financial reports, and so on. Only the FDA monitors drug companies. Only the FCC lives in the world of TV networks, day in and day out.

American government mirrors what goes on in the community at large, to a greater or lesser degree. Planning and system in government grew up alongside of planning and system in business. Big business controlled its parts, units, and divisions through formal rules. Workers punched time clocks and followed instructions; modern labor law "legitimized, while it regulated, patterns of workplace order and command relationships."[3] The administrative state is the public, official form of a pervasive private reality.

How Leviathan Grew: A Brief Sketch

It is hard to think of a more striking change in government and the legal system over the last century or so than the rise of the administrative agency. The differences from a century ago till now, however, are mostly in scale and scope. Administrative agencies as such are as old as the nation. There were administrators and agencies of government when George Washington was president. The post office was a major branch of government then, and it is still a big operation today. Each cabinet office in the federal government was and is an administrative agency of its own. The same was and is true in the states.

Today, there are millions of jobholders in the civil service. The federal work force under Washington, on the other hand, was a tiny handful of men. The staff of Pickering, Washington's postmaster general, consisted of one assistant and one clerk. They took care of all the agency's business.[4] In general, administrative process in the early days of the republic was weak and inefficient.

One of the biggest responsibilities of the federal government in the nineteenth century was managing and selling public land. The General Land Office in Washington presided over an empire of land—millions and millions of acres. It supervised dozens of local land offices. Public land was supposed to be disposed of in an orderly way. First, the land was to be surveyed and mapped. Then the president would declare the land ready for sale. At that point, it would be auctioned off to settlers and buyers. But local offices were poorly run, on the whole, and badly staffed. Congress was always stingy with expense money. One surveyor complained in 1831 that he did not even have decent storage space for his papers: "roaches, and crickets" had "free access"; mice made "beds out of old field notes . . . papers are thrown into old boxes and put out of the way: the roof leaks . . . and injures the books and papers."[5]

The states did at least as poor a job with their own lands. There was no tradition of a trained civil service, and government was simply weaker than its greedy customers. The land office was a primitive operation—a far cry indeed from, say, the Internal Revenue Service today, which commands an army of lawyers, accountants, agents, and banks of computers, and has vast powers of audit and enforcement.

From the dawn of American history, regulating business was one of the jobs of the administrators. Even the early colonists were eager to have quality control of important goods. Under the *Laws and Liberties of Massachusetts* (1648), the selectmen of Boston and other towns that shipped pipe staves abroad were empowered to name two men from each town, "skilfull in that commoditie," to act as "viewers of pipe-staves." All pipe staves for export had to pass before the watchful eyes of these viewers, who could reject staves that were "not merchantable" because of "worm-holes," or were poor in size and quality. For example, staves had to be four and a half feet long, three inches and a half "on bredth . . . without sap," and "in thickness three quarters of an inch"; they also had to be hewed "well and even."

In the eighteenth and nineteenth centuries, cities of any size had somewhat similar laws for the inspection of basic commodities (butter, coal, bread). A Connecticut law of 1822 provided for local inspection of a huge array of products: beef, pork, butter, lard, fish, hay, flour and cornmeal, lumber, barrels for fish, sawed shingles, potash and pearl ash, and "onions put up in bunches." Local government also levied taxes, laid out roads and kept them up, and issued licenses to taverns, inns, and gristmills. Each township or county also had its "overseers of the poor." These local citizens administered the "poor laws," the primitive welfare system of the day. They raised local taxes and spent the money on relief for the sick and the destitute, though in a bare-bones, minimal way. Since every additional "pauper" cost money from local pockets, towns looked with a jaundiced eye on poor people who moved in from outside. Instead of the Welcome Wagon, newcomers could be warned to get out of town; if they did not listen, they could be "removed"—dumped bodily across the township line.

Cities, counties, and towns performed other important administrative tasks. Education was one of them: running the local school system. Until recently, the federal government left education pretty much alone, financially and otherwise. Even centralized state control developed slowly. The schools were doggedly local affairs. Police, and law and order generally, were traditionally given over to local administration. In the nineteenth century, as the economy expanded, so did state administrative law. There were commissions to regulate banking, state lands, canals, bridges, and insurance companies. Connecticut in the 1840s had a commission of three ("annually appointed by the general assembly") to visit and check every bank in the state.[6] Insurance regulation was a particular concern of the states. States regulated many aspects of the insurance contract and the insurance business; the work was often handed over to an administrative body, the insurance commission.[7]

Cities and states welcomed the first railroads with open arms. But from about the 1850s on, control of the railroads became an important policy issue. The New England states set up the earliest railroad commissions, in the 1860s. Connecticut, for example, gave a three-man commission power to inspect the state's railroads, though mostly to check on safety and repair of equipment. The commission had limited enforcement power and no power over freight rates and passenger fares.[8]

The next wave of railroad commissions, in the 1870s, was far more potent. The most noted of these were in middle western states. These were the product of the so-called Granger movement; farmers and shippers lashed out in anger and frustration, accusing the railroads of abuse of power, of crude profiteering. The Granger commissions of Wisconsin, Illinois, or Iowa were far from toothless. The Illinois Railroad and Warehouse Commission, for example, had broad authority over railroads and grain elevators in the state. Besides general inspection power, the commission had power to enforce state laws, which included actual regulation of rates. Indeed, one law set a maximum charge for storing grain—two cents a bushel per month; and another law, for railroads, outlawed rate discrimination.[9]

The Granger laws were fairly radical for their day—or so railroads and warehousemen thought. Business challenged the Granger laws in court, charging that they were unconstitutional. The famous case of *Munn* v. *Illinois*[10] reviewed the right of the state to regulate grain elevators. Here the Supreme Court turned back the challenge to the Granger laws. Under Illinois law, grain elevators had to procure a license to do business, and the law fixed storing and handling prices. The court refused to strike down the law. Regulation—even price fixing—was acceptable, so long as the regulated business was "affected with a public interest." That is, a business with a crucial or vital place in the social or economic scheme could not claim immunity from public intervention. The principle of *Munn* was broad enough to cover most forms of administrative regulation.

The Interstate Commerce Commission Act (1887)[11] was a landmark in the history of administrative regulation. Indeed, this was a landmark in American history generally. The ICC act, though much battered and amended, is still basically in force. The original law created a federal (national) commission, the Interstate Commerce Commission, to regulate railroads. The statute laid down the general rule that all freight rates and passenger charges had to be "reasonable and just." It outlawed rebates, kickbacks, price discrimination, and other practices which had kindled the anger of farmers and shippers.

What stimulated the federal government to enter the field of railroad regulation? State regulation of railroads had generally failed. The early railroads were small, local lines linking two towns, rarely crossing state boundaries. New Jersey, for example, chartered a "Belvedere and Water Gap Railroad Company" in 1851;[12] New Hampshire incorporated a "Concord and Portsmouth Railroad" in 1855.[13] But gradually, local railroads merged and consolidated; big sharks swallowed up little fish, and the railroad barons strung together large interstate networks. A few names, like "Atchison, Topeka, and Santa Fe" (now the Sante Fe Railway) remained for many years to remind us of the older stage. At any rate, the individual states had neither the legal nor the political muscle to control these giant railroads. They had become a national concern.

The commerce clause of the Constitution gave Congress power to regulate commerce "among" the states. This was taken to mean power over interstate movements of vehicles and goods. The Supreme Court had for many years emphasized the negative aspect of the commerce clause: the commerce clause prevented states from impeding the flow of commerce across state lines. Now came the positive side: the power of the national government to regulate commerce itself. The ICC act was not the federal debut in regulation or in the administrative business, but it was a major step in a fateful direction.

Some historians feel that we have tended to look at the ICC through the wrong end of the telescope. They claim it was in fact *not* an attempt to tame the railroads—*not* a reform law passed in the public interest. Rather, the railroads benefited from the law. The ICC put a lid on competition; its regulatory actions were a protective cocoon for existing railroads. It guaranteed friendly guidance from a sympathetic agency, decent profits, and orderly markets for all.[14]

Some parts of this thesis are quite plausible, though it no doubt goes too far. Laws like the ICC Act cannot be totally one-sided. Railroads had a powerful voice in Congress; so did farmers and shippers, in the aggregate. Both groups influenced the law. The ICC Act, as is typical, was some kind of compromise. Each side gained something—and lost something, too. This much is clear. The farmers and shippers gained some measure of control over rates and practices. The railroads gained order and protection. Administrative regulation, in general, strikes a compromise between battling interest groups. The results are almost never all one-way. The hard question is to assess who won the most, and why.

In any event, the ICC Act foreshadowed the rise of the administrative state. In the twentieth century, the pace accelerated. The Food and Drug Administration dates from 1906; the Federal Trade Commission Act was enacted in 1914. The New Deal of President Franklin D. Roosevelt, in the 1930s, was the next great watershed. Congress created new and powerful agencies. Some reflected twentieth-century technology—for example, the Federal Communications Commission (1934), which controlled "communications by wire and radio," later adding television. Others reflected the great social changes and reforms of the New Deal—for example, the Securities and Exchange Commission, which regulates stock exchanges and the sale of stocks and bonds by corporations; the National Labor Relations Board, with its powers over collective bargaining; and the Social Security Administration.

The New Deal is in many ways still with us. And every presidency since Roosevelt has added to the stock of agencies. Under Lyndon Johnson (1964), the Office of Economic Opportunity was created to run the "War on Poverty." The War on Poverty is dead now, but many of the Johnson programs (like Medicare and Medicaid) remain, and are administered by vast bureaucracies. The Equal Employment Opportunity Commission (EEOC) was created in 1964 to enforce the civil rights laws.[15] OSHA (dealing with occupational safety), ERISA (pension and retirement plans), and EPA (environmental protection) are other recent examples of "alphabet soup" agencies. Eugene Bardach and Robert Kagan describe the legislation of the 1960s and 1970s as a "quantum leap" in federal action to protect public safety. They mention not only OSHA (1970), but also the Water Pollution Control Act (1972) and the Surface Mining Control and Reclamation Act (1977).[16]

Meanwhile, administrative agencies have multiplied like rabbits on the state level, too. The occupational licensing boards mentioned earlier are all state agencies; the great rush to enact licensing laws began in the 1890s. The states have their own laws on corporate securities ("blue-sky laws"), and they are in control of many areas of life (zoning is one) that the federal government leaves alone. Some state regulatory agencies have tremendous significance: the Texas Railroad Commission, despite its name, controls oil and gas in Texas; it has power to stop the production of oil "in excess of . . . market demand," which gives it fantastic economic leverage.[17]

The result is a huge melange of boards and agencies, on every level of government. President Reagan's administration roared into office with promises to cut the bureaucracy back. So far (1984), his troops have hardly made a dent on Leviathan. Not a single major agency has been dismantled. "Deregulation" has had some notable successes—air fares and bank interest are two prominent examples— but the administrative core of the state remains firm.

A Typology of Administrative Bodies

There are so many agencies, their work is so various, and they operate in such different ways that it is almost a hopeless task to try to describe them in general terms. One useful way to classify them is by subject matter. Thus, some agencies are concerned with economic regulation (ICC, SEC), others with welfare (for example, the Social Security Administration); still others manage public resources (for example, the Bureau of Public Lands). Again, some regulating agencies regulate single industries (railroads, banks); others regulate business in general (SEC, OSHA).

Another important way to distinguish among agencies is to look at their structure. Some agencies are independent; others are not. An agency is legally independent if it is not attached to an executive department. Independence means the executive cannot control the work of the agency. The president appoints interstate commerce commissioners; once they are installed in office, he is not their "boss," and they do not have to obey his commands. The Social Security Administration, on the other hand, is part of the Department of Health and Human Services. The administrator makes policy; but he can be overruled—or even fired—by the secretary of HSS, who is his boss, or by his boss's boss, the president.

We can also draw a distinction between "friendly" and "hostile" boards and agencies, if we remember not to take these terms too literally. "Friendly" boards and agencies are manned by the very people the board or agency is supposed to regulate. The Interstate Commerce Commission is not "friendly," in this sense. By law, no one connected with the railroad business can sit on the commission. The state boards that license druggists, plumbers, or optometrists are a different story. Druggists, plumbers, or optometrists control these boards and fill all or most of their seats. For example, the State Board of Optometry in California consists of nine members, appointed by the governor. There are to be three laymen ("public" members); but the other six must be registered, practicing optometrists.[18]

There are good historical reasons for the difference between the two types of agency. Licensing of plumbers was probably the plumbers' own idea. They wanted to keep out amateurs, enhance their own prestige, control the work, and hold prices steady and stable. These are mostly economic goals, not very different from some of the goals of labor unions or of workers generally. But not all occupations are able to band together and form effective unions. Against whom could

druggists, doctors, or plumbers call a strike? Whom could they ask
for a raise? They can best achieve results by forming trade groups and
by persuading the legislature to license their occupation, vesting in a
board of practitioners the power to decide who gets licenses, and how
and why. This puts control of membership and work conditions firmly
in friendly hands.

At least part of the thrust to regulate railroads, on the other hand,
was "hostile." It came from shippers and merchants who feared the
railroads—who thought railroads had far too much power for the good
of the country. Of course, there is more to the story of railroad regulation than that. Many concessions were made to the railroads as the
ICC Act journeyed through Congress. But the hostile element
remained part of the package. This is true of economic regulation in
general.

Whatever the origin of railroad regulation—or regulation of public
utilities, airlines, and so on—what happens in practice? Whom do the
commissions serve? One popular theory is that the regulated industry
tends to "capture" the agency and bend it to suit industry purposes.[19]
The ICC becomes the creature of the railroads; television networks
take over the FCC. The puppets shove aside the puppet master and
make him dance on their strings.

There is some truth to this charge. For one thing, regulators have
to live with their subjects. They learn to see things through their
subjects' eyes. Also, commissioners are supposed to regulate businesses, not kill them. A gas or electric company applies to a state
power commission for a rate increase. It presents facts and figures
about rising costs: coal, oil, labor are all more expensive. If the commission accepts the facts and figures it will grant the increase, more
often than not. The commission, after all, is responsible for the health
of the industry. The gas and electric companies are privately owned
and must show a profit. Then, too, some commissioners come from
the industry they regulate, and many expect to go back there when
their terms are up. They are reluctant to be tough and unyielding.
Historically, the public or consumer interest has been weak, diffuse.
Who, after all, has spoken up for John and Jane Q. Public, day in and
day out, at the agency? Nobody. Yet lobbyists and lawyers for industry have always been there, pressing their cases. Only in recent years
has a strong—even strident—consumer lobby emerged.

There is some empirical evidence in support of the "capture" idea.
For example, David Serber[20] studied California's Department of
Insurance and the way it handled consumer complaints in 1969. He

paints a depressing picture. The department leaned overboard to accommodate insurance companies; consumers who made noise were treated as cranks by the staff. The staff systematically disfavored women, blacks, lower-class people, and anybody who seemed "inarticulate or angry."

This was a small state agency, and the data came from 1969. Is the situation changing? There are signs that it is. The consumer movement is stronger than it was in 1969. External controls over administrative agencies are also more vigorous.

Control of Administrative Behavior

Administrative process is everywhere in the modern world. It is the fastest-growing part of the law, yet in some ways the least visible. Administrators have a great deal of power. Even some lowly clerk at the bottom of the ladder can at times exercise considerable authority. To someone who wants a pension or a dog license or a zoning variance, or to a company that wants to float bonds or build a new plant, the power of administrators seems boundless—almost out of control. One of the biggest issues in administrative law is, How tightly should agencies be kept in check? Who will do the job, and how?

Administrative agencies are subject to both inside and outside control. Inside control is control built into the structure of an agency. Higher officials supervise lower officials. Inspectors and auditors monitor the working bureaucrats. Reports, spot-checks, reviews, and internal audits prevent corruption or sloppy work. At least one hopes so.

Outside control begins with the governing law. Controls and limits are written into the text of the law for each specific agency. Thus, the Federal Trade Commission has power to prevent or stop "unfair" methods of competition; but the FTC Act also specifically gives businesses whose methods are challenged the right to appear and fight, with lawyers, at formal hearings.[21] There are also more general controls. The Administrative Procedure Act, first passed in 1946, applies pretty much across the board. It sets down rules of procedure that all agencies must follow. For example, under the APA, an agency must publish "descriptions of its central and field organization"; and it must make public its rules of procedure and inform the public where people can pick up necessary forms. All this appears in the Federal Register. The agency must also make public its rules and regulations, and it has to give notice when and if it intends to change these rules. The

Federal Register, which has run to as many as 75,000 pages a year, is hardly the six o'clock news; but at least it is accessible to lawyers and specialists. Agencies have to report in it the gist of any of their new rules; and they must give the public a chance to object or to make comments in writing.

Congress, then, with its statute-writing power, is the most obvious outside control over federal agencies. Congress passes the laws that make the agencies; it can repeal those laws and kill its creatures. It can give them new marching orders any time it wishes. Congress (after intensive lobbying from industry) told the Consumer Product Safety Commission in 1981 to lower safety standards for power lawn mowers. The commission has no choice but to obey.[22]

Some controls are inside the agencies but outside the regular chain of command. It is possible to give controllers or inspectors great independence, even though technically they belong to the organization they seek to control. The army and navy have inspectors general. So do many government agencies. The Inspector General Act of 1978 created such offices in cabinet departments and in some agencies (EPA, for example).[23] The IG is authorized, among other things, to "receive and investigate" complaints about waste or abuse. The IG is supposed to keep secret the identity of whistle blowers.

This form of control is based in part on the concept of the "ombudsman." The word, if not the idea, comes from Scandinavia. Many private institutions—Stanford University, for example—have set up such posts for themselves. The ombudsman is an official who is independent and (hopefully) independent-minded; he hears complaints from employees or others and tries to deal with them somehow. Presumably he has no ax to grind and his recommendations are fair and impartial. How much actual power he has depends on the particular institution.

Judicial review is perhaps the best-known form of outside control of administrative agencies. Most of what is called administrative law, as taught in law schools, is really the law of judicial review. A person or company dissatisfied with an agency decision first must exhaust procedures or appeals inside the agency. He then has one more chance: he can try his luck in court. Most statutes setting up administrative agencies provide for or imply the right of courts to review such agency decisions. The Administrative Procedure Act itself provides for review; and the Supreme Court has held that a right to review is implied unless Congress firmly and explicitly says otherwise. This happens from time to time. Congress declared that certain decisions of the

Veterans' Administration were absolutely "final and conclusive." No court had "power . . . to review any such decision."[24] This, however, is highly unusual.

Getting a court to review the NLRB or SEC or ICC is not a simple matter; one does not just snap one's fingers and file a complaint. Many roadblocks stand in the way. To begin with, there are procedural problems. One is the concept of "standing." Not everybody can complain about what an agency does. To have standing (the right to complain) usually means the complainant must show a financial stake. If the Department of the Interior decides to let Hilton Hotels build a lodge in Yellowstone Park, can I complain as a backpacker and bird-watcher? Probably not; I have no standing. The mere fact that I like to use Yellowstone, or have gone hiking there, or plan to go, is not enough. Rules of standing are complicated; as they broaden or narrow, the scope of judicial review broadens and narrows in turn. For a while, federal courts were quite liberal about standing, stretching a point to allow groups who represented "the public" to intervene in decisions, even though they had no financial stake. This opened the door to conservation groups that opposed power plants, and to church groups or just plain viewers who complained about the policies of some TV station. But recently courts seem to be having second thoughts and backing off somewhat.[25]

Also, the scope of judicial review is narrow. Courts do not second-guess the agencies. If the FDA decides a drug does not work and takes it off the market, the manufacturer can try to persuade a court to overturn the decision. But as a general rule the court will not rehash the evidence; it will not ask whether the drug works or not. The court will mainly check the agency's *procedures*. Did FDA follow the Administrative Procedure Act? Did the FDA do what Congress told it to do, and in the right way? Was its decision supported by some evidence? If the answer to these questions is yes the court will not overturn the agency's decision.

All well and good; but in fact the line between procedure and substance—between decisions of "law" and decisions of "fact"—is quite fuzzy; and some courts review agency work in a bold and assertive way. Before the New Deal, courts were on the whole hostile to administrative agencies; they scrutinized their work rather carefully (some would say too carefully). During the New Deal, the Supreme Court reflected this hostility in a number of notable instances. The Court did not want Congress to "delegate" its essential powers to agencies. Perhaps the most notorious New Deal decision was *Schech-*

ter Poultry Corp. v. *United States.*[26] Here the court declared the
National Industrial Recovery Act unconstitutional and ruined one of
the keystones of Roosevelt's program.

Schechter and similar cases raised storms of protest. In the long
run, President Roosevelt won his point. The old, conservative judges
resigned; the president appointed new ones more in tune with his
views. The Court lost most of its taste for savaging administrative
agencies. After the New Deal period, a long honeymoon set in for the
agencies. Courts were reluctant to intrude into administrative decisions except in extreme cases. They refused to interfere in agency
decisions if they were the least bit defensible procedurally and had
any shreds of evidence to back them up.

That honeymoon now seems to be over. This is a generation of
diminished deference. Individuals and groups on the outside are more
active than before in fighting the agencies in court; and the courts
themselves are taking a more active role in controlling administrative
behavior. A Washington lawyer, in 1974, spoke for most lawyers when
he talked of a "strong impression" that judicial review was tougher
than before: the courts fancied themselves "as watchdogs at least
comparable to the stature of the agencies."[27] Most observers would
agree.

Why is this so? Courts change their behavior in response to changes
in the outside world. We can mention a few factors:

(a) The public generally has lost some of its faith in administrative
process. Administrative process, of course, is here to stay; but more
and more people think of it as a necessary evil at best. Administrative
process is "red tape," "bureaucracy," "Big Brother"; it is waste, fat,
inefficiency. Politicians of both parties find it convenient to run against
"bureaucracy." The movement to "deregulate" has been mentioned.
There is an urge to turn back the clock—to reverse the trend toward
more and more state control of economic life.

The movement toward deregulation has not so far made a major
impact on the scope of regulation. But it does represent a reaction
against government that has wider meaning. The Reagan administration is determined to shrink the size of government, cut hundreds of
pages out of the Federal Register, and stop the flood of rules and
regulations. These aims seem to be politically popular. They are, of
rourse, easier said than done.

(b) Judicial review is expensive and time-consuming. Only a big
drug company has the money to attack an FDA ruling. In recent years,
new actors have entered the stage, representing new groups—con-

sumers, for example. Of course, no single consumer has the time, money, or skill to battle against the giant agencies or lock horns with the great corporations. But when consumers band together, the story is quite different. Where would environmental law be without the pressure of groups such as the Sierra Club? Particularly important are the "public interest" law firms, organized to fight legal battles on behalf of consumers. There are only a few of these firms, but they make a big splash in the courts.

(c) Again, a change in public attitude lies behind this trend. Consumers band together because there is a consumer movement; that is, some consumers feel angry at business or government and want to take action to make their weight felt. Courts defer less to agencies because segments of the *public* defer to them less than before.

Recently, there has been much discussion about whether agencies are responsive enough to the public. This is a tricky subject. Often when people complain about unresponsive agencies they mean that the agency does not respond to *them*. But an agency may ignore group A because of pressure from group B, which is pulling in the opposite direction. In such a case, we can easily, but mistakenly, imagine that the agency is performing poorly because of technical, structural, bureaucratic reasons. But the agency *is* responsive; what is wrong (from our standpoint) is its pattern of response. Technical reform will not cure the problem. What is needed is political reform—giving group A more power, or exerting pressure on our own (if that is what we want).

On the other hand, there really does seem to be something about a bureaucracy that slows down its actions and toughens its outer skin. After all, the whole point of making agencies independent is to free them from short-run political control. The point of a civil service is to loosen the grip on them of politicians and of the general public. This can work all too well. When we regularize promotion and tenure—when we make internal controls stronger than external controls—we run the risk of distorting the incentives of those who staff the bureaucracies. Individual creativity is discouraged and downgraded; outstanding performance becomes risky. Timid, bureaucratic minds dominate the agency. Those who stick to the rules and never get in trouble are rewarded. Policy change becomes almost impossible.

Bureaucracy is at the heart of modern law and government. A vast civil service, mindless and invisible, grinds away in thousands of tiny offices, churning out rules and applying them, like a troop of blind army ants, following instinct. The work of life, to be sure, could not go on without this corps. But some say the bureaucracy squeezes vital juices out of the economy, and commits—day in and day out—nagging, petty acts of tyranny. Is there some way to give the modern state a human face? Is effective, efficient, and fair government possible? No one is sure of the answers.

7

*Federalism and
American Legal Culture*

ONE OBVIOUS, STRIKING fact about the American legal system is
that it is organized on a *federal* basis. A federal system is a government and legal system in which the central, national government shares
power with states, provinces, or sections, each of which is to some
degree sovereign in its own right. There are quite a few countries in
the world organized on a federal system. One of the best examples is
Canada, our northern neighbor. Australia is also a federal republic.
So is Switzerland. Other countries are federal only on paper. The
Soviet Union is supposed to be a federation, made up of individual
"republics" (Russia itself, Armenia, Estonia, and so on). Each Soviet
republic, in theory, even has the right to secede. In fact, Moscow
calls the tune; and the sixteen or so republics have precious little to
say about their destiny, their politics, or even the organization of their
courts. At the other extreme are such loose groupings as the European Economic Community. Here the *general* government is relatively weak, and the individual countries (France, Italy, Germany,
and the rest) keep almost full control of law and politics. But this may
change over time; indeed, the central government of EEC has already
gotten more powerful than many people ever expected.

The United States is one of the most truly federal countries. The
national government sits in Washington; but the state governments,
in the fifty states, are far from being empty shadows. The states have
governments, in charge of their people and land. Within their spheres
they are supposed to be "sovereign"—that is, in full control.

In many ways, the states echo the structural patterns of the federal government. They all have constitutions of their own. They have legislatures (though they are not called by the name Congress); each has a chief executive (though his title is governor, not president). Each state also has its own court system. Each has a cabinet, an executive staff, and a flock of administrative agencies. Of course, the states are sovereign or independent within rather narrow limits. The national (federal) government is more powerful, employs vastly more men and women, and taxes and spends much more. It is only Washington that sends out and receives ambassadors, coins money, owns guided missiles and aircraft carriers, and tries to "fine-tune" the economy. On the other hand, the federal government does not arrest speeders, grant divorces, or probate wills; it does not pass zoning laws; it does not foreclose mortgages, repossess television sets, or put people on trial for robbing gas stations. It does not do most of the ordinary, workaday jobs of the law.

Federalism, as it has evolved in this country, is a complex and interesting system. It is also a good example of the interaction between structure and culture, within our system of laws.

Federalism: The Formal Plan

The basic story of the American Constitution is well known. After the Revolutionary War, the former colonies became independent states. They set up a central government, under the Articles of Confederation. This central government was weak; real power stayed in the states. Most people considered the experiment a failure: there was fear of anarchy as the separate states began to squabble in an unruly way, unrestrained by a strong central authority.

The Americans (or many of them) resolved to try again. A convention was called and a new plan drafted: the Constitution of 1787. It gave more power to the central government. It is still an open question exactly *how much* power was intended for the national government. Clearly, the drafters meant to give real power, but also to keep a good deal for the states. They proposed a clear-cut division between the two levels of sovereignty, spelling out what the general government could do and what was left to the states. Some powers, of course, would have to be shared. Many details of the division were left rather obscure.

The center had power over war and foreign relations; it had power to levy taxes, run a postal system, and coin money. It also had some smaller powers important to the legal system—power to lay down "uniform" rules for naturalization and "uniform laws on the subject of bankruptcies"; also power to grant patents and copyrights.

The Constitution also set up a separate court system for the central government. At its head was a (federal) Supreme Court, along with "such inferior courts as the Congress may from time to time ordain and establish" (Article IV, Section 1). These courts would have jurisdiction over questions of federal law. They would handle admiralty cases as well. Admiralty cases were maritime cases—about affairs on the high seas or the business of ocean commerce. In England, these cases went before a special court, the court of admiralty, whose powers were in America given to the federal courts. The national courts also had jurisdiction to decide cases "between Citizens of different States." This is the so-called "diversity jurisdiction." The idea here was that the federal courts would provide an impartial forum, free of state jealousies, rivalry, and chauvinism. The federal courts, unlike state courts, would not show bias against "outsiders"—people from other states.

The Constitution also listed some sovereign acts specifically forbidden to the states. They were not to coin money or levy any taxes on imports or exports (except "what may be absolutely necessary for executing . . . inspection Laws"). Commerce was to pass freely from state to state, without barriers or costs. The states were also shut out of foreign policy: they were not to "enter into any Treaty, Alliance, or Confederation" or any "Agreement or Compact . . . with a foreign Power." They were not to wage war, except with congressional consent. Foreign affairs were handed over to the central government.

There was a good deal of opposition at the time; but the Constitution was ratified nonetheless. The hope was that the central government would be strong enough to keep the country from disintegrating into little quarreling baronies—strong enough for that, but no more. The states had control of their domestic affairs, and of everything not specifically granted to the central government. That reserve, most people thought, was a vast and important domain.

Federalism: History and Culture

Federalism, of course, is much more than a formal plan. It is also a tradition, and it is an important facet of our legal culture. In fact, federalism as a structure would be meaningless or empty unless federalism were also part of the culture. To understand federalism in this country—how it grew and how it changed—it will not do simply to tell how the constitutional plan has altered over time. Indeed these changes (on paper) are fairly small. The Constitution of 1787 is still very much with us. It will soon celebrate its 200th birthday; but it has been amended only fourteen times since 1800. By now, it is by far the oldest written constitution still in force anywhere. There are much older countries, but most of them (like France) have suffered constitutional upheaval time and time again. There is no American Third Reich or Fifth Republic. There is still the first and only American republic. Except for the Civil War—and even then—the Constitution stood like a rock.

Or has it? The *words* are the same—but the music? Can a plan set up in 1787—in the horse-and-buggy age, when men wore powdered wigs, and before the Industrial Revolution got going—really still suit us today? In fact, the reality of federalism has drastically altered, and the culture of federalism along with it.

This is precisely what we would expect. Massive social and economic changes have taken place in the last two centuries. Technology alone would necessarily change the reality of federalism. Telephone, telegraph, radio and television, jet airplanes, computers—all these make it possible for the first time to govern a continent from a single nerve center. The power of Washington, D.C., in the twentieth century would be unthinkable without these innovations. Swift means of travel and communication have created mass markets across the country and stimulated the consumer economy. The American population is restless and mobile. People ceaselessly cross state lines, by train, plane, and car, looking for new jobs, visiting relatives, searching for sunshine and scenery, and so on. If there is to be any control over means of travel and the national economy, it will have to come from the center.

Social change, culture (attitudes), and legal structure are bound together in so many ways we cannot ever really disentangle them. None of the three basic elements of law—structure, substance, or culture—has meaning without the others. Federalism is a structural fact. It also generates substance (rules about state and national powers). These in turn influence the legal culture. At the same time, it is the legal culture (what people think and believe) that makes federalism a living part of law—a structure with meaning. And the legal culture is not static. It changes along with society.

Federalism in the first half of the nineteenth century was a far cry from federalism today. The national government was a tiny dot on the legal map. Washington, D.C., was a miserable village, with muddy roads, appalling summer heat, and few permanent inhabitants. The federal government was pathetically small by modern standards. The Department of the Treasury in 1801, which "far overtopped any other administrative agency," contained more than half the civilians who worked for the federal government. It had 78 employees in its central office, and 1,615 in the field.[1] In 1829, the whole body of federal employees in Washington, "from the lowliest clerk, messenger, and page boy to the President," and including congressmen and senators, was 625.[2]

In short, the central government played second fiddle to the states. The states loomed much larger in peoples' lives than the federal government. People thought of themselves as citizens of Virginia or Pennsylvania first, as Americans second. The national legal system was like the tiny brain of a giant dinosaur. There was not much in the way of a central nervous system. This lack became even more pronounced as one traveled west. In the early nineteenth century, people in a state like Kentucky, separated by mountains from the eastern seaboard, saw little use for a central government and were rather bitter about its revenue laws (which they largely ignored). But we should not exaggerate the point. Mary Tachau has studied the federal courts in Kentucky during this period; she found in these courts a surprising level of strength and activity.[3] Still, in most respects the state government was the heart of public life, the national government distant and weak.

In one regard, the West was more national-minded in the later nineteenth century, for a rather different reason. Local culture and local tradition were thinner in the West than in the East and in the South. The population of the West was a migrant population. People there had no western roots; there was no state patriotism of the Virginia type. Americans were rolling stones. What could devotion to Montana—or love for Montana culture and tradition—mean in 1890, when most people who lived there had literally just arrived? Even today state "patriotism" varies greatly from state to state, depending on cultural tradition. There is tremendous local pride—almost nationalism—in parts of New England and the South. In California or Arizona most people are raw newcomers who came for sunshine or jobs, or at best the children of newcomers. The idea of a California "patriot" is absurd in a way that the idea of a fanatical Texan is not.

American legal culture is local in another sense. Judges and lawyers are locals. There is no national career line for judges. State judges cannot cross the border: once a Delaware judge, always a Delaware judge. There is no way to transfer to Pennsylvania. Even federal judges tend to be locals: the district judge in North Dakota is a North Dakota man. The lower bench is even more parochial: a judge of Aroostook County, Maine, will serve there all his life unless he gets a promotion; he will not take up court in Kennebec County. (In some states, however, the chief justice or a court administrator can shift judges around temporarily, to clear up backlogs.) Lawyers also tend to be local. A lawyer who practices in Memphis, Tennessee, will not take cases in Louisville, Kentucky. Some big-city law firms now do have branches—often in Washington, D.C.—but this is still the exception.

It is true that major law schools are "national": they draw students from all over the country and ignore the law of the state they sit in. Only a handful of Yale's students will practice in Connecticut, even though the school is in New Haven, Connecticut. Yale students will learn very little about Connecticut law in the classroom.

Young lawyers are great travelers. In an earlier day, they flocked to new settlements out west. Today, many will leave home for New York or Washington or other centers of practice. But young lawyers do not wander very long. Once the tumbleweed days are past, they take root in one place and stay there. Each state admits lawyers to its own bar only; some states once admitted county by county. A Georgia lawyer is a layman as far as Oregon is concerned. Lawyers move occasionally, but they do not automatically get "reciprocity." They may have to take the bar exam over again, like the rawest recruit. In general, lawyers are pretty much bound to one jurisdiction, just as the judges are.

This state of affairs makes American legal culture quite parochial; it tends to keep alive aspects of local legal culture. This point is vividly illustrated by a recent study of delay and congestion in trial courts.[4] The researchers wanted to find out why filed cases had to wait so long for trial in some cities, while in others there were only short delays, or none at all. In other words, some courts were slow, some were fast—but why? The scholars started out with hunches about the reasons; but none of these, surprisingly, panned out, either in civil or criminal cases: "Neither court size, nor trial rate nor judicial case load, nor use of settlement conferences, differentiates faster from slower courts."[5] Then what does? The scholars fell back on what they called local legal culture: "informal court system attitudes, concerns, and practices." Judges and other courtroom hands had old, deep-seated habits and ideas. The pace of case decision was different in different cities, but judges and lawyers knew only their own cities. What happened someplace else never came to their attention. Thus, local legal culture was slow-moving—a kind of legal molasses. Fads like the hula hoop or disco dancing race across the country; local legal culture barely crawls.

In some ways, then, courts and lawyers in different communities are sealed off from each other. But we must not carry the point too far. The federal court system is fairly uniform, and it enforces national policy. Federal courts follow local law in "diversity" cases; but the Federal Rules of Civil Procedure (and of Criminal Procedure) govern courtroom behavior and the local rules of procedure do not. Nor do federal courts bow down to local opinion and local prejudice, in matters on which Washington (or the national Constitution) has spoken. This became dramatically clear after the *Brown* decision in 1954. Some federal judges were segregationists and resisted the Supreme Court decision as much as they could; others, however, acted with great honor and courage and refused to defer to local norms.[6] As a whole, the federal lower courts were much more willing than the state courts to carry out civil rights policy in an honest, consistent way.

The country is not *legally* unified—at least not as a matter of theory or technicality—except at the federal level. But it is definitely unified in economic life. There is also a common language, and the culture is generally the same from coast to coast. There are strong regional differences, of course; but TV and internal migration are tending to level these off as time goes on.

The economic unity of the country is especially basic. People and products stream across state borders. There is no legal way for one state to keep out the goods of other states. The Constitution expressly forbids it. Vermont cannot put import taxes on New Hampshire goods. Colorado cannot exclude the products of Utah. At most, a state can stop rotten fruit and sick cows at its borders. Beyond this, it cannot go.

Nor does a state have power to keep out unwanted people, any more than unwanted goods. Oregon has no right to chase migrants from Ohio away. At one time, states were able to keep out "paupers" (or try to); but the Supreme Court put an end to this practice years ago.[7] No state, said the court, can "isolate itself from difficulties common to all . . . by restraining the transportation of persons and property across its borders." According to the Constitution itself, if a criminal escapes into another state he has to be extradited—that is, "delivered up," on demand of the governor, to the "State having Jurisdiction of the Crime."[8]

The Constitution also provided for the return of fugitive slaves, although it included them rather delicately in a more general phrase: persons "held to Service or Labour." They were to be "delivered up on Claim of the Party to whom such Service or Labour may be due."[9] Congress accordingly passed a number of fugitive slave laws to put this provision into effect. These were controversial laws, wildly unpopular in parts of the North. Attempts at "slave catching" in the North sometimes led to outright defiance, or even bloodshed. No issue put a greater strain on federalism than this one.[10] Slavery and race pitted state against state, region against region. The Civil War by no means ended the conflict.

The states have not always been free from protectionist impulses. That is, they have often tried to wriggle out of the constitutional plan, passing laws to benefit their own residents at the expense of people in other states. Some cities and states in the nineteenth century tried to tax to death out-of-state peddlers or put special burdens on "foreign" corporations (that is, corporations from other states). A Virginia law of 1866, for example, required agents of "foreign" insurance companies to get licenses; the companies had to deposit bonds with the treasurer of the state. The Supreme Court upheld the law,[11] partly on the grounds that "issuing a policy of insurance is not a transaction of commerce" and thus is not "interstate commerce," off limits to the states. More recently, protectionist measures have done more poorly in the courts. They have failed economically as well. American borders are as weak as pieces of string.

These borders are meaningless in other ways, too. They are never great cultural boundaries, as is the case in Europe. Every single state (except Hawaii, a collection of islands) has a straight line somewhere on its borders. Western states are mostly lines on a map: Wyoming and Colorado are rectangles, plain and simple. Rivers separate Wisconsin and Minnesota, Kentucky and Ohio, Missouri and Illinois; but even these natural boundaries do not divide one civilization or language from another. North Dakota and South Dakota are separate states, but not separate cultures. They do have different criminal codes, divorce laws, and tort laws, and different court systems and procedures, at least in detail: differences in legal culture tend to persist over time. But in some ways these differences are not terribly important, except to lawyers. In any event, they are not closely meshed with differences in economic or social structure in the two Dakotas.

Legal differences between the states, then, tend to be rather minor, on the whole. This is after all a single country. The state laws are like dialects of a single language. (Louisiana is in some ways an exception.)

A man with a strong Boston accent can tell a southerner a mile away; but the two of them can still talk easily to each other. The border with Canada means much more, legally speaking, than does the straight line between North and South Dakota; and the border with Mexico is legally very wide and very deep—much wider and deeper than the Rio Grande and much, much harder to cross.

Federalism and the "Market" for Laws

The central fact of American federalism is worth repeating: the United States is by and large an economic union, by and large a social union, but not a *legal* union—or at least not completely. State laws are, or can be, rather similar; but this is, first, because of deliberate choice and, second, because conditions in the states are fairly similar. A state is free to be different (if it wishes), within its zone. This was very much the case in the early nineteenth century; since the 1860s, the central government has gotten stronger and stronger and there has been a steady, marked change in relations between states and the federal government. It is obvious why this took place. Changes in technology and socioeconomic structure paved the way.

When all is said and done, the states still have a reservoir of power. This makes possible what we might call a "market" for laws. The states compete with each other for "customers," by passing competing laws. And one state can frustrate the policy of others by offering for sale (so to speak) a cheaper, better, or simply different brand of law.

Nevada is, in a way, an extreme example.[12] Nevada is a large but barren state, mostly mountain and desert. It was admitted to the union in 1864. There is some mining in Nevada and some cattle here and there munch at sparse grasses, but basically there is not much to do for a living in the state. The population in 1900 had fallen to about 42,000. Still, this wilderness of sagebrush and ghost towns had one great ace in the hole: it was a sovereign state, like all the others. It had a governor and a legislature. It had the power to pass whatever laws it wanted. This was a kind of natural resource, just as much as silver or gold.

Specifically, Nevada could compete with its neighbors—especially California, the giant to the west—by passing laws that California did not have or did not want. It could legalize behavior that was illegal in California. Hence Nevada, either deliberately or by happy accident, stumbled into its present role. First, it became a divorce mill, as early as the 1920s. This was not a new idea. There had been divorce mills—places where divorce was quick and easy to get—in other states in the nineteenth century: Indiana, the Dakotas. Those divorce mills eventually collapsed beneath the weight of moral indignation.[13] Moral indignation has never been big in Nevada.

Nevada is also the motherland of legal gambling in the United States. Today, gambling and its spin-offs are by far the largest industries in the state.[14] Thousands and thousands of pleasure seekers from California fly or drive there across the Mojave Desert. Jets bring hundreds of thousands to Reno and Las Vegas, from all over the country and abroad. Nevada allows its counties (except Clark County, where Las Vegas is located) to legalize houses of prostitution. No other state has gone this far officially. Nevada also competes for the marriage business. It requires less time and fewer formalities than California, and it allows anyone over sixteen to get married without parental consent. The marriage age in California is eighteen: California couples who want to elope head straight for the Nevada border. They bring along their wallets, and the newlyweds pump still more money into Nevada's economy.

Nevada is only one blatant example of how the "market" works. Delaware is another case in point. This tiny state, clinging by its fingertips to the base of Pennsylvania, is the "home" of thousands of corporations, including great corporate giants. All sorts of companies are chartered in Delaware without any real connection to the state— even (let us say) a Denver bus company or the like. Why is the state so popular? No secret: around the turn of the century, Delaware deliberately passed lenient corporation laws. This attracted companies like bees to honey. They set up "headquarters" in downtown Wilmington, Delaware, in tiny cubbyholes, for the most part. (The real head offices were elsewhere.) And there they are to this day. Their taxes, low as they are, are a boon to the Delaware economy.

We can note another consequence of the national "market" in laws. Until recently, New York had stringent divorce laws. Basically, adultery was the sole grounds for divorce. Year after year, there was pressure to loosen up on these laws, to bring them in line with those of other states. There was also strong pressure on the opposing side— from the Catholic church, for example. One reason why New York held out so long was the availability of the escape hatch in Nevada— at least for those with enough money for the trip. In other words, New York stumbled into a kind of rough compromise. The strict divorce laws remained on the books, making their moral statement; but the shoe did not pinch too hard: rich New Yorkers went to Reno and got their divorces anyway. Needless to say, this arrangement was not completely satisfying, especially for people without much money. Nevertheless it lasted for generations.

In other words, the legal "market" has both advantages and disadvantages. On the one hand, a state can forge ahead of its neighbors: it can act, as Justice Louis Brandeis once put it, as a "laboratory" of social reform, while conservative states, for their part, can retard reform.

This was what happened in labor law, for example, before the New Deal. Organized labor gained political power in the northern industrial states; and these states passed the first tough child labor laws. Southern states had no such laws on their books; or if they did, they enforced them fitfully. The northern states were afraid of runaway factories; they were worried that textile mills and other plants would pack up and go south, where wages were low and where children could work in the mills. In general, the southern states did not adopt the welfare and labor statutes that became standard in the North and West, or accepted them much more slowly. Since capital and labor could easily flow from North to South, the federal system was a drag on reform. Or so it seemed to northern liberals.

It was a frustrating situation. The southern states were an escape hatch: they nullified the effectiveness of northern labor laws, just as Nevada nullified that of New York's divorce laws. The remedy had to be on a national level—that is, federal laws. Congress obliged. It passed a statute in 1916 which prohibited the interstate shipment of goods made in factories that used child labor. But a conservative Supreme Court, in *Hammer* v. *Dage* nart*,[15] threw the law out. Congress, said the Court, had no power to pass such a law. The case set off a storm of protest. There were attempts to get around *Hammer* v. *Dagenhart* through the taxing power or through constitutional amendment. For one reason or another these measures failed. Effective control of child labor, on a national scale, was achieved only during the New Deal period, in the 1930s.

Child labor was a controversial subject; but in other parts of the law—which were more "lawyerly," less politically visible—there were more successful movements to come to grips with the problem of legal disunity. The best examples of "success" were in commercial law, in the Uniform Laws movement, described in Chapter 5. The success of some of these laws, and in particular the Uniform Commercial Code, means that commercial law has at last become in essence a national legal subject.

Federalism in Recent Times

The "market" effects we have talked about are still with us, as the example of Nevada shows. But their influence has gone down considerably, because the role of the central government has gone up and up. Federal control of economy and society is pervasive; traditional ideas of states' rights impede the power of Washington less and less. The Constitution did not give the federal government much regulatory control, on the surface. It doled out power in teaspoons. The central government could regulate commerce "with foreign Nations, and among the several States, and with the Indian Tribes" (Article I, Section 8). "Among the several States" was assumed to mean commerce that flowed across state lines. But interstate commerce was the exception, not the rule, in the early nineteenth century. Commerce was mostly local trade.

In addition, Congress (before the ICC Act) showed little inclination to regulate even interstate commerce; and the Supreme Court up until the New Deal tended to take a narrow view of congressional power—not narrow enough to please extreme "state's righters," but certainly narrow from the modern standpoint. For example, in *United States* v. *E. C. Knight Co.*,[16] a Sherman Act case, the government had moved to break up the so-called Sugar Trust. The American Sugar Refining Company had already gobbled up most of the country's sugar refineries; and it had just gotten its grip on four more, which would give it 98 percent of all sugar refining capacity in the country.

This certainly looked like a monopoly under the Sherman Act, but the Supreme Court held against the government: Congress had power over "commerce," and the Sugar Trust was engaged in manufacture, not commerce. Of course, a monopoly of manufacture necessarily affected commerce; but the court brushed this point aside.

This narrow view of the commerce clause and of federal power over national affairs is now completely discarded. The federal government exercises vast control over the economy, and the legal barriers are almost meaningless. Interstate commerce is the dominant form of commerce; and both Congress and the Court have now reduced the effect of the interstate commerce clause, as a limitation on national power, to a thin, thin wisp of its former self. This process began in earnest in the 1930s, and has gone very far indeed.

For example, the Civil Rights Act of 1964 outlawed race discrimination in stores, restaurants, hotels, and other public places. Where did Congress get power to tell some tiny snack bar—some southern greasy spoon—that it had no right to exclude black customers? This was indeed a problem under our federal system. Congress chose to solve it by resting its power on the commerce clause. Any restaurant that served interstate travelers fell under the act; so too if the "food which it serves . . . has moved in commerce." This meant that if the soup cans on the shelf or the meat in a roast beef sandwich or the box of Rice Krispies had ever crossed state lines, then the restaurant came within the terms of the Civil Rights Act.

This line of argument was logically flimsy but ethically powerful; the nineteenth century, or even the early twentieth century, would have found it absurd. The modern Supreme Court bought the argument eagerly and swallowed it whole. The case was *Katzenbach* v. *McClung.*[17] In this case, a place called Ollie's Barbecue, in Birmingham, Alabama, made legal history; it was the subject of the test case in which the Supreme Court upheld this aspect of the Civil Rights Act of 1964. After this case, it was clear that the commerce clause was no longer a serious restraint on Congress. When it came to enforcing national policy on an issue as sensitive as civil rights, the courts would impose no restraint.

But the commerce clause is far from dead in its negative sense. It still operates as a limit on what the *states* can do. States are not allowed to discriminate against the goods of other states. California still cannot bar Florida oranges. And state regulations that burden interstate commerce unduly—for instance, a weird rule about mudflaps on trucks, or restrictions on the length of interstate trains as they run through the state from outside—have been struck down by the courts.[18] In a landmark case in 1951, the Supreme Court reviewed an ordinance of Madison, Wisconsin. The city banned all supposedly pasteurized milk unless it was processed and bottled at "an approved pasteurization plant within a radius of five miles from the central square of Madison." An Illinois milk company challenged the law. The Court struck down the ordinance. The concept of "preferential trade areas" was "destructive of the very purpose of the Commerce Clause." The ordinance put a "discriminatory burden on interstate commerce"; hence, it had to go.[19]

This is a difficult, technical area of law. The courts have been struggling to find some reasonable middle ground. The states should have some right to run their own affairs—make their own policy. But the national economy comes first. Where is the line to be drawn? Can New Jersey prevent landfill companies from dumping "solid or liquid waste which originated or was collected outside" New Jersey? The

Supreme Court said no.[20] Can a state prefer its own people in allocating scarce natural resources? Montana charged its residents $30 for a license to hunt elk; outsiders had to pay $225. In this case, the Supreme Court said yes.[21] The line-drawing process continues.

Today, the federal government is a vast taxing machine, sucking up billions upon billions of dollars to support its great enterprises and to feed its millions of mouths. The tax money goes primarily for two main objects: welfare and defense. The weapons of a nuclear power, in this dangerous world, are obscenely expensive. Only the federal government can afford them; only the federal government is a player in world affairs. Arkansas has no atom bomb, no ambassadors, no say in international politics. But international politics is a matter of life and death, and so is international trade. These facts feed federal power and cut down the relative importance of states.

Since the New Deal of the 1930s, more and more areas of American law, government, and life have crossed an invisible line, from state responsibility into the federal domain. Before the New Deal, welfare law was as local as local could be. It was hardly even centralized at the state level; townships, cities, and counties ran the show. The depression wrecked local finance. Social security moved in. Today, the federal government is the dominant partner in old-age pensions, unemployment relief, and most other social programs.

Education, too, was once exclusively the affair of local school boards, with some degree of state supervision. In any event, the federal government had no say in the matter. In 1950, Congress passed a law granting money to "impacted" school districts. These were districts with special "financial burdens" because of some federal activity (an army base with heaps of kids, for example).[22] In 1965 came a dramatic change, the Elementary and Secondary Education Act.[23] This provided money for school districts generally, whether impacted or not. From that point on, federal money and federal rules—about bilingual education, race segregation, handicapped children, and so on—began to transform the law and practice of educational administration. The Department of Education is now a cabinet post, spending billions and overseeing dozens of programs.

At one time, too, nothing was more solidly local, more exclusively under state and city control, than criminal justice. The local police took care of murder, robbery, and rape—and gambling and drunkenness, too. There were only a few federal crimes (smuggling, illegal immigration) in the nineteenth century; the federal government did not even have its own prisons before 1891. It boarded its few prisoners in state prisons. Today, crime itself has gone interstate in many respects. Federal crimes became more significant in the twentieth century, because of laws against driving stolen cars across state lines and laws against drugs, draft evasion, and income tax fraud. There is a powerful Federal Bureau of Investigation; the federal government even plays some role in financing local crime fighting. The Law Enforcement Assistance Act (1965) and the Omnibus Crime Control and Safe Streets Act (1968)[24] pumped money into state and local governments. The 1968 act stated that crime was "essentially a local problem," but that the high incidence of crime was a threat to the "peace, security, and general welfare of the nation." This justified a program of federal support for local law enforcement. In the 1980s, it seems clear that no major program of government is completely "local" any more.

Yet the old balance is not completely dead. Federalism still has some hold on legal culture. There is an intense tradition of government close to home. The Constitution tried to build a system of "checks and balances." Executive, legislature, and judiciary would control and monitor each other. State governments would balance the federal government; the federal government would keep states in control.

All this was part of the original plan. The founders distrusted unbridled power. They rejected the divine right of kings or kinglike rulers. They preferred a kind of warlord system, that is, a government made up of little pieces—of small fiefdoms—without overall plan or direction. Even in the nuclear age—in the world of the 1980s—there is something to be said for the plan. Much battered by history, it has not given up the ghost. At this date (1984), there is some sentiment for changing direction—for reversing the trend. There is nostalgia for an older federalism, a federalism tilted more strongly toward the states. It has the ironic title of "new federalism." So far, only a few small steps have been taken in this direction. Whether the "new federalism" will be a major trend, or only a tiny chirping in the night, remains to be seen.

8

Inside the Black Box:
The Substance of Law

*T*HE STRUCTURE OF law, the court system, legal procedures, legal history, the place of law in society—all of these are important subjects. But at the core of the legal system are its actual operating rules—the *substance* of law. What behavior does the system try to control? How does the law influence behavior? What conduct does it encourage or discourage? These are key questions in any society.

The legal system affects our lives every day. This is especially true when we take a broad view of law, defining it as all *public* social control. The system is of awesome bulk, and it touches on many matters, big and small, as the tale of the trip to the grocery in Chapter 1 made clear. The law also operates on many levels. Imagine yourself living in Omaha, Nebraska. You are, of course, a citizen of the United States of America. You are under the Constitution of the United States—under its protection and also constrained by the kind of government it sets up. As an American, you are under the wing—or the thumb—of the federal statutes. These statues run to something on the order of 25,000 pages of small print. True, most of this has nothing to do with you or your life, directly or indirectly; but a surprising amount of it does affect you. You may, for example, neither know or care about the law of patents; but inventions that were patented under these laws—from telephones to computers to safety pins—most definitely matter to you.

The federal statutes are only a start. There are also more than 450 volumes of Supreme Court cases and well over a thousand volumes of lower federal court decisions. Here even less of the contents concerns most of us personally; but in this great mass of words, there are undoubtedly decisions (on race, on war and peace, on the economy) that do affect our lives one way or the other. Then there are the federal regulations, volume after volume; and decisions of administrative agencies and tribunals on food and drug matters, the income tax, labor law, civil rights, stock markets. It is literally impossible to count these.

Yet this is only federal law. You are also under the jurisdiction of Nebraska. It, too, has a legal system. The Revised Statutes of Nebraska fill a good-sized shelf. A Cumulative Supplement was published in 1980. This contained only the changes in the law of Nebraska that had gone into effect in the previous few years; yet the book runs over 2,200 pages all by itself. There are also the reported cases of the Nebraska Supreme Court (several big shelves); and the rules, regulations, and decisions of state agencies. We are not yet done: there is the City of Omaha, too, with its ordinances and its local rules, regulations, and decisions—about schools, about traffic, about local sanitation, about where you can build a house and where you cannot, and so on.

All this amazing mass of material has to be organized in some way. Otherwise, nobody could teach law in law school and lawyers could not navigate their way through the mess. It is perfectly clear that no lawyer can ever hope to "know the law." Every lawyer knows some of it, of course; and a specialist lawyer knows some of it well and precisely. But even the most learned lawyer is ignorant about most of our law. What the lawyer does know (or should know) is the limits of what he knows. He also knows how to "look up law," how to find out when he does not know, and how to deal with law once it is found.

The written laws, in other words, are like entries in a gigantic dictionary. Most people know some of the words—the easy, everyday words. Specialists know the words that belong to their specialties (biologists know biological words, gourmets know food words, soccer players know soccer words). The same is more or less true of the law. People in general know the easy words (*judge, jury, contract, mortgage, murder*). They also know some simple rules. Lawyers know a lot more: they know the basic principles, the stuff everyone learns in law school. Specialists know their fields—tax law, for example. But the tax man knows little or nothing about food and drug law or admiralty law or the law of prisoners' rights.

We have been talking about the visible, written parts of the law.

But lawyers are not just people who look up law. Many lawyers operate day after day without looking anything up in a book. They have experience; they have gone through the ordinary processes a hundred times before. They have closed dozens of house deals, or probated dozens of estates, or handled a hundred divorces, or filled out countless tax returns. They also know how the legal system actually works in their towns. They know whom to see, what to do, what forms to fill out, when to wait quietly and when to move swiftly and soon. Their practical knowledge is a vital part of their skills, as vital as "knowing the law."

Classifying Law

The Romans were probably the first people to address the problem of reducing law to a system. Long before the Romans, of course, societies had laws and codes of law. But, as far as we know, people like the Babylonians or the Hittites did not write treatises about law, or try to organize legal knowledge in some systematic way. The Romans did. They organized and classified their laws; and they did so in a useful, persistent way.

Classical Roman law, for example, drew a line between the "law of persons" and the "law of things." William Blackstone, whose *Commentaries on the Law of England* tried to sum up English law for a lay audience in the middle of the eighteenth century, used the same distinction; and it is also found in many basic civil codes in Europe and Latin America. In Louisiana, too, the first part (Book I) of the Civil Code is called "Of Persons," and includes (among other things) rules about marriage, divorce, and minor children. Book II is called "Things and the Different Modifications of Ownership"; it is basically about property law.

Civil law scholars (mostly European) have always been interested in classifying law. They have searched for some rational, systematic way to break law up into subjects or parts. The common law shows a lot less zest for this task. Of course, over the years, the common law reached an uncomfortable size. When this happened, scholars in England tried to take it apart and put it together in some handy way, restating the whole in convenient form. Blackstone was one of these scholars. He borrowed his arrangement, essentially, from civil law. His *Commentaries* were wildly successful, especially in this country. There were many "American" editions, that is, versions of Blackstone with special notes on American sources and differences. After independence, American jurists tried their hand at the Blackstone game, this time with respect to American law. The most notable treatise of this kind was James Kent's *Commentaries on American Law*, first published between 1827 and 1830. This work, in four volumes, was arranged more or less like Blackstone's *Commentaries*. It, too, ran into many editions.

Blackstone was a good popularizer but not much of a legal philosopher, at least not by European standards. Still, his book was far more systematic than most English attempts to cope with the common law as a whole. The so-called abridgments of the law were another method of setting out the basic rules. The word *abridgment* might seem a bit ironic, since some of the abridgments ran into many volumes. They were arranged as simply as possible: alphabetically, by topic.

This idea, too, carried over into America. Nathan Dane put together an *Abridgment of American Law* in the early nineteenth century, with the same general organization (or nonorganization). Even today, lawyers have available huge legal encyclopedias as reference books. One of these is *Corpus Juris* which (along with its continuation, *Corpus Juris Secundum*) tries to cover the whole of American caselaw. *Corpus Juris* is arranged alphabetically, by topic, like a dictionary or encyclopedia; so are many digests of state or multistate law. The second edition of *American Jurisprudence*, one of the major digests, is eighty-two volumes long; the first volume begins with "Abandoned Property," the last volume ends with "Zoning and Planning."

Alphabetical arrangement means that the arranger has no overall theory for joining the pieces together; he must still carve the huge bulk up into segments or parts. Otherwise, one could not even list things alphabetically. Like flour or sugar, law has to be packaged in boxes or sacks before one can handle it. Conventionally, there are dozens and dozens of such packages; but most of the categories (like "Abandoned Property") are of minor importance. A few categories are of major significance; they constitute big, basic subdivisions of law. These also, for the most part, define the chunks of subject matter which are contained in the basic courses taught in American law schools.

Contracts. Contracts is the body of law that by and large concerns voluntary agreements. Most people understand more or less what it means to enter into a contract. They realize that a contract is a bargain or agreement between two people (or more) to do some work, to buy or sell goods, to put up a building or tear one down, or to perform any one of countless other activities, which one person or company promises to do in exchange for a counterpromise (usually a promise to pay money).

Over a century ago (1861), the great English jurist, Sir Henry Maine, published a book called *Ancient Law*. In a famous passage, Maine described the evolution of law over the centuries in "progressive" (that is, modernizing) societies. The development went "from status to contract." What he meant was that legal relations in modern societies do not depend primarily on birth or caste; they depend on voluntary agreements. Elizabeth II is queen of England because of an accident of birth; but it is not an accident of birth that I make payments on a used yellow Plymouth; it is because I agreed to buy the car, on my own, as an adult, quite willingly.

In this sense, a regime of contact is fundamental to modern society. The whole economy—more, the whole social system—rests on it. But a regime of contract, a system of contract—that is, an economy organized around voluntary agreements, governed mainly by the market—is not the same as the law of contracts as conventionally defined and taught in law schools. The law of contracts deals with only certain aspects of the market, and with certain kinds of agreement.

In legal terms, a contract is a promise (or set of promises) that the law protects and enforces. If I promise to deliver a carload of lumber and the buyer promises to pay me a certain price, and I do not deliver the lumber, I have "breached" my contract. The buyer can sue me for damages—if he chooses.

To make a valid contract, generally speaking, we need at least two parties; both have to have legal "capacity." A small child or an idiot cannot legally enter into a contract. One side must make an "offer"; the other side must "accept" it. *Offer* and *acceptance* are ordinary English words, but they have specialized, technical meanings in law. A department store ad which announces an "offer" of a sewing machine for sale at a low price, as a "Thursday Only Special," is probably not making a legal offer. For one thing, there is no actual promise to sell the sewing machines. If, for example, the public gobbles up the stock, the store does not have to sell sewing machines to disappointed customers.[1] An "offer," however, has to be legally a promise.

"Offer" and "acceptance" are promises, then, and they must be supported by a mysterious substance called "consideration." This is an intricate legal concept, hard to define in a sentence or two. The underlying idea, however, is fairly simple. Each party to a contract makes his promise "in consideration" of something which the other one promises. If I offer to sell my old car for $2,000, and the buyer accepts (promising to pay $2,000) the "consideration" on each side is clear. But if I promise to give my daughter a handful of diamonds because I love her, there is no "consideration" for my promise; she contributes nothing in return. (Love, alas, does not count in the law of contracts.) Here, if I fail to deliver (or die before I get a chance to) she has no right to sue me or my estate and claim the diamonds.

There are, of course, many other issues in the law of contracts. Samuel Williston's treatise on contract law—the leader in the field for many years—lumbers through volume after volume. There is, however, some question whether all this lore matters very much in the world of affairs. In a classic article, Stewart Macaulay explored the behavior of businessmen in Wisconsin. He found that many of them tended to avoid or sidestep (formal) contract law and contract doctrine. They especially shied away from suing each other, even when they had a "good case" according to law. The reason was not at all mysterious. Businessmen depended on each other; they lived and worked in networks of continuing relationships. A manufacturer might buy paper clips, pens, and office supplies from the same dealer, year in and year out. Suing at the drop of the hat, or arguing excessively, or sticking up for abstract "rights," was disruptive; it tended to rip apart these valuable relationships. Also, there were norms, practices, and conceptions of honor and fairness that businessmen customarily followed. These were more subtle, more complicated, than the formal norms of the lawyers.[2]

"Contract law" is a standard first-year course in every law school. Yet it is probably less important a part of the living law than other fields which build on contract law or contract ideas. One of these fields is commercial law. This is the branch of law that concerns the buying and selling of goods, especially sales for credit and on the installment plan; it also deals with checks, promissory notes, and other "negotiable instruments." Another related field is the law of bankruptcy and creditors' rights. A bankrupt business or individual goes through a process that wipes the slate clean and allows the bankrupt to begin again. Even more important, the bankruptcy process is designed to ensure fairness to all of the creditors. It tries to avoid a dog-eat-dog struggle over the assets of wrecked businesses and failed debtors. Bankruptcy law is a federal concern and is administered in the federal courts. Another rapidly growing field is the law of consumer protection. Still other fields concern themselves with special

kinds of contract—for example, contracts of insurance. Insurance contracts, like the insurance business, are quite heavily regulated and
subject to distinctive rules.

Torts. Tort law is usually described as the law of "civil wrongs,"
and it is hard to give a more exact definition. I commit a tort if I hit
somebody accidentally but carelessly (with my fists or my car); if I
falsely call someone a thief or put this in writing (slander and libel); if
I have somebody maliciously arrested, or invade somebody's privacy,
or trespass on someone's land without permission.

This is a more or less ragbag collection of behaviors, which have
little in common except that they are all defined as wrong and do not
grow out of a contractual relationship between victim and "tortfea-
sor." They are also "civil" wrongs, which means they are not crimes
(at least not necessarily). If I wander onto somebody's land by mistake
and trample on something valuable, I may have to pay; but I have not
committed a crime and I will not go to jail. It is not a crime for me to
back out of a parking space and dent somebody else's fender, unless
I did it willfully and recklessly. But of course I have to pay. Some
torts *are* crimes, especially if the behavior is reckless or malicious.
The ordinary tort is not.

A tort is conduct which causes injury and does not measure up to
some standard which society has set. Everything listed in the last
paragraph is a tort, but some torts are more important than other
torts. The heart of tort law is the action for personal injury—a claim
against a person or company for hurting my body in some way. Probably 95 percent of all tort claims are for personal injury. Auto accidents, nowadays, are responsible for most of them. Formerly, railroad
and work accidents were the most prolific sources. Indeed, the law of
torts was insignificant before the railroad age of the nineteenth century—and no wonder. This branch of law deals above all with the
wrenching, grinding effects of machines on human bodies. It belongs
to the world of factories, railroads, and mines—in other words, the
world of the Industrial Revolution.

Basically, then, the railroad created the law of torts. Not a single
treatise on the law of torts was published before 1850, either in England
or the United States. Early tort cases often came up out of railroad
accidents. Nicholas Farwell, who worked for the Boston and Worcester Railroad, lost his hand in a switchyard accident, sued the railroad,
and got nothing; but *Farwell* v. *Boston & Worcester Rr. Corp.* made
legal history.[3] In this case, the chief justice of Massachusetts, Lemuel

Shaw, announced the American version of the "fellow-servant" rule. Under this rule, an employee could not sue his company for work injuries if the accident was caused by the carelessness of a coworker (a fellow-servant). This was, of course, the usual situation in a factory or mine or on the railroad. Hence the rule protected employers against almost all claims of injured workmen.[4]

Despite the rule, industrial accidents in which workers like Farwell were mangled by machines were the most fertile source of tort cases in the nineteenth century. In the twentieth century, the fellow-servant rule was replaced by an administrative system—workmen's compensation—and the auto accident moved to center stage. Lately, two subfields of the law of torts have grown rapidly: medical malpractice and products liability (injuries caused by defective foods, toys, appliances, drugs, or other commodities). A study of jury trials in Cook County, Illinois (Chicago and its suburbs) between 1960 and 1979 documents how auto accidents dominate in the lower courts. Of the civil jury trials in that period, 65.5 percent were auto accident cases. Products liability cases rose from 2.3 percent to 5.8 percent at the end of the period; medical malpractice rose from 1.4 percent of the load to 3.5 percent.[5] These last two categories, however, make a noise in society out of all proportion to their numbers; the rise in medical malpractice cases generated a sense of crisis in the profession and led to reform efforts in many states, including attempts to put a ceiling on the amount that plaintiffs can recover from doctors and hospitals.

A fundamental concept of tort law is "negligence." This means, roughly, carelessness. Basically, if somebody causes me harm I can sue him for damages only if he was negligent. He has to be at fault. If he was as careful as he should have been (as careful as the imaginary "reasonable man"—the yardstick for measuring negligence), then I cannot recover for my injury.

Thousands of cases have turned on what does or does not amount to negligence. In the twentieth century, the concept has gone into something of a decline, especially in products liability cases. More and more, courts impose "strict liability"—that is, a victim can recover even if there was no negligence and if the manufacturer was as careful as is humanly possible. If a company makes jars of pickles and has good quality control, it can still happen that one jar out of a million is bad, slips through the net, and makes someone sick. The company has not been negligent, in nineteenth-century terms. But modern cases insist that the company must pay.

The Law of Property. The old common law was preeminently the law of real property; and the distinction between "real property" and "personal property" was a crucial one. Generally speaking, real property means real estate—land and buildings—but it also includes such things as growing crops. Everything else—money, stocks and bonds, jewelry, cars, carloads of lumber, IOUs, bank deposits—is personal property. We all have a stake in real estate, since we all live somewhere; and we work, study, and travel somewhere, too. Everyone is a renter or an owner, or lives with renters or owners. But for most of us, personal property means more than real estate. It seems odd, then, that as far as the law is concerned the word *property* means primarily real property; personal property is of minor importance.

Actually, personal property is legally a minor field precisely *because* personal property has become so important. There is no single, special field of law devoted to personal property. Personal property is what contract law, commercial law, and bankruptcy law—yes, and torts, too—are all about. But there are so many special rules about real estate that it makes sense to treat this as a separate field of law.

Property law is still one of the fundamental branches of law, and real estate is a significant branch of law practice. Yet property law is a mere shadow of its former self, legally speaking. In fact, one of the major developments in our system, if you take the long view, is the relative decline of real property law. In medieval England, it would have been only a slight exaggeration to say that land law was the law of the land. When Blackstone published his *Commentaries* midway through the eighteenth century, one whole volume (a quarter of his space) was devoted to land law. A modern Blackstone would shrink the topic to a fraction of this bulk—5 or 10 percent, at most, of the total law.

Medieval England lived under a feudal system. Power and jurisdiction—the cornerstones of wealth and position in society—were based on land and land alone. The "lord" was a person who held an estate— a person with ownership, mastery, control over land. A person without land was a person with no real stake in affairs of state. The common law, as the royal law courts expounded it, had little to say to men and women without land, who were the majority of the English population. Even in this country, at one time, only persons who had interests in land were entitled to vote or hold office. The New York constitution of 1777, for example, restricted the right to vote for state senators to men who owned "freeholds" with £100 or more, free and clear of debt (Article X). All this, of course, has ended; land is only one form of wealth. A great and powerful family is one that controls mighty enterprises, rather than one that rules vast estates.

Property law still covers a rich and varied group of subjects. To begin with, it asks: What does it mean to "own" land? How can I get title to land and how can I dispose of it, legally? There are issues about deeds, joint ownership, and land records and registration; and problems of land finance, including rules about mortgages and fore-closures. There is the law of "nuisance," which restricts me from using my land in such a way as to hurt my neighbors, pouring smoke or sending bad smells onto his land, for example. There are the law of "easements" and the exotic law of "covenants" (especially those that "run with the land"): these deal with rights a person might have in his neighbor's land—rights to drive a car up his driveway, to walk across his lawn, or to keep him from taking in boarders. These are not rights of ownership; rather they are "servitudes"—restrictions or exceptions to the owner's rights, in favor of those of another.

The common law was ingenious in carving up rights to land into various complex segments called "estates." These could be either time segments or space segments. A "life estate" (my right to live in a certain house, for example, until I die), is a time segment; so is a three-year lease of a farm or apartment house. Space segments include air rights (the right to build on top of certain property) and mineral rights (the right to dig underneath it). Nowadays, the condominium is also popular; I can own a slice of some building thirty stories above the ground. The common law was also quite ingenious in devising forms of common or joint ownership, with subtle technical differences between them.

There are also all sorts of "future interests" known to the common law. Suppose I leave my house to my sister for life, and then to any of her children who might be alive when she dies. The children have a future interest; that is, the time they will get the house is postponed to some far-off date. But the future event is certain to happen, and thus the future interest can have value and reality now, while my sister is very much alive. The law of future interests developed in a most gnarled and complicated way. Its intricacies drove generations of law students to quiet despair.

Another important, fairly new, branch of property law is the law of "land use controls." It deals with the limits imposed on what peo-ple can do with their property. This was an issue in the law of nui-sance; but modern controls go far beyond this. Zoning is a familiar type of land use restriction. Zoning ordinances date from about the time of the First World War; they are now almost universal in cities and villages. Zoning ordinances divide towns into zones designated for different uses. If my neighborhood is "zoned" residential, I cannot build a factory or run a restaurant on my property. If the zone is restricted to single-family dwellings, I cannot even run a rooming house or rent out apartments.

The Law of Succession. This field, the law of wills and trusts, is closely related to property law as such. It is the branch of law which, essentially, considers how property is passed along from one generation to the next. In the United States, there is a strong system of private property. Property is allocated among individual owners, by and large; this practice is unlike that in many societies, where land is generally owned in common or by clans, families, or tribes. We tend to own our land and homes outright, along with whatever else we possess, from rings and wristwatches to stocks and bonds and money in the bank. Since it is a fundamental rule (alas) that we all die in the end and take nothing with us (the Pharaohs tried and failed), this property must somehow move on at our death.

One way to make this happen is to execute a will. You, the owner, will decide, for the most part, what should become of your worldly goods when you die. This is the principle of "freedom of testation." You decide—but you must do it in a certain way. If you forget to make a will (or botch the job of drawing it up), you have died "intestate," and the state will distribute the property for you according to a fixed scheme set out in the statute books. Intestate property passes to the heirs at law, the nearest surviving relatives. If you leave behind a large enough estate, the government takes a bite of it, too, in the form of taxes.

A will is a formal document. It must be made out just right, and in most states it needs two witnesses. In about half the states, mostly in the West and South, you can also execute a will without witnesses, the so-called holographic will. This kind must be written entirely by hand by the testator (the person whose will it is); no typing is allowed. If you have a valid will, you can disinherit any relatives you choose. Except in Louisiana a parent can, with a stroke of the pen, cut off his children without a penny. A husband or wife cannot be cut off so easily. The surviving spouse has rights to a share of the estate, and it is not easy to disinherit her totally.

"Trusts" are arrangements which, in essence, transfer property to a trustee (often a bank), to invest and to manage. The trustees pay the income to one or more "beneficiaries," who are quite passive; they sit back and collect the money. Trusts are gifts, and rich people use them as part of a general estate plan—their scheme for orderly disposition of their property. Many trusts are "testamentary," that is, part of a plan contained in a will. Others are set up long before death; but even these generally have death and death taxes in mind. The law of trusts goes together with the law of wills, both in law school and in the lawyer's office; both are aspects of "estate planning." Lawyers who specialize in this branch of practice search for the best, cheapest, and most effective way to carry out the wishes of their clients, at the same time avoiding the buzzards of taxation as much as possible.

Estate planning is basically law for the rich. Most people do not have enough "estate" to need the fanciest tricks of the trade. Adults who have money or property do need wills; but many people do not bother with them. In Cuyahoga County, Ohio (Cleveland is the main city) a study in 1964–65 found that almost a third of the estates probated lacked wills.[6] The percentage of "intestacy" was probably higher in the general population; many people who die leave so little money that the family does not bother with probate.

Sociolegal scholars have paid little attention to the law of succession. This is unfortunate. It is a crucial branch of law—as vital to social continuity as DNA is to survival of the species. Since all of us eventually die, society must reproduce itself every generation—not only biologically, but also socially and structurally. The basic process is far from mysterious. Social norms and structures cross from generation to generation through education, child rearing, and other processes that mold the new generation in the shape of the old one. But the inheritance of property also plays a crucial part. Without the laws of succession, there would be no such things as "old money," aristocracy, or "good families." Each generation would start over, and social structure would be fundamentally altered.

Perhaps for the better, perhaps not. But life would be different, in a revolutionary way. Even socialist countries allow some inheritance of property. And the middle class, too, has a stake in the law of succession. The law permits money to flow across time, and specifies how this is to be done. Without succession, there would be no heirlooms, no old family homes, no gifts left to grandchildren for college.

Perhaps just as important as the rights of inheritance are the limits on inheritance. There are complicated rules about estate taxes. The larger the estates are, the more taxes they pay, but there are important escape valves. One of these is the unlimited right to give to charity, tax-free. Without this right, the great foundations would not exist. Other rules limit dynasties of wealth in their duration. No trust, except for a charity, can last forever. The limiting rule is called the rule against perpetuities.

Family Law. This branch of law borders on the law of succession. Most people, after all, leave their money to relatives. Family law is concerned with marital property, including the community property systems of California and other western states. What rights does a husband or wife have in the money or income of the spouse? This field also concerns marriage and divorce, child custody, and childrens' rights.

Family structure is changing rapidly, and family law changes with it. Divorce, for example, was once rare and difficult to get. Indeed, in the early nineteenth century some states did not grant divorces at all except through special acts of the legislature; one state, South Carolina, simply allowed no divorce. Even in "easy" states, divorce was based on the so-called fault system. A married person who wanted a divorce had to go to court and prove some "grounds" for divorce. Divorce was available only to "innocent" parties, whose spouses were guilty of adultery, desertion, cruelty, habitual drunkenness, or whatever else was on the statutory list. Some states were much stricter than others. In New York, one of the strict states, adultery was practically speaking the only grounds for divorce.[7]

The nineteenth century moaned and groaned about rising divorce rates; in retrospect the rates seem ridiculously small. Only in the twentieth century has divorce become an everyday affair. But for at least a hundred years—since the 1870s or so—most divorces have been consensual. That is, there was no real contest; the courtroom proceedings were a mere ritual, a sham. The alleged grounds were often faked. Courts knew all this, but they closed their eyes to it and let the system run its course. There was a heavy, rising demand for divorce, while the stigma attached to divorced status steadily weakened. In recent years, state after state has adopted a so-called no-fault system. There is no longer any need to prove grounds—or indeed to prove anything. All that is required, essentially, is the fact that the honeymoon is over—that the marriage has broken down irretrievably. Divorce is now legally as well as socially routine. It is not even called divorce any more in California; the new name is "dissolution of marriage."

Easy divorce does not mean easier problems for family law. Indeed, changes in family structure, which lie behind the divorce explosion, brought certain dilemmas closer to the surface. Custody disputes are if anything more common and acrimonious than in the days before no-fault divorce. The basic legal principle is that the child's best interests come first; but in the modern world that does not carry us very far. We can no longer assume, as we once did, that "best interests" almost always means mother. Joint custody is one of many new ideas which the system is trying out, to cope with problems of the children of divorce.

The Law of Business Associations. The corporation is the dominant form of business enterprise today—the dominant employer, the dominant force in the economy. It is also the main concern of the law of business associations. Corporations take many forms; but they have in common limited liability and a division of function between the owners of shares and the actual managers of the company (unless the managers themselves own the shares). Corporations are legal entities. They are "persons" in the eyes of the law, and can sue and be sued in their own names. Limited liability means that shareholders cannot lose more than the value of their shares, no matter how many debts the corporation accumulates. Shareholders, in other words, are not personally liable for the corporation's debts.

At the time of the Revolution, and for several generations afterwards, setting up a corporation was not easy. The incorporators had to follow a long, laborious route. Corporations were chartered one by one; each charter was a special law passed by the state legislature. Most of these early corporations held "franchises": they were little monopolies, with the right to build a bridge over some particular river or a railroad between this town and that. It seemed only right to deal with them case by case. The law was also quite strict about their powers. They were not allowed one step beyond what their charters specifically said.

Today, corporation law is entirely different. Basically, it is much more permissive. Anybody who wants to form a corporation fills out a form or two, pays a small fee to a state official, and that is that. Corporations, generally speaking, can last forever and can do whatever they wish, provided it is not downright illegal. Courts will generally uphold the business judgment of management. Tricky questions still arise, to be sure, about the rights of shareholders and about the duty of officers toward their companies, creditors, and others. There

is also a significant measure of federal control. The Securities and
Exchange Commission monitors the issue of public securities—stocks
and bonds offered to the public. SEC rules are designed to promote
honest disclosure of financial facts, in order to prevent the kinds of
stock fraud once all too common among the gaudy wheelers and dealers of Wall Street.

The corporation is not the only form of business association. Most
law firms, for example, are partnerships. The rights and duties of
partners, in relation to each other and to third parties, raise many
legal problems. The law of "agency," too, is closely linked to business
associations. This is the branch of law that deals with principals and
agents. If a pedestrian is hit by a truck that belongs to Acme Toothpick, Inc., the pedestrian will almost certainly sue the company (the
"principal") even though the actual tort was committed by the driver
(the "agent"). Can the pedestrian sue the truck driver instead? Yes,
but the company has more money and is a better target. And the
company is liable for the acts of its agents. This is the doctrine of
respondeat superior—"let the superior [principal] answer"; or, in cruder
language, "soak the boss."

This much seems clear. But it assumes the driver was actually on
company business. This is usually but not always the case. Suppose
he had borrowed the truck to take his boy to a ball game. The driver
is off on a "frolic," as the law quaintly puts it. Is the company still
liable? In other words, if you hire people to work for you, what is the
exact scope of your responsibility for what your agents do? The law of
agency explores this and similar questions.

Public Law

European legal scholars make much of the distinction between
"public" and "private" law. The distinction goes back to classical Roman
law. Private law concerned the rights and interests of individuals;
public law concerned the Roman state. From this standpoint, most
fields we have discussed in this chapter fall under the heading of private law. A divorce case is *Smith* v. *Smith*, husband and wife; tort
cases are mostly between person and person, or person and company;
so, too, are struggles over title to land. But when the government
brought a huge lawsuit trying to break IBM up into smaller parts (the
Reagan administration finally abandoned the suit), this was definitely
public law.

Theorists in common-law systems make much less of the distinction between public and private law. And, as many scholars have pointed out, as time goes on the distinction has less and less relevance. There are few, if any, fields today that are purely private. Government is a silent—or noisy—partner in every branch of law, to a greater or lesser degree. Land law is essentially private; but zoning is public. Tort law is private, but dozens of statutes on safety regulation and the like affect the course of private lawsuits. And so it goes.

Lawyers' work, too, shifts more and more from the private to the public side. There is, for example, taxation—a bloated monster of a field. The federal government spends hundreds of billions of dollars every year; so do the states and the cities, in the aggregate. The money has to be wrung out of taxpayers. Taxpayers wriggle and resist. As a consequence, tax law may well be the single largest field of law, in terms of effort, dollars involved, and the bulk of statutes and regulations, however one measures it. It is also a field of awesome technicality. The Internal Revenue Code, the key to all of Uncle Sam's billions, is the longest, most difficult statute in the whole federal armory.

Taxation is one among many great fields of public law. There is antitrust law, concerned with monopolies and restraint of trade. There is regulation of business in general, public utility law, and such specialties as food and drug law, maritime law, and immigration and naturalization law. Public law also includes bankruptcy and consumer protection law and most of the rules and structures that bear on labor relations. The growth of public law is bound up with the rise of the administrative state. All through this book, we have seen examples of public law at work. Constitutional law and civil liberties are two key fields in this large area, and they merit fuller discussion in a chapter of their own.

9

Crimes
and Punishments

FOR THE LAYMAN, the criminal side of the legal system is in many ways the most familiar aspect of American law. In fact, when you mention law or the legal system, the trappings of criminal justice— police, courtrooms, juries, trials, prisons and jails—spring naturally into people's minds. The drama of the trial has fascinated people for centuries. Crime and punishment are frontpage news, and are the subject of hundreds of plays, movies, and books. There is a great novel called *The Trial* and another called *Crime and Punishment*. No novel worth reading is called *Antitrust Suit* or *The Broken Lease*.

Criminal justice is a vast, complex system. Briefly, it is that part of the legal system which, first of all, marks off certain behavior as wrong or "criminal"; second, takes steps to control or prevent that behavior by threats of punishment; and third, if prevention fails, tries to catch and to punish the wrongdoer. Familiar as the system is in some of its aspects, in others it is obscure and much misunderstood.

To begin with, what *is* a crime? Every country—and in the United States, every state—has its own special list. The list is part of an elaborate statute which is usually called the penal code. The code describes conduct that is illegal and therefore criminal; it also sets out punishments. The federal government has its own code, which is fairly specialized: it does not cover ordinary crimes, but only crimes against federal laws, like smuggling or tax fraud. The District of Columbia has its own criminal code, much like that of the states.

Some crimes are in the penal codes of every state: murder, manslaughter, robbery, burglary, rape, arson, and so on. Others are less universal. The Georgia code makes it a crime "to be a peeping Tom" or to invade a person's privacy with acts "of a similar nature."[1] The Georgia code also deals with the sale of obscene literature, shooting guns on Sunday, illegal use of credit cards, necrophilia, sale of Molotov cocktails, and dozens of other offenses.

What is criminal in one society need not be criminal in another. It is a serious offense in the Soviet Union to speculate in foreign currencies. In our country, on the other hand, the same act may be done by currency dealers as part of their quite respectable business. For medieval Mongolians, it was a crime to urinate into water or ashes. Americans would find this tasteless at worst, but hardly a crime. Definitions also vary with time and circumstances. It was once illegal to own gold in this country. This is no longer the case. During the Second World War, wages and prices were frozen and it was a crime to charge more than the "ceiling" price. There are no such restrictions today.

Are there some acts which are crimes universally, that is, which every society defines as criminal? Yes and no. It would be hard to think of a society that did not forbid murder, the wrongful killing of another human being. But each society has its own definition of murder. Not every intentional killing is murder. A soldier can lawfully kill during wartime; citizens are allowed to kill in self-defense. Infanticide is murder, but abortion is not. (Many people think it should be.) In some societies, it is not murder to kill for revenge or to get rid of someone who has brought dishonor on the family. There are societies in which it is not a crime to kill baby girls or to dispose of old people who have outlived their usefulness.

Many crimes listed in the penal code are acts which shock the conscience. Murder is a prime example. But different societies have different consciences, as the last paragraph shows. And not every listing in the penal code carries the same moral freight. The codes are motley collections. There are many regulatory or economic offenses which are unknown to most people; and most of us will never run up against them because they affect small groups or particular occupations, like druggists or taxi drivers or used-car salesmen. Other acts (shooting deer out of season, picking rare orchids, overtime parking) are well known, but do not shock the conscience as, say, murder does. These are crimes only because the state so defines them; murder would be (in a sense) a crime even if the laws against it ceased to exist. It is a crime, in other words, in people's minds and hearts.

The great, classic crimes are part of the social code, whatever their status in the legal code. The layman *knows* them as crimes. He has a rough working knowledge of what constitutes murder, even though he does not understand the law's technicalities and distinctions. Cold-blooded killing is murder, we know, although few of us can tell the difference between first-degree and second-degree murder, or what "malice" means, or what level of insanity excuses an act of killing.

Punishment, too, is variable. It depends mostly on how serious the crime. Seriousness is not inherent in the criminal conduct; it is a social judgment. Legally speaking, serious crimes are called felonies; less serious crimes are called misdemeanors. The exact line between them is a matter of legal definition. In California, a felony is a crime which can be punished by death or by a year or more in prison; all others are misdemeanors, except for some petty acts (traffic violations, breaches of ordinances) which are called offenses. Offenses carry less of a punishment than crimes and have less of a stigma. A history of parking tickets is not a criminal record.

Functions of Criminal Justice

Why do we have criminal justice? What functions does it serve? The short and obvious answer is that this is the system that guarantees law and order. Criminal justice substitutes for private violence and vengeance; instead of "taking the law into their own hands," communities turn to specialized people and agencies who do the job for them.

Every society has deviant behavior; every society has people who behave in ways which society (or its leaders) cannot tolerate. In simple societies, there are no specialists or specialized agencies (like the police) to enforce social norms. The anthropologist E. A. Hoebel has described the system of handling deviance among the Eskimos. They have no police, no judges, no obvious courts. But when someone steps out of line, some member of the community, more or less self-appointed, may punish on behalf of the community—perhaps even killing the "criminal."[2]

Clearly, this system would not work in a complex society like ours. Crminal justice takes the handling of most violence away from private citizens and concentrates it in the hands of the government. This serves to protect the great mass of people against the bad and the strong. It also makes revenge, blood feuds, and lynching illegal. It is also an obvious opening for oppression and tyranny, for the so-called police state: if the state has a monopoly of violence it may misuse or overuse it. History, alas, is full of examples.

Outlawing private violence is not an either-or affair; it is the product of a long evolution—a process—and it is even now not complete, if indeed it ought to be. There are those who defend a certain amount of private vengeance, as the popularity of Charles Bronson's movie *Death Wish* shows. But private citizens and laymen play less and less of a role in criminal justice; the task is more and more in official, professional hands.

The most obvious function of criminal justice, then, is control of dangerous behavior—dangerous, of course, as the particular society sees it. Another function is to set out and enforce a moral code. Prostitution is a crime—but why? It is not physically dangerous in the sense that murder is; unlike burglary, it does not threaten the property system or take away people's hard-earned goods and money; it does not violate the sanctity of the home. Indeed, some people think prostitution should be stricken from the roster of crimes, because it is not dangerous to life, health, or property. Yet other people—probably the majority—want to keep it on the books as a crime. Prostitution, they insist, is morally offensive; and one business of criminal justice is to announce and enforce rules of morality. The penal code is full of crimes whose main point is moral: they offend the moral interests or tastes of some fraction of the public.

Criminal justice is also concerned with order and discipline. It is not dangerous or immoral to park overtime on a busy street or to go through a red light when no traffic is coming. It is neither dangerous nor immoral to hunt deer out of season or to catch a fish that is too big or too small. The word *order* implies a kind of rationing system. There are not enough deer or fish to go around. There are not enough parking spaces for everybody. We need rules to prevent overuse.

Rules of order are common in our society. For example, there are rules against talking in public libraries. Talking is a harmless activity; if there were only one or two people in the library, probably no one would care if the users had a nice conversation. But to keep order we have to restrict this harmless activity—in other words, ration it or forbid it altogether. The legal system provides this kind of order; and the criminal justice system enforces it. Breaches of order are punished, not so drastically as more serious crimes—hanging and long jail terms would be out of place—but punished nonetheless.

The word *discipline* applies to a special kind of order. We "discipline" behavior when it violates rules of order that have some flavor or nuance of immorality or danger. Rules against public drunkenness are a good example; for many years this was the commonest "crime" of all—the one most frequently punished.[3] Another crime against discipline is disturbing the peace. The line between dangerous behavior and undisciplined behavior is of course very fuzzy; and disturbances of the peace can range from drunken singing on the sidewalk to something close to a riot.

Perhaps all these functions can be summed up in a single formula, and fitted into one huge macrofunction. They are all concerned with keeping society on an even keel, protecting its structure, and safeguarding its boundaries. Stealing is a crime; and if it is punished, a special service is rendered to people who have property worth stealing. Criminal justice protects the property system and the value system; it is the watchdog of the house, guarding the furniture, the pictures on the wall, and the peace and contentment of the residents.

Criminal justice, then, is vital to any social system. It is essential to welfare capitalism; but it it is also a pillar of socialism in Hungary or Cuba, of the police state in Chile, of apartheid in South Africa, of Moslem fundamentalism in Iran and Saudi Arabia. Whatever the system, criminal justice supports it. That does not mean that criminal justice (or law) is by nature conservative, that is, inherently an enemy of change. In fact, patterns of power and wealth change constantly in the United States, through tax laws, for example, or through other forms of legislation. Many of these changes are slight, but they are changes nonetheless. The legal system is not against all change; rather, it tries to control the process. It stamps some methods of altering structure and rules as fair and legitimate—for example, those that come about through acts of Congress or court decisions. It outlaws all others—riots and revolutions, or robbing banks. Criminal justice is the strong arm of the law, its main weapon against these outlaw methods.

In our modern welfare state, criminal justice has a special role in enforcing rules about the economy. Many "economic crimes" are best looked on not as dangerous or repulsive acts, but as activity subject to rules of rationing or of order. Thus, in Rhode Island, it is an offense to catch lobsters without a license or to take a lobster less than three and three-sixteenths inches long, "measured from the rear of the eye socket along a line parallel to the center line of the body shell."[4] There are countless other examples, in state and federal laws. But why make these technical regulations part of the criminal process? One reason is that criminal justice is *public* justice; it requires *public* litigation. The plaintiff is "the people" or "the commonwealth" or "the state";

the state sets the process in motion and the state pays the bills.

This makes criminal justice useful in situations where private citizens do not have financial stakes high enough to encourage private enforcement. If a butcher runs a crooked scale and cheats every customer a nickel or two per pound of meat, no customer would sue—even in small-claims court—for what he loses on three pounds of hamburger, or a two-pound steak. But if using crooked scales is made a crime, the state can prosecute and control this offense, for everybody's benefit.

Types of Crime

There are a number of conventional ways to classify crimes. One is to ask what interests have been injured by the crime. Thus we speak of crimes against the person and crimes against property. Crimes against the person contain an element of force, of physical contact: murder, manslaughter, rape, kidnapping, robbery, assault. Crimes against property include the various forms of stealing (burglary, theft, shoplifting, embezzlement), and frauds, extortion, forgery, receiving stolen property, and arson—a serious, dangerous crime, which seems to be increasing greatly in our cities. There are also crimes against public order, or against the administration of justice. These include disorderly conduct, prison escape, rioting, resisting arrest, and perjury.

We also speak of crimes against morality. Examples are gambling, drunkenness, prostitution, and drug abuse. In many states, the law also forbids various kinds of "unnatural" or immoral sexual behavior: incest, sodomy, and so-called statutory rape. We can also speak of "regulatory" crimes: violations of weights and measures law, adulterating food, criminal monopoly, and so on. Regulatory law is a rapidly growing area. It is a product of the administrative state, of a sense of social interdependence, and of a desire to protect public health and safety. There is a newfound interest in conservation, too—in the beauty of the country and in the preservation of the national heritage; hence laws against littering, against killing bald eagles, against tearing down historic houses. There are also regulations of billboards and other forms of outdoor advertising. Each state has its own special interests to protect. Florida, for example, with its tropical coastline, has a total ban on the taking of sea turtles' eggs; and an elaborate statute protects the manatee, a lovable but endangered creature which is the official "state marine mammal."[5]

Among serious crimes (felonies), property crimes clearly predom-

inate; they account for more arrests than all other categories. Police
in San Jose, California, made 6,034 felony arrests in 1981. Of these,
1,046 were for burglary, while larceny, forgery, fraud, and receiving
stolen property accounted for more than a thousand more. There were
1,644 drug arrests (359 of these associated with marijuana). There
were about 1,100 arrests for crimes against the person: 46 of these
were for murder and manslaughter and 128 for rape; the crimes of
robbery (416) and aggravated assault (553) were much more significant. There were 158 drunk-driving arrests, 373 "weapons violations," and 157 arrests for parole and probation violations. Sex and
morality crimes made a poor showing, on the whole, except for drug
offenses. There were 57 arrests for "sex perversion," one for "unlawful intercourse" (statutory rape), 26 for "lewd and lascivious conduct,"
and 4 for bookmaking.

Arrests, of course, do not tell us how many crimes were reported
to the police or how many were actually committed. We can learn
some of this from "victim" studies, which ask people if they have ever
been victims of crime, whether or not they reported the crime to
authorities. In 1977, Californians claimed they reported only 57 percent of the rapes suffered, 38.6 percent of the assaults, 50.9 percent
of the burglaries, and 20.8 percent of the household larcenies.[6]

Arrests also vary because of policy decisions. The police arrest any
murderer or burglar they get their hands on, but not every speeder,
gambler, or public drunk. Arrests for crimes against morality or public order may rise and fall more dramatically than arrests for murder
or burglary. Gambling is always with us, but San Jose, California,
arrested only six gamblers in 1981. In many cities, the police normally ignore, or wink at, gambling, prostitution, pot smoking, and
certain other offenses. Then suddenly some scandal rocks the town
and makes big headlines; a crackdown follows because of the public
outcry; and the arrest rate for the crime zooms—for a time.

Crimes against morality or public order make more of a splash in
arrest records, if we look at arrests for petty offenses (misdemeanors).
In San Jose in 1981, for example, there were 22,862 misdemeanor
arrests. They included 5,952 arrests for being "drunk in public," 280
for prostitution, 655 for liquor law violations, 183 for indecent exposure, 389 for "lewd conduct," 183 for vagrancy, and 160 for disturbing
the peace.

Almost all of us accept without question the idea of punishing
crimes against the person; and there is not much controversy about
burglary or theft. Crimes against morality are another story. These

are much more sensitive to ebbs and flows of public opinion—to shifts in the moral climate. This is why arrest rates zig and zag so radically, especially for laws against "victimless crimes." Many people argue it is wrong to punish acts simply because they are "immoral." Morality is "not the law's business," as the title of a book by Gilbert Geis puts it (1972). There is a movement to wipe most of these laws off the books—to decriminalize adultery, fornication, and "unnatural" sex, at least between consenting adults. Some would legalize gambling, prostitution, or the use of drugs like marijuana or cocaine. Many people resist this movement, of course, and oppose decriminalization.

We sometimes hear people talk about the "Puritan heritage" of the country. This heritage gets blamed for what some people feel is an unhealthy tendency to meddle in private lives and punish people if they choose styles of life outside the mainstream. In fact, the history of victimless crime law is not a simple line of descent from the colonial past. It is rather a story with surprising twists and turns.

The Puritan colonies, in the seventeenth century, were in fact very much concerned about crimes against morality. No crime in Massachusetts Bay was punished more frequently than fornication. Thus we read, for example, that in Salem, Massachusetts, in 1655 the court ordered Cornelius Hulett to be "whipped ten stripes on some lecture day in seasonable weather, for fornication with Elizabeth Due."[7] These were small, gossipy communities; the clergy had leadership roles; and in general law made little or no distinction between sin and crime. Hulett was only one of hundreds who were whipped, fined, put in the stocks, or forced to marry, because of the "crime" of fornication.

If we leap forward to the nineteenth century, we get a different picture. Laws against fornication and adultery were still on the books. But there seemed to be little appetite for enforcement. In some states, the crimes were redefined: in Indiana, for example, adultery was against the law only if it was "open and notorious." In other words, adultery could not be punished unless the adulterers flaunted themselves before the public. The law was much less concerned with secret sin. Vice was tolerated if it kept in its place. In every large American city there were red-light districts. Prostitution was illegal in these cities; but it was "tacitly tolerated" and "relatively undisturbed" so long as it stayed put in the districts. Despite sporadic outbursts or morality and occasional riots, brothels were "almost as much a part of social life as the cocktail lounge is today."[8]

The situation changed rather dramatically, beginning in the late nineteenth century. There was a new birth of interest in outlawing and punishing victimless crime. In 1873, Congress passed the so-called Comstock Law, which made it a federal crime to mail any "obscene, lewd, or lascivious" book, or "any article or thing . . . for the prevention of conception." In 1895, Congress prohibited the interstate sale of lottery tickets. In 1907, Arkansas passed a law making it a crime to manufacture, sell, or give away "any cigarettes or cigarette wrappers or papers to any person."[9]

There was more to come. The famous Mann Act[10] made it a federal offense to transport any woman across state lines "for the purpose of prostitution or debauchery, or for any other immoral purpose." Under the Harrison Act,[11] it was illegal to buy or sell narcotics, except with a doctor's prescription. For the first time, practically speaking, the law made outlaws out of drug addicts. The climax of the purity movement came just after the First World War: the Eighteenth Amendment to the Constitution (1919) launched the "noble experiment" of Prohibition. This was the end point of a long struggle for temperance. Congress sent the amendment to the states in November 1917; Nebraska, the thirty-seventh state, ratified it in January 1919, and put it over the top. National Prohibition actually began in January 1920. The Eighteenth Amendment and the supporting laws slapped a total ban on the "manufacture, sale, or transportation of intoxicating liquors" in the United States. Congress also passed a law (the Volstead Act, 1919) to enforce prohibition.[12]

It is one thing, of course, to pass a law and quite another to enforce it. The troubles of Prohibition are legendary, and most historians consider it a dismal failure. It certainly did not get rid of alcohol, although there is a good deal of dispute about its actual impact. It clearly fostered corruption and scandal. After a decade or so of misery, the country got rid of it, in the Twenty-first Amendment (1933). Another failure (in the long run) was the red-light abatement movement, which flourished around the time of the First World War. This was a campaign by reformers and moralists to get rid of vice and prostitution once and for all. Tough new laws were passed, and armies of the righteous closed down the Barbary Coast in San Francisco, Storyville in New Orleans, and other notorious vice districts, at least temporarily. (Sin had a way of popping back, in the end.)

The movement had just about run its course by the 1930s; a reaction set in. In recent years, the pendulum has swung in the opposite direction. Many states have taken the criminal label off fornication and adultery. A few states have all but given up the fight against marijuana. The gay rights movement has also made some progress. Some states have stopped punishing homosexual acts among consenting adults. The struggle for legitimation continues; but opposition is also strong and highly motivated.

It is far from obvious what lies behind these movements and countermovements. They begin in the dark and mysterious world of social attitude. If we knew what brought on the "sexual revolution," we would understand more about the legal reaction, too. One thing is plain: we cannot blame history or the Puritan heritage for our backwardness (if that is what it is). Nor can we blame the law for the current conflicts, the public disputes and debates. Many people feel that the looser laws on personal behavior are extremely dangerous to society—that they weaken family life, endanger public morality, and threaten the very health of society. This may or may not be true. But again, even if it is true, it is a mistake to blame the laws. The legal system plays a part, but only a derivative one. The laws are symptoms; they are not the disease. Law responds to social movements, to forces that come and go, to deep rhythms and great powers that lie outside of the system itself.

The Criminal Process

So far we have talked mostly about laws on the statute books. Let us turn now to the criminal process, and take a look at the life cycle of a typical felony case, in California.[13] We begin, of course, with the crime itself—a burglary, let us say. Somebody breaks into a house in Atherton, California, and steals jewelry, silver, and hi-fi equipment. The people who live in the house come home and find to their horror that somebody has broken in. They call the police.

All too often, alas, this is nearly the end of the story. Most break-ins are never solved; no arrests are made; the goods are never recovered. There is data for New York City on this point. In 1971, victims reported 501,951 felonies to the police; in four cases out of five, nothing more happened. The police made 100,739 felony arrests. Some of the people arrested were charged with more than one reported felony. Still, the police were able to "clear" by arrest only 111,824 of these half million felonies.[14]

Our householders, let us assume, are among the lucky few. The police take notes, go off, and—lo and behold—in due course they find a suspect and arrest him. The police now "book" the suspect—that is, they record the charges, photograph the man, and take his fingerprints. He goes before a magistrate, who tells him about his rights. This judge may also set bail; and he may arrange for a "public defender," who will act as the suspect's lawyer. Sometimes the suspect will hire his own lawyer, if he has the money to do so.

The district attorney's office will make the next move. The staff will have to decide whether the case is strong enough to act on. Is there enough evidence to make prosecution worthwhile? If not, the case must be dropped. Let us suppose the DA thinks he can get a conviction. Before the man can be brought to trial, there is one more major hurdle. This is the "preliminary examination."

The preliminary examination is a kind of pretrial trial. It starts when the prosecutor files an "information," that is, formal charges. These proceedings, too, take place before a "magistrate," usually a municipal or police court judge. There is no jury. The magistrate hears what the prosecution has to say. He does not decide whether the accused is actually guilty. He has three choices: if he feels the prosecution has no case, he can dismiss the charges and let the accused go free; he can knock the case down to a misdemeanor; or he can decide that the state does have enough of a case, so that it pays to go on to a full-scale trial. To do this, the case must be transferred to another court, a court for felonies. In California this is called Superior Court.

In many states, this "information" method is not used. Screening is done by a grand jury. The grand jury is made up of laymen who are picked at random, like the members of an ordinary jury. The number of jurors varies. Texas law calls for not less than fifteen or more than twenty.[15] Grand jurors serve for a limited time. The prosecutor shows his stuff to the grand jury and asks for an "indictment" against the accused. The grand jury decides whether to indict or not to indict. If it indicts, the case will go forward for felony trial. This alternative method is also on the books in California; but the "information" method is much more common and is much preferred.

The prisoner's case will be finally decided in Superior Court. The judge may, of course, dismiss the matter here, too, either on his own account or because the prosecution decides not to press charges. The defendant can plead guilty and end the matter that way. His lawyer can file any one of a number of "motions" on points of law. He can, for instance, file a motion to suppress certain evidence, on the grounds that the state gathered it illegally. This motion usually fails; under the Victim's Bill of Rights in California, passed in 1982, the failure rate should be even greater than before.

Most felony cases do not get this far. Only a small minority actually go to trial. The rest fall by the wayside. Yet trials are the most dramatic and familiar way of deciding on innocence or guilt. Not all trials go on before a jury. The defendant can waive his right to a jury. The judge will then handle the case by himself. This is called bench trial. If the defendant does not choose this route, the court proceeds to pick a jury.

A jury usually consists of twelve men and women chosen from the community. They are supposed to be totally impartial. Lawyers on either side will question prospective jurors; and the lawyer can "challenge"—that is, demand dismissal of—any who seem unsuitable for one reason or another. A certain number, too, can be "peremptorily" challenged, that is, for no legal reason at all. Defendant's lawyer may have a hunch that this sour-faced, mean-looking man would be deadly for his client; he can get the man excused by peremptory challenge. In Minnesota, for example, a defendant charged with an offense "punishable by life imprisonment" is entitled to fifteen of these challenges; the state can have nine. In all other cases, defendant can have five, the state three.[16]

When the jury is chosen, the trial begins. Both sides present their cases, usually through lawyers. They cross-examine each other's witnesses. The judge sees to it that the trial runs smoothly and correctly. He makes rulings on points of law and decides any questions that come up on points of evidence. A policeman may want to testify, for example, about something he heard a witness say. If the defendant objects, claiming that this testimony is "hearsay," the judge will decide which side is right.

At the end of the case, the judge "instructs" the jury. That is, he recites the legal rules that are supposed to guide the jury in reaching a decision. Unfortunately, such instructions usually do not instruct very well. In past times—in the early nineteenth century, for example—judges gave the jury genuine explanations of the relevant law. Today, judges simply shovel out to the jury a mess of canned, stereotyped formulas, written in dense legalese. Legally speaking, these instructions are quite accurate; whether the jurors can possibly fathom them is doubtful. Curiously enough, in many states the judge will refuse to explain them any better even if the jury begs and pleads.[17]

In any event, the case now goes to the jury; and for the first time the jurors are truly in the driver's seat. They retire from the courtroom and deliberate in private. Generally speaking, a jury verdict has to be unanimous. Sometimes a jury "hangs"—that is, the members fail to agree. When this happens, the prosecution will either start over again with a new trial or give up completely. In Kalven's and Zeisel's major study of jury behavior, it was found that juries, overall, hang about 5 percent of the time. They acquit roughly a third of the defendants and convict the rest.[18]

How the jury goes about deciding is mostly a secret. Some jurors have been willing to talk about what happened in the jury room; and social scientists have studied the process with various techniques, including the use of experimental juries that are given hypothetical cases to decide. There are obvious drawbacks to research that uses make-believe cases. But they do have one powerful advantage: researchers can manipulate variables one at a time, for scientific purposes. This cannot be done with the messy materials of real life.

Some of the research findings are of uncommon interest. They shed light, for example, on the hung jury. If only one juror holds out for conviction or acquittal, the jury does not end up hung. The sole dissenter—the "minority of one"—has a "lonely and unattractive" role. The other eleven are almost sure to convert him to their side. Support from even one other juror makes a big difference to the hold-out.[19]

Legally, the power of the jury is clear. If it finds the defendant not guilty, the defendant goes free. The jury decision is final. No matter how wrong or how foolish it seems, there is no appeal. If the jury convicts, the judge sets a date for sentencing. A convicted defendant can also try to appeal on the grounds of error at the trial. Generally speaking, "error" means legal error; it is not enough to say the jury was wrong or failed to do justice. An appeal court does not try the case over or redecide issues of fact.

The more serious the case, the more likely that the defendant will appeal. Practically everybody sentenced to death will appeal; in some states, these appeals are automatic. But overall only a small minority of losing defendants go on to a higher court. The rest give up and take their medicine.

Plea Bargaining and
the Guilty Plea

It is a striking fact that trials, as described above and as the public knows them, are not the usual way a defendant's fate is decided. Most men and women behind bars did not get there because a jury put them there. They got there because they pleaded guilty. In some parts of the country, up to 90 percent of all convictions come about this way.

How does this happen? Why do defendants plead guilty? Sometimes they plead guilty out of shame, hopelessness, or remorse. But in the overwhelming majority of cases, the guilty plea is part of a "deal"—part of the practice called "plea bargaining" or "copping a plea." The prosecutor agrees to press for a lighter sentence, or to drop some charges, or to give defendant a break in some other way: this is in exchange for a guilty plea, which avoids trial by jury. Plea bargaining has pushed the jury trial into a small corner of the criminal process. The big cases—the headline cases—still go before a jury: the trial of Patricia Hearst or of John Hinckley, who tried to kill President Reagan. Ordinary cases, like the case of our house burglar, are unlikely to go to a jury. And the jury's role has been steadily shrinking over the years.

Plea bargaining is controversial. Some people defend it. Most people arrested, they say, are guilty anyway. Why bother with a trial? Why waste public money? Plea bargaining is a compromise: both sides give a little, get a little. Trials take time; there is always the chance of some slipup. It is best (for both sides) to avoid it.

On the other hand, a growing number of people feel that plea bargaining is a disgrace. "Law and order" people think it shows too much softness toward defendants. Dangerous criminals "cop a plea" and slip through the nets. Others claim that the process is unfair to the innocent. One study claimed that up to one-third of the people who plead guilty would be acquitted if they went to trial.[20]

This is a startling conclusion. But it does not mean that these people were in fact innocent of the crime—only that they had a legal excuse or that the evidence was weak. In any event, plea bargaining (so the argument goes) makes a mockery of criminal process. It certainly does not fit our image of due process or our picture of the adversary system. In general, as Herbert Jacob has put it, in the criminal justice system today "the most important decisions are made in private—either in the prosecutor's office or in the judge's chambers."[21] Justice consists in the main of deals by lawyers in the back rooms or the courthouse corridors.

It is no surprise, then, that demands for reform come from all sides. Some prosecutors have tried to end plea bargaining. In Wayne County, Michigan, the prosecutor ordered his staff not to bargain in any case where defendant used a gun. The attorney general of Alaska, in 1975, banned the practice of plea bargaining entirely. The voters of California, in a 1982 initiative ("Proposition Eight"), adopted a "victim's bill of rights" which, among other things, restricted plea bargaining. It has also been proposed that plea bargaining should come out of the closet; that it should take place more openly, with the judge participating all along.[22] We can expect more reforms and reform proposals in the future.

But do reforms actually work? Milton Heumann and Colin Loftin studied the Wayne County experiment. Did it really curb plea bargaining in Detroit? Their answer was, "Sort of." Plea bargaining in the literal sense was cut back. But "other mechanisms came into play" which were, they felt, "functional equivalents" of plea bargaining. Through a "mix" of techniques, the system "managed to digest" the new policies without really changing its ways.[23]

Why did this happen? Then again, why do we have plea bargaining in the first place? To many people the answer is simple. They assume that plea bargaining is a recent innovation and that it is a response to crowded conditions in urban courts. They connect plea bargaining with a deterioration in criminal justice over the last twenty years or so. Actually, plea bargaining is not as recent as most people think it is; and it is not found only in crowded urban courts.

In fact, there was never a golden age of full, fair trials. True, in 1800 or 1850 most defendants charged with serious crime did go before a jury. But trials were short, routine, cut-and-dried. Historical research on this point is skimpy, but consistent. John Langbein found these slapdash trials in eighteenth-century England; another study confirmed this with a bit of research in the late nineteenth-century records of Leon County, Florida (Tallahassee is the county seat). The average trial there took about half an hour. Case after case paraded before the jury. Few defendants had lawyers. Justice was careless and swift.[24]

In other words, hasty, routine processing did not begin with plea bargaining at all. Plea bargaining changes the style and the place. Quick, rough justice has moved from the jury box to the corridors of the courthouse, to judges' chambers, to the offices of lawyers.

Plea bargaining itself goes back a century or more. One study found it, for example, in Alameda County, California, in the 1880s.[25] Judges in the county even talked about the way they gave "credit" for guilty pleas. Plea bargaining was not as pervasive as it is now—not even close to it—but it was by no means rare.

There is plea bargaining in England, too, apparently; but in other systems of law, on the continent of Europe, there is nothing exactly like it. Plea bargaining depends on a central feature of our system: the guilty plea. In some legal systems, there is no such plea. Of course, a defendant can confess his crimes, and a confession is powerful evidence of guilt; but, at least in theory, the state must still prove its case. Our system is different. The guilty plea is accepted as truth; except in very rare cases, it puts an end to the proceedings. Once a defendant pleads guilty, the trial is over. There is nothing left but sentencing.

The guilty plea, too, goes back many years. In 1839, in New York state, one out of every four criminal cases ended with a guilty plea. By the middle of the century, there were guilty pleas in half the cases. In Alameda County, one out of three felony defendants pleaded guilty as charged in the decade 1900–1910. In the 1920s, guilty pleas accounted for 88 out of 100 convictions in New York City, 85 out of 100 in Chicago, 70 out of 100 in Dallas, and 79 out of 100 in Des Moines, Iowa.[26] It has kept its dominance ever since. In short, we can trace a steady, marked decline in trial by jury from the early nineteenth century on.

The Professionalization of
Criminal Justice

Why is trial by jury declining? This is, in part, only one aspect of a larger, long-term trend—the professionalization of criminal justice. If we could go back in time two centuries and watch criminal justice at work, we would be struck by how much laymen—amateurs—dominated it. There were no public prosecutors in England. If somebody robbed a storekeeper, the storekeeper himself had to prosecute. There was nothing like the modern district attorney. If the storekeeper did nothing, the case simply vanished. There were also no defense attorneys; and the jury, of course, was a panel of amateurs.

In the United States, unlike England, there was a public prosecutor, the district attorney, from colonial times on. But even this was usually a part-time job; and private prosecution was quite common well into the nineteenth century. Police science as we know it did not exist in colonial times and in the early republic. Indeed, neither did the police. The first police force, in the modern sense, was established in London, England, in 1829. New York City had a police force by 1845. Even so, the New York patrolman was "essentially an amateur, . . . little more than an ordinary citizen delegated with legal power."[27] It was not until the twentieth century that police forces became truly professional, that is, specially trained for their work.[28]

Today the system is full of professionals: public defenders, probation officers, social workers, detectives. Criminal justice makes use of "science" in the most literal sense: ballistics authorities, pathologists working for the coroner's office, fingerprint experts. In short, the center of gravity has moved dramatically away from a system controlled by laymen to a system controlled and dominated by experts of various sorts. The decline of the jury (and the grand jury, too) is part of this general development. Plea bargaining, then, is merely the modern, professional version of routine processing. It is the same process, in essence, as the slapdash trials of Leon County, Florida, in the nineteenth century, but under new and professional management.

Punishments and Corrections

Conviction by judge or jury is not, of course, the end of the line. The defendant now faces his sentence. In many ways, this phase of the process is more important to the defendant than what went before. Most defendants, after all, plead guilty. Their only question is, What will the punishment be?

Generally speaking, the law vests great power and discretion in the judge. He has many options and much leeway. Some defendants will pay a fine and some will get "probation," a kind of conditional freedom: this will be especially true of first offenders. Only a minority will actually go to prison or jail. In the New York City study, covering 1971, half of those who pleaded guilty and one-third of those convicted at trial "walked out of court without being sentenced to jail or prison."[29]

We are used to thinking of prison or jail as the basic punishment for serious crime. Yet before the nineteenth century, imprisonment was rarely used for punishing criminals. Jails were for people who could not pay their debts, or for people waiting for trial and not out on bail for one reason or another. In colonial Massachusetts, criminals were whipped, fined, put in the stocks, branded with a hot iron, and in especially serious cases banished or hung. This was true in England, too. The mother country made heavier use of the gallows, and also "transported" convicts to the colonies, notably Australia.

The modern prison or penitentiary was a nineteenth-century invention (if *invention* is the right word). The United States was among its social pioneers. An early example was the "penitentiary house" at

Walnut Street prison in Philadelphia, with sixteen little cells for soli-
tary confinement. The classic penitentiaries of this period, the first
third of the nineteenth century, were Cherry Hill in Philadelphia and
Auburn and Sing Sing in New York state. These were huge, forbid-
ding structures with thick outer walls and strong cells with iron bars.

In these dour prisons, convicts lived one to a cell. They lived in a
world of total silence and isolation, broken only by hard labor. During
the entire term in prison—and this could be years—not a word was
supposed to be spoken. Life in this quiet tomb was completely regi-
mented; each day was exactly like the next, every prisoner getting up
at the same time as all others, going to bed at the same time, wearing
the same uniform, eating the same food. It was in theory a kind of
radical surgery, meant to separate the prisoner totally from the corruption and rot of society. The iron discipline of prison would give
the prisoner a chance to repent and to learn new habits of life.[30]

In its classical form, the penitentiary system did not last very long.
The "Big House" remained, architecturally speaking; we recognize it
clearly in dozens of Hollywood prison movies and from such living
museums as San Quentin. By the time of the Civil War, there were
clear signs that the "silent" system would have to be abandoned. For
one thing, it would not work unless prisoners were housed one to a
cell. But this was expensive; and the legislatures were far too stingy.

When the silent system disappeared, so did the theory that isolation and regimentation at hard labor would cure criminals of their
habits. The late nineteenth century turned to new schemes of reform:
parole, probation, the indeterminate sentence. These were geared
toward dividing convicts into two classes—the hopeless incorrigibles
and those who could be saved—and sifting out the savable ones. New
York began to experiment with the indeterminate sentence in the
1870s. In its developed form, it rested on a simple idea: the judge
would no longer fix the defendant's sentence. Rather, he would prescribe some minimum (one year, as a rule). In prison, the convict
would be carefully observed—graded and marked like a schoolchild,
in a way. If he behaved and showed the right character, he would
earn a light sentence and early release. If not, he would rot in prison.
Some people, so the theory went, should never be released. That
would be as senseless as letting loose "people suffering from lep-
rosy."[31]

The indeterminate sentence spread rapidly. Along with it went
the parole system—a program to let promising convicts out early,
under supervision. Probation was another reform. It gave convicted

criminals (especially first offenders) a chance to escape prison altogether. Probation, too, was (at least in theory) a kind of supervised freedom at the end of a rather taut string: a wrong move, and the criminal justice system would jerk its end of the string and the probationer would land back in jail. Still another innovation was a special court for young people, called the juvenile court. The first true court of this kind was established for Cook County, Illinois, in 1899. By 1945, every state had juvenile courts.

These reforms had one trait in common: they were relatively professionalized. They also vested great discretion in parole boards or juvenile judges or probation officers. These reforms also shifted emphasis from the offense to the offender. Decisions were highly subjective, and varied from case to case, from defendant to defendant. Probation officers, for example, were not bound by narrow, legal rules of evidence. They were allowed to investigate the entire background and character of the defendants. Early probation reports in California show graphically the kind of evidence the probation officer gathered. We read in one instance that a sixteen-year-old boy, in 1907, smoked about ten cigarettes a day, masturbated, had been to a house of prostitution three times, and read magazines, but had no library card.[32] This information was all legally irrelevant, but it could mean the difference between freedom and iron bars.

Still, probation *was* a reform—a step toward leniency. In operation, it might be unfair and arbitrary. But it kept some people out of prison and saved their lives or their souls. Partly because it was so subjective, so discretionary, a reaction has set in in recent years. Decisions of parole boards, too, have been criticized as far too random, too personal, for a system of justice and due process.

Even more important has been the reaction from the law-and-order side. The rampaging crime rate frightens and outrages people, as it should; fear of crime focuses attention on any part of the system that can be accused (however unfairly) of "coddling criminals." The indeterminate sentence rested on a kind of faith in rehabilitation. At least *some* prisoners would benefit from prison: prison experience would reform them. Rightly or wrongly, hardly anybody believes this any more.

The demand now is for harsher measures. This means long, flat sentences. California, among other states, has gotten rid of the indeterminate sentence. Parole, too, is under attack: Maine has abolished its parole board, and so has Illinois. Some states have tried mandatory sentences for certain crimes, insisting that all criminals who use guns, for example, must go to jail. Like programs to abolish plea bargaining, these changes in law never quite work out as advertised or hoped. It is still too early to tell how determinate sentencing will work, in states such as California. It is doubtful, though, that it will affect the crime rate—even by a hair.

Class, Race, Power, and Criminal Justice

The criminal justice system is where law most openly shows its teeth. Here is the policeman's club, the iron bars of San Quentin, the gas chamber; here is the jailhouse and the riot squad. The army of civil authority is the police. The police have tear gas and guns. They are the enemies of crime; but they can also turn their force against dissent or against the weak and powerless. History, alas, makes it clear that society can and does use power for evil ends. The police state is all too real, in every part of the world.

What about the United States? Does criminal justice treat people fairly? Does it fall more heavily on the poor and the powerless? On black people and other minorities? On women, as compared to men? Many studies have tried to answer these questions scientifically. As noted in Chapter 4, the results are surprisingly inconclusive, especially on the matter of race. There may well be biases in the system, but they are fairly subtle and covert today. The days of lynch mobs are, happily, over. Still, nobody should be surprised to find race prejudice in criminal justice. If it is present in society as a whole, why would criminal justice alone be free of this curse? On the surface, the argument for bias is quite strong. In 1979, blacks were 10.1 percent of the adult male population; but 48 percent of the inmates of state prisons were black.

Why should this be so? Is it because blacks are weaker than whites in economic and political power? As Austin Turk has pointed out, "powerlessness" does not explain very much. Women have less power in this society than men, yet women make a very feeble showing at crime.[33] Indeed, in 1979, women were only 4 percent of the country's prisoners. These figures do not prove much unless we know how much crime women (and blacks) actually commit.

Still, we are left with a disturbing question. What accounts for the huge disproportion between the experiences of blacks and whites in regard to criminal justice? Can we really rule out bias? A recent study went over more than seventy research projects that had tried to ferret out race prejudice in the sentencing process alone. Some of these studies came to the conclusion that there was race prejudice; some came to the opposite conclusion. Hence at the present time, we have to say that the case is not proven—at least as far as the aggregate performance of the system is concerned. There are surely individual judges, however, who betray bias against race.[34]

Why is the question so hard to answer? One reason may be that bias comes in many forms. There can be bias in the rules themselves. Rules may be tilted in favor of (say) landlords and not tenants, or in favor of the state and not defendants. This bias would affect outcomes even if judges, police, and prosecutors applied the rules fairly. Or the rules might classify as criminal certain patterns of behavior that are more common in some communities than others. Or crime may be more of a temptation among people who are poor, downtrodden, despised, and shut off from legitimate opportunity. If we look only at the way the rules are applied, the system might seem quite fair— more so than it really is.

Another possibility is that bias is subtle and works at an early point in the process. Suppose the manager of a boutique catches a well-dressed white woman in the act of stealing a hat. He may quietly take back the hat and show the woman out with a firm warning, rather politely. Later he finds a black teenager shoplifting. This time he delivers the boy straight to the police. If this happened consistently, throughout the city, arrest figures would suggest that most shoplifters were black. That, of course, would be misleading. Or the police themselves might have a double standard as between rich and poor, black and white, in deciding whether to book a person or let him go. This is not to say that the police in any town actually behave this way, merely that it is possible—that bias in the system may not be easy to see or to measure and that it may relate to factors more elusive than the simple variables of race, sex, and class.

The Rights Revolution

We hear a lot today about the "rights revolution," about tenderness toward criminal defendants, about the way courts "coddle" criminals, about due process of law. How much of this is real and how much is talk? When we ask whether trials are basically fair, we must remember that most people accused of crime never go to trial. Their rights are decided in other ways—often through plea bargaining. For those who do go to trial, there is strong evidence that the law really does show more concern for defendants' rights than it did in past generations.

The basic rights of defendants are, of course, quite old. The Bill of Rights—attached to the federal Constitution nearly 200 years ago—is a kind of mini-code of criminal procedure. It prohibits cruel and unusual punishment, unreasonable searches and seizures, and excessive bail. It guarantees trial by jury and the writ of habeas corpus (a protection against illegal imprisonment). Compared to justice in other countries, and especially in the dictatorships, American criminal justice is a shining example, and always has been.

No country is perfect, or even close to it. There is much to be ashamed of in our national past, as there is in every country. There is, in particular, a sorry record of police brutality and unfair prosecution. There is also a history of lynch law. The vigilantes were not as admirable as some people think. Groups and individuals with unpopular ideas often had to suffer in the past. In general, the system has often cut corners. Sometimes, at least, corner cutting ends up convicting the innocent.

But the past is dead. One has to ask, What are the trends? In what direction is the system heading? The *formal* rights of defendants have expanded enormously, especially since the 1950s, with the Supreme Court under Earl Warren leading the way. In *Miranda* v. *Arizona*,[35] the Supreme Court tried to improve the rights of people arrested by police. The police must inform the suspect of his constitutional rights, including his right to say nothing. If this warning is not given, the court can refuse to allow what the defendant said to be used as evidence. It has become a standard practice for police to give the "Miranda warning" to anyone picked up for a serious crime.

Some people doubt that this has done much good. The police simply mumble a verbal formula. Perhaps; but *Miranda* was only one of a whole series of decisions by the Warren court (and like-minded state courts); the net effect of the cases as a whole may be far greater than the effect of any single decision. Police and prosecutors today seem more sensitive to due process than in the past. In *Gideon* v. *Wainwright*,[36] the Supreme Court took another bold step. When a person is accused of a serious crime (a felony), he or she has a right to a lawyer. If there is no money to hire one, the state must provide, and pay the bill. This case, at least, did have an effect—if not on the system in general, then on thousands of lives and thousands of cases.

The criminal justice system is headline news, and the subject of great controversy. Crime (especially crime in the streets) is a terrible social problem. At the same time, the country is in the middle of the "rights revolution"—an expansion of due process. People who speak for the poor, for black people, and for other racial minorities complain bitterly about the behavior of police, prisons, and the rest of the system. The system, in other words, is under attack from both the right and the left—from those who think it is too soft and those who think it is too hard.

The result of this ferment is a whole package of changes, in opposite directions. One example is bail reform. A person who is arrested and charged with a crime does not always sit in jail until his case comes up; he is often released "on bail"—that is, after he puts up some money as security. He forfeits the bail if he does not show up for trial. The Eighth Amendment forbids "excessive bail"; but even a fairly modest amount of bail looks excessive to somebody poor or unemployed. Bail makes a tremendous difference. People out on bail can prepare their defense better; they can also go about their daily lives. A person in jail is suffering a kind of punishment, even if he is found innocent in the end. He loses freedom, and he might also lose his job. Hence, some reformers have proposed letting people go free before trial, on their word of honor, if they seem like good risks. People with ties to the community are not likely to skip out on the court. Release of this kind, now quite common, owes a great deal to the Manhattan Bail Project of the 1960s, sponsored by the Vera Foundation. Congress passed a Bail Reform Act in 1966 for the federal courts; other communities have their own versions.[37]

There have been other attempts to humanize the system. Changes in the indeterminate sentence and in parole are in part attempts to control arbitrary processes: prisoners resented their dependence on faceless boards or unseen experts. There is also a prisoners' rights movement, which led to the establishment of grievance procedures in prisons and helped curb some of the worst prison excesses. Especially in California and a few other states, prisoners have become politicized and have demanded changes in prison administration. Courts have been sympathetic to some of these demands, and have expanded the scope of due process within prisons.[38] There have also been pressures to toughen the system—to sharpen its teeth. This too has brought some results—changes in plea bargaining and indeterminate sentencing.

But reforms have a depressing tendency to dribble out into nothing. Malcolm Feeley has reviewed the evidence on the impact of bail reform, sentence reform, and "pretrial diversion," that is, the plan to siphon off certain defendants before trial (for example, those with mental problems or alcohol problems), referring them to more appropriate social agencies. He found that planned changes or reforms accomplished very little. Of course, important changes do occur in the criminal justice system, but they are usually "unheralded as by-products of seemingly unsuccessful efforts, or as the consequence of general social change.[39]

In truth, the criminal justice system is hard to deal with, in either direction. This is the message of Feeley's book. He looked at hard-line reforms as well as soft-line reforms. New York, under Governor Nelson Rockefeller, passed a Draconian drug law, meant to put pushers in jail. This law (and others like it) had, on the whole, as little effect as the softhearted laws. There was "little measurable deterrent effect on narcotics use"; the law was "astronomically expensive to administer, and it led to harsh sentences for marginal offenders." In 1979, the law was repealed.[40] Failure has also been the experience, by and large, of perennial attempts to put teeth into laws against drunk driving. Experiments in tougher enforcement sometimes work—as experiments—but the system soon lapses back into its old ways.[41]

We can compare the criminal justice system to a leaky garden hose, full of holes. If you try to turn up the pressure at one end, the extra water squirts out of holes in the middle. In many ways, the criminal justice system is just such a leaky hose.

Is it really a system at all? The word *system* suggests some sort of rational organization, some sort of overall coordination. Criminal justice is a pseudosystem at best. Nobody is really in charge. Everybody can frustrate the work of everybody else. The legislature can pass laws, but cannot enforce them. The police can arrest people, but they have no way to guarantee prosecution. The prosecutor can prosecute, but cannot be sure the court will convict. The judge can sentence people, but cannot keep them in prison. The jury can disregard the judge; the judge can disregard the jury. And so it goes. The system, in short, is "decentralized, fragmented, made up of bits and pieces." It is "like some . . . primitive beast, with primeval power to regenerate; snip off a leg, an arm, an organ here and there . . .—the missing part simply grows back. No brain is in control, no central nervous system."[42] For better or for worse, this seems to describe the system as it is.

10

*Constitutional Law
and Civil Liberties*

NO ONE CAN write about or discuss the American legal system
seriously without taking account of a document which is a few years
short of its 200th birthday: the American Constitution. The Constitution was ratified in 1787, which makes it the oldest written constitution still in force. It is certainly the most legally active. It is not, of
course, exactly the way it was in 1787. The Constitution has been
amended twenty-six times; some of the amendments (the Fourteenth, for example) have been extraordinarily important. But when
we consider how the world has changed since 1787, twenty-six
amendments do not seem like a lot. Twelve of these had been added
to the Constitution by 1804; there have been only fourteen since.

A note of caution: when we talk about the influence or effect of
the Constitution, we must remember that the Constitution is only a
piece of paper by itself. There is no magic in words and phrases. It is
not the American Constitution that is powerful, but the constitutional
system. It is a system made up, first, of public attitudes toward the
Constitution, and secondly, of behavior patterns and institutions that
have grown up around the Constitution. The Constitution itself,
important as it is, well crafted as it is, could not and cannot account
for the constitutional system.

The experience of other countries proves this point. Dozens of
countries have written constitutions; but some of these are bad jokes
played on the public. The constitution of the Soviet Union, for example, has as many glittering, noble phrases as any other. It promises

all sorts of liberties and rights. But it has very little to do with living law or the structure of power in the Soviet state. In this regard, the Soviet constitution has plenty of company. On the other hand, the British have no written constitution, no firm "guarantees" of liberty. Parliament in theory is utterly supreme—more powerful than the Soviet state is, on paper. Yet Britain is a democratic country, and the rule of law is as healthy there as in almost any state.

Whatever the situation in other countries, in this country constitutional government is a strong force to be reckoned with. It is part of the fabric of American life. The American Constitution is living law because it is enforced; the Russian constitution is not. Some of the enforcement comes through the courts, by means of "judicial review." The courts are not the only guardians of the constitutional system, but they are a powerful and important one. Indeed, when people talk about the Constitution as living law, they usually mean doctrines and understandings that courts have invented, developed, and spread.

These doctrines and understandings may be rooted in the text of the Constitution (and in theory they must be). But the Founding Fathers would hardly recognize them. What would Jefferson say if he were told that under the protection of the First Amendment, a magazine can print pictures of naked people making love? What would he make of the argument that the death penalty violates the Eighth Amendment? Or, for that matter, that the commerce clause allows Washington to tell farmers how many peanuts they can grow?

The Constitution, in short, is what the judges say it is, as Chief Justice Charles Evans Hughes once bluntly put it. What they say is said in the context of actual cases. Actual cases arise out of real disputes between real litigants. They are always a product of their times. They reflect the social issues of the day, and thus these issues are the immediate source of constitutional law.

This is a basic fact of our constitutional system. It is important not to stress judges and courts unduly. Constitutional behavior is more than judicial behavior. Constitutional law begins outside the courtroom: it begins with claims of constitutional right. Also, traditions of behavior and understanding exist that are independent of judges and courts. The First Amendment guarantees freedom of speech; so do all the state constitutions. Yet the Supreme Court did not decide an important free speech case until *Schenck* v. *United States.*[1] Schenck was convicted of violating the 1917 Espionage Act during the First World War. Schenck was opposed to the war and mailed a document out to draftees attacking the war and the draft.

By then, the First Amendment was over a century old. Yet the federal courts had said almost nothing about the meaning and limits of freedom of speech. During those years, the federal government took many actions which would be considered gross violations of our rights today. On the other hand, there was never general censorship of the press during peacetime. Wide-open political debate was always possible, on a scale that few countries achieve even today. Freedom of speech, then, was part of our basic tradition. The essential point is this: constitutionalism is more behavior than theory, at any given time.

But one should look at theory, too. The place to begin is with the Constitution itself. Its basic idea is simple. The Constitution is the supreme law of the land. It is the highest authority. No person, and no branch of government—not the president, not Congress, certainly not the corner policeman—has the right to set the Constitution aside; its words and its rules are law. The courts are guardians of the Constitution. They have the right to check unconstitutional actions—to declare them null and void.

This is the famous power of judicial review. In *Marbury* v. *Madison* (1803),[2] the great chief justice, John Marshall, first exercised this mighty power against an act of the United States Congress. The issue was a technical one: did the Supreme Court have the power to issue a certain kind of legal writ, called a mandamus, against the secretary of state? An act of Congress gave them power to issue such a writ; but the Constitution (as Marshall read it) restricted the Supreme Court to appeals, except for a few narrow, specific exceptions. Thus the act of Congress conflicted with the Constitution, and Marshall boldly set it aside. During the period of the Marshall court, the power of judicial review and its exercise evoked enormous controversy. But the case— and the principle—held firm.

Judicial review is, of course, not just a federal power. State high courts exercise it, too, with regard to their legislatures, not to mention city hall and the various state agencies. The power is now so deeply ingrained in our system that it is hard to imagine our legal world without it.

Nonetheless, it is still subject to debate. For one thing, judicial review is countermajoritarian. Nobody elects the Supreme Court. The voters elect congressmen, senators, presidents to govern them. Why should the Court overturn what the public decides, through its representatives? True, the Constitution is the highest law of the land. But only the most naive believe that the Supreme Court merely "interprets" the text, that is, inquires what the document means or meant to the people who wrote it. The Court goes far beyond interpretation. The Court invents and expands constitutional doctrine; some of this doctrine is connected to the text by gossamer threads, if at all.

The Supreme Court, and courts generally, have immense power. Many scholars and political figures think the courts go much too far. They want more "restraint." They want the court to confine itself to what the Constitution "actually means." But what is that? Is it even possible to detect a "meaning" for these ancient words? And must the meaning be the same now as it was in 1787? The world has changed. Should the Constitution stay the same?

Hundreds of books, articles, essays, statements, manifestos, and judicial opinions have wrestled with the problem of judicial review, and how to justify it in a democratic society. Some scholars think the Court has a duty to enforce basic human rights, text or no text, and especially the rights of minorities. Majority rule, they say, is a good idea in general; but there is nothing absolute about it. The majority is not always right. Freedom is a value which everybody ought to enjoy, whether the voters think so or not. The rights of minorities are especially important, they would add, in a country like the United States, where people of different races, religions, nationalities, lifestyles, and political beliefs all have to live together. We cannot allow a majority to squash minority rights. The Supreme Court must insist that these rights are respected. That is what freedom means.

There is no question that the Court, in large part, agrees with this view. Indeed, minority rights are one of the great themes of constitutional history. In case after case, the issue turned on the claims of some member of a despised minority, or the litigant was a person who held hateful opinions or was weak, deviant, or powerless. In *Yick Wo* v. *Hopkins*,[3] a Chinese laundryman in San Francisco made legal history; in *Gideon* v. *Wainwright*,[4] it was a middle-aged, drunken nogood; in *Terminiello* v. *Chicago*,[5] a rabid racist and anti-Semite. Through the cases parade an amazing battalion of underdogs: outcasts, the downtrodden, or those who are just plain different—Jehovah's Witnesses, sharecroppers, pornographers, rabble-rousers, "reds," and born-again troublemakers.

Some scholars also look to the court as the only place in this society where we can expect cool, rational, high-minded debate on controversial issues, sometimes issues so hotly disputed that they threaten to tear us apart. The Court and the Court alone is strong enough and independent enough to tackle these issues. The justices have life tenure. They draw their paychecks no matter who is president, no mat-

ter who controls Congress, no matter what the Gallup poll reports
about public opinion. Laurence Tribe, championing the court and its
work, put it this way: "By debating our deepest differences in the
shared language of constitutional rights and responsibilities, we create the possibility of persuasion and even moral education in our
national life."[6]

This may be a trifle overstated. The Court is certainly aware of
political feeling. It has done more than its share of backpedaling, and
it has given way to prejudice at times. Its overall record on civil liberties is far from perfect. Yet its sensitivity to enlightened opinion
may be one of its strengths. Many people feel that social justice, overall, gets a far better shake in the courtroom than in the back rooms of
politics.

It is possible, then, to justify the astonishing power of courts, even
in a democratic society. The power is not random or willful; decisions
are reached after careful consideration of many factors, including legal
ones. The debate goes on, as it has since *Marbury* v. *Madison*. It will
continue. Meanwhile, the Court does its work; and the country, by
and large, accepts the results.

Another point is worth making: there is a big difference between
long-run and short-run values. The Constitution tried to set up a plan
for the long haul. Short-run pressures pour in every day, on Congress, the president, and the rest of the government. This tempts
them to hasty actions which they may live to regret. The Constitution
(fiercely guarded by the courts) can cancel or prevent mistakes of the
moment; we may be all better off in the end when we are forced (by
the court) to resist short-term temptation.

An analogy may be helpful: Two friends set out for a party on New
Year's eve. One of them, as he knows, has a drinking problem. He
gives his friend the keys to the car, and says: "Don't let me drive if I
get drunk—no matter what." At the party, he drinks too much, as he
foresaw. Drunk, he demands the keys. But the promise was "constitutional"; even though he begs, coaxes, and pleads, the friend refuses
to give up the keys. The drunken man is angry, disappointed. He
complains loudly that his friend is unfair. After all, it is *his* car; they
are *his* keys. But in the cool, pearly light of morning, he will be glad
his friend refused him and stuck to his guns.

The Constitution and the courts that enforce it are of course the
keepers of the keys.

Stepchildren of Research:
The State Constitutions

If you study constitutional law or constitutional history in college or law school, you study the federal constitution, and the way courts interpret it. Yet every one of the states has its own constitution, too. State constitutions are significant documents in their own right. They are the highest law within the state. State courts have the last word, by and large, on questions of state constitutional law. The California Constitution affects the rights and duties of more than 20 million residents; and the California Supreme Court, its prime interpreter, is an important institution indeed.

State constitutions are by no means pale imitations of the federal Constitution. Of course, the states have been influenced by the Constitution of 1787. For example, they all have bills of rights, patterned more or less on the federal bill of rights. This is, in a way, repayment of an ancient debt; the federal bill of rights drew heavily on some of the early state constitutions, for example, Virginia's. Since 1787, the federal Constitution has been a powerful model. But the state constitutions differ greatly from each other and from the federal Constitution, both in structure and in detail.

There are many provisions in state constitutions that have no counterpart in the federal document. Many states, in the second half of the nineteenth century, enacted special restrictions on the power of their legislatures. Some legislatures had been, alas, quite corrupt and richly deserved distrust. Maryland, in 1851, took away the legislative power to grant divorces, set up lotteries, spend money for canals and railroads, or go into debt by more than $100,000.[7] Many states outlawed "local or special laws" or "private" laws. (Congress still has this power; it can, and does, pass laws that apply to only a single person.)

Many states also put constitutional limits on the form of laws. No law could cover more than one "subject," and this subject had to be "expressed in the title."[8] The point was to keep a crafty senator or assemblyman from slipping some pet provision into a bill and getting it by the senate or assembly unawares. Whether a statute covers more than one topic is a fairly subjective judgment. Hence this provision gave the judiciary another meat ax to butcher legislation.[9] The clause, in state constitutions, has been a fertile source of litigation. It has no equivalent in the federal Constitution.

State constitutions, on the whole, have had more tangled histories than the federal Constitution. The federal Constitution has been a model of stability. It has been amended, but never overthrown. Only a few of the states (Wisconsin is one) have made do with a single constitution. Louisiana, at the other extreme, has had nine or ten, depending on how one counts. The Louisiana constitution of 1864 was replaced in 1868; the constitution of 1868 was replaced in 1879; this one only lasted until 1898. The 1898 version had 326 articles; it fixed the governor's salary at $5,000, and had twenty-eight separate provisions that dealt with the government of New Orleans.

This was a classic case of constitutional bloat. It was a far cry from the federal model, in which the document sets out a basic framework of government, lists basic principles and rights, and then leaves it at that. Constitutions like Louisiana's in 1898 are actually a kind of superstatute. No wonder that these constitutions are continually tinkered with or replaced. These detailed constitutions are terribly brittle. The federal Constitution, broad and sweeping, bends with the wind and does not break.

Amendments

The Constitution is the highest law of the land; but it can be amended. Under Article V, Congress can propose amendments, which go into effect when "ratified by the Legislatures of three fourths of the several States." This is the method which up to now has been followed every time. There is an alternate way, which starts out with a constitutional convention; it has never been used. In either case, the amendment process is tough and slow; many proposals never succeed. The Equal Rights Amendment seems doomed to be the latest example.

The states, too, have methods of amending their constitutions. California is a special home for one of these, the "initiative." This is the power of voters themselves to propose and pass amendments to the state constitution.[10] Amending the constitution is almost a way of life in California. In every general election, the California voter finds on the ballot "propositions" to amend the constitution. Sometimes there are a dozen or more of these. It takes a big effort, however, to get a proposition onto the ballot. The organizers have to collect a great number of signatures: they need voter signatures totaling at least 8 percent of the number of votes for all candidates in the most recent election for governor. But obviously it can be done, since the ballot is usually crowded with propositions. Some are trivial, some significant. "Proposition Thirteen"[11] cut property taxes to the bone, and shook up the whole system of state finance.

The Flowering of Judicial Review

Marbury v. *Madison*,[12] John Marshall's great decision, is a convenient starting point for talking about judicial review. After *Marbury*, despite grumbling in state courts and among Thomas Jefferson's followers, judicial review won general, if gradual, acceptance. It became a swift and mighty sword in the hands of the courts.

But at first the sword almost grew rusty from disuse. It was more than fifty years until the Supreme Court clearly struck down a piece of federal legislation. This was the infamous *Dred Scott* case (1857).[13] The Court, in an opinion written by Chief Justice Roger B. Taney, held (among other things) that the Missouri Compromise was unconstitutional.[14] The case also held that black people could not be citizens of the United States. Taney's views on slavery, race, and territorial politics, as expressed in *Dred Scott*, were totally obnoxious to antislavery forces in the North. No decision in the Court's long history has been so thoroughly reviled, then and now.

During the long latency period between *Marbury* and *Dred Scott*, judicial review was not totally dormant. The Court did use its power, from time to time, to void *state* statutes. Article I, Section 10(1) of the Constitution provides that "No State shall . . . pass any . . . Law impairing the Obligation of Contracts." This clause was intended to prevent states from going too far in protecting debtors against creditors, especially during times of economic crisis.

The Supreme Court read the clause very broadly. In *Fletcher* v. *Peck*[15] the Court applied the clause to land grants. Georgia's legislature in 1794–95 transferred huge tracts of so-called Yazoo lands to speculators, for a low price. Some of the legislators took bribes. Later the voters turned the rascals out of office. The next legislature tried to undo the land grant, declaring it null and void. By this time, a good deal of the land had passed into the hands of new investors who were not part of the original deal; many of them lived out of state. The Supreme Court labeled the original grant a contract, and refused to let Georgia undo it. In *Dartmouth College* v. *Woodward*,[16] the Court went even further. It held that a legislature could not tinker retroactively with the charter of a corporation (charters were issued, at the time, in the form of statutes). The Court also decided some contract-clause cases more strictly concerned with debtor relief; here, too, they sometimes boldly overturned the policy of individual states.

Contract-clause cases were among the most critical constitutional cases decided before the Civil War. There were also scattered cases on the scope of state and federal power over interstate commerce, and, more generally, on the relationship between the two spheres of government. The issues have an antique flavor: runaway slaves; control of the newfangled steamboats, puffing their way in the waters between New York and New Jersey; toll bridges and turnpikes. But the problems of mapping the jagged boundaries between state power and the federal government are with us yet.

After the Civil War, the triumphant North pushed through three amendments to the Constitution—the Thirteenth, Fourteenth, and Fifteenth. The Thirteenth Amendment abolished slavery and "involuntary servitude," except as punishment for crime. Under the Fifteenth Amendment, the right to vote could not be "denied or abridged" by reason of "race, color, or previous condition of servitude." The Fourteenth Amendment (1868) undid the *Dred Scott* case and made a citizen out of anyone born or naturalized in this country. It forbade states from depriving anyone of "life, liberty, or property, without due process of law." States were also not to "deny," to anyone "within [their] jurisdiction," "the equal protection of the laws." Nine-tenths of modern constitutional law seems to have burst forth like a rocket from the two pregnant phrases *due process* and *equal protection*. A massive social revolution would ultimately hang on them, or be made to hang.

The Civil War was itself a source of change. A weak, part-time government, idling in the swampy village of Washington, was forced to mobilize itself and run a great war. The war destroyed slavery, and ruined the economy of the South. In the North, a farming region with a few mills and machines swiftly became the center of an industrial society—a society of mines, railroads, factories, and rapid communication. The very basis of social life slowly but inevitably altered. The war had not brought this on, of course; but perhaps it speeded up the process. And a dramatic new age of judicial review began.

As late as the 1860s, the Supreme Court decided only four or five constitutional cases on average each year; by 1890, they were deciding about twenty-four.[17] Under Chief Justice Fuller, the Court declared five federal acts unconstitutional in a single decade (1889–99), together with thirty-four state laws and four municipal ordinances.

This great expansion of judicial review, in the late nineteenth century, pivoted on the "due process" clause. Doctrines sprang out of these few words like rabbits from a magician's hat. The draftsmen of the Fourteenth Amendment were almost certainly thinking only of procedure when they used the words *due process*. They were thinking of fair trials in courts of law. But by the turn of the century, the phrase had come to mean something quite different, and vastly greater. As the court saw it, an "unreasonable" or "arbitrary" law amounted to a deprivation of due process. Only the justices, of course, could say what was unreasonable. Too great an infringement of "liberty of contract," for example, violated the Constitution. Out of such bricks, the court built a structure which, in effect, made rugged free enterprise part of the constitutional scheme.

Not, of course, consistently; and not without loud voices from left and center crying out against the court's work. In some notorious instances, the Court used "substantive due process" to tear the guts out of popular laws—laws passed to give labor more power against capital. The high-water mark, perhaps, was *Lochner* v. *New York*[18] in 1905. The issue was a New York statute regulating bakeries. Among other things, it restricted the killing hours some bakers worked. Under the statute, no one could be "required or permitted" to work in a bakery more than sixty hours a week, or more than ten hours in a day.

The Supreme Court voided the law. Justice John Marshall Harlan, dissenting, pointed out that the majority had brushed aside evidence of subhuman work conditions: how bakers suffered from flour dust in their lungs; how "long hours of toil" produced "rheumatism, cramps, and swollen legs"; evidence that bakers were "palefaced," had delicate health, and "seldom" lived past fifty. Oliver Wendell Holmes, Jr., also dissented; to him, the majority rested its case "upon an economic theory which a large part of the country does not entertain." This was the theory of pure free enterprise. Holmes himself was sympathetic to this theory; but he did not wish to raise it to the level of constitutional principle. To the majority, however (speaking through Justice Rufus Peckham), none of this mattered. The health arguments were a sham. The statute was fatally flawed. It interfered with "the freedom of master and employee to contract with each other." A regulation of "hours of labor" of this kind violated the Fourteenth Amendment.

Some state courts (Illinois, for one) were even more active, constitutionally, than the Supreme Court, along the same lines of doctrine. Labor and social laws seemed to fall like tenpins at the turn of the century. But it is hard to measure the actual impact of *Lochner* and its fellow travelers. Most statutes, in fact, survived constitutional challenge. Many were never tested at all. On the other hand, we can never know what statutes did not pass—or passed in weakened form—because legislators in Illinois or Tennessee or Rhode Island were afraid the courts would strike them down. Perhaps, too, the opposite sometimes happened: a legislature passed a "radical" law to please some constituents, hoping deep down that the court would kill it and take them off the hook.

One thing *is* clear: challenges to the validity of laws were common from the 1880s on, and had not been common before. They became, in effect, part of the life cycle of important laws. There was no turning back. Judicial review got stronger and stronger in the twentieth century. It did so, first of all, in terms of sheer volume: more statutes reviewed; more statutes struck down; new doctrines, some of them very bold, very sweeping. In a single year (1915), the Supreme Court voided twenty-two state statutes.[19] The pace continued. An active, intrusive Supreme Court became a permanent part of the landscape.

What it is active *about* has also changed, and dramatically. In the Great Depression of the 1930s and during Franklin D. Roosevelt's New Deal, the country shifted to the left. Power flowed from the exhausted cities and states to Washington. The Supreme Court at first refused to get the message. In a series of cases, the Court nullified key New Deal statutes. For example, in *Schechter Poultry Corp.* v. *United States*,[20] the court swept off the books the National Industrial Recovery Act of 1933.

Once more there was great anger in the country—and in the White House, too. Roosevelt hit on a plan: he would "pack" the court (increase its size) by appointing new justices—men more to his liking, who would neutralize the "nine old men" who then sat on the court. Under the plan, the president was authorized to appoint one new justice for every sitting justice over seventy. There were six of these in 1937. But for once, his political sense had failed him; the court-packing plan was attacked from all sides as a threat to the independence of the justices and to the whole American system. The plan was hastily abandoned and soon died.

In the end, Roosevelt won his war against the Court. He was elected president four times, and the "nine old men" simply could not outlast him. He got his court without packing it; the Supreme Court after 1937 first rather meekly submitted to—then willingly and even eagerly embraced—the expansion of national power and the scope and methods of the regulatory state. Congress and state legislators could do as they liked with the economy; the Court would not say no.

This attitude was expressed in a line of cases whose climax, per-haps, was *Williamson* v. *Lee Optical*.[21] William O. Douglas, one of Roosevelt's appointed judges, wrote the opinion. The facts turned on an Oklahoma law regulating the eyeglass business. No one was allowed to make eyeglasses or fit them except a licensed optometrist or ophthalmologist, or without having a prescription from one of these. The law was supposed to protect the public, and it had some vague connection with health; but these were rather skimpy grounds. The real motives seemed basically anticompetitive: opticians ("artisans qualified to grind lenses, fill prescriptions, and fit frames") were the target of the law, and it hurt them badly in their business. The Supreme Court as it was in 1900 might have gone over the law with a fine comb and could well have struck it down. The Court of 1955, on the other hand, was not of a mind to interfere. Douglas brushed aside all objec-tions to the act. Let Oklahoma do what it wants: "The day is gone," he said, when the Court made use of "due process" to "strike down . . . laws, regulatory of business . . . because they may be unwise."

Williamson is still the law of the land; and the Court, so far, has not gone back on it, spirit or letter. The Court takes a hands-off approach to laws that regulate business. But the energy saved, so to speak, simply flowed into other fields of action, into the so-called social issues: race relations (especially after *Brown* v. *Board of Edu-cation,* in 1954); the rights of criminal defendants; civil liberties in general; sex discrimination; and a motley collection of cases on what we can call, for want of a better term, personal life-style.

Here the Court has been active indeed. It has hacked away at dozens of old taboos. Laws against contraception and abortion were declared unconstitutional.[22] *Furman* v. *Georgia*[23] blew away the death penalty, though the court retracted considerably later on. All of these decisions have been in the highest degree controversial. Has the court gone too fast, too far? Many scholars—and citizens—think so. Others defend the Court. The noisy debate goes on.

As of now (1984), it is the conservative wing of the country that finds the Court most offensive. William French Smith, President Reagan's first attorney general, complained in 1981 that the Court had "overstepped the proper bounds." It had made up "fundamental rights" out of thin air—"the right to marry, the right to procreate, the right of interstate travel, and the right of sexual privacy." These rights are highly "subjective"; the Court drains power from Congress and state legislatures and draws this power to itself.[24] Others, of course, disagree with Smith. They approve of the results, and of the methods, too.

The mechanics of the new jurisprudence are easily described. Almost all of the bold new cases rest, however precariously, on the two great phrases of the Fourteenth Amendment: "due process" and "equal protection." Modern constitutional law balances on these few words, like an elephant standing on a dime. The Court treats these phrases as wonderfully prismatic. It reads concepts and results into them that would stagger the men who drafted the text.

But this is true of the whole of constitutional law. The death penalty cases rested on the Eighth Amendment, which forbids "cruel and unusual punishment." It never occurred to the Founding Fathers that hanging was "cruel and unusual." The gallows was standard for murder in the eighteenth century. Indeed, at the time the Constitution was adopted there were dozens of capital crimes, including burglary and rape in many states. The Bill of Rights itself presupposes capital punishment. This is clear from the very words of the Fifth Amendment. No one can be held to "answer for a capital . . . crime," without "presentment or indictment" by a grand jury. Every state in the Union used the gallows at the time the Constitution was adopted. Hangings were public events.

In this and other instances, the Court inflates the meaning of the text like an accordion. Yet some clauses have expanded only modestly or lie completely inert. In a few instances, the Court has dramatically narrowed the meaning of a provision, or retracted a previous expansion. This was true of the contracts clause. The Court made heavy use of the clause before the Civil War. After the war, the clause cropped up in cases on the debts of southern states, which the bankrupt states were struggling to avoid. Then the clause fell more or less asleep. And in the 1930s, during the Great Depression, the Court nearly destroyed its meaning altogether.

The case was *Home Building & Loan Ass'n* v. *Blaisdell*.[25] In the background was the agony of economic crisis and the catastrophic collapse of real estate values. Hundreds of thousands of people could not make the payments on their homes or their farms. Banks and creditors threatened to foreclose. Minnesota passed a law in 1933 which in effect postponed most foreclosures. This was exactly the kind of law the contracts clause was about. But the Court refused to interfere. The Minnesota law was a "reasonable" attempt to "safeguard the economic structure upon which the good of all depends." History and precedent were swept away because of the Court's sense of crisis.

Civil Rights and Civil Liberties

We tend to think of the Supreme Court as a strong arm of defense for the downtrodden—as the very soul and armor of civil liberties. Yet this is a surprisingly recent role. Decisions about freedom of speech, freedom of the press, freedom of religion, and the like, were extremely rare in the nineteenth century. A good case can be made that the Court's record, until fairly recently, was timid and patchy. There was little in it to excite the admiration of civil libertarians.

Words, after all, do not enforce themselves—even constitutional words. Repression of unpopular opinion was far from unknown in our history. The Sedition Law[26] is a case in point. This law, passed during the presidency of John Adams, made it a crime to publish any "false, scandalous and malicious writing or writings" about the president, Congress, or the government, or any writings intended to defame them or bring them into "contempt or disrepute." The government used the law to harass opposition newspapers. The courts uttered hardly a peep of protest; the law died only because the opposition won power and repealed it.

One can add other instances. The South was harsh on abolitionist opinion. Under the Virginia Code of 1849, for example, it was a crime for a free person, "by speaking or writing," to "maintain that owners have not right of property in their slaves." Many southern states restricted "inflammatory" (antislavery) writings and newspapers.[27] The first Civil Rights laws (passed after the Civil War) were emasculated by the courts.[28] In *Reynolds* v. *United States*[29] and other cases, the Supreme Court upheld strict laws directed against the Mormons. The Justices did next to nothing about the "red scare" during World War I and the 1920s. "Subversives" and "reds" went to jail; the Court affirmed their convictions. The Court was less than heroic in the 1950s, during the McCarthy era and throughout the "cold war" period.[30] It accepted racial segregation in *Plessy* v. *Ferguson* (1896), and ratified the disgraceful treatment of the Japanese during World War II.[31] These were hardly proud chapters in Supreme Court history.

Nevertheless the United States *was* a free society in the nineteenth century. It was a very paradise of freedom compared to most countries, before and after. History is full of examples (Hitler and Stalin come to mind) of what murderous, evil government can stoop to. Nothing in our domestic history sinks so low. It is not sugarcoating our history to stress the fact that few countries have a better record; most have been far, far worse.

The Bill of Rights was never a dead letter. Trials were fair, on the whole, even though they did not meet today's more exacting standards. Concepts of rights change over time. We define liberty today to include rights our grandparents never thought of in that connection. In 1890, for example, no one read the Constitution as limiting the right of the state to control sexual behavior.

In the nineteenth century, there was probably more consensus than there is today about the limits of rights. Of course, we do not have precise information about past public opinion on issues of freedom of speech or defendants' rights. There were no Gallup polls; and our sources—newspapers, court cases—are almost certainly biased. What we can say is we do not find much inclination to kick against the traces. Deviants lay low; the most they hoped for was immunity from arrest. They did not dream of legitimacy. Courts were not, on the whole, hospitable to rebels. Judicial activism, in the field of civil rights and civil liberties, took a long time to warm up.

At first, federal courts did not have the power (never mind the inclination) to enforce basic rights against the states. This was decided in the famous case of *Barron* v. *Baltimore*.[32] The Supreme Court ruled that the Bill of Rights bound the federal government but not the states. A citizen could not bring an action in federal court claiming that the state had taken his property or infringed his basic rights. The states had their own constitutions, their own bills of rights. But *Barron* v. *Baltimore* closed the door on hope for a single, national standard.

Barron v. *Baltimore* is still law, technically speaking. But later developments took away most of its bite. Today, citizens can enforce their basic rights against the states in federal court. Our old friend the Fourteenth Amendment, with its supple, expansive provisions, was the vehicle of change—specifically, its due process clause. In a series of cases, the Supreme Court held that certain aspects of the Bill of Rights were so "fundamental" that the due process clause scooped them up and swallowed them whole. In this way, the Fourteenth Amendment bypassed *Barron* v. *Baltimore*. Justice Benjamin Cardozo, in *Palko* v. *Connecticut*,[33] one of the key cases, said that freedom of speech was "the matrix, the indispensable condition, of nearly every other form of freedom." Hence, said the Court, any state that impairs freedom of speech steps over the line and violates "due process of law." In this way the First Amendment, which covers free speech, became the national standard.

Over the years, the Court has slowly but steadily "incorporated" more and more provisions of the Bill of Rights into the Fourteenth Amendment, thus imposing them on all fifty states and vesting enforcement power in federal courts. Most of the provisions on criminal justice have been incorporated bag and baggage. There are a few exceptions. The Fifth Amendment requires indictment by grand jury in criminal cases. In *Hurtado* v. *California*,[34] the Court refused to read this requirement into the Fourteenth Amendment. This decision still stands.

So much for the technical side of the story. But "incorporation" is more than a device. It means, first of all, greater sensitivity to rights; it also means that the federal courts have assumed broad powers. The Supreme Court leads the way. It has built up a rampart of rules giving national scope to the Bill of Rights and lending its weight to one underclass after another: blacks, women, the poor, and, most particularly, those caught in the web of the criminal law. The most dramatic developments came after 1950. Many are associated with the Court under Earl Warren, appointed chief justice in 1953 by President Eisenhower.

Of course, one man cannot be responsible for so strong a trend— even if the man is chief justice. Not even the whole panel of nine justices can claim the credit or take the blame. Courts are *instruments* of social change. They deal with issues that other people raise; they do not, on the whole, invent policies. They give policies a legal basis, and help to carry them out. The 1950s was the decade of the civil rights movement. Black people had become more militant. This militance was one of the great social realities behind the *Brown* case. In the years since then, other minorities and underclasses have claimed their rights. On these social foundations, the Court has built its house of doctrine.

The Supreme Court has no power to promote its own docket. It does have the right to pick and choose among the thousands of cases that beg for the ear of the Court. This right to choose is a source of great power. But a case before the Court is at the end of its line, not the beginning. Each case is about a real problem, issue, or claim which began in the world outside the Court. To be sure, when courts show they are receptive to a certain type of claim, they encourage people to bring more such claims to court.

For example, the *Brown* case dealt, on the surface, only with Jim Crow schools. It outlawed segregation in public schools; and in fact, for years, it had only moderate success in achieving this goal. But the case also delivered a powerful message to the black community. The message was that the Court was willing—even eager—to advance the cause of racial justice. Still, it was the black community and its allies that had to act. It takes nothing away from the Court to recognize that it had these partners—the groups and individuals that demanded constitutional rights. The "rights revolution" is the result of a partnership between an active court and an active society.

To explain where law comes from, what it does, and where it is going, one always has to look at social context. The law of obscenity is another example. The Court has been struggling with this issue for about thirty years. The First Amendment protects freedom of speech. In most states the sale of "pornography" or "obscene" books and pictures is a crime. Oklahoma, for example, prohibits selling "obscene, lewd, lascivious, filthy, or indecent" matter.[35] Where is the boundary line between obscenity, which can be forbidden, and free expression, which cannot? How far can people go, in words and pictures, before they lose the protection of the First Amendment?

The Court has never come up with a satisfying answer. The issue is on the whole surprisingly recent. The Supreme Court did not deal with it squarely until 1957, when it decided *Roth* v. *United States*.[36] Litigation on the point was rare in the nineteenth century. There were dirty books and dirty pictures; but they stayed in the closet, so to speak. Obscenity rarely showed its face in public.

Apparently a Pennsylvania case decided in 1815 was the first ever reported on the subject.[37] Another early case, in Massachusetts (1821), dealt with a book called *Memoirs of a Woman of Pleasure*, but better known as *Fanny Hill*. For more than a century after the Massachusetts case, this famous erotic book, written by John Cleland, continued its underground life. It passed from clammy hand to clammy hand. In December 1923, two New York booksellers, Maurice Inman and Max Gottschalk, were arrested, convicted, and fined $250 for selling *Fanny Hill* (along with two other "classics," *A Night in a Moorish Harem* and *Only a Boy*).[38] During all this period, rarely if ever did anyone claim that the constitutional protections were broad enough to cover *Fanny Hill*.

Then, in the 1960s, *Fanny Hill* went dramatically public, and this time with a difference. The publishers demanded (and got) constitutional protection. In the years after 1960, there was a great wave of obscenity cases. *Fanny* was the star of some of these cases. And generally speaking, the courts made an honest woman of her. The First Amendment, it turned out, was sweeping enough in its scope to protect this "woman of pleasure."[39]

By this time, *Fanny* was about 150 years old—about the same age, in fact, as the First Amendment. Yet their definitive meeting took place only in the 1960s. The words—of the book and of the First Amendment—were the same as they had been since the eighteenth century. But society had changed, and with it legal doctrine; and the very meaning of freedom of speech had altered in the course of time.

Despite *Fanny's* triumph, the obscenity issue has never been finally resolved. Legal doctrine on the point is a hopeless muddle. The courts have been unable to find and announce workable rules and workable limits. It is clear, of course, that standards have dramatically shifted. A generation ago, a mild movie comedy, *The Moon is Blue*, provoked an uproar simply because the word *virgin* was uttered on the screen. Today "adult" bookstores, peep shows, and pornographic movie houses exist in every town of any size. Customers can see and buy hard-core pornography, magazines, and books for every brand and off-brand of sex—in living color, if you please—and all without crackdowns or raids. This rank permissiveness shocks and disgusts millions of people. Obviously, millions of others disagree, but quietly: they vote by watching and buying hard-core products. Those who prefer tradi- tional morality tend to blame the courts for the flood of pornogra- phy—for stretching the First Amendment so that it protects this "filth." No doubt the courts do deserve some credit or blame. The courts have opposed censorship; they have vetoed restrictive laws; they have allowed very broad standards. But the major change has been, unquestionably, not legal but social. There is a demand for these movies, books, and magazines; and, what is more, customers want to buy cheaply, easily, legally, and openly. For the most part, their views have prevailed.

The issue is by no means a simple one. The Court faces, here as elsewhere, a difficult question: where to draw the line. There are, after all, bluenoses who want to censor Shakespeare, who find *Catcher in the Rye* too raw for high-school libraries, who want to ban any movie that even hints at sex. In one of the Supreme Court's obscenity cases,[40] the movie in question was *Carnal Knowledge*. A major studio produced it; it was a serious, important film on serious themes, and obscene by no stretch of the imagination. Yet the defendant had been convicted for showing this movie in Albany, Georgia. The Supreme Court reversed the conviction. Another case, *Erznoznik* v. *City of Jacksonville*,[41] wrestled with the problem of drive-in movies. Jack- sonville, Florida, banned movies if they showed "the human male or female bare buttocks, human female bare breasts, or human bare pubic areas," whenever the screen was visible from a public street. The Supreme Court felt the rule went much too far: taken literally, it would ban a film containing a "picture of a baby's buttocks . . . the opening of an art exhibit . . . shots of bathers on a beach."

On the whole, the Court has tried to move cautiously in this delicate and controversial field. It does not wander too far ahead of elite public opinion. It does not give either side everything it wants. It certainly rejects the standards of prudery; but it has also never said that anything goes. This is in general the posture of the Court in civil liberty cases. The Court can lead public opinion, and it often does. It shows the way. It acts as teacher or vanguard. But it cannot march all by itself, way ahead of the rest of the crowd.

This is especially true because courts have only limited power. They make pronouncements, but somebody else must carry them out. Enforcement, however, is crucial. Real rights are more important than rights on paper. What happens to Supreme Court doctrines when they reach the street, the station house, the chambers of trial court judges? Generally speaking, there is a lot of slippage between command and execution; but whether the gap is scandalously large or tolerable depends on the time, the subject, the people, and the place.

One historical example might be useful. The case is *Bailey* v. *Alabama*,[42] decided in 1911. Lonzo Bailey was a poor black farm-worker, working in Alabama for a white landowner. He quit his job in the middle of the growing season and was arrested for breaking his contract "fraudulently." This was a crime in Alabama, under a statute passed with people like Bailey in mind. The whole point was to tie black farm-workers to the land, at least during the growing season—to make it impossible for them to quit, whatever their reasons.

The system smacked of serfdom, or even slavery. It had been going on for years. But a tiny band of progressive lawyers made a test case out of Lonzo Bailey's problem. They took the case all the way to the Supreme Court. Here Alabama lost. The court declared the law unconstitutional; the justices felt it was part of a system of peonage, forbidden by federal law. Black people in the South and their allies had won a great victory.

But in fact nothing happened to the underlying problem. Bailey, of course, went free. Alabama tinkered with its law, making small, cosmetic changes. Other southern states simply ignored the decision. The southern labor system continued, just as before. Southern peonage lived on.[43] *Bailey*, in short, was "ahead of its time." It gave liberals a warm glow, a sense of accomplishment. But there was no movement, no organization, no plan to follow through, no muscle and will to enforce the case. Thus, in a real sense, it died on the vine.

More than forty years later, the Supreme Court decided *Brown v. Board of Education*.[44] The court ordered race segregation to end in public schools. It was also the first of a series of cases that banned segregation everywhere. What happened after *Brown* was nothing short of a revolution—an incomplete revolution, to be sure, but a revolution nonetheless.

Brown, in other words, did not suffer the fate of the *Bailey* case. It did not fade away. Why? Not because of anything in the opinion, in the doctrines announced, in the way it was written, in its style, or in its craftsmanship. The answer lies elsewhere—in changed social conditions and, especially, in the civil rights movement. The great events that followed *Brown*—the sit-ins, marches, protests, the constant litigation, the struggle in the South and the North—put power and passion behind the concepts of *Brown* and made them a working reality. The "revolution" happened because of the partnership between court and constituents, between legal force and social force.

Here and Abroad

A final word, this time about American constitutional law as an export commodity. Our system is old, as systems go; and since it began, it has served as a model for other nations. When the countries of Latin America broke away from Spain, they often adopted written constitutions. The United States Constitution was an important source of ideas for these documents. Unfortunately, dictatorships in many of these countries make a mockery of constitutional guarantees. The words speak of liberty, equality, and justice; but the state ignores or suspends these guarantees.

The Latin American countries come out of a different legal tradition—the tradition of Spain and the civil law. Judicial review, American style, is alien to them. Nonetheless, in some countries (for example, Colombia and Costa Rica) courts have played a strong constitutional role. From 1910 to 1953, the supreme court of Colombia invalidated over fifty statutes, in whole or in part. In other countries (Ecuador, Paraguay), judicial review has never taken hold.[45]

After the Second World War, Germany, Italy, and Japan also wrote new constitutions. In each case, there was a strong imprint of American ideas about constitutional systems. We had, after all, won the war; we had armies stationed in the losing nations. Bloody, repressive regimes had been overthrown. Control of centralized power was an aim of the occupying forces.

The new constitutions included provisions for judicial review. Germany and Italy established special "constitutional courts" to exercise this power. It was a startling break with national tradition. The German court, after a rather slow start, now shows strong signs of "activism"; it exercises power with a certain relish. It has, for example, jumped into the abortion issue as boldly as the United States Supreme Court. However, it has come out on the other side: in February 1975, it struck down liberal abortion laws, in the constitutional interests of the unborn child.[46]

Other postwar courts have so far been quite cautious about their novel powers. In its first twenty years, the Japanese supreme court was constitutionally almost inert; it almost never disapproved of legislation on constitutional grounds.[47] But this reluctance, too, may be slowly eroding. In general, the new constitutional courts (Cyprus and Austria are other examples) tend to grow stronger, more assertive, more self-confident over the years.

These overseas versions of judicial review have naturally attracted the attention of scholars. We hear a lot about "American influence." It would be wrong to put too much weight on this point. Of course, American example has been significant. But context, too, is important. Societies are all undergoing rapid social change. In many ways, we live now as part of a single world culture. In every major country of the West, populations are much more mobile than before and wealth is widely, though unequally, distributed. Old patterns of authority are decaying—very fast in some places, more slowly in others. Jet airplanes, computers, and satellites have turned the world into a single village, at least in some respects.

Judicial review did not spring up in the United States by magic. By now it is a tradition; but it did not start that way. There was no such thing as judicial review in England, any more than in Spain or in Germany. It developed in this country almost from scratch. It grew because, in some mysterious way, it worked. Certain social conditions (and legal tools) made possible the American pattern. If these conditions reproduce themselves in, say, Germany or Japan, and if the tools are there, we would expect some sort of parallel development. Hollywood movies and Coca-Cola conquered the world because they appealed to people. No one forced them down alien throats. Foreigners turned out to have much the same tastes, good or bad, as Americans. No one should have been surprised. Judicial review is an export of a similar type, in some ways, though on a higher plane, one hopes.

11

On Legal Behavior

WE HAVE SPENT a good deal of time so far on legal rules and on the structures that make and carry out those rules. But, once again, it must be emphasized that a legal system is more than structures and rules. Rules, after all, are supposed to be followed—at least some of the time. The key element in any legal system is behavior—what people actually do. Otherwise rules are nothing but words; and the structures are a ghost town, not a living city. There is no way to understand a legal system—including ours—unless we pay attention to what we might call "legal behavior."

The term *legal behavior*, as used in this book, means behavior influenced in any way by a rule, decision, order, or act given out by somebody with legal authority. If I behave in some way, or change my behavior in some way, because of something the law commands—or because of some government action, or some message or order coming from government or from the legal system or from some functionary in it—then this is legal behavior. If I am driving along the road and see a speed limit sign—or spot a policeman—and slow down, this then would be legal behavior.

It would also be legal behavior, though of a somewhat different sort, if I saw the policeman and started going 100 miles an hour, to give him the slip. After all, here, too, I am reacting to something going on in the legal system. It is also legal behavior, of course, to file income tax returns, sue somebody, register to vote, and do countless other ordinary and extraordinary acts.

There are many things we might want to know about legal behavior. One question is this: It is plain that some laws are obeyed and some are disobeyed. How do we account for these facts? Why do people obey some laws and not others? This is an important question, because most of us have an interest, most of the time, in seeing that the rules are obeyed. (This is, of course, not universally true.)

Actually, we should try to steer clear of the words *obey* and *disobey*. They can be somewhat misleading. Legal behavior is more than a matter of obeying and disobeying. One example will do to show this point. When married life has been too bumpy for a couple, they may consider divorce. In almost every state, today, there is a no-fault system, which makes divorce fairly easy to get. It is a matter of filing papers in court, paying a small fee, going through certain formalities, and waiting a while. If neither party makes a fuss, which is almost always the case, the court dissolves the marriage, splits up the property as agreed, issues custody orders if there are children, and so on. The man and woman are free now to marry again.

Clearly, all of this activity—going to court and getting a divorce—is legal behavior. Certainly the couple followed forms and rules. But we would hardly say they "obeyed" the law. The law does not order anybody to get a divorce. What it does is tell you how to get one if you want one. Thus it makes no sense to talk about obeying or disobeying the law in this instance. Rather, we should talk about using (or not using) the law of divorce. And, in general, except in criminal law and in certain provisions of regulatory law, legal behavior is more a matter of using or not using than of obeying or disobeying.

Not that obeying and disobeying are unimportant. It seems clear that the legal system would collapse if everybody disobeyed certain laws, such as laws against violent behavior, or if so many people disobeyed that the law lost its point completely. There is, in fact, a lot of crime, lawlessness, and deviance in our country. But we are still a long way from anarchy.

Some laws, of course, are more widely obeyed than others. There are many examples of laws that "nobody pays attention to." Prohibition is often cited as the best example of a major law which came to grief because of massive disobedience. Prohibition, the "noble experiment," was a total ban on selling or dealing in liquor. It went into effect in 1920. By most accounts, it was a dismal failure. Millions of people kept right on drinking. Bootleggers and gangsters took over the liquor business. In 1928, there were 55,729 prosecutions for violations of the National Prohibition Act in federal courts, and more than 48,000 convictions. Most of these were resolved by fines; in any event, prosecutions were a drop in the bucket compared to the number of violations. Some scholars even feel that liquor consumption went up during Prohibition. This was probably not true; but the mere fact that one can make the argument suggests that violation was widespread indeed.[1]

Prohibition is, of course, not the only example of a law widely flouted. Marijuana laws have been called the "new Prohibition." John Kaplan's 1970 book has that phrase as part of its title. Kaplan reports on a survey in a California city (1967–68), where 49 percent of the males and 32 percent of the females between eighteen and twenty-four had tried marijuana. Yet marijuana was strictly illegal.[2] Thousands—maybe millions—of drivers ignore the national speed limit (fifty-five miles an hour). Yet these laws are not dead letters: they are enforced somewhat, even though imperfectly or sporadically or unfairly.

Many "dead" laws are not, after all, as dead as we may think. Even during Prohibition, many people (perhaps most?) obeyed the law. And the law had an important effect on legal behavior, including the behavior of people who regularly broke the law: it changed the time, manner, and mode of their drinking. After all, before Prohibition it was legal to drink openly or in public. During Prohibition, drinking had to be kept more or less secret. Today, even where the "pot" laws are enforced very weakly, nobody dares light up in front of a policeman at high noon. Similarly, nobody drives 100 miles an hour when the police are around.

Obedience and disobedience are not matters of black and white. There are all sorts of shades of gray. The speed limit is a good example. The national speed limit, of course, is fifty-five miles an hour. But by custom, fifty-five does not mean fifty-five; it means (more or less) sixty. Most people drive at sixty; some drive even faster—at sixty-five or seventy. Technically, they are violating the law. But what if the speed limit were raised to sixty-five, or if there was no limit at all? In this case, no doubt many people would drive at seventy-five, or eighty or ninety, on the open road. Probably, then, the speed limit has some effect on the behavior of drivers, even though they "disobey" the law. It seems to dampen some of their passion for speeding. How much is an open question.

Similarly, how "ineffective" are the laws against marijuana? People say, rather loosely, that these laws are "not obeyed at all." But of course this is wrong. We have no idea how many people would smoke marijuana if it were completely legal to do so. There must be some timid souls who are deterred even by weak enforcement; there must be some people who refuse to smoke because it is against the law. The laws, then, have a real effect on behavior, including the behavior of violators. The law influences conduct, for better and for worse. Poor old Prohibition, on history's ash heap, probably made more of a dent on behavior than anybody gives it credit for.

Much the same can be said about use and nonuse of law. There are rules, doctrines, provisions that are used or not used, as a matter of individual choice. A woman can either make out a will or not, as she sees fit. The law certainly does not insist on a will. A study of Cuyahoga County, Ohio (Cleveland), which took a sample of 659 estates closed in 1964–65, found that 31 percent of them were "intestate"— that is, the deceased never bothered to make out a will.[3] When a marriage breaks up, the couple can simply live apart, or they can get a divorce. It is up to them.

The law of divorce is, in a way, a kind of commodity: the legal system offers it for sale to the public like a bar of soap or a car. The public can buy or not, as it chooses. A lot depends on the product— and on the price. A divorce costs money. It also has a value: without a divorce, nobody can legally remarry and start a legitimate new family. The rules about divorce and divorce procedures affect the cost of the law and the benefits it brings; these costs and benefits influence whether or not people "buy." Recently, divorce has become easier and cheaper. This influences the number of "sales." But of course a happily married couple does not rush out and get a divorce just because divorce is cheaper than before—or even free.

No law is 100 percent effective. We always have to tolerate a certain amount of slippage. The amount we can tolerate varies tremendously from one type of behavior to another. Let us take speeding as our example again. We tolerate a high level of violation. This does create problems—accidents, for one thing—but though literally millions of people break the law every day, it does not produce a crisis in society.

Contrast this with skyjacking. This is a very rare crime, committed by a tiny handful of disturbed people—terrorists, extremists. The potential pool of violators is and always will be small. But even a tiny violation rate (one out of a billion) is simply intolerable; it could throw the whole transportation system into chaos. Society spends millions of dollars and devotes thousands of hours of effort to try to prevent *all* skyjacking. The toleration rate is very low. The same is true of political assassination.

Influencing Legal Behavior

What can we say about the factors that influence legal behavior? First of all, both *communication* of the law and *knowledge* of it are essential. It makes no sense to say that I obey or disobey a rule, use it, or evade it, unless I know what it is. The rule, in other words, has to be communicated to me and I must have some knowledge of its contents.

In communicating information about legal rules, the size of the audience is crucially important. Some rules of law apply to only a few people; others apply to a whole class; some apply to everybody. If a rule applies only to a small group (manufacturers of lipstick, for example), it is easier to make the rule known to those it affects, especially when it is possible to pinpoint and locate everybody in the audience. A rule which is supposed to reach the whole public is harder to get across, and communicating it is much more expensive.

The way the rule is communicated is also important. Some rules are, in fact, common knowledge; they are part of very general, very early learning. Most rules—and all the technical, detailed administrative rules—have to be specially delivered to the audience. There are all sorts of ways to do this: a sign that says "No smoking" is one way; a presidential speech is another. Some rules or orders are delivered to their audience in the flesh; a policeman, for example, stands at the intersection, in the midst of traffic, and tells people when and how to move.

The form of a rule also has a bearing on its communication. A rule which is specific is better at conveying its message than a rule which is vague and general. The extreme case is the speed limit. It is posted in big letters at the side of the road, and its message is simple and direct: "55 MPH." We have little doubt that this rule reaches its audience. At the other extreme are subtle, difficult, vaguely worded doctrines of law. The Uniform Commercial Code, for example, provides that a court need not enforce an "unconscionable" clause in a contract.[4] Only lawyers, by and large, know that there is such a rule; even they have no way of knowing exactly what it means. It has no earthly way to reach a larger audience.

Knowledge of the Law

How much do Americans know about their own legal system? One survey carried out in Michigan (1973) reported, to nobody's great surprise, that the general public knew less about law than law students did; and that better-educated people knew more about law than the less-educated. This was hardly news, but at least it confirmed people's guesses. The study also provided some bits of detail. People seemed to have a better grasp of criminal matters than of civil matters. Take, for example, this question: "If a person remains silent when questioned by the police, may his silence be used against him in court?" The right answer is no, and 82 percent of the subjects knew this. On the other hand, people were asked whether a car dealer could simply repossess a car parked on the street if the buyer missed a payment; 71 percent said yes, which is the wrong answer.[5]

A Texas survey taken slightly earlier found important class differences in what people knew about law. It is disheartening to learn that poor people know very little about their rights. For example, nearly 40 percent of the low-income blacks who were surveyed thought police had a right to search their houses whenever they wanted to, which is certainly not the law.[6] These answers may reflect either pure ignorance or (sad to say) a degree of realism. That is, low-income people may experience law in a way that leads them to expect injustice. Their answers are technically wrong, but match their experience.

Knowledge of law, like knowledge of anything else, is a matter of degree. We are not surprised to find that people are fairly ignorant about the legal system. But they do have enough working knowledge of law to get by. On the whole, people tend to know more about rules that are relevant to themselves, their groups, and their jobs and situations. Taxi drivers are likely to know (more or less) the taxi regulations and the rules about taxi licenses. A policeman knows the laws of arrest better than a plumber does. A plumber knows more about building codes than a policeman. A person in the export-import trade knows very little about taxi licenses, arrests, or plumbing rules, but a lot about export-import law. And so it goes.

What about rules that apply to everybody? Some are common knowledge. The aspects of law "everybody" knows are, in a way, the most primitive—the most closely connected to general customs and norms. Everybody above the age of five or so knows that the law forbids stealing—that it is a crime to rob a gas station. Details of the law, where to find the law, exactly what the law says—these are things most people may not know. They also probably do not know or understand technical distinctions—such as the difference between first- and second-degree murder or the nuances that separate burglars from robbers. They know that a check has to be endorsed (signed on the back) before it can be transferred; but they may not understand the various refinements of the concept of "negotiability" which lie behind the practice of endorsement. Still, the guts of these rules are part of everyday life in society.

These very basic, very elementary rules, are part of general and early learning. Even grade-school children have some idea about the rules and what they are. One study asked children of various ages, "What is a rule?" A boy in primary school gave this answer: "A rule is not to run around, not to hit anybody, not to break anything." Another question was "What would happen if there were no rules?" A second-grade girl said: "Then people would go around killing other people, and . . . stealing things, and . . . kidnapping people." These young children, then, have a clear sense that some behaviors (killing, stealing) are forbidden.[7] They learn these things in early childhood from their parents, teachers and friends, and from TV.

But not all rules are learned this way, of course; and most are not learned at all. Otherwise, there would be no need for lawyers and other experts. In fact, nobody can know all the rules, or even one percent of them. The federal government alone produces hundred of new regulations every year, some of them tremendously complicated. The new rules and regulations are printed in the Federal Register, which runs to thousands of pages a year. It is also a very technical, very boring book, hardly something to keep on your bedside table. But lawyers will keep up with rules and regulations in the area of their specialties. A food-and-drug lawyer or a corporate tax lawyer makes sure he knows the latest "regs" on the subject; he also keeps a loose-leaf service with up-to-date material. He probably reads reports of the latest, most important cases.

These lawyers are important to the business world. They are middlemen—brokers of information. They store up knowledge of legal rules and pass them on to clients when and as needed. In this regard, of course, they are like any other experts:—doctors, auto mechanics, engineers. Lawyers are rules experts. They are, of course, not the only rules experts in society. Tax accountants are experts on tax rules; they compete with lawyers for business. There are many other examples. Every big company probably has many people working for it whose job is to keep up with rules and regulations of one kind or another: labor rules, business law rules, regulations of all sorts. Some of these people will be lawyers; some will not.

Most people have working knowledge of the most essential rules; lawyers and knowledge brokers take care of the rest. But, as the Texas survey suggests, there is no reason to assume all is for the best. There are large knowledge gaps, and they can be socially destructive. In general, more sophistication about law and legal process would be useful, if only to educate voters and make them better judges of policy. Ignorance and misinformation can be hazardous to society's health.

Once in a while mistakes in legal knowledge can be shown to have terrible consequences. Joseph Wambaugh's book *The Onion Field* (1973) is the history of a crime, the brutal murder of a policeman in California. The killer, according to Wambaugh, misunderstood the state's "Little Lindbergh Law." This was a law about the punishment for kidnapping. The killer thought he had already committed a crime that could land him in the gas chamber, just by kidnapping the policeman. If this was true, he could not be any worse off for getting rid of the man, and he would benefit by eliminating a witness. This was a mistake about the law, and it led to a needless murder.

People in society probably have many wrong beliefs and ideas about law. There is, in a way, a kind of legal folklore in every society, including ours. The folklore consists of notions about the law that are baseless or distorted, for one reason or another. Some people think it is illegal to sign a document in pencil. In fact, this is perfectly OK, though for obvious reasons it is also a bad idea. Or they may think they are not allowed to leave a hospital unless they pay the bills. In fact, they can. The hospital is not a prison and has no right to hold people prisoner. The folklore of American law is an intriguing subject which nobody, apparently, has systematically explored.

Sanctions

Suppose a norm or rule has been communicated to the necessary audience. People now know it, at least well enough to understand what is expected of them. At this point, the choice is theirs—to obey or not to obey, to use or not to use. Which will they choose? For simplicity, let us concentrate on obedience to criminal rules.

First of all, there is probably no rule or law in the land which everybody follows all of the time. If there was such a norm, there would be no point making it a law in the first place; people would obey it on their own. At the same time, it is hard to think of a rule or law universally disobeyed. Almost everything falls in the middle. Of course, that middle is very broad. Every driver has broken traffic rules, and probably frequently. On the other hand, few people (fortunately) have tried their hand at murder.

What moves people to make the choices they do? What pushes them in the direction of obeying some norm, or disobeying it? Why are some laws observed more than others? The simplest and most general explanation is in terms of "sanctions," that is, rewards and punishments. People follow rules because they are afraid what will happen if they break the law. In other words, the law and its sanctions deter them.

The word *deterrence* conjures up certain images: we think of fines, jail, and other forms of punishment. The word *sanctions,* however, covers more than punishment. It also includes rewards. The positive side of sanctions (rewards, incentives) is less obvious, because the literature stresses the criminal law; and when we think of law at all, we tend to think of the criminal side. But incentives are an important part of the legal system. Government at every level hands out billions of dollars in subsidies. To encourage people to save energy, we give them a tax break for insulating their homes, rather than putting them in jail if they do not cooperate. If farmers are growing too much cotton or peanuts, we pay them to put land in the "soil bank." The law makes heavy use of incentives, mostly tax breaks or subsidies.

Do rewards and punishment work? The answer is yes—as a general proposition. In case we need it, there is plenty of proof—first, in everyday experience, and second, in the scholarly literature. For example, suppose that the faculty in a university community blatantly disobeys the parking rules. If the university jacks up the fines and increases its police force, the violation rate is sure to decline.[8]

We can take the following for granted: if there is a rule that includes some kind of punishment for breaking it, and if we increase the punishment, keeping all other factors the same, the new level of punishment will increase the deterrent effect. That is, some people (not everybody) will stop doing the deed, out of fear of punishment. Similarly, an increase in rewards will stimulate a desired behavior if all other factors are held constant. If a state offers $10 apiece for coyote skins, it will get a certain number of skins. If it raises the offer to $1,000 a skin, and nothing else changes, there will be a bigger harvest of skins. If we raise the fine for overtime parking from $5 to $20, at the same level of enforcement, some people will think twice about violating the rules. If we get serious and start towing cars away, there will be an even greater effect.

So much is obvious. The real issues are more difficult and complex. We know that threat of punishment deters people; but we do not know how much, in any given case. Nor do we understand who is deterred, and why. Yet these are the crucial questions. Argument rages over whether capital punishment is an effective deterrent or not, or effective enough to be worthwhile. The Supreme Court, by a five-to-four vote, threw out all of the country's death penalty laws in *Furman v. Georgia*.[9] Thurgood Marshall, one of the five in the majority, asserted that there was no justification for the death penalty, partly because it did not deter. Some scholars agree with Marshall; others disagree. One economist, Isaac Ehrlich, went so far as to claim that every execution prevents between eight and twenty murders.[10] Other researchers have vigorously disputed these claims, and with much plausibility.

The death penalty is an emotional issue; feelings run high on both sides. It is not easy to sort out facts from emotions. The situation is probably this: capital punishment, as a general proposition, does deter—that is, it does have an impact on behavior. If a dictator suddenly announced that anybody on the streets after dark would be shot, and if he meant business, people would scurry for cover as soon as the sun started sinking in the west. This is obviously true.

But this is not really the issue. The issue is not whether the death penalty is effective compared to no punishment at all. Nobody suggests letting murderers go free or punishing them with a slap on the wrist. The question is whether capital punishment adds an *extra* deterrent, compared to life imprisonment or a long "jolt" in prison. Or, if it adds something, does it add enough to make it worthwhile? On this question, we have little information. The death penalty has been rare in this country for a generation or so, and there is no way to know how much it enters into the calculations of potential criminals. Many people object to killing prisoners, on moral grounds. Ethical issues, of course, have no scientific answer. That does not make them unimportant.

We talk about the way punishment deters people; but what we really mean is the threat of punishment. After all, very few people actually go to jail. The literature on crime speaks about two kinds of deterrence, "general" and "special." General deterrence is deterrence in advance: people obey the law because they know there is such a thing as punishment. Special deterrence is after the fact: a criminal is caught and sent to jail. If he "learns a lesson" and goes straight, he has been specially deterred.[11]

General deterrence is more important than special deterrence. Sending a thief to jail may or may not get thievery out of his system. There are, in fact, lots of backsliders ("recidivists"). What the thief does, however, is far less important than the presumed effect of jails and punishment on millions of other people, who think twice before stealing, out of fear. The Internal Revenue Service, with a loud clang of publicity, often indicts a few prominent tax evaders right before April 15. The idea is general deterrence—putting the fear of the Lord, so to speak, into taxpayers. It probably works.

What is important, of course, is not the actual sanction, but what people know or think about sanctions—the knowledge and notions they carry around in their heads. A completely secret system of punishment, if such a thing were possible, would not change anybody's behavior. This points up a weakness in much of the literature on deterrence. Scholars have tried to prove that harsh punishments cut down the crime rate. They cannot run experiments, so they try to find "natural" experiments. They compare, for example, the situation in two or more states. They look at the average prison term in State A, and compare it with the term in State B; then they look at the crime rates in these states. Does the tough state have less crime?[12]

But this is tricky business. In the first place, it is not easy to measure crime rates in any state. Comparing the rates compounds the problem. Secondly, all sorts of other factors besides punishment influence crime rates. Thirdly, unless the differences in prison terms from state to state are extremely great, criminals are unlikely to know the differences. Suppose State A gives out, on average, prison sentences 12 percent more severe than those in State B. If burglars and thieves are not aware of the different levels of severity, then we should not expect any difference in the behavior of potential criminals as between the two states. And if it takes a team of social scientists to discover the precise levels of severity, would a pickpocket or shoplifter know the same facts simply by intuition?

The reverse of this point is a kind of scarecrow or bogeyman effect. People are deterred by sanctions that are not really there—people only think they are. A study of subway crime in New York City found this "phantom effect." When the city put more policemen in subway cars, the crime rate went down, even during hours when the police were not actually there.[13] Of course, a phantom effect is not likely to last; it will wear off as soon as people learn the true picture.[14]

When people talk loosely about the punishment for some particular crime, they often mean the official level of punishment—that is, the simple, blunt words on the law books ("five years in prison"). But punishment is both more and less than that. It is a complex process— a whole package of events—that an arrest sets in motion. A woman is picked up for shoplifting; she is taken to a strange, scary place; she is held in a cold, filthy cell; her name gets into the newspapers; she misses work and may lose her job; the neighbors gossip about her case. All this can happen even if the police or the prosecutors or a jury let her go in the end without any "punishment." As Malcolm Feeley put it, in a study of a New Haven court, in the "lower criminal courts the process itself is the primary punishment."[15]

Process *is* punishment, no question; this makes it even harder to compare deterrent effects across state lines. It is easy to compare the statutory words in, say, Connecticut and Mississippi; harder, but still possible, to compare average sentences in the two states; much harder, and almost impossible, to compare real punishments. Shoplifting may carry more shame in a small town than in a big city, where life is more anonymous. Even "one year in prison" is not the same thing everywhere. Some prisons are harsher than others. There are maximum security prisons where life is as tough and brutal as outside on the streets. Some prisons are filthy and corrupt; their guards are vicious; prisoners are victimized and raped. Then there are "model" prisons, well run, with more freedom and humanity. In theory at least, the kind of punishment experienced in prison should make a difference in both general and special deterrence.

Deterrence is a psychological concept, at bottom. It is a guess about the way people will react to certain expectations. It obviously varies with the individual. People do not all react alike. Punishment, for example, is stigmatic: it imposes shame. But the impact of stigma is quite variable. An arrest might ruin a respectable businessman for life. It might humiliate him to the point of suicide. On the other hand, a young, street-wise thief might accept arrest as a cost of doing business. These assumptions are at least plausible.

People today are rightly worried about crime. There is no question that the problem is serious; there is an explosion of crime in our society—robbery, burglary, even murder. There is also little doubt that the crime rate has taken a huge jump from about the time of the Second World War. This may, in fact, be more or less a worldwide trend; the crime rates in London, Stockholm, and Sydney, Australia, though much lower than ours, have also risen dramatically in this period, according to a careful study.[16]

What should be done about crime? For many people the solution is obvious: tighten the screws. Punishment deters; we need more punishment. The idea is simple and attractive. The question is, Can it, and should it, work?

For better or for worse, tightening the screws is more easily said than done. The legislature can try to toughen the system; but it cannot make punishments stick. The legislature does not catch or prosecute criminals, or carry out trials, or run the jails. The individual parts of the system can all frustrate each other. The system, to repeat, is like a leaky hose.

Evidence of this fact keeps mounting up. Malcolm Feeley, in his studies of reforms in criminal justice, found a record of repeated failure. Laurence Ross, in an interesting essay, analyzed studies of traffic crackdowns on speeders and drunk drivers; most of the crackdowns failed. When there is a move to control discretion at one point in the system, discretion simply shifts to another point: "The serpent held by one coil of his body may wriggle more energetically elsewhere."[17]

We can call this the problem of the "cadres." We talk as if a law or rule is a simple order which goes directly from some commander (the legislature, say) immediately to a subject—someone supposed to listen and obey. But in fact the process is rarely that simple, at least in our legal system. The process is more like chains of complex molecules. When the legislature orders longer jail sentences for drug pushers, it sends a message down the chain of command. The people in charge at each stage (the cadres) have the power to misunderstand, to pervert, to divert, to drag their feet, to frustrate the order. They may do this either consciously or unconsciously. It is a general problem of bureaucracy, and is especially severe in criminal justice because the system is so loose, so gangly, so uncoordinated.

There is another problem with "tightening the screws." The layman forgets that punishment can be self-defeating; it may have toxic side-effects. In theory, a vicious, brutal prison should do a better job of deterring than a "country club" prison; but it may also make inmates more criminal—more likely to commit crime when they get out. We frequently hear that juvenile halls and jails are schools for crime; if this is so, it is another side effect of harshness. Probation, after all, is not a school for crime.

The stigma and shame of a criminal record are also punishments, in theory, and should deliver extra deterrence. In practice this, too, does not quite work out. The stigma can close so many doors that the ex-con is forced back to crime. Elliott Currie, among others, has suggested an incentive system instead—basically, more and better jobs. This might produce results where extra toughness fails.[18]

The Deterrence Curve

Another point about rewards and punishments is worth making. We assume that if we jack up the threat of punishment, or punishment itself, we get some additional deterrent. That is, if we make a parking ticket $10 instead of $5, there will be less parking violation. Can we tell in advance how *much* less?

The simple answer is no. It depends on the social setting, the circumstances, who the people are. Even if we know all this, we have no way to predict the amount of deterrence that more punishment buys. One thing is clear: the relationship is not simple and linear. Doubling the fine does not double the effect. It may or may not. It may produce much more than double, or very much less. There is no known way to predict.

There are, however, typical patterns; and they seem to be more or less curvilinear. Suppose there is a $5 fine for parking overtime on Main Street; suppose the police catch one out of every three violators. Suppose, too, that half the drivers disobey the rules. They have two chances out of three of succeeding; and if they are caught, the fine is low. (Assume, to keep things simple, that the drivers know these facts.) What happens if enforcement stays the same, but we raise the fine to $50? Do we get ten times more compliance?

Almost certainly not. Half the drivers are already obeying, despite the pitiful fine. They are already deterred, or are law-abiding people for other reasons. We are concerned, in other words, with only half the drivers. They may be a tougher group.

Still, $50 is real money. We cannot expect ten times more results; but we do get improvement. Suppose now only one out of four parks overtime. Raising the fine to $100 would flush out a few more—but probably not many, since only hard-core cases are left. To get at this group, we might start towing cars away. This is a big leap forward. Overtime parkers now have to pay a big fine and run around the city to reclaim their cars—a colossal nuisance. Nonetheless, a towaway system brings about little change, because there are not many drivers left to deter. The curve has flattened out. If we try more severe punishments—taking away licenses or putting people in jail—we would get only piddling results. There are too few left to deter. At some point, the curve becomes almost perfectly flat.

Transfer this reasoning to a more serious crime, for example, rape. The punishment for rape, assuming most rapists are caught, is, let us say, five years in prison. This is already quite severe. Most men do not rape. Rapists are sick, violent people. There are only a few of them, compared to the general population. Morality and fear of heavy punishment already prevent most rape. Only a few people are left for new deterrence to work on. Some of these are hard-core cases—really sick men, who have trouble controlling their violent urges. If we double the punishment and make it stick, we get *some* fresh deterrent effect, but probably not very much. The curve has already flattened out. In theory, the effect of greater punishment will never be zero; but in practice, for some crimes, the effect is very close to zero. Whether we have reached that point with rape, for example, is a difficult question.

Capital Punishment

The debate about capital punishment is so loud and so passionate that it is worth spending a little more time on the subject. For many people, the basic issue is a moral one. They are against putting people to death, regardless of its effect on deterrence. Similarly, some people favor capital punishment regardless of evidence: they feel that killers deserve death as a matter of justice. But there is a large group in between, who would be for or against depending on whether the penalty worked.

Does fear of the gallows, the gas chamber, the electric chair, the firing squad, keep people from killing? (Murder is, practically speaking, the only capital crime left in this country.) Our homicide rate is scandalously high. We kill each other at a shocking rate—compared to the Japanese or the Belgians, for example. Moreover, the killing today is far greater than in the past. Violence may be as American as apple pie, but we go in for more pie than before. In Philadelphia, for example, in the years 1839–1901 only 3 persons per 100,000 were accused of criminal homicide each year. In 1969–71, however, 1,499 people were accused—a rate of 25.7 per 100,000.[19] Government statistics estimate there were about 8,000 homicide victims nationally in 1950, and more than 20,000 in 1978.[20] There are some problems with all of these figures; but the differences between time periods are so vast that there is no doubt about the general trend. We live in a golden age of murder.

Crime is a national scandal; yet the actual number of murderers is nonetheless quite small. It is not hard to think of reasons why—moral scruples, fear of revenge, and the likelihood of severe punishment, short of the death penalty. These are more than enough to keep most of us away from violent crime. The curve, in other words, has flattened out enormously. This means that the added bang which the death penalty might provide is apt to produce little fresh deterrence. In other words, a person can argue against the death penalty on many grounds—because of moral or social scruples or assumed side effects, but also because it may not work very well. It is not necessary to argue that the death penalty does not deter. This would be questionable in principle, and it skates on very thin empirical ice.

Most discussions of the death penalty are, in a way, unnecessarily abstract. They ignore the facts of this particular society. The death penalty may work efficiently in some societies, which use it quickly, mercilessly, and frequently. It cannot work well in the United States, where it is bound to be rare, slow, and controversial. This point gets lost in the shouting and the arguments.

To deter, a threat must be real. If we ticket an illegal parking spot once every thirty years, we cannot expect anybody to be afraid to park there. The death penalty is seldom used here, and it has gotten more and more uncommon here over the years. This means that it is probably a feeble extra deterrent. In order to pack more muscle, we would have to put it into effect reasonably often, though how often is not easy to say. But because it is so controversial, it is unlikely that this will ever take place in this country, at least in the foreseeable future.

A bit of history may illustrate this point. The death penalty was never as common in this country as in England and other countries. It was, to be sure, much more widespread at one time than now. At the time of the Revolution, people could be hung for dozens of crime; there were 113 separate offenses that carried the death penalty in South Carolina in 1813. By 1850, the list was down to 22.[21] The northern states were stingier with capital offenses. In practice, murder and rape were the only important crimes that carried the death penalty. As far back as the early nineteenth century, there was a movement to get rid of the death penalty. Some states—Wisconsin is one—have never had it at all.

A law on the books is one thing; actual hangings are another. Here, too, the South was more lavish with death penalties than the North. The chief victims were slaves. South Carolina put 296 slaves to death between 1800 and 1855—64 for murder, 46 for insurrection, 31 for burglary, 28 for assault, 17 for arson, 21 for poisoning, 17 for rape. (In 72 cases, the exact crime is unknown). By contrast, Massachusetts, with a white population twice as large as the black population of South Carolina, executed only 28 people between 1801 and 1845.[22] This is less than one a year.

Public opinion, especially in the past, is a slippery and elusive topic. There were of course no Gallup polls in the nineteenth century. But we do know something about the behavior of the system then, as well as the rhetoric of public debate. Behavior and rhetoric both suggest that support for the death penalty has suffered a long-term decline in America. The number of people actually put to death has gone down steadily. In the decade of the 1930s, 1,667 prisoners were executed. As late as 1951, there were 105 deaths from capital punishment. In 1966, there was only one. After that time, capital punishment almost, though not quite, ground to a halt.

The main reason was the success of the legal campaign against the death penalty. In 1972, in the famous case of *Furman* v. *Georgia*,[23] the Supreme Court dropped its bombshell. The Court struck down as unconstitutional every death law in the country, and made a clean sweep of death row. It was a startling decision and a close call: the majority was a bare five out of nine justices, and the decision was so fragmented that it was hard to tell exactly what was decided and why. In fact, every justice wrote a separate opinion.

A few justices felt that the death penalty was "cruel and unusual," or had somehow become cruel and unusual in the course of social evolution. This made capital punishment unconstitutional under the Eighth Amendment, in all circumstances. Most justices did not support this view. In fact, the majority—the five justices on the winning side—said all sorts of things, some contradicting the others. One basic theme was that there was too much discretion in the system. The death penalty was thus imposed in arbitrary, unpredictable, almost irrational ways. It also fell too heavily on black people, on underdogs, on the unpopular. Some justices argued that it was a poor deterrent, or that it was immoral, or that enlightened public opinion had turned against it, and so on.

Some of these arguments rest on empirical assertions—statements of fact—at least in part. For example, is it really true that the death penalty offends "enlightened" public opinion? Of course, there is no standard for judging what is and what is not "enlightened." What is "enlightened" to one person is foolish or bigoted to another. At any rate, only one thing was clear after *Furman:* capital punishment was dead—for the time being.

It did not stay dead. The soaring crime rate breathed new life into it. Public opinion (enlightened or otherwise) apparently turned. Capital punishment began to do better in public opinion polls. Most state legislatures showed their disagreement with *Furman* in the most direct possible way: they passed new death laws. They had to take account of *Furman*, and they tried to write less offensive statutes. In this sense, at least, the decision was a powerful force. But it failed to put the issue to rest.

In 1976, the Supreme Court decided a new batch of cases on the
death penalty. The lead case was *Gregg* v. *Georgia*.[24] In many ways,
the results were just as chaotic as *Furman's*. The Court split badly,
and the justices wrote many separate opinions, ranging all over the
lot. The court ruled on several new kinds of statute. It accepted some
and struck down others. Most of the justices were not willing to go
the last step and destroy the death penalty absolutely and finally and
under all circumstances. Beyond this, the law is still quite murky.
Later decisions have not cleared up the murk.

Meanwhile, legislatures have not been idle either. The issue is
still alive and very active politically. In many states, new statutes are
passed in every session. Governors veto some bills. Some vetoes are
overridden. There are endless court cases. More and more prisoners
sit on death row. Few are put to death; blizzards of suits, claims,
writs, and petitions pile up delay after delay. Meanwhile, since 1976
and up to the time of this writing (1984), more than a dozen people
have been executed, starting with Gary Gilmore in Utah, who (at the
end) had given up the struggle. The sixth, Charles Brooks, was executed in Texas in December 1982, by lethal injection, a novel mode
of execution. The pace quickened a bit in 1983 and 1984, and some
observers expect the harvest of executions to increase in the future.

Forces on both sides are strong and dedicated. The death penalty
is a rallying cry for "law-and-order" people. Determined enemies of
capital punishment fight them at every step of the way. The result is
a kind of stalemate. The death penalty is still law in most of the states;
but it is not common, and not easy to carry out. Nobody can be put
to death smoothly or quickly, no matter how vicious he is, how hei-
nous his crime. In the 1950s, it was already possible to hold the exe-
cutioner off for years; legal moves seemed almost endless. A famous
instance was the case of Caryl Chessman. Chessman was sentenced
to die in California on May 21, 1948. Not until twelve years later, in
May 1960, did he lose his final hope and die in the gas chamber.

Today, there are dozens of Chessmans—men who have spent years
(some a decade or more) on death row, fighting their fate. The end of
the torture, one way or another, is still in doubt for almost all of them.
But meanwhile this number continues to grow. Over a thousand prisoners have the death penalty hanging over their heads. They wait and
fight in court.

In a real sense there *is* no death penalty in the United States
anymore, not in a form that the Founding Fathers would recognize.
What we have is a half-dead penalty, which is tied up in so many

knots because of controversy that it is hard to see how it can ever be unraveled. A death penalty of this sort is surely not much of a deterrent compared to a genuine life sentence—that is, life without possibility of parole. A real death penalty—one that worked, one that had a strong effect on criminal behavior—would have to be more certain and more swift.

But there seems little chance of such a death penalty now. The opposition is still quite strong. Too many people (including judges and juries) find the death penalty awesome, frightening, extreme. No doubt many people who tell pollsters they favor the death penalty would shrink from it on an actual jury. Our tradition of due process, whatever its deficiencies, stands in the way of any "quick and dirty" solutions. Would anybody deny careful review and appeal to a person sentenced to death?

The situation, then, is confused, uncertain, endlessly complex—and as a result, frustrating to both sides of the argument. Both sides grumble and complain, and no wonder: neither side can, for the moment, win a meaningful and decisive victory. Yet this situation reflects current social reality. Society is of two minds on the subject. The law faithfully mirrors public hesitation, disagreement, and doubt, just as it reflects its deeper convictions.

The death penalty is an extreme example of a more general issue in deterrence theory; and it also points up problems in the plan, so popular today, to make the legal system more effective by toughening its spirit. Many scholars have worked on deterrence theory in recent years. They tend to agree that deterrence is no humbug: if we jack up real penalties, we will definitely scare away a certain number of customers, just as a price rise would scare off some buyers. In the real world, this is a mighty big *if*. "Severity" is easier said than done. The system is too complex to move easily and quickly. Severe laws can be controversial (like the death penalty); they may produce nasty, unwanted side effects. All of this makes deterrence hard to measure and hard to predict, and also hard to harness and control.

12

Legal Culture: Legitimacy and Morality

*N*OT ALL LEGAL behavior can be explained in terms of reward and punishment. To some extent, we are indeed animals that respond to the carrot and the stick. But we are also moral and social beings. Moral and social factors—motives from inside and the messages we get from other people—are important in explaining how we respond to legal acts. They may, in fact, be more important than rewards and punishments.

The social factor is of primary importance. Reduced to its simplest form, this means that people care what other people think. No man or woman is an island. We are all powerfully influenced by other people in our lives: family, friends, neighbors, coworkers, fellow students, members of our church. All of us feel their silent and not-so-silent pressure. This pressure may push us to obey the law or to disobey, or to use the law in particular, patterned ways.

There has been much talk, for example, about the influence of peer groups—a phrase that refers, basically, to the people around us, the people we consider to be our group (*peers* means "equals"). We know from everyday experience that the group has a tremendous influence. Such a term as *delinquent subculture,* for example, is merely an elegant way to express a simple idea. The point is this: it is a kind of punishment if your friends taunt you, laugh at you, treat you as inferior; it is a real and strong reward when they admire you and praise you. If you belong to some big-city gang whose code gives high marks to macho behavior—breaking the law, acting tough, defying the police—but gives low marks if you tattle or are "yellow" or refuse to go along with some illegal caper, you are more likely to violate laws than other people who are not gang members. This is because breaking the laws in your case represents conformity to group norms; and if you conform to *official* norms—that is, act "good"—you are breaking the law of your group.

Even outside the gang context, we can use similar ideas to help account for delinquency: the adolescent chooses rebellion because it "allows conformity to the standards of an alternate social system," which (for a number of reasons) suit his psychological and other needs more than the mainstream system.[1] And the delinquency label, when it is pinned on an adolescent, only serves to isolate him from respectable society and makes it more likely that his real rewards will come from the members of his group, and only from them.

There is nothing startling, then, in all this, either as theory or as practice. Everybody likes to be rewarded and practically everybody wants to avoid punishment; a whipping is a whipping whether it comes from the state or from the people next door. The groups we belong to are, in a way, miniature societies, with tiny "governments" and "laws" of their own. If we follow gang norms instead of the norms of the "real" government, we are in a way simply choosing among competing rulers. Very often, the scarier and more threatening government is the one that sits on your doorstep. After all, for most people, it may be easier to avoid or evade a policeman than to get out from under disapproval (or worse) coming from friends, neighbors, or parents. And in many prisons, gang leaders are more effective rulers of the prisoners than the warden or guards.

This much seems fairly obvious, though there is not much research directly relevant. It is sometimes possible to show how other people influence legal behavior. Johannes Feest, for example, did a little study of traffic behavior in Berkeley, California. His study showed that people drive one way when they are alone, quite another when other people sit next to them. Among drivers who were alone, only one out of ten came to a full stop at a stop sign; when someone shared the car with the driver, full stops rose to 21 percent.[2]

In other words, people do not obey traffic rules only because they are afraid of the police. They also respond to the person sitting next to them—to what that person thinks and feels, what that person says about the driver's behavior. Some of us will go through a red light late at night, with nobody around and nobody with us, but would never do the same by day, police or no police.

Feest gathered his data by sitting in a parked car and watching how drivers behaved. He did not talk to the drivers, and we do not know who the other people were who influenced the driver. No doubt they were relatives or friends. A study by Lionel Dannick, however, suggests that even a stranger can affect behavior, simply by being nearby. Dannick did research on pedestrians in New York City. Pedestrians often crossed the street illegally, that is, when the sign said "Don't walk." But if the experimenters planted somebody to stand on the corner and cross only when the sign said "Walk," the rate of violation dropped dramatically. Contrariwise, when the "plant" clearly broke the rule, the rate of violation went up.[3] Violators, in other words, "reinforce" other violators; and compliers do the same.[4]

We have to draw a distinction, of course, between the effect of other people on our own behavior and the effect of our own ideas about right and wrong. Of course, what we see when we stand on the corner or peek out from a parked car is people's behavior; their motives are invisible. Why is it that somebody stops himself from jaywalking, when he sees other people who obey the rule? Perhaps he wants to avoid embarrassment, and of course it is embarrassing if people see you breaking rules. But the "good" people are also teachers, of a sort: they show us that the rule is alive, that it means something to them, that they choose (for whatever reason) not to break it. That may influence the way we feel about the rule.

The point, in other words, is that peer pressure (or other messages from the crowd) may in the long run change our thoughts as well as our behavior. The civil rights laws have forced hotels and restaurants to open their doors to people of all races; there was a time when many of them—and not only in the South—refused to let black people in. The fact that these hotels and restaurants must not discriminate does not in itself change bigots to nonbigots; the owners may still feel the same way about race. But coercion creates a new situation—it changes public behavior—and when this happens, real or imagined peer pressure may start to work on people's minds. A segregated restaurant first becomes illegal, then impossible, and finally unthinkable. At that point, the battle against Jim Crow restaurants is over for good.

Legitimacy and Morality

To state explicitly what has been assumed so far, and what is plain common sense: ideas about right and wrong, about morality, about legitimacy, are very important in explaining how people behave. Most of us (one hopes) would not steal, cheat, murder, or set fire to buildings, whether or not there was any chance the police would catch us and whether or not there was any chance that peers would find out and disapprove. We would do the right thing because we want to, because of the voice inside, because we have been taught to avoid evil deeds and this lesson took.

The penal code, in other words, is not the only source—or even the main source—of ideas about right and wrong. We learn the moral code from our parents and teachers, and we drink in ideas simply by living in society. Every community has its own definitions of right and wrong, and every community has its own way of imparting them to members. Ideas of right and wrong are constantly changing; and it is interesting to watch them shift, bend, and change colors. Some norms (about killing and stealing) are very stable, of course; others (about sexual behavior, for example) seem much more changeable.

In any event, our consciences are powerful motors. Most of us want to do what is right, and if this means obeying the law, then we will obey. Conversely, there may be times when people feel strongly that the law is wrong or immoral. Conscience can lead to disobedience as well as obedience. There are many examples in our history. People have often gone to jail as a matter of conscience. In protest against the war in Vietnam, for example, many men refused to register for the draft. It was a way to oppose what they felt was an immoral war; they were willing to suffer punishment rather than obey.

We obey—and want to obey—what is *right*, and also what is *legitimate*. These two words do not mean the same thing. Social scientists and legal scholars—at least since the days of Max Weber, the great German sociologist—talk a great deal about *legitimate* rules and about *legitimacy* in general. But the words are not always used very precisely, and there are many definitions floating about in the literature. The imprecision is so great that at least one scholar, Alan Hyde, feels that the whole concept should be junked as useless and confusing.[5] Of course, no single definition of legitimacy is right or wrong, but the concept still strikes us as having a core of value. Basically, when people say that laws are "legitimate," they mean that there is something rightful about the way in which the laws came about. Legitimacy is mostly used as a procedural concept, in other words—or, if you will, a legal one.

An example will make this clear. What makes a law passed by Congress "legitimate"? Not what is *in* the law—that might be foolish, shortsighted, or deficient in all sorts of ways. No, the law is legitimate because Congress passed it; for most of us that is enough in itself. In other words, we do not question the legitimacy of a law so long as it was regularly passed by Congress or a state legislature or a city council.

We can push this idea further, and ask *why* a law passed by Congress is legitimate. If we put this question to people, they might answer with something like this: because Congress is elected in free elections, or because the law is what the majority wants. Very few members of the public have thought deeply about political theory; but they do have vague, commonsense ideas floating around in their heads. In any case, the legitimacy of law rests on the way it comes to be: if that is legitimate, then so are the results, at least most of the time. And what is true for legislative bodies is also true for actions of the president, rules of the Seattle school board, and decisions of the supreme court of Arkansas: all are legitimate insofar as the public accepts them as part of the normal, rightful way of doing public business.

The binding force of these legal acts comes, then, from the procedure or from the institution, not from what the acts do or say. Obeying a rule because it is legitimate is not at all the same as obeying it because it is moral or ethical, or even because it is fair. In fact, we should probably distinguish carefully between various ways in which a rule or act can be "right." People in their legal behavior do follow the voice of conscience. But conscience is a complicated organ; its voice is made up of many tones.

Legitimacy is only one of these factors of conscience. Another we can call "civic-mindedness." This is the notion that we ought to obey some rules for social or patriotic reasons. Civic-minded people are willing to take fewer showers and let their lawns die if there is a water shortage; they enlist in the army during wartime; they resist the impulse to throw beer cans on the trail in Yellowstone; they pay taxes on time and in full. For some people, this is a powerful impulse, even in situations where there is no chance violators will get caught and no peers are around to wag their fingers. For others, of course, such a motive is weak or absent.

"Morality," strictly speaking, is a somewhat different motive. This may perhaps be the most powerful and important factor of all: obedience to rules for moral or religious reasons. It is our moral training that explains why most of us do not cheat, steal, murder, or lie. It is why Mormons refuse to drink, why Jews refrain from eating pork, why Catholics do not divorce. The normative structure of society is as important as its political structure, and just as essential.

"Fairness" is still another concept. Sometimes I might feel that a rule deserves support because of some purely formal characteristic—for example, because it affects everybody in the country, and why should I be different? If the government imposed a five-dollar tax on every man, woman, and child, some people might decide to pay because they felt it was only fair to do so, whether or not they thought the tax made sense, was morally sound, or good for the country. Still another conscience factor is what we might call "trust." This is the feeling that we should go along with some rule or order because of faith in the authorities. They know so much, and we know so little. If they tell us to do something, they must have a good reason; and we should go along, whether we understand the reasons or not. If the government says a fifty-five-mile speed limit saves gas and saves lives, then that must be true.

These factors are all different from legitimacy, and they are all motives for obeying or disobeying law. Motives are invisible; but motives or attitudes are social facts as much as behavior is. What people think is as real as what they eat and how they vote or swim, only harder to observe or to measure. Like all attitudes, these are not poured in concrete. They change over time. Different ages and types of people have them in different degrees; and they also rise and fall with the social tides.

Many people feel, for example, that trust is in short supply today. Studies have suggested that people have been getting more cynical. They are less likely than before to say that they believe the authorities. One study asked people "How much of the time do you think that you can trust the government in Washington to do what is right?" In 1964, 14 percent said "always"; 62 percent said "most of the time"; only 22 percent said "only some of the time." Six years later, in 1970, only 6 percent trusted the government "always"; 47 percent said "most of the time"; the doubters who said "only some of the time" had risen to 44 percent.[6]

Trust probably declined even further after 1970. It is hard to know how much; but most observers sense a definite loss of confidence in government, and in experts and authorities of all sorts, though perhaps in the last year or two there has been a slight upturn. In California in 1981, the governor of the state (after much controversy) gave an order for aerial spraying of pesticides on parts of northern California. The problem was the insidious medfly, whose larvae threatened to chew the fruit industry to death. The public was told that the spray was harmless, that there was nothing to fear. A generation earlier, almost everybody would have accepted this as gospel; it was the governor's word and the word of the scientists employed by the state. In 1981, many people simply refused to believe; some people left the area in panic; blind faith was in short supply.

What follows from a loss of trust? Will distrustful, dissatisfied people break the law? Not necessarily. People can comply even if they are dissatisfied with the system.[7] There is some reason to be skeptical about the so-called spillover effect. This is the hypothesis that people who think one part of the legal system is unfair or illegitimate, or who do not trust it in one regard, will disobey or lose faith in the rest of it.

In a way, this seems plausible. People frequently make this point about laws that are badly or unfairly enforced; they claim that this leads to disrespect for law in general. Supposedly, this was a side effect of Prohibition. We hear the same argument about marijuana. In fact, there is little or no evidence for the "spillover" effect. If you think the marijuana laws are unfair or ridiculous, are you more likely to cheat on your income tax, park overtime, or shoot your brother-in-law? It seems unlikely. There may be spillover into "neighboring" areas of legal behavior: a person with contempt for marijuana laws may be more likely than others to use cocaine or break the liquor laws. A dope pusher will hardly shy away from illegal gambling. But we are not sure how far these "neighborhoods" extend.

It is logical to assume some connection between the way we behave and what we think about the moral status of law. In one classic study, Harry V. Ball studied landlords in Honolulu. The city was under rent control at the time. Ball found that landlords who thought rent control was unfair tended to act accordingly: these were the landlords who overcharged their tenants.[8]

This shows *some* relationship between attitude and behavior. But exactly what relationship? We have a chicken-and-egg puzzle here. Which comes first, the moral attitude, or the lawbreaking? The sense of unfairness may be one way a landlord soothes his conscience. Ball assumes the sense of unfairness led landlords down the path to lawbreaking; but the causation might go the other way around: landlords who violated came to excuse themselves by blaming bad law. The Honolulu data do not show which way the causal arrows point.

The Inverse Factors

We have discussed a variety of inner motives for legal behavior— morality, fairness, trust, civic-mindedness, legitimacy. Each of them, as the discussion implies, also has its opposite: mistrust, illegitimacy, a sense of unfairness, and so on. We assume that the more we make people think of a law as moral, trustworthy, and legitimate, the more likely it is that they will comply. Similarly, an increase in a sense of a law's unfairness or illegitimacy should weaken the feeling of duty, leading to less obedience (or none) or—if the moral feelings are strong enough—to actual defiance or revolt.

This is plain common sense. It is confirmed by experience as well. At this time (1984), the law requires young men to register for the draft. Many feel strongly that the law is wrong for one reason or another, and they refuse to register. Some men have openly defied the law. In our society, there are legitimate ways to express these feelings. There was a challenge to the draft law in court, for example; it failed. Failure to register is a stronger and more dangerous statement of opposition. Those who oppose nuclear power from civic motives, and who distrust the government, have used tactics that range from sullen acceptance to acts of sabotage.

The spillover effect, then, is most uncertain. Loss of faith is not necessarily across-the-board. When people become disgusted or mistrustful toward one law or one part of government, they do not necessarily turn outlaw. A few do; many do not. Some people turn to other avenues for expressing dissent. These may be, and often are, legal channels. Thus there is a *transfer* of legitimacy. People who lose faith in Congress, city hall, or the bureaucracies may turn to the courts, for example. That is, they "judicialize" their problems.

In the medfly crisis in California, the state government announced it would spray a pesticide (malathion) over the counties near San Francisco Bay. They assured the public that malathion was safe. The spraying (they said) had to be done; the alternative was a horrendous economic calamity. Some people, of course, believed every word of this. Many people did not. Was the government lying, to protect big fruitgrowers at the expense of the citizen?

As it happens, the spraying went off as planned. The opposition did not take this lying down. They went to court. This is a common strategy for the disgruntled; in many cases, it is almost the only one. It is the way the battle against capital punishment is carried on. As the malathion case shows, the strategy does not always work (the case was lost), but it can at least achieve delay. The battle against nuclear power plants goes on and on; court tactics make nuclear power more costly through delay and through obstructive measures that are all perfectly legal, though sometimes extremely legalistic. The enemies of the death penalty, too, count on delay. They try measure after measure to keep the men on death row alive.

Yet in one sense much of this (paradoxically) implies more trust, not less—trust in the courts. The Sierra Club and the other environmental groups would not waste time and money on litigation if they were cynical about court systems, or if they trusted the courts as little as they trust the secretary of the interior. The trend toward judicialization is a sign of a loss of legitimacy and trust with regard to government in general. It is also a sign of a transfer or shift of legitimacy to courts.

Legitimacy and Conscience
as Force

How strong are our feelings of legitimacy or trust, or conscience in general? Common sense tells us that we have more attachment to some norms than to others. Most of us would not kill except in dire emergency, if then; but we are nonchalant about breaking the speed limit. These differences make it hard to say much, in general, about how people resolve conflicts among the various motives for legal behavior. Everything depends on the circumstances, the situation, and the particular rule. People who feel that speeding is dangerous and antisocial, and who are afraid of the police, are still willing to go seventy miles per hour if the situation is serious enough.

If sanctions, the people around us, and our inner feelings all pull in the same direction, then the norm will be tough and durable indeed. This is basically the case with norms against killing. The law takes murder very seriously and punishes it severely. Conscience is against it, too; and neighbors and friends share the general revulsion against killing. Hence this norm is one of the strongest known.

It is not easy to go much beyond this simple point. Suppose conscience pulls one way and the law pulls another: who wins? Is the threat of punishment more powerful than appeal to conscience? There is no general answer. An occasional researcher has tried to study the question experimentally. In one such project, two researchers used college students in Florida as their guinea pigs. The students were allowed to grade their own quizzes in a course. Without the students' knowledge, the teachers were able to check the scores against self-graded ones and find out how much cheating was going on. Quite a bit, it turned out. Some students were then threatened with spot-checks and punishment; this cut down cheating considerably. Others were given a moral pep-talk. This hardly worked at all. Punishment was much more powerful than conscience.[9]

But this hardly proves the general case. In fact, the general case is unprovable, because the term *punishment* does not refer to a single, constant factor and neither does the term *conscience*. There are many types of conscience, and many ways to try to evoke conscience. They cannot be summed up in a single formula. Sometimes in the midst of a war appeals for sacrifice have been tremendously successful; and many people have been willing to die for their country. At other times and under other circumstances, moral appeals and sermons simply fall on deaf ears. Wage-price guidelines, for example, have often been dismal failures; they need strong sanctions to back them up.

Also, sanctions come in all shapes and sizes, from money rewards to fines, jail, whipping, and even the gallows. Some sanctions terrify us; some have very little bite. Some incentives are strong and some are weak. Again, much depends on the circumstances.

The Florida study, then, could not provide a general answer to the question, since it pitted only one sort of moral appeal against one sort of sanction. We do not know what happens when there is conflict between state sanctions and private conscience, between conscience and the pull and tug of group loyalty, between peer pressure and the government. Conflicts of this kind are everyday occurrences. Nothing is more common than to find ourselves in the middle, torn between a feeling that we ought to obey (or disobey) the law and contradictory messages coming from the people around us or from government. There are no rules on how to resolve these conflicts, and there are no general research findings that tell us how people do resolve them.

Civil disobedience is an important social fact in our history. Civil disobedience is an open challenge to law, but one based on principle. A person who civilly disobeys does not deny that the laws he attacks are formally valid. But he feels that they are so repulsive morally or so harmful to society that the citizen has a higher duty to disobey. The higher duty may be grounded in religion. The Mormons in Utah in the nineteenth century believed that God permitted and encouraged men to have several wives. The idea was enormously offensive to the rest of the country; but the Mormons stuck to their guns and defied the authorities until their church itself retracted. The Boston Tea Party, the abolitionist movement, civil rights, draft protests—the historical record is full of examples of civil disobedience. Some of it has been extremely effective in changing the law or in teaching the larger society a moral lesson. It is enough to mention Martin Luther King and the black protest movements of the 1950s and 1960s.

Civil disobedience is not always nonviolent. The Boston Tea Party destroyed private property. John Brown was willing to kill in his crusade against slavery. However, there is no question that nonviolence adds strength to civil disobedience. This was the lesson taught by Mahatma Gandhi in India, and applied since then in many countries. One reason is that nonviolence expresses, in a particularly dramatic way, the morality of civil disobedience. It expressly denies any spillover effect. It is a way of saying, We object to *this* law, but not to law in general. The protesters in fact are deeply committed to order, justice, and organized society. But they assert, with their words and their body language, that there exists one exceptional case of official law that is too morally corrupt to survive.

Law and Morality

We often hear talk about the conflict between law and morals. Many writers stress how different law is from morality, and how much the legal code differs from the moral code. Others insist that law cannot be separated from morality, or even that unjust rules or an unjust regime cannot be law. There are complex and fascinating issues here, which are at the core of the philosophy of law.[10]

The relationship between legal codes and the moral norms and customs of society—and specifically, of United States society—is a simpler, less normative issue. It is obvious that the law embodies a moral code, and does so explicitly. The law books of any state and of the federal government—and of other countries, too—make this point in the most elementary way. Murder, theft, rape, and income tax fraud are immoral—and illegal as well.

But every complicated society (and ours is certainly complicated) has more than a single moral code: it has many different ones. People disagree, sometimes quite bitterly, about which code should prevail and how to deal with competing moral norms. Some disagreements over norms can be compromised; or the norms can be treated as equal. The law, for example, is neutral on the subject of religion, by and large. It does not require anyone to practice any faith. In many societies there were, or are, state religions; and those who hold unorthodox beliefs and follow unorthodox practices are persecuted, sometimes to the point of death.

But in other situations, neutrality is impossible. The law cannot be both for or against something at the same time. This means that conflicts arise continually between law and morals, or rather between law and the morals of some part of the population. The polygamy dispute was one example. Before the Civil War, abolitionists clashed with those who defended slavery. There have been innumerable other examples.

One of the most poignant instances today is the abortion controversy. The Supreme Court, in *Roe* v. *Wade*,[11] held that the Constitution, our highest law, protects a woman's right to have an abortion, at least in the early months of pregnancy. The Court struck down state laws that interfered with this right. Many people feel *Roe* v. *Wade* was a wise, just, and—yes—moral decision. But many people were outraged. To them, abortion is nothing more or less than murder and any law that permits it permits the worst possible crime, the slaughter of an innocent being. Obviously, these believers in the "right to life" cannot accept the present law, which goes against their own moral code. "Prochoice" people, on the other hand, believe just as strongly in the justice of their cause—in the sanctity of a woman's right to control her own body.

There is a sense, however, in which law and morality clash, even without sharp differences of opinion of this sort. Most of us would probably agree that it is wrong to tell lies or to cheat at cards. Neither of these is a crime; neither is found in the penal code. Some lies are so gross or harmful that they may amount to slander, and card-cheating may, under some circumstances, amount to fraud; but these are exceptional situations. Why does the law leave lying and cheating alone? Why not at least a small fine? Is overtime parking really worse than cheating at poker or bridge?

Perhaps these examples prove that law and morality are different spheres and have different aims. But there is another explanation, too. If we made card-cheating a crime, we might set off some nasty consequences. People might start informing on other people. We would give great discretion and power to police if we let them arrest people for lying. We would open the door to blackmail and corruption. We might punish people beyond what they deserve.

Notice that these are all statements about morality. In other words, when "immoral" acts are left out of the penal code it is not because of some inherent difference between law and morality, but because there are many competing moral principles and we have to make choices among them. These are real choices; and society makes them all the time, though not always correctly, by any means. The Mann Act[12] made it a federal crime to "transport" a woman across state lines "for the purpose of prostitution or debauchery, or for any other immoral purpose." This law was supposed to help stamp out "white slavery": the practice of forcing women into the degrading status of prostitution. The act probably had no impact on prostitution. It probably did open the door to blackmail, which is another evil, and a serious one.

The legal system is based on social norms; it has to be. It reflects principles and ideas which fit ideas about morality held somewhere in society. But not necessarily by everybody. Morality is an abstraction. Debates and conflicts are hard, specific, concrete—about abortion, the death penalty, polygamy; about drug laws, gambling, pornography, the military draft, prostitution. The list is long and the struggle is hard. But the issue is not whether or not the law should enforce morality. Of course it should; it must. The issue is, *Whose* morality, and how?

To put it another way: in a complex, pluralistic society—a society made of up all sorts, shapes, and tastes of people, with many ways of life—how far should the legal system go in upholding a single, official moral code? Many people would answer rather quickly, "Not far at all." We should live and let live. An open, democratic society can and should tolerate different ways of life.

Not everybody, of course, would agree with this philosophy. In fact, nobody agrees with it entirely. After all, there are people whose personal moral code allows or even requires them to rob banks, burn buildings, and skyjack planes "for the cause." Even the Ku Klux Klan or the American Nazi party has "principles," which the rest of us find repulsive. We see no reason for the legal system to accommodate these views, aside from the rights of free speech; and there is no reason why we should.

On the other hand, a live-and-let-live philosophy will accommodate a range of viewpoints—a variety of beliefs, opinions, and styles of life. It is not a case of *one* code of norms, or else infinity. The issue is not that general. Victimless crime, for example, is at least in part an issue of minority rights. Our legal system is based on the idea of limits: the majority has moral and physical power, but the wishes and needs of minorities must be protected, too. Where are the limits? No one can say. But many of the most strident conflicts today turn on issues of the "social revolution," which is considered in Chapter 14.

13

The American Legal Profession

*T*HE AMERICAN LEGAL profession is the largest in the world, in absolute numbers. It may also be the largest in the world in proportion to population. There are over 600,000 lawyers practicing in the United States. The growth of this profession, what lawyers do (and don't do), and the professional ethics and practices of the bar cannot be ignored, then, in any discussion of the nature of American law.

The American Bar: A Thumbnail Historical Sketch

There was a time, long ago—a golden age, if you will—when there were very few lawyers in what is now the United States. In some colonies, especially those dominated by the clergy, there was a good deal of hostility to lawyers. It may or may not be significant that Plymouth Colony, in the seventeenth century, expelled its first lawyer, Thomas Morton, for various "misdemeanors," including trading with the Indians, drinking to excess, and other "beastly practices."[1]

Yet the lawyers found a niche for themselves, despite their unpopularity, as they would do time and time again. By the eighteenth century, they had become quite indispensable in a country whose lifeline was the sea and which depended heavily on its trade with the West Indies and its mother country. Wherever there is business, trade, or dealings with government, the American lawyer plays a role. After Independence, the legal profession took a quantum leap in size. There were only 15 lawyers in Massachusetts in 1740, serving a population of about 150,000. In 1840, a century later, there were 640 lawyers, ten times as many in ratio to the population. The big push came after the Revolution.[2]

What was true in this one state was no doubt true in other states as well. In the nineteenth century lawyers increased far faster than population. Sometime before 1900, their numbers crossed the 100,000 mark. In the twentieth century, and especially in recent years, growth has been even more explosive. Betwen 1960 and 1970, the number of lawyers increased by about a third; new admissions to the bar grew by an astonishing 91 percent between 1970 and 1975.[3] About 40,000 new lawyers a year are added to the swarm. The total number of lawyers may have doubled in the last twenty years or so. From 1920 to 1970, there was about one lawyer for every 750 people in the country; in 1980, there was about one for every 440 people.[4] If this trend continues, the whole country might in the end consist of lawyers. Fortunately, that day is a long way off.

Where are these lawyers, what are they up to, and what kinds of work do they do? They are mostly in big cities, mostly in private practice, mostly handling the affairs of business firms. Some private practitioners are "solos," who work by themselves. Others work in law firms as partners or as "associates," lawyers who work for the partners on salary and hope to "make partner" some day. A smaller number of lawyers work as "house counsel." That is, they are lawyers on the payroll of one particular company. They are lawyers with a single client, their company. The number of these lawyers also seems to be growing fast. In 1951, there were 11,000 house counsel; in 1979, 50,000.[5] AT&T had 895 lawyers on its payroll in 1981; Exxon had 454; General Electric, 340.[6] Governments—state, federal, and local—also hire thousands of lawyers. Other members of the bar have jobs related to law, but not quite of it: these include insurance claims adjusters and FBI agents. A few lawyers teach, or write about law. Judges are lawyers, or rather ex-lawyers. And, of course, some lawyers never quite make it, or choose not to; they dribble out of the profession into business, real estate, or insurance, or even further afield.

The work habits, life-style, and collective behavior of lawyers has, naturally, changed a good deal over the years. Nowadays, most lawyers never see the inside of a courtroom. They give advice and, if possible, keep clients out of litigation. In the early nineteenth century, lawyers' work centered much more on the courtroom than today. Judges in many parts of the country "rode circuit." That is, they went from county seat to county seat, hearing cases. Lawyers traveled along with them. Abraham Lincoln rode circuit in Illinois.

In such a system, bench and bar formed a cozy little unit. The lawyer had no clients "on retainer." He picked up clients as he went along, if he was lucky. When he came to town, the lawyer would perhaps scarcely have a chance to get down from his horse when two or three clients who wanted his services might rush up. A good lawyer, with a quick mind and aggressive tactics, could earn a reputation on circuit and get clients and business this way.[7]

The traveling lawyer, of course, had no time or place to do research, few books, and no staff of clerks to help him. His brains and his mouth were his assets. Speeches to the jury were important; a silver tongue was a definite advantage. The most famous lawyers in the first half of the nineteenth century were those known as great orators. Daniel Webster was one of these talker-lawyers. In the higher courts, speeches might go on for hours, even days. Alexander Hamilton argued for six hours before a New York court in Albany, in a criminal libel case (1804). In the *Dartmouth College* case (1818), Daniel Webster spoke on behalf of the college for three to five hours; his speech, especially its ending, has gone into legend. According to one account (probably exaggerated), the audience "dissolved in tears"; when Webster finished, the whole courtroom was so overcome with emotion that for a while no one could speak.[8]

Some courtroom speeches have come down to us; by modern standards, they seem flowery and overblown. But in those days before radio and television, speeches were entertainment; they were also the key to a lawyer's reputation. With his oratory, he could catch the eye and ear of potential clients.

Lawyers of course were more than orators. Law was a job for quick, clever people—young men with good heads on their shoulders, who knew their way around. Law was an easy profession to get into. Lawyers scrambled for any kind of work they could get. They searched titles; they defended petty criminal cases; they collected debts. They oozed into any crack or cranny of the business world they could find. They bought land and sold land, on their own or for investors. George Gale, a Vermont lawyer who settled in Trempealeau County, Wisconsin, in 1851, "acted as a kind of real estate broker . . . as a one-man mortgage company . . . as a collection or serving agent on the lands."[9] Lawyers also went into politics, and took political jobs when they could. They were all over Congress, the statehouses, the county seats, the city halls.

Even before the Civil War, of course, not all lawyers were cast in the mold of Abraham Lincoln—country lawyers who rode from town to town on horseback. There were rich, established lawyers in big cities, harvesting the commercial practice of the seaports. Alexander Hamilton, in the years around 1800, was one of these lawyers. He dealt, for example, with problems of marine insurance—policies written on ships and cargo. This lucrative work, with its tang of salt water and money, was worlds apart from the petty land deals and debt collecting that were staple work for the prairie lawyers.[10]

A few lawyers, as early as the first half of the nineteenth century, avoided the courtroom altogether. They specialized in book work, office work, business planning. After the Civil War, the rise of big business created new legal demands, and hungry lawyers rushed to fill them. In this period, from roughly 1870 on, the "Wall Street lawyer" came into prominence. This new breed of lawyer had a new style of work. Practice and professional life revolved around clients, mostly businesses and businessmen, not around judges and fellow lawyers.

It was a natural process. Business needed skilled hands to solve the thousand and one legal problems that confronted them. A big company like Standard Oil or Sears Roebuck or United States Steel, as it traveled the road from shop or store to interstate giant, had the greatest needs of all. In this country, only lawyers had the necessary skills. The legal problems of a large enterprise are continuous. Lawyers for big business are not hired for this case or that; rather, they are kept on retainer.

The great enterprises were willing to pay well, and they wanted to stay out of court. They wanted their counsel to know their business inside and out; they wanted to steer a clear course among the reefs and shoals of the law and the hazards of competition. Lawyers were valuable to big business, not because of any gift of gab, but because they were shrewd at business deals, creative in drawing up papers, nimble at finance and the securities market, sophisticated about government and rules. Railroad receiverships, deeds of trust, municipal bond issues—none of these had the glamor of a murder trial, or the homely interest of a suit to replevy a horse. But Wall Street was built on these drab, essential pillars of paper, sweat, and guile.

Daniel Webster and Alexander Hamilton worked by and for themselves. The Wall Street lawyer worked, more and more, in partnership. Before the Civil War, there were a few two-man firms. Once in a while, the partners tended to specialize: one acted as the courtroom man; the other as the office or inside man. After the war, there was a slow expansion of firms. By 1900 or so, all major cities had firms of some size. New York, of course, led the way. The firm of Carter, Hughes and Dwight listed fourteen lawyers in *Hubbell's Legal Directory* for 1903—eight partners and six associates. Sullivan and Cromwell had ten lawyers on its payroll. The biggest firm in Denver, Colorado, was Dines and Whitted—two lawyers and three associates. In Chicago, two firms had seven lawyers each.

Size carried definite advantages. One man could have only so much knowledge and skill. A large bank or steel mill needed more than one man could provide: a firm could better cover the relevant aspects of law. And only a firm was likely to have manpower and brainpower enough to cope with a major bond issue, or merge two giant businesses, or reorganize a sprawling network of railroads.

It was almost as if a hormone was at work on the legal profession, pushing the growth of firms. The process continues. In the 1960s, according to one survey, there were forty-three American law firms with 50 or more lawyers each. Twenty of these were in New York City. The largest law firm, Shearman and Sterling, was made up of 125 lawyers—35 partners and 90 associates on salary.[11] This seemed immense at the time, a "law factory" of massive proportions. But the biggest firms today utterly dwarf it in size. In 1980, Baker and McKenzie, with headquarters in Chicago, had 512 lawyers, and branches in eleven cities.[12]

Baker and McKenzie is unusually cosmopolitan. Most law firms, even large ones, stick to a single office. At most they have a branch or two. But the habit of branching is definitely on the march. In 1982 Sullivan and Cromwell, besides its mother office on Wall Street, had branches in Washington, D.C., London, and Paris. San Francisco firms had branches as close as Palo Alto, and as far away as Hong Kong and Riyadh. This is at the upper end of the scale. At the popular end, there are now a number of "law clinics," with offices in many neighborhoods—a very recent development. There is talk about putting mini-offices in department stores, too, so that a person can buy underwear, get glasses, eat a sandwich, and consult a lawyer, all under a single roof. The Wall Street lawyer of 1900 would surely whirl in his grave.

What Lawyers Do

The big firms grow bigger; but thousands of lawyers still work on their own, as "solos." There are also tiny firms and middle-sized firms.

There are lawyers in big cities, and lawyers in sleepy towns. Thousands of young people pour out of law schools every year and take the bar examination. In California alone, 3,622 men and women passed this test in the fall of 1982. These new recruits take up all sorts of jobs and fill many slots. Not all of them, of course, will stay in law.

The profession is, and always has been, quite diverse. There are many legal worlds. To begin with, there is the world of the big firm, the "Wall Street lawyer." There are, of course, "Wall Streets" all over the country—La Salle Street in Chicago, Montgomery Street in San Francisco. There are "Wall Street" firms in Houston, Atlanta, Boston, Los Angeles, Denver, and so on.

These big firms recruit their lawyers, by and large, from the "national" law schools—schools with big reputations and long traditions, like Harvard and Yale, and brash newcomers like Chicago and Stanford. A few state schools have elbowed their way into the ranks of the elite (Michigan, Berkeley). We know in general who the clients are: big corporations and wealthy families. We know in general what the work is: it includes securities law, antitrust law, bond issues, mergers, tax work, international trade. But we have little systematic knowledge. Researchers hardly ever pierce the curtain of privacy. Sociological literature on the big law firm is small indeed.[13]

In both big and little firms, there will probably be some litigation. How much is uncertain. Business lawyers used to pride themselves on staying out of court. But there has been a litigation boom in recent years at the larger firms. In 1978, at the Cravath firm in New York—one of the largest firms—40 percent of the lawyers were working on litigation, double the manpower effort of the past.[14] Cravath was up to its neck at the time in a monster lawsuit—the government's attempt to hack IBM's "monopoly" to pieces—and the work load in litigation was probably somewhat out of the ordinary; but other firms also report increases in their trial and courtroom work. This is a response, among other things, to increased regulation and to new causes of action. Sears Roebuck had no sex discrimination suits in 1930.

Another staple of law practice is real estate: buying and selling houses or (on a more sophisticated level) concocting elaborate deals for shopping centers, suburban developments, and office buildings, or converting luxury apartments into condominiums. Estate work is also common to big firms and little firms alike—writing wills and trusts, guiding the dead through the dark rivers of probate. Big firms handle these affairs for captains of industry and for great old families. Middle-sized firms do the same for the medium-rich—manufacturers of plastic novelties, owners of restaurants, car-wash companies, apartment buildings. Small-town lawyers handle farm estates. And so on.

Big firms and solo practitioners are alike, curiously enough, in one key regard: they are generalists. In medicine, the specialists have more prestige and make more money than "GP's," or doctors who practice "family medicine." The law is different. Big firms make the most money and enjoy the highest status, yet they are general firms, or at least general-business firms. Their senior partners earn as much as half a million a year, or more. Specialization is not the way to the top. On the other hand, big law firms are *internally* specialized. They are rather like clinics or hospitals. This is one reason why the firms grew large in the first place.

Some branches of practice, to be sure, do tend toward spcialization. There are lawyers who carve out niches in almost any and every conceivable area of law. Lawyers have specialized in patents, will contests, tax appeals, divorce, civil rights. There are lawyers who work on export-import trade, on chartering ships, on show business ("entertainment law"), on trademarks and copyrights. There are so-called "boutique" firms, especially in Washington, which specialize in certain types of administrative law. There are "PI" (personal injury) lawyers, who confine themselves to tort cases growing out of accidents or bring products liability and malpractice suits. Some lawyers do nothing but sue airlines.

On the other hand, few lawyers are totally specialized. This is one finding from a massive study of the Chicago bar. Criminal prosecutors are exceptional in that they stick to criminal work and do not stray into other fields. But even patent lawyers have more than one string to their bow; only 40 percent of those in the survey restricted themselves totally to patents. Only 22 percent of the corporate tax specialists did nothing else.[15]

Big-firm lawyers cover many fields and many problems. But there are areas they definitely do not touch. One is divorce. Wall Street does very little family law, except perhaps to mop up financial fallout when millionaires split. It is the lawyers in smallish firms and in law clinics, and the solos, who handle "one-shot" clients—couples who want a divorce, victims of car crashes, people arrested for drunk driving.

Some lawyers with one-shot clients struggle to make ends meet; others earn heaps of money. The better-known personal injury lawyers do very well indeed. They take cases on a "contingent fee" basis. That is, the lawyer gets nothing if the client loses; but if the client wins, the lawyer takes a hefty chunk of the winnings, often one-third. This is true whether the case is settled or goes to trial. If the recovery is big—a New York jury awarded \$4,848,000 in a medical malpractice case in 1979[16]—so is the fee. It does not take many cases of this type to put a lawyer in clover.

Money, of course, is not everything, and "PI" work never carries the prestige of a Wall Street practice. Partly this is because Wall Street has a richer, more elegant clientele. Tort lawyers serve all classes, top to bottom. Criminal lawyers, in particular, dirty their hands with the less savory citizens. And all "one-shot" lawyers face the problems of recruiting new business. Their clients come and go; the lawyers need constant infusions of fresh blood. After all, no one gets run over by trains, divorced, or arrested for murder consistently. Wall Street firms keep their clients "on retainer"; their business is steady, year in and year out. Of course, they scramble for new business and fight to keep old business. But the struggle is, on the whole, genteel. What is more, they do not hustle in public. In fact, they hate publicity. A flamboyant style hurts them more than it helps. The opposite is true for tort lawyers, criminal lawyers, and divorce lawyers.

Who Are the Lawyers?

Since the early nineteenth century, law has been a prominent way to get ahead in this society, a means of upward mobility. Young men on the make have shimmied up this greasy pole, which has been a bit easier and less slippery than other alternatives. Who were these men? In the first place, the word *men* is to be taken literally. For much of our history, *lawyer* meant "white male." Not a single woman was admitted to the bar before the 1870s, and precious few blacks.

Indeed, when women tried to break into this all-male club, they met resistance and reluctance, to say the least. One pioneer was Myra Bradwell, wife of an Illinois lawyer and mother of four children, who applied for admission to the bar in 1869. She passed the exam, but the Supreme Court of Illinois turned her down. Women, especially married women, were not suitable lawyers. Like lunatics and children, they were under "disability"; they themselves lacked full legal rights. Besides, women lawyers were unthinkable: practice would endanger the "deference and delicacy with which it is the pride of our ruder sex to treat her." Mrs. Bradwell appealed to the United States Supreme Court, but did no better there. The traditional family, according to Justice Bradley, was "founded in the divine ordinance, as well as in the nature of things." This meant that women belonged inherently to "the domestic sphere" (the kitchen, in other words).[17]

Opinion changed, but slowly and grudgingly. In the same year that Myra Bradwell was shut out in Illinois, Iowa admitted Arabella Mansfield to practice. The first woman lawyer in Illinois was Alta M. Hulett (who was unmarried); she broke the barrier in 1873. The University of Michigan decided to admit women to its law school in 1870; Yale's law school followed in 1886, Cornell's in 1887.

Despite this, the bar stayed largely a man's world. As recently as 1960, less than 3 percent of the country's lawyers were women. Change did not take place until the 1970s. In 1965, 4 percent of the country's law students were women; in 1973, 16 percent; in 1979, 32 percent. A trickle of women begin to show up on law faculties, in big firms, and on the bench. In 1981, President Reagan appointed Sandra Day O'Connor of Arizona, a graduate of Stanford University's law school, to the United States Supreme Court. She was the first woman ever to sit there. The chief justice of California as of 1984 is a woman (Rose Bird). In 1967, no American law school had more than two women on its faculty. Most had none at all. But in 1979, only four accredited law schools had *no* women teaching; ten schools had six or more women professors.[18]

Black lawyers were rare birds, too, in American history. John Mercer Langston was one of the first. Langston was the son of a white plantation owner and a slave woman. He became a lawyer in Ohio in 1854; later, he served as the first head of the law department of Howard University, which opened its doors after the Civil War and trained a small corps of black lawyers.[19]

Progress here too was painfully slow. In 1965, blacks made up 11 percent of the population, but less than 2 percent of the legal profession and only 1.3 percent of the law students, nearly half of these in all-black law schools. At this point, the doors began to open a bit wider, both in law schools and at the bar. Some law schools devised special programs to get and train black students and help correct the extreme imbalance at the bar. In 1977, about 5 percent of the law students in the country were black; many of these—perhaps most—would have been shut out of places in law schools if the schools admitted students purely "by the numbers."[20] Chicanos would have fared just as badly. There is, of course, controversy over this kind of "benign discrimination." It was an issue in the famous *Bakke* case, in which a white student complained of racial quotas in medical school admissions.

Law firms, in the past, were as discriminatory as law schools, and even more so. Through the 1950s, most were solidly WASP. Jews were taboo, Catholics suspect and rare. Jews tended to have their own firms, some quite large. Barriers in the big firms have by now largely crumbled. Barriers against women and blacks are more stubborn, but are definitely receding. At any rate, they are no longer blatant and overt. True, many firms settle for a "token" woman or black. But even a token is important; it soon proves to the firm of Chicken and Little that the sky will not fall in if a black or a woman joins the firm.

But equality of opportunity is not an easy goal. Structural barriers are not quickly dismantled. The cost of legal education is one of these barriers. Tuition alone at top private schools was over $8,000 a year in 1983–84. The Chicago survey reports some disquieting facts. Lawyers tend to come from the families of businessmen, teachers, professionals; they are not sons of grocery clerks or coal miners' daughters. Over 73 percent of the practicing lawyers in Chicago come from "solidly middle-class or upper middle-class homes," far more than if lawyers were selected from Chicago families at random. Many come from lawyerly or professional backgrounds. And the percentage of lawyers from working-class backgrounds may be going down, not up.[21]

Becoming a Lawyer

In England, there is a sharp distinction between two kinds of lawyer: barristers and solicitors. Barristers, in their wigs and robes, act as courtroom lawyers; solicitors do everything else, but cannot appear before the higher courts. Solicitors, on the whole, are less tony and prestigious than barristers; but only solicitors deal with clients face-to-face on a regular basis. A few American states once made distinctions between ranks or classes of lawyers (New York, New Jersey, Massachusetts, Virginia); but by the middle of the nineteenth century these had all died out and we were left with a single category: lawyer.

It was not a hard label to earn. In the nineteenth century, the law was fairly wide open, as professions go. To some extent, it flatters the nineteenth-century lawyer to call him a professional. Nowadays, the road to the bar is a long, hard grind—first college, then three years of law school (if you can get in), then a cram course, then the bar examination itself. In many states, the bar exam is itself quite a hurdle. Of those who took the California bar exam in the fall of 1982, 52.5 percent failed to pass it.

Admission to the bar was a different beast entirely in the nineteenth century. Legal education as we know it did not exist in 1800. The way to the bar was through apprenticeship. The young man who wanted to be a lawyer "read law" in a lawyer's office. He sat in the office for a period, and plowed through a number of law books. Often, the apprentice made himself useful doing the lawyer's drudge work: copying documents, writing out pleadings, running errands. In the days before typewriters, telephones, stenographers, Xerox machines, and word processors, a lawyer *needed* clerks. If the clerk was lucky, he got some actual training out of the deal. Not all clerks or apprentices were lucky.[22]

In most states, the bar examination did not do much filtering; it was hardly a significant hurdle. A few states (Indiana, for one) got rid of it altogether for a while. Elsewhere, it was short and not very tough. Young Salmon P. Chase, later chief justice of the United States, was admitted to the bar in Washington, D.C., around 1829. Seldom, he wrote, "has any candidate for admission to the bar presented himself for examination with a slenderer stock of learning." Chase had spent time in the office of William Wirt, then attorney general, as a "student-at-law." He read Blackstone and a few other books. Wirt "never examined me. Only once did he put a question to me about my studies." The "bar examination" itself was just as perfunctory. Justice Cranch asked him a few questions; Chase answered them, but "not very well." The judge said "You must study another year." But Chase begged for mercy: "I have made all my arrangements to go to the Western country and practice law." The judge "yielded"; and Chase was sworn in.[23] Those were the good old days.

Legal education in a school setting developed only slowly, though in a sense it can be traced to the end of the eighteenth century. Two streams of education ultimately flowed together. The first was a kind of glorified clerkship. It came about in this way: A few lawyers *liked* teaching clerks, and were good at the job. They spent less and less time with clients, more and more time with their clerks. They took on extra clerks, for pay, in order to teach them law. Finally, the law practice withered away, and the office turned into a school.

This is more or less the story of the famous Litchfield School, the first law school in the country. It was founded by Judge Tapping Reeve in Litchfield, Connecticut, in 1784. It lasted until 1833, and was quite successful in its day. The Litchfield School had little in common with modern law schools. In looks, it was modest: a simple, frame building, much like a country schoolhouse. There were no entrance requirements, no prerequisites, no final examinations. Litchfield used the lecture method. The full course took a bit more than a year. There were lectures every day. Students copied down as much of the lectures as they could. On Saturdays, there were quizzes covering the work of the week. Instruction was, needless to say, intensely practical.

There were a number of other schools on the Litchfield plan, in all parts of the country. Eventually, they died out. Their influence merged with the other stream—instruction in a university setting. Here Blackstone was an early model. To be sure, his Oxford lectures in the mid-eighteenth century were not meant for the training of lawyers. They were rather for the educated layman. But his example gave a strong push to the notion of learning law at a university. Blackstone's lectures were the source of his *Commentaries*, which were fantastically successful, on both sides of the Atlantic. American colleges and universities began to copy the Blackstone idea. The first American chair of law was at William and Mary College. A holder of this chair, St. George Tucker, published an American edition of Blackstone in 1803, up-to-date and with American notes and additions.

Harvard, however, was the first university with a separate department of law. In its early years, from about 1816 on, legal education at Harvard was a kind of mixture of Litchfield and Blackstone. Its intellectual pretensions, of course, went beyond those of Litchfield, especially under Joseph Story. Story was the first professor to occupy a new chair endowed by Nathan Dane (1829). Story was a justice of the Supreme Court of the United States, and he wrote many learned but ponderous treatises. Despite Story and his successors, Harvard Law School in the middle of the nineteenth century was not the tough, rigorous Harvard of *The Paper Chase*. When Joseph Hodges Choate entered Harvard Law School in 1852, he found the standards "very low." "There were absolutely no examinations to get in, or to proceed, or to get out. All that was required was the lapse of time, two years, and the payment of the fees." [24]

All this changed radically in 1870. In that year, legal education as we know it was born. It sprang from the brain of Christopher Columbus Langdell, who became dean of Harvard Law School in that year. Langdell worked a revolution in legal education. He invented the case method, practically speaking, in which students read and discussed published reports of cases decided by appellate courts. These cases were collected in casebooks, and Langdell put the first one of these together. He also insisted on the so-called Socratic method of teaching—teaching through questions and answers. Lectures were out.[25]

He also, in a way, invented the law professor. Before Langdell, judges and practicing lawyers taught law. Usually they kept their "real" jobs; teaching was a sideline. Joseph Story was a sitting justice of the Supreme Court during the years he taught at Harvard. Other professors came to teaching after careers in judging or practice; Chief Justice Joel Parker of New Hampshire was appointed to a Harvard chair in 1847, at the age of fifty-two.[26] Langdell put an end to this practice. He hired James Barr Ames, almost fresh out of law school, for his faculty. Ames had no practical experience at all. Langdell believed in him—not as a lawyer but as a teacher. Law, to Langdell, was a science; it had to be taught by people adept in the science. Whether they had dirtied their hands in practice was irrelevant.

Langdell's methods were novel and disturbing; they evoked bitter opposition, even at Harvard. Gradually, the opposition died down, and the Langdell method won out over all of its rivals. By the second decade of the twentieth century, the Harvard case method was almost universal. It remains dominant to this day. To be sure, there have been many changes in curriculum. Some schools have also experimented with a more "clinical" approach, teaching a few courses through real or simulated casework. But the core of the Langdell method has been remarkably resistant to change.

Law schools also tightened their standards after the Langdell revolution. A definite curriculum was established; classes were taught Socratically and topped off with a final exam. The Langdell method was austere, abstract. Langdell's conception of law as a science divorced the study of law from the grubby world of practice—and also from politics, history, economics, and social context. His schools taught only legal principles; the social environment was banished from the law school, exiled to the rest of the university—for example, departments of politics or government. Yet in other ways the new-model law schools were tied more closely to their universities. Nineteenth-century university law schools were independent kingdoms, on the whole. They ran themselves; they collected their own fees; they had almost nothing to do with their universities, except to share their names.

Meanwhile, law school pushed out clerkship as the high road to the bar. In 1850 there were 15 law schools in the country; in 1870, 31; in 1900, 102. In 1981, the American Bar Association accredited some 181 schools. Apprenticeship is virtually extinct. In a few states, notably California, there are many unaccredited schools. Some are "proprietary"—that is, they make money, or try to. Their entrance requirements are low; but so are their success rates in training students for the bar.[27]

There are, then, some 200 American law schools. They are much the same, only different. They are remarkably similar in curriculum and method. They also tend to impose the same general requirements: a college degree, and the Law School Admission Test (LSAT). This test began its reign of terror around 1950; a good score is a must for admission to all but the weakest law schools. Law schools are on the other hand quite different in prestige, money, and power—and in quality of faculty and students, at least on paper. A tremendous surge of applicants in the 1960s and 1970s battered at the doors of law schools. The stronger, older schools were able to "skim off the cream." In 1979, for example, there were 72,000 applicants—many more than could hope to get in. This flood now seems to have crested; but the demand is still very strong.

Schools differ in other ways, too. Harvard, Yale, and Chicago can afford huge research libraries; small schools cannot. For a long time, the rich schools were mostly schools for the rich; but public legal education has a distinguished history, especially in the Middle West (Michigan, Wisconsin, Minnesota), and in the West (California). In the late nineteenth century, many schools were founded to teach law at night. There were twenty of these schools by 1900, and many survive to this day, though they usually offer day courses, too. Their students were mostly drawn from the working class. Out of these schools came the immigrant lawyers, Polish, Italian, Jewish, Irish, and Greek, who often went back to their neighborhoods and served their ethnic constituents. Graduates of these schools rarely make it to Wall Street or La Salle Street. The big firms are staffed with graduates of national schools, not these "local" schools.[28] But the night schools and other local law schools have been breeding grounds for local judges and politicians; thus, in their own way, they wield great influence and power. Their alumni run the statehouses, or at least city hall.

The Organized Bar

Lawyers, like Americans in general, are joiners. Yet the bar did not have a strong, permanent organization until the 1870s. The first modern bar association was the Association of the Bar of the City of New York. It was founded in 1870 by what one lawyer called "the decent part of the profession." This "decent part" had boiled over in indignation because of the plague of corrupt lawyers, judges, and politicians in Boss Tweed's New York. A few years later, in 1878, "seventy-five gentlemen" of the bar, meeting in Saratoga, New York, founded a national group, the American Bar Association.

Bar associations in their early days made no attempt to recruit the mass of American lawyers. They were basically clubs of like-minded, high-minded lawyers. Indeed that was their point: they kept the riff-raff out and admitted only the "best elements" of the profession. The purpose was reform—drafting better laws, fighting against corruption, raising the prestige of the profession.

They had other, less defensible, ideas. The ABA has a rather shameful history of snobbery and bias. In 1912, through carelessness, the ABA admitted three black lawyers; when the leadership realized what had happened, they tried to undo this dreadful mistake, since the "settled practice" was to "elect only white men." The three blacks were allowed to remain, but future applicants had to reveal their race, to prevent any more "mistakes." The ABA also took reactionary stands on matters of free speech and political dissent. Its record during the Cold War was unenviable. Instead of standing up for the Bill of Rights, the ABA resolved, in 1950, "that all lawyers attest to their loyalty with an anti-Communist oath."[29]

The ABA in fact represented the upper crust of the profession. It stood for their values. Early on, the ABA promoted codes of ethics for the bar and tried to upgrade the lawyer's reputation by defining, and upholding, ethical conduct. This had its good side and its bad side. The good side was the struggle for honesty and higher standards. The bad side was elitism, a kind of dogged conservatism on professional issues, and a failure to consider the rights of consumers of legal services. Even the ethics were class-biased. Under the old ABA canons of ethics, advertising was forbidden. Wall Street, after all, did not need to advertise. The small lawyer did, but the ABA was not concerned with his wishes. The ordinary layman, too, was disadvantaged: it was hard for him to find out what lawyers had to offer. The rule, in other words, made sure that "knowledge would remain unevenly, and unfairly, distributed."[30] The bar did not like price competition, either. In many states there were tables of minimum fees. Price cutting was unwelcome.

The ABA today has come a long way since the 1950s. But it is still not an association of all American lawyers. No one has to join. More than half the practicing bar now joins and pays dues, however. Under pressure from inside and out, the ABA has changed its tune. It is no longer a club for white males; it is open to any American lawyer. The bar has also done some reexamination of its ethical codes. The so-called Kutak Commission proposed a major revision; the bar in 1983 refused to accept it, but the debate opened up discussion on matters the bar once accepted without question. The outside world, too, has intervened. In 1976, the Supreme Court struck down minimum fee schedules.[31] The next year, the Court killed the ban on advertising, too.

This was the case of *Bates* v. *State Bar of Arizona*.[32] John R. Bates, with his partner Van O'Steen, ran a "legal clinic" in Phoenix, Arizona. His ads in the paper ("Do You Need a Lawyer?") touched off the case. Bates won, and since then more and more lawyers advertise. There are even ads on TV. Obviously, these ads are not aimed at rich Americans, let alone General Motors or IBM; they appeal, for example, to the man arrested for drunk driving, a person who has never had a lawyer, and has only the vaguest idea how to get one. Advertising makes the old-time lawyer squirm, and its virtues are certainly debatable. What it will mean to the profession in the long run remains to be seen.

The ABA is a national organization of lawyers; there are also state, county, and city bar associations. In more than half the states, starting with North Dakota in the early 1920s, the bar has been "integrated." This has nothing to do with race; it means that lawyers cannot practice unless they join their state bar and pay dues. The integrated bar gets rich and fat with these forced contributions. It is in theory better able to control its members and keep them on the straight and narrow path. Some lawyers are skeptical. Many states have rejected the idea, and the plan has been attacked as a kind of "closed shop" for lawyers—an infringement of individual rights and autonomy. The debate continues.

Lawyers have always insisted, to a skeptical world, that they are mostly honest, skilled, high-toned. There are of course rotten apples in every barrel; but the bar insists on the right to pick them out itself. The bar's record in doing so is spotty, at best. State bar associations and state judiciaries are the ultimate enforcers; the ultimate sanction is disbarment, that is, losing the right to practice law. In 1961–62, the fifty states disbarred 74 lawyers and suspended 9.[33] In 1978, according to Deborah L. Rhode, agencies received 30,836 complaints serious enough to warrant opening a file; but only 124 lawyers in the whole country were disbarred.[34]

Only a few lawyers, then, pay for their sins. Yet complaints brought and satisfied must be the merest drop in the bucket, unless lawyers are upright to an impossible degree. The disciplinary agencies are, in Rhode's view, "grossly unresponsive" to clients and their complaints. Lawyers punish other lawyers for very flagrant violations—stealing a client's money, for example. For most other offenses, and for plain incompetence, lawyers are (understandably) quite gentle with themselves. And many rules are simply not enforced.

For example, under professional codes of ethics, it is wrong for a lawyer to farm out a case to another lawyer and split the fees. That is, if a client brings a case to Lawyer X, Lawyer X should handle it himself. But if he does bring in another lawyer for some reason, they must divide the fees in a way that reflects the actual work done by each of them. In New York, according to a study of personal injury lawyers, the rule is "systematically broken." Moreover, there is a "tacit understanding" not to treat this violation "as a serious matter"; the organized bar will discipline only truly outrageous cases.[35]

The Social Role of Lawyers: Do Lawyers Run the Country?

From the very beginning of the republic, lawyers have swarmed all over government—federal, state, and local. In Indiana, for example, seven out of the first eight governors were lawyers, eleven out of the first thirteen lieutenant governors, eight of the first nine senators, and forty-five out of sixty-one congressmen, up to the 1850s.[36] Many presidents, from John Adams to Richard Nixon and Gerald Ford, have been lawyers; no other profession has contributed so many presidents. Abraham Lincoln and Franklin D. Roosevelt were lawyers. Lawyers have served in droves as secretaries of state and cabinet members. They have occupied offices down to the lowliest township level, in numbers far, far outstripping their "proper" share.

This is no accident. For one thing, the business of lawyers is intimately connected to the business of government. Government makes and administers law; law is what lawyers know. For many lawyers, too, a political career goes hand in glove with a private career. If a Chicago woman who is a doctor or dentist goes down to Springfield to serve in the Illinois assembly, she hurts her career quite badly. If she is a lawyer, it may have the opposite effect; politics may be good for an assemblywoman's law business, especially if she has partners back home. She gets a reputation as somebody who knows the right people and who knows the ropes—a lawyer who can get things done.

This works for federal service also. A lawyer appointed to a high position in the State Department, or the Department of Transportation, or the Department of Housing and Urban Development, is not interrupting his career. The job may in fact be a step up the ladder. He learns what to do, whom to know. When he leaves government service, he often gets a fat partnership in a major law firm. Experience in a regulatory agency like the ICC or the SEC, or the Internal Revenue Service, or the antitrust division of the Justice Department makes a lawyer more valuable to private clients. Lawyers often end up working for companies they used to regulate. It is no surprise when an attorney general becomes chief counsel for IBM, or when a manpower specialist at the Pentagon becomes a partner in a firm whose clients build missiles and tanks.

In recent years, lawyers have lost a little of their dominance in Congress and state legislatures. In 1966, 26 percent of state legislators were lawyers; in 1979, 20 percent. By 1980 or so, lawyers made up less than half the members of Congress for the first time in years.[37] One reaon is that these jobs (Congress, the state legislatures) have gotten tougher. They are definitely full-time now, certainly in Congress; for the first time in our history, state political positions may interfere with a lawyer's career.

This trend may continue. For now, lawyers are still as common as sparrows in government; wherever one turns, one stumbles over lawyers, either inside the bureaucracy or outside of it, acting as attorneys for companies with government business. Many people think lawyers have perhaps too much influence in America. Lawyers, on the whole, have a terrible image. The poet Carl Sandburg asked rhetorically why the hearse-horse "snickers" when he carries the lawyer's bones. Even worse things are said about lawyers. "Superlawyers," the powerful Washington firms, are suspected of running the country, and on behalf of their big, nasty clients. Lower down, we hear about shysters, ambulance chasers, ticket fixers. The criminal bar has its own special, odious image. Lawyer-politicians combine two bad reputations in one. The Watergate scandal made matters worse: the connivers who surrounded Richard Nixon—and President Nixon himself—were mostly members of the bar, their morals dulled by "blind ambition."

Still, the ethical practices of lawyers are probably no worse than those of other professions. Lawyers bring some of the trouble on themselves by claiming too much—by claiming, in a sanctimonious way, that they are interested only in justice, not power or wealth.

They also suffer guilt by association. Their clients are often people in trouble. Saints need no lawyers; gangsters do. Companies that wheel and deal—or pollute rivers—need lawyers more than stable, law-abiding firms. Happy couples do not see lawyers; divorcing couples do. And so it goes.

Lawyers are certainly a help to their clients. But in the aggregate, are they good for the country? What difference do lawyers make? Are we better or worse off than countries with fewer lawyers? Are there too many lawyers, in short, for our own good? It is not easy to answer these questions. A few studies give a clue or two. Some scholars have tried to measure the behavior of lawyers in state legislatures and compare it to the behavior of nonlawyers. Do lawyers in the Tennessee assembly, say, vote and act in ways systematically different from the other assemblymen? If they do, we might decide that legal training shapes a certain personality, a certain cluster of opinions; if you fill up a legislature or agency with people of this type, you bend it in some particular way.

On the whole, the studies turn up negative results. There are few, if any, differences between the way lawyers and nonlawyers vote and behave in state assemblies.[38] The job of being a legislator and the social situation—pressure from voters, for example—bend the lawyer, not the other way around. A few studies have come up with differences: lawyers are more independent politically, more reform-minded, more effective, more active in sponsoring legislation, as compared to nonlawyers.[39] But even these results do not show that lawyers share some special ideology or that they influence how the country runs.

It is intriguing to compare the American profession with the bar in other countries. Japan is an amazing contrast. In 1960, Japan had a population of over 90 million—and only 9,114 lawyers, concentrated in a few large cities.[40] The situation has not changed very much since then. There are more than twenty times as many lawyers in the United States per 1,000 population. And the Japanese seem content to keep down the number of lawyers. In 1980, 30,000 Japanese students took the entrance exam for the Judicial and Legal Training Institute. This is a prerequisite for admission to the bar. A mere 500 passed.[41]

Yet Japan is no primitive country. It is an industrial giant. Its huge industrial firms sell cars, radios, cameras all over the world. Sony or Nissan Motors, if they were American companies, would have hundreds of lawyers on their payroll or at their beck and call on Wall Street.

Obviously, lawyers in the United States do things that are not done—or not done by lawyers—in Japan.

It is not clear what these things are. Supposedly the Japanese do not like to litigate, but neither do American businesses; and litigation does not begin to account for the number of American lawyers. Obviously, the two countries define lawyers' work very differently. The Japanese do quite nicely without an American-type legal profession. We can conclude that there is no inevitable, necessary connection between a legal profession of the American type and modern society, or capitalism, or the welfare state, or industrial society. Rather, our profession is at least in part unique or peculiar, shaped to the characteristics of American society. But exactly how or what these features are is not at all clear.

This is not to say that lawyers make no difference to the United States. Clearly they do. Six hundred thousand lawyers do not sit around twiddling their thumbs. They work; they accomplish; they do. A culture has grown up in this country which somehow depends on this crowd of lawyers. Our business system, unlike Japan's, cannot get along without lawyers; and the social system, too, is curiously dependent on the bar. Would we be better off, then, with fewer lawyers? There is no answer. Without the lawyers, this would be a different society, in a different sort of world.

Lawyers and Social Justice

The business of lawyers is justice. That, at least, is what they claim. A man or woman accused of crime or of tax fraud, or hounded by government in some way, or sued by a nasty neighbor, wants fairness, justice, a crack at vindication. Only a good lawyer can get these for him. Of course, a smart lawyer can pervert justice, too, in some cases. This also happens.

In fact, the business of lawyers is both justice and injustice. They are on all sides of every issue, on both sides of every case. Some lawyers are attracted to lost causes, like moths to a flame—men like Clarence Darrow, "attorney for the damned," who defended anarchists and murderers.[42] There are left-wing lawyers, like William Kunstler, who take up the causes of clients despised by most of the rest of society. There are ACLU lawyers, who defend free speech for left wing and right wing alike; some of their clients, the American Nazis, for example, spit on everything the ACLU stands for and loves.

Thousands of lawyers, however, work for the status quo. They represent American business, especially big business, and the people who own great wealth. They work for oil interests, computer companies, real estate syndicates. We sometimes hear it said that lawyers are by nature conservative. It is more accurate to say that lawyers, like most people, are anxious to make a living. They go where the money is; and the money is concentrated at top levels of business and society. Lawyers gravitate to whatever regime is in power; in this sense they are conservative, but only if the regime is conservative. In a Communist country, the lawyers tend to be faithful party members. And of course there are exceptions. There are, as we said, left-wing lawyers, dissident lawyers. Some lawyers have even been prominent revolutionaries, men like Fidel Castro or India's Nehru.

Law and lawyers are expensive. Many people who want or need a lawyer have trouble paying the price. Justice is for sale; but in a just society it should not be totally for sale. The state thus provides a lawyer, free of charge, to anyone accused of a serious crime who cannot afford his own lawyer. Many states had long recognized such a constitutional right; in 1963, in the famous case of *Gideon* v. *Wainwright*,[43] the Supreme Court imposed it on all the states. Today, "public defenders," who are on the state payroll, defend most people charged with serious crime.

For civil cases, the situation is more complicated. A few lawyers have always made it a practice to do some work free for poor clients. Since the late nineteenth century, some cities have had programs of legal aid. The Legal Aid Society of New York began as an organization called Deutscher Rechts-Schutz Verein, in 1876, to help out German immigrants. It broadened its scope over the years, and changed its name officially in 1896. By 1913, there were forty active societies, all over the country, and growth continued afterwards.[44] But though these societies did good work, they merely scratched the surface. The poor were basically shut out of civil courts. Even the small-claims movement was not much of a help.

A major change came during the "War on Poverty," in the 1960s, under President Lyndon Johnson. The Office of Economic Opportunity established neighborhood law offices to serve poor clients. Bright young lawyers staffed these offices. In 1974, the work was transferred to a new body, the Legal Services Corporation, chartered and paid for by Congress. As of 1981, the corporation funded 320 legal aid programs and 1,200 neighborhood offices, all around the country. It paid for 5,000 lawyers and 2,500 paralegals. The price tag was $300 million.

From the start, there was controversy over the program. Land-lords were annoyed when poverty lawyers helped tenants fight evic-tions. Conservatives thought it was absurd to pay one agency of government in order to bring lawsuits against the rest of the govern-ment. They considered poverty lawyers radicals, whose main aim was to drum up "activist" lawsuits, not to help the poor with ordinary legal problems. Many political leaders agreed. OEO lawyers had the annoying habit of fighting city hall. Some governors, too, tried to get rid of the program in their states. One of these was the governor of California, Ronald Reagan. Later he became president; and as presi-dent, he proposed cutting off all federal money, leaving the states in charge of legal aid if they chose to support this kind of program. So far (1984), Congress has balked, and successfully. But the funds have been drastically cut.

The "public interest" lawyer is another departure from past prac-tice. There are now a number of law firms organized for the "public interest." They do not represent private clients. Rather, they repre-sent "the public" (as they define it): people who want to preserve wilderness lands in Alaska or who oppose nuclear power plants. They speak up for the snail darter and the black-footed ferret; they tilt lances against government red tape in housing and welfare administration. They fight for convicted murderers and for victims of discrimination.

Who pays for these lawyers? The government contributes some-thing; foundations contribute something; members of organizations (the Sierra Club, for example) contribute their share. There are only a handful of these firms. One study found about "40 charity-sup-ported public interest law firms" in 1973. They averaged ten lawyers each.[45] The number has grown a little since then; but public interest lawyers make up no more than a tenth of one percent of the practicing bar. These are truly little Davids, up against the Goliaths of govern-ment and big business. Their opponents have thousands of lawyers and tremendous resources. Financially speaking, too, the public-interest bar leads a hand-to-mouth existence.

Yet these firms have accomplished miracles; they have done heroic work (some think too heroic). They have brought giant enterprises to a halt. They delayed the Alaska pipeline, and have helped kill nuclear power plants and projects to develop wilderness areas. They have forced the government to shift direction or change programs in many different ways. They have helped revolutionize the law of landlord and tenant. They have monitored the work of dozens of agencies.

One sign of their success is the bitterness of the opposition. Another is the rise of conservative counterparts. "Public interest" firms on the right have sprung up in recent years, to counterbalance the liberal firms. The Mountain States Legal Foundation in Denver, Colorado, was one of these counterbalances. James G. Watt, President Reagan's first secretary of the interior, served as its president before he entered the cabinet. The foundation "defends free enterprise." It believes in "privatization" of the public domain, assigning more of the public lands to "mineral development," or leaving the land in the hands of ranchers.[46] It is, in other words, a kind of mirror image of the Environmental Defense Fund or the Natural Resources Defense Council. Imitation is the sincerest form of flattery.

14

Law and
Social Change

*I*T IS OBVIOUS to the naked eye that we live in a period of very rapid social change. There is change in every aspect of life—social life, the family, sex, technology, politics, the economy. Why the world is changing so fast, compared to older times, is a complicated question. But whatever the reason, mankind and womankind are speeding along on a fast-moving train, and there are no signs that the train is slowing down. Nor is there any way to stop it and get off. The relationship between law and social change needs a good deal of careful thought and analysis.

First, a theoretical question about that relationship. Does law lead in the process of social change, or does it simply follow along? In other words, can we point the finger of praise, or of blame, at law and the legal system for what is happening in the world? Is law a motor— or one of the motors—generating social change? Or does social change originate in the larger society, spilling over into the legal system—a system which merely adjusts or accommodates itself to big changes taking place outside?

Nobody can give full, final answers to these questions. As a matter of general theory, this book takes the point of view that major social change begins outside the legal system, that is, in society. The legal system is not wholly autonomous. It is not a world in itself. It is not insulated from outside influence.

To be sure, many people argue that the law is tough, conservative, and resistant to change. They sense a good deal of autonomy in the system. Experience suggests a rather different story, at least over the long haul. The legal systems of Western countries have been completely transformed since the Middle Ages, most notably in the years since the Industrial Revolution began. When we look at the changes, it is clear that over the centuries the legal system has been carried along by great waves of social force. Social movements sweep across it with the strength of a mighty sea. The legal system may seem like a mighty warship to those on deck, but its power shrinks to nothing compared with that of the ocean it sails on and the wind and weather all about.

Of course, we can carry this point of view too far. We need not downgrade the power and importance of law—in this culture, at least. We must keep in mind the tremendous size of the legal profession; the vast bulk of the substantive law; the striking way in which political, social, and economic issues somehow end up as lawsuits; the massive activity of administrative agencies; the ceaseless creation of new norms by Congress, states, and cities. All of this must have some independent impact—some impact of its own—on society.

What *is* the place of law in society? A purely social theory of law takes the legal system to be some kind of puppet, dancing on its master's strings. Social forces are the puppet masters. The picture may be somewhat overdrawn. A parable may provide a better image. Imagine a town on the banks of a swift, wide river. The people who live in the town want some way to cross the river. They want to reach people on the other side, to buy and sell goods, to travel to other places, and so on. The only way across is by ferry, which is slow and inefficient. The townspeople get together and demand a bridge. Taxes are levied; contracts are let; the bridge is built. Now both sides of the river are linked.

Clearly, the bridge did not get built by itself. It owes its existence to the political process, and social demand called the bridge into being. But once the bridge is in place, spanning the river, it begins inevitably to have its own, independent effect on community life. People construct their lives around the bridge. They move back and forth across the river. Some people live on one side and shop on the other. Some people commute to jobs on the opposite side. The towns on both sides grow larger and become more interdependent.

The bridge is now a familiar presence; it is part of consciousness and tradition. Poets write poems about it. Young people cannot remember a time when the bridge was not there. They *expect* a bridge; they find it natural. They take for granted the flow of people, goods,

and cars from bank to bank—the freedom to cross the river at will.
The bridge determines once and for all exactly where and how people
cross. It excludes all other crossing points. The ferry is long since
gone. The bridge has drilled itself into people's minds and taken root
there. In other words, it affects more than their way of life; it affects
the way they look at the world—what they expect, how they live,
how they think.

The bridge is a metaphor for law and the legal system. Social forces
in the larger society create it, shape it, twist it and turn it, pull it and
push it. But these forces produce a system that becomes itself a part
of social life; once in place, the system works its own influence on
society, on how we live, how we think, how we feel. This independent effect of the legal system does not mean that the social theory is
wrong. The legal system is not autonomous, not independent of society. It is not a system all to itself, insulated from the life of society.
The legal system does not march to a separate drummer. It is a part
of the social order, a soldier in the army of society. But its sheer size
and presence, its importance, its scale, its interactions with the rest
of the social organism give it a meaning beyond that of some limp
marionette. Law is society's servant, to be sure. But it is not a quiet,
invisible servant in an old-fashioned household; it is the noisy, bump-
tious work force of a factory.

The legal system has clearly played a role in the American economy and society. J. Willard Hurst's classic study of the lumber business in Wisconsin is full of lessons on this point.[1] The law did not
make the lumber industry; it was the other way around—that is, the
law was bent to suit the needs of the industry, because that is what
dominant opinion wanted. But like the bridge in the story, once the
legal system was in place, it channeled development along set lines.
There were old, familiar notions of contract and property: and although
the law was sometimes changed and restructured to suit the needs of
industry, these changes nonetheless took place within a tradition of
law and legal action. Thus, the legislature made use of its old power
to grant franchises by giving lumberers exclusive rights to improve
streams and use these streams for the transport of logs.[2] Law also
"offered ordered procedures for exploring facts, mustering evidence,
defining values and the range of value choices, and setting decent
bounds and terms for controversy."[3] In other words, law defined the
rules of the game; and in the short run at least, the players all accepted
these rules, just as one accepts—and must accept—the bridge, and
where it is, in the game of crossing the river.

In some respects, of course, the metaphor of the bridge is misleading. Generally speaking, law is far more flexible than an ordinary bridge. It is perhaps more like a pontoon bridge, which we can move somewhat, upriver or downriver, if the need is great.

The general thesis of this book, then, is that law follows social change and adapts to it. Yet it also crystallizes and channels social change; and plays an important role in community life. After all, it is through law, legal institutions, and legal processes that customs and ideas take on a more permanent, rigid form, like the bridge—or the pontoons—in our story. The legal system is a structure. It has shape and form. It lasts. It is visible. It sets up fields of force. It affects ways of thinking. When practices, habits, and custom turn into law, they tend to become stronger, more fixed, more explicit. They can be imposed on people who do not share the customs and habits, or are downright hostile to them. Law has its hidden persuaders—its moral basis, its legitimacy—but in the last analysis it has force, too, to back it up. Custom can also be powerful; but in complex societies custom is far too flabby to do all the work—to run the machinery of order. Law carries a powerful stick: the threat of force. This is the fist inside its velvet glove.

Revolution and Evolution in Legal Change

Thus far, the term *social change* has been used without explanation. Of course, there is no single process of social change. There are many kinds of change. Some social change is total, cataclysmic—revolutionary, in a word—breaking sharply with the past. Other forms of social change are incremental, evolutionary, step-by-step. There are also all grades in between. Social change in the modern world, unless appearances deceive us, is racing along faster than in older, traditional societies. We live in an age of constant revolution.

There are legal revolutions, too, as well as social revolutions. The Russian Revolution (1918) destroyed czarist society, and the czarist laws came tumbling down, as well. The Soviets wiped out all the old codes, and—temporarily, at least—established a new, radical form of justice. No sudden change on this scale ever took place in this country. Our own revolution was not as sharp a break with the past, legally speaking. Independence brought about a change in government, of course, and some dramatic innovations (the Constitution, for example); but the ordinary legal system kept on as usual. Rules, court procedures, daily routines were hardly disturbed, except where there was actual fighting. The common law was like a clock that kept on ticking all through a raging storm.

A real revolution brings about the kind of drastic, sudden change a war does. But for the sake of drama, we often talk in terms of "bloodless revolutions," legal and social—the civil rights revolution, the Industrial Revolution, even the so-called sexual revolution. These expressions are obviously somewhat overheated, but they express an underlying point. Social change does not move at a uniform pace. It accelerates and decelerates. There are fairly static periods and periods of rapid change, such as the Civil War and the two World Wars, and the Great Depression and the New Deal of the 1930s. Major changes in social relations and in the economy almost inevitably produce major legal change. Between 1954 and 1970, the law of race relations altered completely. The so-called sexual revolution came at about the same time; it, too, has had major legal fallout.

Today, we seem to live in an age of constant acceleration. But over time, even small differences add up to big ones. If we compare American law today with the law as it was in 1800, we are stuck with the fact of change—enormous, fundamental, revolutionary change. But no single step was of revolutionary size; there was nothing to compare with what happened in Russia in 1918 or China in the late 1940s, when the whole order crumbled at once.

Race Relations

Exactly how does law respond to social change? What is the mechanism? There are no general answers. One can trace some aspects of the relationship by following the course of race relations in the United States, or—to be more exact—black-white relations. The story is long and complex, and in many ways quite ugly. Most black Americans are descendants of slaves. They were brought to this country from the seventeenth century on. They were Africans, kidnapped, turned over to slave traders, and brought here or to the West Indies in the dirty, crowded holds of slave ships.

The law of slavery was discussed in Chapter 3. As was pointed out there, slavery was unknown to England or to the common law. Many whites, however, came to the colonies as indentured servants. Servitude was a kind of temporary slavery: a servant was bound to his master or mistress for a specific period, often seven years. At the end of this time the servant went free. Some blacks probably had this status in the beginning.

But from the beginning, too, there were signs of a different status for blacks; and from the very first, the line between servant and slave was a color line. By the middle of the seventeenth century, it was clear that some blacks were slaves, not servants. A slave is a servant for life, a servant who can never work off his status. In Virginia, at least some African blacks were treated as slaves before there is any evidence that law officially recognized slave status.

Court records from about 1640 show this custom clearly. In 1644, there is mention of a mulatto boy named Manuel, sold "as a slave for-Ever."[4] In 1662, a Virginia statute made one aspect of the relationship official: slave status was to be inherited; children of a black slave mother would be slaves themselves from birth. The same statute recognized the color line in another way. Anyone who committed "fornication with a negro" was to be fined twice the usual fine for fornication.[5]

Another law, in 1667, dealt with Christian slaves. Suppose a black slave became a Christian. Was he then free "by vertue of baptisme?" The answer was no: baptism did not "alter the condition of the person as to his bondage."[6] The slave might be free in heaven, but not here on earth. Later laws hammered home the legal reality of slavery. Slaves could not vote, hold office, own property. They were chattels, pieces of property; they could be bought and sold, given away, mortgaged, or rented out. They could be left to an heir by will or transferred by deed. The colonies spelled out these rules in elaborate codes of laws.

Meanwhile, slaves arrived by the boatload and the local population multiplied. On southern plantations, slaves made up the basic work force. They provided the muscles for planting and harvesting; they were the servants in the master's great house or in town. In fact, there were slaves in every colony—in New York, Massachusetts, and Rhode Island as well as in the South. But only in the South—in Maryland, Virginia, the Carolinas, Georgia—did slaves make up the bulk of the labor force. In the middle of the eighteenth century, 40 percent of the population of Virginia were blacks; some 96 percent of these blacks were held as slaves.

The differences between North and South became sharper after the Revolution. All of the northern states abolished slavery. There was some reaction in the South, too, against slavery. Some slaveholders took seriously the rhetoric of the Revolution, with its doctrines of inherent, inborn rights. A few southern slave owners set their slaves free or wrote their slaves' freedom into their wills. George Washington was one of these; his will provided that at the death of his wife all the slaves he owned "shall receive their freedom."

But these were exceptions. Slavery kept a powerful hold on the
southern mind; and the economy needed black bodies. King Cotton
demanded slaves. Slave codes became stricter and stricter in the
nineteenth century. Fear of slave rebellion and of northern abolitionists made the South more stubborn and defiant in the years before
the Civil War. Slave states by law discouraged manumission (setting
slaves free), and even moved to abolish it. The South barely tolerated
its free black population. Like slaves, they could not vote or hold
office. They could not testify in court against a white man. In many
southern states, if a slave got his freedom, he was required by law to
leave the state and never return. The actual practice was somewhat
more lenient, but the message was clear: slavery was the natural condition of the black. Finally, Arkansas, just before the Civil War, passed
a law to expel its few free blacks.[7]

The South imposed many restrictions on antislavery activity. It
resisted attempts to reform or limit slavery. The slavery issue, in general, poisoned relations with the North. Two issues, perhaps, stand
out: the problem of the fugitive slave, and the spread of slavery to the
territories. Northern abolitionists were dead set against returning
runaway slaves; slaveowners insisted on their rights; northern courts
were caught in the middle. The territorial question raged on for at
least forty years, from the Missouri Compromise (1820) to the Civil
War, in 1860. The South, of course, lost this long and bloody war.
Slavery was finally abolished; emancipation was rammed down white
southern throats.

But the white South did not give up its privileges so easily. When
the war ended, the old oligarchy held fast to power—at least for a
while. The defeated states (starting with Mississippi) passed new race
laws in 1865 and 1866, the so-called Black Codes. In these laws the
white legislatures somewhat grudgingly conceded that slavery was
dead and that blacks could marry and own property. But they tried
to keep the old social system alive, as far as they could. Blacks would
be slaves without slavery—landless peasants, forced to work for white
masters. In Mississippi, any "freedmen, free negroes and mulattoes"
who were over eighteen but had no "lawful employment or business"
were declared "vagrants." A vagrant was liable for a large fine, up to
fifty dollars. If he could not pay—and few blacks had any cash—he
would be hired out to anybody who would pay the fine. The employer—
often his old master—would recoup the fine from the black man's
wages. Through this and other legal requirements, the South planned
to force blacks to go back to work under their old arrangements.

But war emotions were too fresh in the North for these laws to prevail. The North insisted on repeal of the Black Codes. The South was forced to accept three new amendments to the federal Constitution which ended slavery and guaranteed civil liberties to the blacks (the Thirteenth, Fourteenth, and Fifteenth). Blacks were to be full citizens; they had to share in political life. Federal troops patrolled the South.

Blacks were indeed legally free, as never before. They could go to school, start businesses, come and go as they pleased. At least this was true on paper. But southern blacks were still at the bottom of the heap, still poor and illiterate, still treated as inferior by whites. During Reconstruction, blacks voted in some numbers. Blacks sat in southern legislatures and even on southern courts; a black man, J.J. Wright, was a justice of the supreme court of South Carolina. These were important developments. In the long run, black political power might have led to better, more equal relationships with whites. But this was not to be.

Racial equality, North or South, was in fact a house of cards. It fell apart at the touch. White people, whether high or low in the social scale and regardless of where they lived, were overwhelmingly opposed to full racial equality. Blacks had never been really welcome in the North; and northern blacks were not treated as equals. School segregation, for example, was an invention of the North, not the South—though in fairness, the North was also the first to repudiate it. The South made little attempt to educate black children, segregated or not.

The legal structure of equality was also a house of cards. When the federal troops marched home, in the late 1870s, white supremacy came back to the South with a vengeance. Black workers were tied to the soil, as before. They were tenants or sharecroppers; they lived from hand to mouth, desperately poor, completely dependent on white landowners. A network of law and legal techniques helped keep blacks in their place; the crushing weight of the law enforcement system added to poverty, illiteracy, and social prejudice, reinforcing the structure of discrimination.

Laws against "vagrancy," for example, were still on the books. Other laws made it a crime for black workers to "defraud" employers by quitting their work on white farms. It was also illegal for outsiders to "entice" workers away from their jobs—by offering them better jobs, for example. In practice, then, black farmhands were chained to white masters.[8]

The formal legal system was hardly any help. In the Reconstruction period, Congress passed a number of Civil Rights Acts. The Civil Rights Act of 1875 was a far-reaching law which banned discrimination in "inns, public conveyances on land or water, theatres, and other places of public amusement." But in the *Civil Rights Cases*,[9] the Supreme Court declared the law unconstitutional. Congress, said the Court, had overstepped the bounds of the Fourteenth Amendment. The amendment applied only to "state action," that is, to acts of public authorities; it banned "discriminative and unjust laws" but not "individual offenses." People were still free to "discriminate," if they wished, in their homes, their social lives, their businesses; the Fourteenth Amendment had no power to reach into these spheres.

By this time, Reconstruction was in full retreat. The resurgent South swept off the table whatever crumbs of political influence blacks had picked up. There would be no more black faces in southern legislatures, no more black judges in courtrooms. Some black officeholders were voted out; a few were impeached. Toward the end of the nineteenth century, the South began to weave a tight new fabric of legal segregation—the Jim Crow laws. These crystallized and formalized the attitudes and customs of the dominant whites. They made a rigid set of rules out of fluid social practice.[10] Any dissenters, white or black, had to face the fact that law as well as custom was against them. Blacks sank further into a swamp of oppression and injustice.

A few black voices were raised in protest in the courts; but the courts turned a deaf ear. In 1890, Louisiana passed a Jim Crow railroad law. Its title was an "Act to promote the comfort of passengers." Its message had nothing to do with comfort, however. Blacks were no longer free to sit in the same railroad cars as whites; the only exception was for "nurses attending children." Black and white otherwise had to be separate. A light-skinned black named Plessy ran afoul of the law. He tried to sit in the white section of a train, but was thrown off, and for his impudence landed in the parish jail of New Orleans. His protests ultimately reached the United States Supreme Court, whose famous (or infamous) decision, *Plessy* v. *Ferguson*[11] was handed down in 1896.

By a vote of eight to one, the Supreme Court gave a green light to segregation. Nothing in the Constitution made Jim Crow laws illegal, it said. So long as facilities were "equal," it did not matter that they were "separate." The law could take into account the "established usages, customs and traditions of the people" especially for "the preservation of the public peace and good order." What these words meant was clear: the southern (white) way of life would prevail. The struggle for racial equality suffered a deadly blow; the highest court in the country accepted, and even praised, the American brand of apartheid.

John Marshall Harlan wrote a passionate, vigorous dissent. He insisted that the Constitution was "color-blind." It neither "knows nor tolerates classes among citizens. In respect of civil rights, all citizens are equal before the law." The Louisiana statute, "under the guise of . . . equal accommodation," was an act of oppression—a device to compel blacks "to keep to themselves while travelling." This, Harlan thought, violated the spirit and letter of the Civil War amendment. It was an evil act, and it would encourage race hatred and violence for years to come.

Harlan's predictions were accurate, but he was swimming against the tide. *Plessy* v. *Ferguson* encouraged the South to continue with its program of segregation. Soon every southern state had an arsenal of Jim Crow laws. Even jails were segregated: Arkansas law called for separate "apartments" for white and black convicts, "separate bunks, beds, bedding, separate dining tables and all other furnishings."[12]

At the same time, the southern states moved to strip blacks of political influence. They destroyed the black right to vote. This was, in theory, illegal; but the South found ways to do it: poll taxes, literacy tests, sometimes sheer terror. Whites were generally excused from literacy and other tests, sometimes by virtue of "grandfather clauses." The Oklahoma version, struck down later by the Supreme Court, required voters to be able to read and write any section of the Oklahoma Constitution. But it exempted anybody who was entitled to vote on January 1, 1866, in any country; and anybody descended from such a voter. Of course, blacks could not qualify this way. The tactics worked. The number of black voters in most southern states dropped off to almost nothing. The rest of the country stood silent.

Stripped of political rights, the southern black was now helpless. A black who dared cross the color line, or who outraged local opinion, ran the risk of sudden death. The bloody law of lynch mob and rope enforced the grim southern code. Lynching was at its height around the turn of the century. Hundreds of prisoners, almost all of them black, were dragged from prison, hung, or burned; local authorities looked the other way. The North was uncomfortable with lynching; many voices, black and white, cried out against the practice; but the southern system was deeply, firmly entrenched and the national will to oppose it was weak and diffuse.

White supremacy was the cornerstone of southern culture—and the southern economy. Segregation survived legally because strong social forces held it in place. A counterattack began early in the twentieth century. It was slow and tortuous at first; but it, too, was persistent. Like segregation itself, it had an important legal aspect and embodied an important legal strategy. The fight for racial justice was a fight for power in society; but part of its strength came from its appeal to morality and its firm commitment to law.

The National Association for the Advancement of Colored People (NAACP) was founded just before the First World War. From the start, it had a strong legal arm. The NAACP defended black rights in court and brought lawsuits to expand those rights. Not all these lawsuits were successful, but some were spectacularly so. In *Guinn* v. *United States* (1915),[13] the NAACP took part in the fight against Oklahoma's grandfather clause. This case was won. But even victories did not produce real change in race relations. Southern states, for example—despite cases like *Guinn*—had plenty of ways to keep blacks out of the voting booth. The United States Civil Rights Commission, in a report issued in 1961, found sixteen counties in the Deep South in which not a single black was registered to vote, even though blacks were a majority in these counties.[14]

Time, however, was ultimately on the side of the NAACP and the black population. The world outside the courtroom was rapidly changing. By 1950, the plantation system was dying in the South. In the twentieth century, blacks migrated north in great numbers, looking for work. The Second World War drew more blacks North, with the promise of factory jobs. The black community developed more and more a deep consciousness of self. Internationally, colonialism was in decline. The Second World War was in part a war against racist ideology. It was jarring and discordant, perhaps, to fight the war with segregated troops; but the system hung on. President Harry Truman ordered the army, navy, and air force desegregated, though this was after the war. By then, broad change was in the air.

A climax was reached in 1954, when the Supreme Court, on one of its most historic Mondays, announced the stupendous, unanimous decision in *Brown* v. *Board of Education*.[15] There was only one opinion. By Supreme Court standards it was very short. It was signed by the chief justice, Earl Warren, recently appointed by President Eisenhower; but he spoke for the entire Court. The *Brown* case dealt with segregated schools.

In the Deep South and in some border states, black and white children had to go to separate schools. Oliver Brown, the black plaintiff, lived in Topeka, Kansas; his daughter, Linda, went to a segregated school.

The Court declared segregation illegal in the schools. That was startling enough—a massive shock to the South. But *Brown* was only the beginning. A chain of decisions struck down race discrimination and segregation in every aspect of public life—in parks, swimming pools, beaches, municipal services. Despite howls of protest from the South, the Court never backed down, never looked back. The cases sent an important signal to the black community and its allies: federal courts would not waver in defense of minority rights. Their doors would be open to blacks, to enforce racial equality. The promise of the Fourteenth Amendment would at last be fulfilled. More: courts would redefine and expand the classic rights.

Enforcement of *Brown* was never easy. The South resisted, dragged its heels, dug in. "Massive resistance" was the slogan in the former Confederacy. In 1962, eight years after *Brown*, not a single black child went to school with whites in Mississippi, Alabama, or South Carolina. Even colleges in these states were still rigidly segregated.[16]

Civil rights had become, quite literally, a struggle. At times blood was shed. Civil rights workers were harassed, beaten, ostracized. Martyrs died for the cause, most of them black. A church was bombed and black children died. There were sit-ins, marches, petitions, riots; nonviolent protest spread throughout the South. Meanwhile, legal struggles went on in the law courts. Both modes of battle were vital. Neither was sufficient in itself. The marchers and battlers needed lawyers; and the work of the lawyers meant nothing without action on the streets.

A generation has gone by since *Brown*. School desegregation is still controversial, still an issue in the country. There are still hundreds of all-black (and all-white) schools. Most now are in the North, products of the neighborhood school system, segregated housing patterns, and "white flight"—that is, the migration of the white middle class to the suburbs. The school bus is one possible technique for mixing the races, but it is bitterly resisted—and not always by whites. The Supreme Court approved of busing in 1971;[17] but this did not end the debate or the constant stream of lawsuits. The Court itself has become, in recent years, a shade more hesitant about this remedy.

In many big cities, public school children are, in numbers, overwhelmingly black. Integration in the *Brown* sense is no longer even possible, at least not inside city limits. Yet this does not mean that

Brown has failed. All-black schools are not segregated schools, in the older sense. They have integrated staffs, and the school boards treat them fairly. Indeed, in some cities, blacks control the boards of education. Black schools face immense problems; but they are not second-class—not Jim Crow—as they were in the South.

Race relations are in constant evolution. The Civil Rights Act of 1964 was a great leap forward. Title II outlawed race discrimination in "any place of public accommodation." This included inns, hotels, motels, restaurants, cafeterias, lunch counters, soda fountains, "any motion picture house, theater, concert hall, sports arena, stadium or other place of exhibition or entertainment," and "any gasoline station." The law was, of course, soon challenged in court. But this time the Supreme Court upheld the statute, and in sweeping terms.[18] The challenger in the second of these cases was a "family-owned restaurant in Birmingham, Alabama," Ollie's Barbecue by name, which specialized in "barbecued meats and homemade pies." This kind of small, local eatery stood at the very limit of the law; but the Supreme Court was willing—even eager—to validate the law to the maximum extent and smash segregation forever.

This time, the barriers in public places really did collapse. The Civil Rights Act took hold. A black man for the first time could drive a car across the country, and eat at any restaurant, stay at any motel. A strong Voting Rights Act (1965) put another nail in the coffin of the old order. The federal government now promised to stand behind the right of blacks to vote. Black political power increased enormously. Blacks began to appear again in legislatures and city halls, where they had been absent since Reconstruction. Political power also grew in the North. Black mayors were elected in Detroit, Atlanta, Los Angeles, Newark, Cleveland, Chicago, Philadelphia.

Race is still a burning issue in American life. Social and legal change have moved in the direction of racial equality. But the movement has not been smooth, even in recent years. There have been many zigs and zags. Segregation is officially dead. There is no chance it will come back to life. But there is still a huge black underclass in every major city and in the rural South; there is still a wide gap between the incomes of blacks and of whites. There are too few black doctors, lawyers, business executives, scientists, architects. More black babies die than white babies. Twice the percentage of blacks are unemployed.

Are new measures called for? Many blacks (and white liberals) say yes. What is needed is an extra helping hand—something that goes beyond desegregation. It is not enough to dismantle legal barriers. Affirmative steps are now needed, positive programs of help. But this touches a raw nerve. Many whites fear and resent these "favors" to blacks. They feel threatened in their jobs or their homes.

The issue came to a head in the famous *Bakke* case.[19] Alan Bakke, who was white, applied to the medical school of the University of California at Davis. Davis had a special admissions program for minorities; it had, in fact, a quota, by which a certain number of places were set aside for blacks and other minorities in each entering class. Davis rejected Alan Bakke's application, but let in at the same time, he claimed, blacks with lower grades and scores than his. This, he felt, violated his constitutional rights.

The Supreme Court obviously found the case terribly troubling. Its decision was fragmented and confused. The Court struck down the Davis system of quotas, and (by a bare majority) ordered the school to let Bakke in. But the justices wrote several separate opinions, and there was no true majority on any major point. A bare majority of the justices felt that some forms of "benign" discrimination were legal; but exactly which ones, and how far a school could go in its affirmative action programs, remained unanswered.

In a sense, then, the *Bakke* case settled nothing, except for Alan Bakke himself, who forced open the door to a medical career. Affirmative action and benign discrimination are living issues, very much unresolved. They are also hotly contested in sex discrimination cases. Most blacks feel a strong claim of right to affirmative action to undo the centuries of injustice; some even feel that they have a right to reparations. They feel that economic and political equality are still far-off goals. They are afraid the country is getting tired of the issue once more, and that progress has ground to a halt.

One thing is clear: changes in race relations since *Brown* have been, by any measure, immense. Unlike many legal "victories" before *Brown,* the earth *did* move, the landscape shifted in a permanent way. How much of this was because of *Brown?* How much credit goes to law and legal process?

It is impossible, of course, to separate cause and effect. The *Brown* case did not start the civil rights movement; that much is obvious. The movement came first, and it "caused" *Brown,* if the word *cause* is appropriate at all. But once in place, *Brown* and later cases played a major role in the developing drama. They played a role like the bridge in our story. Congress added to the structural framework by passing new strong laws on civil rights. This tough, bony structure of law helped channel and concentrate power and influence in society. As more black people voted, it became more difficult for candidates to run for office on a white-racist basis. Race prejudice did not disappear, but it went underground.

This, too, was important. The law not only expressed power, it also expressed ideals; and when power and ideals were united, racism became an outlawed concept. Outlaws sometimes wield their own form of sinister strength. But in this case, they lost their legitimacy; and that loss can be crucial at times. The chain of events since *Brown* helped transform people's thoughts and ideas, their concepts of legal right; it modified their view of law and what they expected the law to perform. Social processes lay behind these changes in legal culture; but legal culture, like the bridge, reinforced these processes, and in time and in turn led to further social change.

Law and the Social Revolution

Tremendous changes have also taken place in recent years in culture, life-style, and social behavior. These changes have gone far beyond race relations, though the civil rights revolution may have been the cause—or effect—of some of these changes. There has been a revolution in customs and habits of life, and notoriously, a so-called sexual revolution, much discussed in recent years. This revolution has taken a number of forms. There is a huge increase in the number of young couples and not-so-young couples who live together without bothering to get married. There is the gay rights movement, demanding legitimacy for the "sexual minorities." Pornography is sold more or less out in the open, and protected by law to a large extent. There are relaxed attitudes toward "dirty" speech, in public and private; a decline in the double standard of sexual morality; and so on.

Our concern is with law—more specifically, with the role legal institutions play either in helping to bring these changes about, in resisting them, in adapting to them, or in altering their form. Of course, we must be more precise in describing our subject. Exactly what is the revolution in social norms and behaviors? Everyone has his own notion. At the core is the idea that certain standards of conduct that were widely accepted in the United States have now broken down. Specifically, what has changed is, first, the idea that a single official code of personal behavior governs (or should govern) the country; second, that the code more or less coincides with the moral commands of traditional Christianity, overlaid with a dose of Victorian morality; third, and most relevant for our purposes, that the government has the right—indeed, the duty—to turn these precepts into legal rules and to enforce them as best it can.

All three of these notions are under sustained attack, and all three have been drastically weakened in their hold on the law. Many illustrations that we might use concern sexual morality, though by no means all. Consider, for example, the legal and social position of minority religions. There was never, of course, any official religion in the United States, and in theory everyone enjoys total freedom of religion. The First Amendment makes a bold, positive statement: "Congress shall make no law respecting an establishment of religion, or prohibiting the free exercise thereof." Some state constitutions are even more emphatic. The Wisconsin Constitution states that "the right of every man to worship Almighty God according to the dictates of his own conscience shall never be infringed"; the state cannot "give preference" to any one religion, or spend any public money on any "religious society."[20] In fact, however, there has always been a semiofficial range of religions in the country; and Americans have found it hard to tolerate "free exercise" for religions that seemed too strange— that wandered too far from the familiar course.

The troubled history of the Church of Jesus Christ of the Latter-day Saints, or Mormons, is a case in point. Joseph Smith founded this religion around 1830. From the beginning, his followers were persecuted; Smith himself was murdered by a mob. The Mormons traveled west, hoping to find a sanctuary. They founded a community in the basin of the Great Salt Lake, in what is now Utah. But they were not destined to be left alone. The Mormons practiced polygamy, which was, they believed God's will. The practice was too much for the rest of the country to stomach. "Mormonism," one Protestant minister proclaimed, is a "great surge of licentiousness . . . it is the concentrated corruption of this land, it is the brothel of the nation, it is hell enthroned."[21] The "free exercise" of polygamy went too much against the grain of American opinion. There was no way the majority could tolerate polygamy, and therefore they could not tolerate the Mormons themselves.

The Mormons wanted only to live their faith in peace. Congress felt otherwise. In 1862, Congress passed the Morrill Act, aimed explicitly at the Mormons, which made polygamy a federal crime in the territories, including Utah.[22] A man named George Reynolds was indicted under the act, convicted, and sentenced to prison. He appealed to the United States Supreme Court. His defense was freedom of religion—his right under the First Amendment.

In *Reynolds* v. *United States*,[23] the Supreme Court affirmed Reynolds's conviction. Polygamy was "odious"; Congress was right to declare it a crime. Merely because polygamy was a tenet of someone's religion did not excuse the practice: if a person believed that "human sacrifices were a necessary part of religious worship," was that an excuse? Or if a wife "religiously believed it was her duty to burn herself upon the funeral pile of her dead husband," would the state allow this to happen?

The Mormons argued, with a good deal of justice, that they were not licentious people at all; they were religious people, who had the highest moral standards. They put enormous stress on wholesome, traditional family life. But the rest of the country refused to believe them. Polygamy, to the ordinary American, was a barbaric custom, and socially dangerous besides. In the *Reynolds* case, the Court noted that polygamy was "exclusively a feature of the life of Asiatic and of African people"; it also "led to the patriarchal principle . . . which . . . fetters the people in stationary despotism."

Here, as is usually the case, the Court no doubt reflected what the country felt as a whole. *Reynolds* demonstrated the limits of national tolerance, which stopped far short of allowing multiple wives. Tolerance meant the right—for white people, at least—to blend into the dominant culture without barriers of caste or class. It did not imply the right to "do your own thing"—to live as a free, unconventional spirit. It never occurred to the justices that Asiatic and African people might claim the same level of civilization—and legality—as white Christians from northern Europe.

Wisconsin v. *Yoder*[24] is a modern case which also deals with offbeat religion. The contrast with *Reynolds* is in some ways striking. Jonas Yoder was a member of a minority religion, the Old Order Amish. Another defendant, Adin Yutzy, belonged to the Conservative Amish Mennonite Church. The defendants lived in Wisconsin. Under state law, children had to go to school until sixteen. The defendants refused to keep their children in school past the eighth grade. They were fined five dollars, and appealed. The case—clearly a test case—went all the way to the United States Supreme Court.

The defense, once again, was freedom of religion. Public high school, or any advanced schooling, was "contrary to the Amish religion and way of life." If defendants obeyed the Wisconsin law, it would "endanger their own salvation and that of their children." The Amish insisted on living in their own church community, "separate and apart from the world and worldly influence."

This time, the Supreme Court was willing to accept the claim. The First Amendment guaranteed the right to live outside the "conventional 'mainstream.'" The state had no power to impose its will on a religion and a way of life "that is odd or even erratic but interferes with no rights or interests of others." The Wisconsin school law was a valid use of state power in general; but the Amish also had rights, and were entitled to be exempted from the law.

The *Yoder* case, as has been often pointed out, has some quite conservative features. The Amish are intensely religious, rural, old-fashioned people. Their values do not offend the majority; in some ways they are merely extreme forms of values admired in the dominant culture. But much the same could have been said about the Mormons. Polygamy itself was a Biblical practice. Despite the differences between *Reynolds* and *Yoder*, it does look as if the 1970s Court was less wedded to the idea of cultural assimilation, more open-minded, more willing to tolerate groups different in life-style from the rest of the country.

Yet there are definite limits to freedom of religion. No court even today would accept human sacrifice or the burning of widows, in the name of religion, any more than was true in 1878. The controversy over cults was heightened by the horrifying events at Jonestown, Guyana, in November 1978: hundreds of followers of a fantical leader committed suicide at his orders, by drinking poisoned Kool-Aid. Nonstandard religions still make most Americans fearful, suspicious. The Unification Church (the "Moonies") has provoked intense legal action as well. The church is under the wing of the First Amendment—but to what extent? Are the tactics of this church—its aggressive recruiting, its dictatorial demands on its members—protected by law? Desperate parents have snatched their children out of the clutches of this church and had them "deprogrammed." Since these "Moonies" are all over eighteen, how can the parents legally do this? Is this not a way of life that young people may freely choose? If so, parents cannot insist that their children must submit to deprogrammers. On this last point, at least one California case quite clearly agreed.[25] But however such questions are resolved, they clearly raise issues resembling those in *Reynolds* and *Yoder*.

Changes in laws about obscenity and sexual deviance also bring the legal system face to face with the social revolution. Chapter 9 discussed the rise and fall of laws against victimless crime and the renewed interest in enforcing the traditional moral code from the late nineteenth century on. Sex and obscenity laws were tightened; abortion was criminalized; stronger laws against gambling and Sabbath breaking were also passed. This movement, which began around 1870, may have been the last gasp of a dying social order. It was perhaps the last stand of a beleaguered concept—the notion that there was, and ought to be, a single basic moral code for the country, essentially the code of Protestant America.

A flood of immigrants, many from southern and eastern Europe, had recently entered the country. These immigrants had their own cultures; these cultures differed from the culture of Old Americans in crucial respects. Joseph Gusfield uses this culture clash to explain why the temperance movement became so strong in this period. He sees it as a kind of Protestant backlash, which snowballed until it reached its peak in the passage of the Prohibition Amendment.[26]

The Harrison Narcotics Act (1914) was another "triumph" of morality; it made criminals out of drug addicts, and was perhaps an even greater disaster than Prohibition, in the long run. Culture clash was a factor in the war on "dope" and "dope fiends." The earliest drug laws—for example, in California[27]—were laws against "opium dens;" the Chinese ran these dens, and to white Californians, opium was one aspect of the "Chinese problem." The drive against marijuana was also aimed primarily at a single ethnic group, the Chicanos; marijuana was supposedly "a direct by-product of unrestricted Mexican immigration." In "areas with concentrations of Mexican immigrants, the fear of marihuana was intense."[28]

The old moral code had no doubt begun to decay, in practice. Behavior, as usual, precedes new law, and is decisive in creating new law. But changes in ideas—in attitudes—shift along with behavior. At one time, there was a standard notion of what respectable behavior meant. Respectable people had moderate sex lives, within the boundaries of Christian marriage. They did not get drunk and disorderly. They did not gamble or take drugs. They worked hard and obeyed the law. Of course, society had plenty of dirty secrets. There were millions of heavy drinkers. Prostitutes sold their bodies on city streets. Gambling and vice were available in every city. There were tramps and hoboes who drifted from place to place. But nobody *defended* vice and drink. People either behaved according to the code or— what is almost as important—they accepted it as the official code; they pledged allegiance to it even if they broke every single commandment.

What happened from the late nineteenth century on was perhaps a subtle change in the legitimacy of the traditional code. More people began to question it, and not just through their conduct; they questioned the code as the norm, the ideal, as well; they attacked its official status. Italian Catholics, for example, saw nothing wrong in a glass of wine. Others leveled more extensive fire on "puritanism" and "prudery." Most of the habits and norms of the new immigrants were not at all offensive—nothing to compare with Mormon polygamy or the Chinese opium culture. Nonetheless, the old elites may have felt that the sun was setting on their empire of values—that the fine old house of American culture was rotting away.

They did not accept their fate lying down. If rot was attacking the house, then the timbers needed reconstruction. The majority turned to law to enforce their code and to shore up their monopoly of moral legitimacy. Law acts as a substitute for informal norms, in a complex society. It is used to keep a diverse population glued together in some reasonable working order, despite all the differences in values and habits. It replaces informal methods—those methods which worked well enough on the tiny island of Tristan de Cunha, or among little clans and groups of hunters and gatherers, or in clubs, families, and groups of friends.

Society turns to law for help in shoring up the house—in preventing further dilapidation. But the law does not necessarily work as expected. The very fact that evokes the use of law—cultural diversity—dooms the legal process to imperfect performance. If the law chooses sides—if it outlaws the codes and customs of a minority—it may meet with severe resistance. Most people think Prohibition was a dismal failure. The Harrison Act has had an even worse history. Most fair-minded people concede this point. It created a black market in drugs and drove addicts into lives of crime; it contributed to urban decay. The policy not only failed; it also did incalculable harm. Perhaps there is no reasonable alternative,[29] but that does not alter the fact that drug laws have failed in their purpose.

As far as sexual morality is concerned, the law has been even more ineffective. The social revolution, it turns out, is not a flash in the pan. The old morality kept on decaying in practice; there were more and more strident demands to legitimize other life-styles. In the last generation, the forces that insist on change have become strong enough to force society and the law to meet their demands halfway. The last word, of course, has not been spoken. "Moral" forces have counterattacked, in force. Pornography is still intensely controversial. So are gay rights. So is abortion—liberalized by the Supreme Court, attacked by the "prolife" movement. The administration of Ronald Reagan is committed to traditional values. Many legal battles lie ahead in Congress, in the courts, in the public mind.

The Decay of Authority

What lies behind the social revolution? Some see it as part of a long-term trend, the general weakening of authority in the United States. It began, perhaps, early in our history. The Puritan colonies were dominated by the clergy, but this situation did not last. When the country became independent, it was a nation without an established church, a nobility, or an aristocracy of birth or merit. Such nineteenth-century visitors as Alexis de Tocqueville were amazed at how "democratic" this country was, which meant, among other things, that the population showed little respect for traditional authority, compared to countries like France. It was a nation of social and political equals; or at least it looked that way to a European, despite the slaves in the South. (The subordinate position of women was an issue most men never noticed.)

Every society has an authority structure. Every society has high and low. No society even comes close to pure equality. There were and are many kinds of authority, many forms of hierarchy, in this country. Millions of Americans are deeply religious, and follow the word of their churches. Learning is respected. So is money. So is political power. There is also the authority of custom, and the authority of traditional morality. These are a kind of inner monarchy, whose word is passed along by parents, teachers, and preachers. For many people, tradition is a powerful source of control.

Authority is hard to measure. It seems that some traditional forms of authority have been slowly losing their grip over time. There is considerable discussion, for example, of the fate of family authority. Clearly, family authority is by no means dead. Father's word may not be "law" any more; but most children do obey their parents. They do their homework and they listen to teacher in school, even if they do not show old-fashioned respect or obey like little Prussians. Most people follow a definite code of behavior. The decline of authority is a matter of degree. Studies suggest a decline in respect for governmental authority, a decline in trust, a crisis of legitimacy; but these problems are perhaps quite selective.

Legal process, in a sense, rushes in to fill the vacuum. It has in many ways replaced other forms of authority. In the colonial period, officials swore to be loyal to their king; they had a personal bond to the crown. The president of the United States takes an oath to support the Constitution. His "king" is a legal document, a symbol of law, rather than any human authority. In this country, ultimate power is supposed to rest with the people; more concretely, it lies in the structure of laws. We pledge allegiance to the flag, but true allegiance runs not to the flag, or to the president, or to some sacred text—or even to God. Rather, our commitment is to a way of governing, a process, a set of procedures, a way of making decisions—to law, in other words. There is a shared understanding that we obey and respect the rules of the game.

These rules hold society together. They are essential nuts and bolts that keep the structure from falling apart. As other authorities weaken, the role of law becomes stronger, as an impartial, impersonal arbiter of disputes. Law is a way out of the dilemmas of politics and controversy. Even if this idea of law above and beyond all politics is a myth, it is still a valuable way to appeal to people's inner voices, to motives higher than their crude self-interest. All this may explain the trend so many have noticed: the trend to adjudicate all sorts of social and economic questions. In court, these questions get answers; and both sides usually respect what the courts decide. Other countries do not have quite the same system. De Tocqueville noticed the American habit in embryo in the nineteenth century. There is no political or social question in America, he said, that does not turn into a judicial one. Today De Tocqueville's insight seems even more obviously accurate. Many people are alarmed by this turn of events; some are proud of what has happened.

In any event, law and (rather surprisingly) the courts stand at the very core of crucial decisions in the United States. These decisions concern policy in many spheres of life, including the major social questions and such sticky issues as obscenity, abortion, sexual deviancy, personal morality, and drug laws—in short, the whole social revolution.

A Modern Instance:
The Palimony Case

Social forces constantly make and remake law. We often see this happening before our very eyes, so to speak. One more example is the notorious "palimony" case of *Marvin* v. *Marvin*.[30] Lee Marvin, the movie actor, and a singer, Michele Triola, lived together in one household for seven years. They were never married to each other. But Michele Triola called herself Michele Marvin, and they behaved in all respects like man and wife. Then the relationship ended. In 1970, Michele Marvin sued Lee Marvin, demanding half of his earnings—more than a million dollars—for the years they lived together. She claimed he had promised her this share in return for her promise to come and live with him, which she did.

The trial court in Los Angeles threw the case out of court. It relied on a long line of prior decisions which refused to enforce such agreements. To live together outside of marriage was immoral in the eyes of the law; and any supposed contract to behave this way was unenforceable. Michele Marvin appealed to a higher court; and the California Supreme Court, by a six-to-one margin, reversed the lower court decision. The trial court, they said, had acted too hastily; Michele might well have a good cause of action. She should be allowed to prove her case. They sent the matter back down below for a trial.

The opinion of the California Supreme Court is technical and full of legal nuances. These subtleties were, of course, lost on the millions of people who read about the case in the newspapers or heard about it on the evening news. Only a handful of lawyers read the actual text. The public did understand one thing, however: Michele's case had opened the door to a new kind of lawsuit. Cohabitation was no longer an outlaw status, on the fringe of respectability and legality. It was or could be a definite legal relationship; rights and duties might flow out of it, and a court would enforce any arrangement the partners reasonably made.

The Supreme Court of California had pushed legal doctrine in a new direction—but why? One point seems obvious to layman and lawyer alike: times had changed, morals had changed. The census bureau estimated that 2.2 million unmarried couples were living together in 1978.[31] The numbers had risen sharply since 1970; cohabitation was becoming more popular, year by year.

The California Supreme Court lives in society along with the rest of us. The justices have eyes and ears; they read newspapers and watch TV. They surely know people—their own children, perhaps—who live together unmarried. Cohabitation is a way of life, like it or not, and it is spreading among all classes of society. When social arrangements change, it is no surprise that legal rights and duties rearrange themselves. The California court argued at various points in its opinion that *Marvin* v. *Marvin* was not really a break with past law. Courts like to stress the continuity of law, even when they create new doctrines. But the Court also frankly referred to the altered social context, to the "radical" changes taking place in "the mores of society."

Michele Marvin's victory in the California Supreme Court did not settle her claim. It now had to be assessed on the facts. The new trial was long and bitter. It made headlines, and was rich in gossip and scandal. Legally speaking, the outcome was something of an anticlimax. Michele Marvin won a modest victory, so modest it was almost defeat. She was awarded something on the order of $100,000. This was small potatoes, compared to the size of her claim. Probably she failed to win more because her evidence was weak. She insisted she and Lee Marvin had come to an "agreement," but she had no convincing proof. In the end, both sides claimed victory. One thing was clear, though it was cold comfort for Michele Marvin: the law had changed. No moral or legal barrier stood in the way of claims like hers, at least in California.

The social revolution had touched one field of law, at one point in space and time. Duties and rights were realigned. The exact realignment was not, as far as we can tell, foreordained with iron logic. The spread of cohabitation meant that the issue was sure to bob to the surface somewhere in the legal system. Legal change was bound to happen; but the California solution was by no means inevitable or predetermined. No one can say the new legal pattern had to take exactly this form, at this time, or that this was the best way to handle the situation. We can say only that arrangements were bound to change—bound to take some new form better suited to the new facts than the arrangements discarded.

What effect, in turn, did *Marvin* v. *Marvin* have on society? The case was famous—notorious, in fact. The *New York Times* ran seventeen articles on the case between 1976 and 1979. *Time* magazine featured it in a story; so did *Playboy;* comedians told jokes about it on TV; cartoons appeared in magazines. The word—or at least some word—got around. Millions of people learned that the law had changed. They learned this vaguely and inaccurately, but they did smell something happening.

What took place next is hardly surprising. Other disappointed lovers took their cue from *Marvin* v. *Marvin.* In the two years after the California case, about 100 lawsuits of the *Marvin* type were filed in various courts.[32] Others were probably settled before getting that far. In many states, cases went up to higher courts on appeal. There the outcomes were mixed. Some states stuck to their guns, at least for the time being. Others—Oregon, Minnesota, New Jersey, and Alaska—climbed on the new bandwagon and followed the line laid down in *Marvin* v. *Marvin*. The cases were establishing a trend.

Did behavior outside the law change after *Marvin?* In one way, it probably did. Some wealthy people with "live-ins" no doubt became more cautious about what they said and did. The case stimulated a few people to consult their lawyers; a few cohabitors drew up contracts with each other spelling out rights and duties and setting out the claims they asserted, if any, to their partner's earnings. Once again, we can invoke the metaphor of the bridge. Social forces bent the law in one direction; but once the law changed, new forces and new alignments emerged; law itself became an influence on conduct. The California Supreme Court responded to social change; it formalized and restated the problem, redefined the issue, and (in a blaze of publicity) gave rise to new expectations. The case also probably helped in a minor way to legitimize a way of life that in the past would have scandalized all respectable people. To be sure, many people still think cohabitation is immoral. No doubt they disapprove of what the supreme court of California did. But the court did not invent, or spread, cohabitation.

Changes in morals, morality, ways of life—changes in culture and expectation—create new demands that press in on legal institutions, including the courts. These institutions then change their behavior, as they are pushed and pulled by rival social forces. Legal rules, processes, and behaviors shift—move right or left, up or down. The new legal situation freezes customs into more solid forms, reinforces certain expectations, sends out new messages, subtly alters culture. It changes ways of thinking and looking at life, the way a prism alters beams of light. This is a constant process in society.

To take still one more example, environmental law is a whole new field that has sprung up in recent years. It originates, basically, with the environmental movement. This movement did not begin inside the legal system. It began outside, in society. It burst into consciousness and spilled over into law. But today this field of law is a big, important, tangible reality. Lawyers and the public talk about "impact statements," "endangered species lists," "clean air amendments," and so on. Environmental law, in turn, provides hooks or handles for environmental groups to use in putting pressure on society to move still further in a particular direction.

The course of sociolegal change is not smooth and painless. It is at best a bumpy road. The environmental movement, for example, is continually embroiled in controversy. Many people think "things have gone too far." They believe that "extremists" have hurt the economy, all for the sake of a few trees or fish. An important countermovement became prominent in the 1970s. Some of its leaders have gained political power. James Watt, President Reagan's secretary of the interior until late 1983, came out of this background. Arguments rage over oil leases in California waters, over coal mines on public land, over nuclear wastes, over the dredging of canals, and so on. Both sides push and pull—in the courts, in legislatures, in the election booth. As they do, they push and pull at the doctrines and rules, the raw material of law. Environmental law is in constant flux.

Every major change in social behavior has an impact on law. And every major change in law has its roots in changes outside of it, in social behavior. The "medical malpractice crisis" is on the surface a purely legal crisis. There has been a rash of lawsuits against doctors and hospitals; these stimulated, or panicked, insurance companies, who raised doctors' premiums sky-high; the doctors fought for legislative curbs on tort suits. But the whole crisis would be inconceivable without deep changes in the organization of medicine. The interaction of doctors and patients, the structure of medical practice, the growth of specialization, the development of modern surgery and pharmacology have all altered the way doctors and patients react to each other; and the legal rules of the horse-and-buggy days were bound to be swept away.

The struggle over the death penalty also shows how courts and law are exposed to outside pressure. In the battles over capital punishment, the courts are often in the spotlight, often in center stage. But they are really not the major actors in the battle, in an important sense. The crime rate, its effect on public opinion, vast shifts of political force—these are backstage, so to speak, pulling the strings.

Still, the sheer mass, the volume, of law keeps growing, one way or another. Where is it leading us? And can we say anything about trends?

15

Epilogue:
The Future of Law in
the United States

M ANY PEOPLE FEEL that law is too much with us, that Americans
are too involved with law, litigation, and legal process for their own
good. Certainly, American society seems to be trapped in a net of
law—more than is true of other countries or was true here in older
times. Some people think we are sinking deeper and deeper into legal
quicksand. A national magazine bewailed the "suing society," in which
"trust is undermined and creativity discouraged" because of endless
litigation.[1] Others think the growth of the American legal system is
rather a matter of pride, a sign of commitment to justice for all.

The first fourteen chapters of this book gave evidence of the pervasive role of law, legal process, and legal institutions in the United
States. Even the simple acts of everyday life—a trip to the grocery
store—presuppose a vast superstructure of law. Law rules both the
ordinary and the extraordinary in this society. Much of the news on
an average day is news of law, to an astonishing degree. Most of what
makes news is what is public; nowadays that is almost sure to be legal
or governmental, or to have some legal or governmental angle. This
is true, too, of natural disasters (so-called acts of God, floods, hurri-
canes, earthquakes) and of major accidents (plane crashes, fires, col-
lapsing walls). Somehow law gets involved. We cannot avoid bringing
up the Civil Aeronautics Board, air controllers, fire ordinances, disaster relief, government inspection of dams and levees, and so on. A
plane crash or any other tragedy is bound to produce a flurry of inves-
tigations. It will also surely bring about a flock of lawsuits. These are

now almost as certain as death and taxes.

Everybody talks about the "litigious society" and about "too much law." Are these any better than impressions? Is there something more systematic we can say about the volume of law? Can it be measured scientifically? There is no real way to take a yardstick to the legal system and measure it. It has no definite beginning, middle, and end. But there are some crude ways to show the fact of growth. There are now over 600,000 practicing lawyers. The sheer volume of statutes, state and federal, can be easily seen, and it is growing. The collected statutes of New Jersey of 1847 fit into one snug volume of about 1,000 pages. Today, the statutes of New Jersey fill an entire shelf.

The population of New Jersey has also grown since 1847. The 1850 census recorded a population of 489,555 in New Jersey: it is over 7 million today. But growth in the laws is more than a question of keeping up with population. The statutes left untouched many aspects of life in 1847 which are densely regulated today. If a state passes a law regulating dry cleaners, the law will apply whether there are 30 dry cleaners in the state or 30,000. Of course, regulation is unlikely if there are, in fact, only 30 dry cleaners. The growth of law is not unrelated to population size; but the relationship is not a simple one.

There were no dry cleaners at all in 1847. There were also no telephones, computers, automobiles, atomic wastes, oral contraceptives, television sets, and so on. The astonishing changes in science and industry since 1847 have blown apart the old limits of law. There was a little bit of traffic law before the automobile; but machines that swarm the streets by the millions and have the power to speed at 100 MPH create problems much greater than any a horse and a buggy can create.

The automobile also expands the zone of personal freedom, in ways we take for granted. For centuries, most people in the world were tied to the soil almost literally. There was no easy way to see the world beyond the crest of some small hill near the family hut or shack. In 1847, even New Jersey farmers or textile workers in Lowell, Massachusetts, were essentially tied to home base. Travel was difficult and slow.

Technology vastly expanded the mobility of the average person. The railroad was already a great advance; but it was the automobile that worked the most fantastic change in our lives. Today, most families own or have access to a car. They can move from city to country, country to city, state to state, almost at will. The car means freedom to explore parks and museums, to visit relatives who moved to Colorado, to go camping, to live in the suburbs and commute to work.

At the same time, the auto generates need for an immense body of rules—rules about auto accidents, rules about auto safety, rules of the road, traffic regulations, parking restrictions, rules about driver's licenses and drunk driving, and so on. All this is part of the price for the vast extension of freedom the automobile brought with it. It is not so obvious, then, that more law, more rules, as such, cut down on personal freedom. This may or may not be true. Some level of regulation is a natural product of new technology—a cost or side effect of machines that expand our freedom and our possibilities. The question is difficult and complex. This book has touched on it here and there, but certainly never resolved it.

Crude as they are, then, all the indicators strongly suggest great growth in the law. The legal system has swollen in size over the years, growing faster than the population; and the rate of growth itself seems to be growing. Administrative law came up almost out of nothing and is now a major force in society. Particularly striking is the explosion in federal law in the last two generations, roughly since the New Deal. The Reagan administration took office in 1981 with a firm resolve to cut and slash. But it has not gotten very far. And no one even dreams of rolling the federal government back to the days of Harding and Coolidge. No such reversal is possible. A conservative government can only hope to keep the state from swelling until it bursts like a giant balloon.

The Litigation Explosion:
Fact and Fiction

One special area of growth is litigation. The clamor over litigation and litigation rates is especially great. Litigation, people say, is rising rapidly, faster than courts can cope, faster than is good for us. There is talk about an "explosion" of lawsuits, about "hyperlexis," a dreadful disease that has "overloaded" the legal circuits.[2] A magazine article quoted earlier puts it this way: "employees sue employers, students sue teachers, taxpayers sue bureaucrats and friends sue friends."[3]

What is wrong with a "litigation explosion," if we have one? First of all, lawsuits might overwhelm the courts and interfere with the orderly administration of justice. Secondly, the flood of cases can disrupt and destroy the ordinary processes of government. Courts take over roles that do not belong to them: they meddle in affairs of state. They move into areas which should be left alone or handled by others. Third, lawsuits can disrupt and destroy normal social relations. Suing your physician, for example, does not make for good relations between doctor and patient.

The people who complain come up with many horrible examples to show what they mean: some point to the busing of schoolchildren, some cite the way courts stop or delay big projects, some refer to the death penalty cases or the abortion case, and so on. Judges themselves—led by Chief Justice Burger—complain of a crisis in the courts. They talk of a crushing burden of lawsuits.

Actually, we know very little about litigation rates in the United States and even less about the way these rates change over time. The litigation explosion may even be in part purely imaginary—a bad dream, a false impression. The gross amount of litigation has certainly been rising over the years. But when we talk about a litigation rate, we must mean some sort of relationship between cases and population. Here the talk about "explosions" has nothing much to back it up. Judicial statistics are poor. Historical statistics (where we have any) are almost worthless. It is hard to say anything about long-term trends.

Litigation rates are definitely rising in one court system, the federal courts. These courts on the whole keep good records. In 1902, filings in federal court came to 19.9 cases per 100,000 population; by 1972, they had gone up to 43.9 cases per 100,000.[4] The rate has continued to rise since then. In 1900, the United States District Courts disposed of 29,094 cases. The volume rose to 152, 585 in 1932 (swelled artificially by Prohibition cases), dropped to 69,466 in 1942, and then began rising again. In 1971 it reached 126,145; in 1980, 189,778.[5]

This boom in federal cases helps give the impression of a litigation explosion. But there is only one federal system, and there are fifty states. The states account for over 90 percent of the lawsuits in the country. Studies of state courts are sparse and somewhat inconclusive. In St. Louis, for example, Wayne McIntosh found a high litigation rate in the early nineteenth century, until 1850. The rate then declined, and bottomed out in the 1890s. Since 1900, there has been an upward trend, but an extremely modest one. Essentially, he concludes, "the litigation rate has remained fairly stable during the last six decades." No explosion here; nor was any explosion found in a study of two California counties, Alameda County and San Benito County, in the period 1870–1970.[6]

The litigation rate is quite an elusive figure. One reason is that it is hard to say exactly what litigation is. For example, there is a high divorce rate in the United States. The courts churn out hundreds of thousands of divorces. Almost all of them are uncontested. Each is a "case," in the sense that somebody files a piece of paper in court, the clerk opens a file, and *Smith* v. *Smith* gets a case number. But 99 times out of 100, nothing will actually happen in court that deserves to be called litigation. The case is completely cut-and-dried. The Smiths and their lawyers work out everything far in advance. There is legal behavior here, but hardly litigation.

The same is true of cases of other kinds: adoption proceedings, petitions to change one's name, and so on. Most tort cases, as we noted, are settled out of court. Even most of those that are filed in court drop out before trial. As with divorce cases, the clerk gives them a file number and they are tallied in court statistics. Yet when people talk about litigation, they usually have in mind genuine disputes resolved in the courtroom before a judge, or a judge and jury. These may not be increasing in numbers at all.

Of course, some kinds of litigations *are* increasing. Judicial review is more common than in the past, as we have seen. In an important way it feeds on itself. If courts are willing to monitor, revise, and oversee what Congress, legislatures, and administrative agencies do, then they encourage social groups to bring their demands into court. People band together to challenge a law they do not like, to stop a highway or a jetport, to force the state of Arkansas to clean up its prisons, to get Alabama to reform its mental hospitals, to prevent the execution of a murderer, and so on. This is a strong trend, and a growing one. In some ways it is unique to this country.

Whenever and wherever a new "field" of law emerges, or a new cause of action, a bulge in cases at the trial level may result. These cases may make a social splash, even when they are not statistically significant. Chapter 14 discussed *Marvin* v. *Marvin*. This case opened a door that had once been shut. In the two years after *Marvin* v. *Marvin*, some 100 cases of the *Marvin* type were filed in various trial courts. This was in many ways an important development. But 100 cases would not show up at all in judicial statistics. There are over a million filings each year in American courts; 100 cases are a spit in the ocean.

What is important, then, are not the numbers, but the types of cases filed. Whole new areas of litigation have opened up in the last decades. Malpractice and products liability have blossomed. The Civil Rights Act of 1964, and associated laws, inspired a flock of novel cases. Before the 1960s, there was the merest handful of cases about race discrimination, and there were basically none at all on sex and age discrimination. Congress and the courts created new rights. Discrimination in the job market was outlawed. Today, employment discrimination is a major field of law. It gives work to hundreds of lawyers and has hatched a whole battery of lawsuits. Compared to the number of divorces, the numbers are insignificant. But many of these cases are huge, class-action cases against great corporations, involving millions of dollars and the structure of whole job markets. Numbers do not do justice to the situation. There are more mice in the world than there are elephants; but each elephant makes a good deal more of a splash.

In general, "megacases" are increasing: monster lawsuits, massive and incredibly expensive. Private antitrust suits are one prominent example. The Sherman Act[7] made monopoly and restraint of trade a crime. The government, of course, had primary powers of enforcement. But Section 7 of the law gave private citizens or companies the right to sue for damages against any person or company who had "injured" them by violating the act. Indeed, the plaintiff could collect three times the actual damages. This was meant to provide incentive to sue, and also to be a sort of punishment for wrongdoers. Yet private suits were not common for many years. They averaged 100 a year in the 1940s. In 1979, on the other hand, there were 1,312—ten times as many.[8]

Private antitrust suits tend to be elephant cases. Some drag on for months, even years. They cost each side tens of millions of dollars. The amounts at stake can be staggering—perhaps more than a billion dollars in a single case. Tons of documents are filed in court. Whole platoons of lawyers are thrown into the fray. Some public antitrust cases are also supercases. One prime example was the great IBM case. It began in 1969, and turned into the all-time champion lawsuit in size. The documents could fill a dozen warehouses. Costs on both sides were staggering. At one time it looked as if the case would never end—that it would literally go on forever. But in 1981, the Reagan administration threw in the towel and the mighty lawsuit fizzled out, after millions of dollars, millions of documents, and millions of hours. This case too made no dent on judicial statistics. It was essentially one case. Obviously, it does not take many megacases of this sort to give off the smell of an "explosion."

On the other hand, lawsuits of some types may actually be declining. Some scholars claim the courts are doing less work on ordinary disputes—contract cases, disputes between landlord and tenant, quarrels between two people who claim the same piece of land, accident cases in which the parties cannot agree, arguments over Uncle Harry's will. The evidence is imperfect here, too, but there are those who argue that the courts are falling down on their job. The ordinary person cannot get justice. Businesses, too, avoid the courts and prefer arbitration.

The courts, then, may be neglecting "issues that affect the quality of everyday life." The phrase is from Laura Nader, in the preface to a book which explores "alternatives"—ways of handling disputes and grievances outside of the court system, everything from the Better Business Bureau to the activities of a congressman's office.[9] Chapter 2 of this book also looked briefly at "informal justice." There are many plans under discussion to improve or revivify the courts and to provide more effectively for popular justice. In 1977, the Department of Justice set up, on an experimental basis, three Neighborhood Justice Centers. They were located in Atlanta, Kansas City, and Los Angeles, and were supposed to be alternatives to courts for resolving minor disputes.[10] More will be heard of this, and other, new ideas in the future.

Perhaps the courts are not doing a good job in small cases, but they certainly play a role in society at large. They are muscling their way—or being pushed into—more and more of the business of government. At the very least, they check and control much of the work of those who do govern. The boundaries between what is traditionally thought of as fit stuff for courts and that which is not seems to be eroding. Areas of life that were off limits to courts in the past are no longer immune to intervention.

We see constant signs of this evolution. Newspapers report the extremes. One man threatened to sue a young woman because she stood him up on a date. Another man tried to sue his own mother and father for "malpractice." They botched the job of bringing him up, he said, and turned him into a psychological wreck. A Yale graduate, disgruntled at something or other, wanted a federal court to wipe his degree off Yale's records.[11] According to the magazine story we quoted earlier, the parents of a nine-year-old girl in Indiana filed a lawsuit because the girl found no prize in a box of Cracker Jack.[12]

The courts usually throw such cases out. They are oddities, freaks; after all, that is why they make the newspapers. But they illustrate one general point: almost anything can end up as a court case today. No area of life is sacrosanct. Courts routinely make decisions about the inner workings of factories, hospitals, schools, and prisons—decisions on subjects unthinkable as the basis for lawsuits a century ago, when these subjects were "private" and beyond the reach of the law or were within the unfettered discretion of public officials.

Courts even intervene in family affairs. In a 1972 case, a fourteen-year-old girl in Minnesota sued her parents in juvenile court. The parents had built themselves a boat and were about to go off with their daughters on a cruise around the world. The girl, Lee Anne, wanted to stay at home with her friends. She went to court and won a partial victory. The juvenile judge allowed her to stay behind, in custody of an aunt.[13]

This is striking, perhaps alarming and deplorable. We can see why many people would condemn Lee Anne's case as outrageous meddling in family affairs. But it is a bit unfair to single out the court. After all, hardly any area of life is beyond the scope of government. The more the government does, the more we need to control it. In most countries, courts do not exercise this power. In most countries, governments are too big, too powerful, too pervasive. The ordinary citizen has no way to gain redress, or even a hearing. There is no meaningful judicial review in Russia or Cuba—or Chile, for that matter. Justice is powerless against the will of the regime.

Courts in the United States, for all their faults, give people at least some realistic way to right wrongs done by the government and by private centers of power. There are, to be sure, other democratic countries where the courts are fairly inactive. Some of these have evolved other means, perhaps, to control the state. But courts are part of *our* system of control, geared to our needs and traditions.

Regular courts may be too expensive and formal for ordinary cases and for day-by-day disputes. But they are well suited for big cases, group claims, class actions. As for the little cases, we do need fresh ideas and new institutions; we need debate and research about dispute settlement, grievance procedures, access to law. Ideas are in the air; some are getting a hearing. We have seen some examples. Change is sure to take place.

The Society of Strangers

A society like ours is one of great interdependence. All of us are in the same boat, in many ways. Imagine, at one extreme, a pioneer family in the nineteenth century—a family, let us say, that lived miles away from its nearest neighbor; that built its own house, grew its own food, wove its own clothing. The parents taught the children themselves, provided their own entertainment, acted as their own doctors, dentists, barbers, nurses—did everything, took every role.

This is an extreme case, and was rare even in the past. But it points up how different our way of life really is. America in the 1980s is a far cry from the world of these pioneers. It is a far cry, too, from the way of life of tribal society, where custom rules, where life is bound to a tiny village and a few miles of woods all about it. Village life is life lived wholly in the so-called primary group, a face-to-face culture. Each man, woman, and child is related by blood or marriage or clan to everybody who matters to that person. Similarly, on the island of Tristan da Cunha, the primary group was the only group. In our society, however, though we are as profoundly dependent on each other as the people in any tribal culture, most of the links in our chain of dependence are strangers, not kinfolk or friends.

We are, in short, a "nation of strangers, a country where the greatest number of potential abuses occurs between people who are strangers to each other."[14] We work for big companies. We buy ready-made food and clothing. Strangers protect us, as police, or threaten us, as criminals, when we walk the streets. Strangers put out our fires. Strangers teach our children, build our houses, invest our money. Strangers on radio and TV or in the newspapers give us our news of the world. When we travel by bus or train or plane, our lives are in the hands of strangers. If we fall sick and go to the hospital, strangers cut open our bodies, wash us, nurse us, kill us or cure us. When we die, strangers put us in the earth.

We accept all this. We are used to it. The environment of strangers is part of our lives. The line between intimate life and impersonal public life is growing a shade indistinct. Strangers even intrude on the most private, inward corners of our lives. Love, sex, and marriage are not immune. Social workers, psychiatrists, marriage counselors—there are thousands of "experts" in these matters; and we are encouraged to go to them with personal troubles. Sometimes, in extreme cases, we may even be forced to go. More and more, a technical, professional, bureaucratic world elbows its way into the last of the private sanctuaries.

This does not mean that there is less space for us to grow as individuals, less scope for us to experiment with ways of life, or less personal privacy, in American society in the 1980s. Quite the contrary. There is probably far greater room for personal autonomy than ever before in history. Certainly there is far more than in tribal societies, or even among the pioneers, whose lives were rigidly constrained by survival needs. Growing food, keeping warm, and staying alive absorbed almost all of their energy. There is far more leisure today, and more options for the average person. But the boundaries between what is supposed to be private and personal and what is not no longer carry the same meaning as before.

And law moves along, following society, responding to these social facts. It is no surprise, then, that in the 1980s no zone is so intimate, personal, or private that it is immune from the staring eye of law. And why not? *Custom* is what we call the norms that regulate face-to-face relationships; *law* is the word for norms that regulate relations among strangers. When customary norms break down, society turns to law. This is the central thesis of this book. A small society, a tribe, a tiny island, can go on from year to year on the basis of shared norms, unspoken premises, rules of behavior made sacred through tradition. Our society cannot do this. Americans hold many things in common, but not enough for automatic governance. The country is just too big. We need (or feel we need) formal, structured ways to govern ourselves. And this means law.

No doubt a lot is gained and a lot is lost, in a social order built up in this way. This is not the place to explore the gains and the losses in detail. Some economists argue that a regulated economy is less efficient in every regard than a free economy, run entirely by the "invisible hand." On the other hand, almost everyone concedes that a fairer, more equitable—or safer and healthier—society requires some degree of control. Almost everybody agrees about some kinds of collective control. We *must* have police. Most of us want a lot more government than that; and a small band on the left believes in almost total collective control. Where to draw the line is a subject of constant political debate; it is one of the major cleavages in democratic society.

In a complex world, freedom does not necessarily mean *no* government control. Paradoxically, law may be needed to maximize freedom. When the air people breathed was fresh and clean, nothing much had to be done to keep it that way. Streams ran pure and clear; there seemed to be no end to wildlife, trees, and space, or to oil, gas, and coal. Those times have passed. The automobile has generated not only new freedom but also new rules. Courts have created or expanded many rights to counterbalance the strength of big government, big business, big unions. There is, and will be, constant tension between freedom and control. But there is no escape from interdependence; the people of this country are tied together in organic knots, and forever. The need for law continues to be great.

The specific role of courts in our society is hard to predict. The future is, as always, cloudy. The particular jobs courts do now may change. Nothing is engraved in stone. Some of the present trends—the heavy use of judicial review, for example—will probably continue into coming years, as far ahead as we can see. Certainly the overall needs will not become obsolete. If not the courts, then some other agency will take over these functions in this or that regard.

Law is a creature of society. Society shows no signs of returning to the simpler habits of bygone days or of advancing toward a state of utopian perfection in which no government is needed. Hence we can expect law, legal process, and the legal system in the United States to continue to occupy a central place. Perhaps the role of law will grow, perhaps not; but it will not shrivel or wither away. And the legal system will continue to bend and turn in response to social change. Courts may change a bit (or a lot) in what they do; taxes may go up, or down; government may expand into this area, retract its horns from that. But short of some mammoth reworking of our way of life, law will be with us for as far ahead as we can see—a massive presence in our lives.

Documents

In this book, we have discussed many different kinds of law, and many sources of law. This short collection of documents illustrates some of the most prominent of these sources: constitutions, legislation, administrative regulations, and case law.

In our legal system, the federal Constitution is the supreme law of the land. It outranks all other sources. No state or federal law, no city ordinance, no administrative rule, is valid if it violates the federal Constitution. Of course, there are also state constitutions, and they have the final word on local, state matters.

The documents in Part I begin with excerpts from the federal Constitution which have a particular bearing on the material in this book. A small portion of the constitution of Oregon illustrates state constitutional law: the section chosen discusses lawmaking through the initiative and referendum—sources of law which are unknown to the federal Constitution. The Oregon material also includes a few typical features of state constitutions which, again, have no parallel in the federal Constitution, for example, the prohibition against "local" and "special" laws.

Legislation is a term that covers a vast range of activity; the documents in Part II give some idea of that range. The Sherman Act, a federal statute of great historical and economic significance, is in form quite general and brief: it sets out a few broad principles, and leaves entirely open all questions of interpretation and administration. The short excerpt from the federal Food, Drug, and Cosmetic Act, with its mixture of broad principle and meticulous detail, shows what modern regulatory law is often like. Title VII of the Civil Rights Act of

1964 is similar in style, and shows how deeply federal law has penetrated into areas of life that were immune from federal regulation in earlier generations. Part II also includes two examples of state legislation. The Idaho statute is a typical workmen's compensation law. Workmen's compensation replaced the old system of dealing with work accidents through private lawsuits. The new system, in Idaho and elsewhere, is an elaborate, detailed, highly "administered" body of law. The brief excerpt from the California Structural Pest Control Board Law is an example of a common and important form of state legislation: occupational licensing.

Part III deals with the administrative process. The main theme is the way in which administrative agencies fill in the blanks in bodies of statutory law, by writing rules and regulations. The three examples given are drawn from the rules laid down by the federal Food and Drug Administration, the Equal Employment Opportunity Commission, and the California Structural Pest Control Board. These examples are keyed to statutes reprinted in Part II.

In our legal system, of course, courts play a major role in interpreting law, which in practice often means making law. Part IV contains four cases; each of them, in its own way, illustrates this theme. In *Brown* v. *Board of Education*, the celebrated school desegregation case, the Supreme Court of the United States boldly made policy, in a decision which is perhaps the most important that institution ever handed down. *Brown* is also an example of judicial review: the Supreme Court swept aside dozens of state laws and city ordinances which required segregated schools, on the grounds that the federal Constitution outlawed such segregation.

In *Dothard* v. *Rawlinson*, the Supreme Court made policy in a somewhat different context. The case presented a tricky issue of sex discrimination; formally, the task was to interpret the policy set out in Title VII of the Civil Rights Act of 1964. In *Louie* v. *Bamboo Gardens*, the Idaho Supreme Court had an analogous job with respect to a broad principle embodied in the Idaho workmen's compensation statute. The facts of the case made the situation difficult—it was a situation on the very edge of the statutory policy. The decision can be read as a kind of reaching out, an extension of principles of liability beyond the text of the statute. Finally, *Marvin* v. *Marvin*, the famous California "palimony" case which was discussed in Chapter 14, shows how courts respond to changing customs and changing times in areas where there is no statute or constitutional mandate to bind them or guide them.

PART I.

The Constitutional Experience

A. Constitution of the United States

B. Constitution of Oregon

A. Constitution of the United States

We the People of the United States, in Order to form a more perfect Union, establish Justice, insure domestic Tranquility, provide for the common defence, promote the general Welfare, and secure the Blessings of Liberty to ourselves and our Posterity, do ordain and establish this Constitution for the United States of America.

. . .

ARTICLE III

Section 1. The judicial Power of the United States, shall be vested in one supreme Court, and in such inferior Courts as the Congress may from time to time ordain and establish. The Judges, both of the supreme and inferior Courts, shall hold their Offices during good Behaviour, and shall, at stated Times, receive for their Services, a Compensation, which shall not be diminished during their Continuance in Office.

Section 2. [1] The judicial Power shall extend to all Cases, in Law and Equity, arising under this Constitution, the Laws of the United States, and Treaties made, or which shall be made, under their Authority;—to all Cases affecting Ambassadors, other public Ministers and Consuls;—to all Cases of admiralty and maritime Jurisdiction;—to Controversies to which the United States shall be a Party;—to Controversies between two or more States;—between a State and Citizens of another State;—between Citizens of different States;—between Citizens of the same State claiming Lands under Grants of different States, and between a State, or the Citizens thereof, and foreign States, Citizens or Subjects.

[2] In all Cases affecting Ambassadors, other public Ministers and Consuls, and those in which a State shall be a Party, the supreme Court shall have original Jurisdiction. In all the other Cases before mentioned, the supreme Court shall have appellate Jurisdiction, both as to Law and Fact, with such Exceptions, and under such Regulations as the Congress shall make.

[3] The trial of all Crimes, except in Cases of Impeachment, shall be by Jury; and such Trial shall be held in the State where the said Crimes shall have been committed; but when not committed within any State, the Trial shall be at such Place or Places as the Congress may by Law have directed.

Section 3. [1] Treason against the United States, shall consist only in levying War against them, or in adhering to their Enemies, giving them Aid and Comfort. No Person shall be convicted of Treason unless on the Testimony of two Witnesses to the same overt Act, or on Confession in open Court.

[2] The Congress shall have Power to declare the Punishment of Treason, but no Attainder of Treason shall work Corruption of Blood, or Forfeiture except during the Life of the Person attainted.

ARTICLE IV

Section 1. Full Faith and Credit shall be given in each State to the public Acts, Records, and judicial Proceedings of every other State. And the Congress may by general Laws prescribe the Manner in which such Acts, Records and Proceedings shall be proved, and the Effect thereof.

Section 2. [1] The Citizens of each State shall be entitled to all Privileges and Immunities of Citizens in the several States.

[2] A Person charged in any State with Treason, Felony, or other Crime, who shall flee from Justice, and be found in another State, shall on demand of the executive Authority of the State from which he fled, be delivered up, to be removed to the State having Jurisdiction of the Crime.

[3] No Person held to Service or Labour in one State, under the Laws thereof, escaping into another, shall, in Consequence of any Law or Regulation therein, be discharged from such Service or Labour, but shall be delivered up on Claim of the Party to whom such Service or Labour may be due.

Section 3. [1] New States may be admitted by the Congress into this Union; but no new State shall be formed or erected within the Jurisdiction of any other State; nor any State be formed by the Junction of two or more States, or Parts of States, without the Consent of the Legislatures of the States concerned as well as of the Congress.

[2] The Congress shall have Power to dispose of and make all needful Rules and Regulations respecting the Territory or other Property belonging to the United States; and nothing in this Constitution shall be so construed as to Prejudice any Claims of the United States, or of any particular State.

Section 4. The United States shall guarantee to every State in this Union a Republican Form of Government, and shall protect each of them against Invasion; and on Application of the Legislature, or of the Executive (when the Legislature cannot be convened) against domestic Violence.

ARTICLE V

The Congress, whenever two thirds of both Houses shall deem it necessary, shall propose Amendments, to this Constitution, or, on the Application of the Legislatures of two thirds of the several States, shall call a Convention for proposing Amendments, which, in either Case, shall be valid to all Intents and Purposes, as part of this Constitution, when ratified by the Legislatures of three fourths of the several States, or by Conventions in three fourths thereof, as the one or the other Mode of Ratification may be proposed by the Congress; Provided that no Amendment which may be made prior to the Year One thousand eight hundred and eight shall in any Manner affect the first and fourth Clauses in the Ninth Section of the first Article; and that no State, without its Consent, shall be deprived of its equal Suffrage in the Senate.

ARTICLE VI

[1] All Debts contracted and Engagements entered into, before the Adoption of this Constitution, shall be as valid against the United States under this Constitution, as under the Confederation.

[2] This Constitution, and the Laws of the United States which shall be made in Pursuance thereof; and all Treaties made, or which shall be made, under the Authority of the United States, shall be the supreme Law of the Land; and the Judges in every State shall be bound thereby, any Thing in the Constitution or Laws of any State to the Contrary notwithstanding.

[3] The Senators and Representatives before mentioned, and the Members of the several State Legislatures, and all executive and judicial Officers, both of the United States and of the several States, shall be bound by Oath or Affirmation, to support this Constitution; but no religious Test shall ever be required as a Qualification to any Office or public Trust under the United States.

ARTICLE VII

The Ratification of the Conventions of nine States shall be sufficient for the Establishment of this Constitution between the States so ratifying the Same.

Done in Convention by the Unanimous Consent of the States present the Seventeenth Day of September in the Year of our Lord one thousand seven hundred and Eighty seven and of the Independence of the United States of America the Twelfth.

ARTICLES IN ADDITION TO, AND AMENDMENT OF, THE CONSTITUTION OF THE UNITED STATES OF AMERICA, PROPOSED BY CONGRESS, AND RATIFIED BY THE LEGISLATURES OF THE SEVERAL STATES, PURSUANT TO THE FIFTH ARTICLE OF THE ORIGINAL CONSTITUTION

AMENDMENT I [1791]

Congress shall make no law respecting an establishment of religion, or prohibiting the free exercise thereof; or abridging the freedom of speech, or of the press; or the right of the people peaceably to assemble, and to petition the Government for a redress of grievances.

AMENDMENT II [1791]

A well regulated Militia, being necessary to the security of a free State, the right of the people to keep and bear Arms, shall not be infringed.

AMENDMENT III [1791]

No Soldier shall, in time of peace be quartered in any house, without the consent of the Owner, nor in time of war, but in a manner to be prescribed by law.

AMENDMENT IV [1791]

The right of the people to be secure in their persons, houses, papers, and effects, against unreasonable searches and seizures, shall not be violated, and no Warrants shall issue, but upon probable cause, supported by Oath or affirmation, and particularly describing the place to be searched, and the persons or things to be seized.

AMENDMENT V [1791]

No person shall be held to answer for a capital, or otherwise infamous crime, unless on a presentment or indictment of a Grand Jury, except in cases arising in the land or naval forces, or in the Militia, when in actual service in time of War or public danger; nor shall any person be subject for the same offence to be twice put in jeopardy of life or limb; nor shall be compelled in any criminal case to be a witness against himself, nor be deprived of life, liberty, or property, without due process of law; nor shall private property be taken for public use, without just compensation.

AMENDMENT VI [1791]

In all criminal prosecutions, the accused shall enjoy the right to a speedy and public trial, by an impartial jury of the State and district wherein the crime shall have been committed, which district shall have been previously ascertained by law, and to be informed of the nature and cause of the accusation; to be confronted with the witnesses against him; to have compulsory process for obtaining witnesses in his favor, and to have the Assistance of Counsel for his defence.

AMENDMENT VII [1791]

In Suits at common law, where the value in controversy shall exceed twenty dollars, the right of trial by jury shall be preserved, and no fact tried by a jury, shall be otherwise re-examined in any Court of the United States, than according to the rules of the common law.

AMENDMENT VIII [1791]

Excessive bail shall not be required, nor excessive fines imposed, nor cruel and unusual punishments inflicted.

AMENDMENT IX [1791]

The enumeration in the Constitution, of certain rights, shall not be construed to deny or disparage others retained by the people.

AMENDMENT X [1791]

The powers not delegated to the United States by the Constitution, nor prohibited by it to the States, are reserved to the States respectively, or to the people.

AMENDMENT XI [1798]

The Judicial power of the United States shall not be construed to extend to any suit in law or equity, commenced or prosecuted against one of the United States by Citizens of another State, or by Citizens or Subjects of any Foreign State.

. . .

AMENDMENT XIII [1865]

Section 1. Neither slavery nor involuntary servitude, except as a punishment for crime whereof the party shall have been duly convicted, shall exist within the United States, or any place subject to their jurisdiction.

Section 2. Congress shall have power to enforce this article by appropriate legislation.

AMENDMENT XIV [1868]

Section 1. All persons born or naturalized in the United States, and subject to the jurisdiction thereof, are citizens of the United States and of the State wherein they reside. No State shall make or enforce any law which shall abridge the privileges or immunities of citizens of the United States; nor shall any State deprive any person of life, liberty, or property, without due process of law; nor deny to any person within its jurisdiction the equal protection of the laws.

. . .

Section 5. The Congress shall have power to enforce, by appropriate legislation, the provisions of this article.

AMENDMENT XV [1870]

Section 1. The right of citizens of the United States to vote shall not be denied or abridged by the United States or by any State on account of race, color, or previous condition of servitude.

Section 2. The Congress shall have power to enforce this article by appropriate legislation.

. . .

AMENDMENT XVIII [1919]

Section 1. After one year from the ratification of this article the manufacture, sale, or transportation of intoxicating liquors within, the importation thereof into, or the exportation thereof from the United States and all territory subject to the jurisdiction thereof for beverage purposes is hereby prohibited.

Section 2. The Congress and the several States shall have concurrent power to enforce this article by appropriate legislation.

Section 3. This article shall be inoperative unless it shall have been ratified as an amendment to the Constitution by the legislatures of the several States, as provided in the Constitution, within seven years from the date of the submission hereof to the States by the Congress.

AMENDMENT XIX [1920]

[1] The right of citizens of the United States to vote shall not be denied or abridged by the United States or by any State on account of sex.

[2] Congress shall have power to enforce this article by appropriate legislation.

. . .

AMENDMENT XXI [1933]

Section 1. The eighteenth article of amendment to the Constitution of the United States is hereby repealed.

Section 2. The transportation or importation into any State, Territory, or possession of the United States for delivery or use therein of intoxicating liquors, in violation of the laws thereof, is hereby prohibited.

Section 3. This article shall be inoperative unless it shall have been ratified as an amendment to the Constitution by conventions in the several States, as provided in the Constitution, within seven years from the date of the submission hereof to the States by the Congress.

. . .

AMENDMENT XXIV [1964]

Section 1. The right of citizens of the United States to vote in any primary or other election for President or Vice President, for electors for President or Vice President, or for Senator or Representative in Congress, shall not be denied or abridged by the United States or any State by reason of failure to pay any poll tax or other tax.

Section 2. The Congress shall have power to enforce this article by appropriate legislation.

. . .

Amendment XXVI [1971]

Section 1. The right of citizens of the United States, who are eighteen years of age or older, to vote shall not be denied or abridged by the United States or by any State on account of age.

Section 2. The Congress shall have power to enforce this article by appropriate legislation.

B. *Constitution of the State of Oregon*

Article IV: Legislative Department

Section 1. Legislative power; initiative and referendum. (1) The legislative power of the state, except for the initiative and referendum powers reserved to the people, is vested in a Legislative Assembly, consisting of a Senate and a House of Representatives.

(2) (a) The people reserve to themselves the initiative power, which is to propose laws and amendments to the Constitution and enact or reject them at an election independently of the Legislative Assembly.

(b) An initiative law may be proposed only by a petition signed by a number of qualified voters equal to six percent of the total number of votes cast for all candidates for Governor at the election at which a Governor was elected for a term of four years next preceding the filing of the petition.

(c) An initiative amendment to the Constitution may be proposed only by a petition signed by a number of qualified voters equal to eight percent of the total number of votes cast for all candidates for Governor at the election at which a Governor was elected for a term of four years next preceding the filing of the petition.

(d) An initiative petition shall include the full text of the proposed law or amendment to the Constitution. A proposed law or amendment to the Constitution shall embrace one subject only and matters properly connected therewith.

(e) An initiative petition shall be filed not less than four months before the election at which the proposed law or amendment to the Constitution is to be voted upon.

(3) (a) The people reserve to themselves the referendum power, which is to approve or reject at an election any Act, or part thereof, of the Legislative Assembly that does not come effective earlier than 90 days after the end of the session at which the Act is passed.

(b) A referendum on an Act or part thereof may be ordered by a petition signed by a number of qualified voters equal to four percent of the total number of votes cast for all candidates for Governor at the election at which a Governor was elected for a term of four years next preceding the filing of the petition. A referendum petition shall be filed not more than 90 days after the end of the session at which the Act is passed.

(c) A referendum on an Act may be ordered by the Legislative Assembly by law. Notwithstanding section 15b, Article V of this Constitution, bills ordering a referendum and bills on which a referendum is ordered are not subject to veto by the Governor.

. . .

(5) The initiative and referendum powers reserved to the people by subsections (2) and (3) of this section are further reserved to the qualified voters of each municipality and district as to all local, special and municipal legislation of every character in or for their municipality or district. The manner of exercising those powers shall be provided by general laws, but cities may provide the manner of exercising those powers as to their municipal legislation. In a city, not more than 15 percent of the qualified voters may be required to propose legislation by the initiative, and not more than 10 percent of the qualified voters may be required to order a referendum on legislation.

Section 18. Where bills to originate. Bills may originate in either house, but may be amended, or rejected in the other; except that bills for raising revenue shall originate in the House of Representatives.—

. . .

Section 20. Subject and title of Act. Every Act shall embrace but one subject, and matters properly connected therewith, which subject shall be expressed in the title. But if any subject shall be embraced in an Act which shall not be expressed in the title, such Act shall be void only as to so much thereof as shall not be expressed in the title.

. . .

Section 21. Acts to be plainly worded. Every act, and joint resolution shall be plainly worded, avoiding as far as practicable the use of technical terms.—

. . .

Section 23. Certain local and special laws prohibited. The Legislative Assembly, shall not pass special or local laws, in any of the following enumerated cases, that is to say:—

Regulating the jurisdiction, and duties of justices of the peace, and of constables;

For the punishment of Crimes, and Misdemeanors;

Regulating the practice in Courts of Justice;

Providing for changing the venue in civil, and Criminal cases;

Granting divorces;

Changing the names of persons;

For laying, opening, and working on highways, and for the election, or appointment of supervisors;

Vacating roads, Town plats, Streets, Alleys, and Public squares;

Summoning and empanneling (sic) grand, and petit jurors;

For the assessment and collection of Taxes, for State, County, Township, or road purposes;

Providing for supporting Common schools, and for the preservation of school funds;

In relation to interest on money;

Providing for opening, and conducting the elections of State, County, and Township officers, and designating the places of voting;

Providing for the sale of real estate, belonging to minors, or other persons laboring under legal disabilities, by executors, administrators, guardians, or trustees.—

PART II.

Federal and State Legislation

A. Sherman Antitrust Act (1890)

B. Food, Drug, and Cosmetic Act

C. Civil Rights Act of 1964, Title VII

D. Workmen's Compensation Law (Idaho)

E. Structural Pest Control Board Law (California)

A. Sherman Antitrust Act (1890)
U.S. Statutes at Large, Volume 26, p. 209.

CHAP. 647.—An act to protect trade and commerce against unlawful restraints and monopolies.

Be it enacted by the Senate and House of Representatives of the United States of America in Congress assembled,

SEC. 1. Every contract, combination in the form of trust or otherwise, or conspiracy, in restraint of trade or commerce among the several States, or with foreign nations, is hereby declared to be illegal. Every person who shall make any such contract or engage in any such combination or conspiracy, shall be deemed guilty of a misdemeanor, and, on conviction thereof, shall be punished by fine not exceeding five thousand dollars, or by imprisonment not exceeding one year, or by both said punishments, in the discretion of the court.

SEC. 2. Every person who shall monopolize, or attempt to monopolize, or combine or conspire with any other person or persons, to monopolize any part of the trade or commerce among the several States, or with foreign nations, shall be deemed guilty of a misdemeanor, and, on conviction thereof, shall be punished by fine not exceeding five thousand dollars, or by imprisonment not exceeding one year, or by both said punishments, in the discretion of the court.

SEC. 3. Every contract, combination in form of trust or otherwise, or conspiracy, in restraint of trade or commerce in any Territory of the United States or of the District of Columbia, or in restraint of trade or commerce between any such Territory and another, or between any such Territory or Territories and any State or States or the District of Columbia, or with foreign nations, or between the District of Columbia and any State or States or foreign nations, is hereby declared illegal. Every person who shall make any such contract or engage in any such combination or conspiracy, shall be deemed guilty of a misdemeanor, and, on conviction thereof, shall be punished by fine not exceeding five thousand dollars, or by imprisonment not exceeding one year, or by both said punishments, in the discretion of the court.

SEC 4. The several circuit courts of the United States are hereby invested with jurisdiction to prevent and restrain violations of this act; and it shall be the duty of the several district attorneys of the United States, in their respective districts, under the direction of the Attorney-General, to institute proceedings in equity to prevent and restrain such violations. Such proceedings may be by way of petition setting forth the case and praying that such violation shall be enjoined or otherwise prohibited. When the parties complained of shall have been duly notified of such petition the court shall proceed, as soon as may be, to the hearing and determination of the case; and pending such petition and before final decree, the court may at any time make such temporary restraining order or prohibition as shall be deemed just in the premises.

SEC 5. Whenever it shall appear to the court before which any proceeding under section four of this act may be pending, that the ends of justice require that other parties should be brought before the court, the court may cause them to be summoned, whether they reside in the district in which the court is held or not; and subpoenas to that end may be served in any district by the marshal thereof.

SEC. 6. Any property owned under any contract or by any combination, or pursuant to any conspiracy (and being the subject thereof) mentioned in section one of this act, and being in the course of transportation from one State to another, or to a foreign country, shall be forfeited to the United States, and may be seized and condemned by like proceedings as those provided by law for the forefeiture, seizure, and condemnation of property imported into the United States contrary to law.

SEC. 7. Any person who shall be injured in his business or property by any other person or corporation by reason of anything forbidden or declared to be unlawful by this act, may sue therefor in any circuit court of the United States in the district in which the defendant resides or is found, without respect to the amount in controversy, and shall recover three fold the damages by him sustained, and the costs of suit, including a reasonable attorney's fee.

SEC. 8. That the word "person," or "persons," wherever used in this act shall be deemed to include corporations and associations existing under or authorized by the laws of either the United States, the laws of any of the Territories, the laws of any State, or the laws of any foreign country.

Approved, July 2, 1890.

B. Food, Drug, and Cosmetic Act
(21 U.S.C.A., Section 350)

Misbranded drugs and devices
A drug or device shall be deemed to be misbranded—

(a) If its labeling is false or misleading in any particular.

(b) If in package form unless it bears a label containing (1) the name and place of business of the manufacturer, packer, or distributor; and (2) an accurate statement of the quantity of the contents in terms of weight, measure, or numerical count: *Provided*, That under clause (2) of this subsection reasonable variations shall be permitted, and exemptions as to small packages shall be established, by regulations prescribed by the Secretary [of Health and Human Services].

(c) If any word, statement, or other information required by or under authority of this chapter to appear on the label or labeling is not prominently placed thereon with such conspicuousness (as compared with other words, statements, designs, or devices, in the labeling) and in such terms as to render it likely to be read and understood by the ordinary individual under customary conditions of purchase and use.

(d) If it is for use by man and contains any quantity of the narcotic or hypnotic substance alpha eucaine, barbituric acid, betaeucaine, bromal, cannabis, carbromal, chloral, coca, cocaine, codeine, heroin, marihuana, morphine, opium, paraldehyde, peyote, or sulphonmethane; or any chemical derivative of such substance, which derivative has been by the Secretary, after investigation, found to be, and by regulations designated as, habit forming; unless its label bears the name and quantity or proportion of such substance or derivative and in juxtaposition therewith the statement "Warning—may be habit forming."

. . .

(f) Unless its labeling bears (1) adequate directions for use; and (2) such adequate warnings against use in those pathological conditions or by children where its use may be dangerous to health, or against unsafe dosage or methods or duration of administration or application, in such manner and form, as are necessary for the protection of users: *Provided,* That where any requirement of clause (1) of this subsection, as applied to any drug or device, is not necessary for the protection of the public health, the Secretary shall promulgate regulations exempting such drug or device from such requirement.

. . .

(i) (1) If it is a drug and its container is so made, formed, or filled as to be misleading; or (2) if it is an imitation of another drug; or (3) if it is offered for sale under the name of another drug.

(j) If it is dangerous to health when used in the dosage or manner, or with the frequency or duration prescribed, recommended, or suggested in the labeling thereof.

C. Civil Rights Act of 1964, Title VII, (as amended)
42 U.S.C. Section 2000e-2

(a) It shall be an unlawful employment practice for an employer—

(1) to fail or refuse to hire or to discharge any individual, or otherwise to discriminate against any individual with respect to his compensation, terms, conditions, or privileges of employment, because of such individual's race, color, religion, sex, or national origin; or

(2) to limit, segregate, or classify his employees or applicants for employment in any way which would deprive or tend to deprive any individual of employment opportunities or otherwise adversely affect his status as an employee, because of such individual's race, color, religion, sex, or national origin.

(b) It shall be an unlawful employment practice for an employment agency to fail or refuse to refer for employment, or otherwise to discriminate against, any individual because of his race, color, religion, sex, or national origin, or to classify or refer for employment any individual on the basis of his race, color, religion, sex, or national origin.

(c) It shall be an unlawful employment practice for a labor organization—

(1) to exclude or to expel from its membership, or otherwise to discriminate against, any individual because of his race, color, religion, sex, or national origin;

(2) to limit, segregate, or classify its membership or applicants for membership, or to classify or fail or refuse to refer for employment any individual, in any way which would deprive or tend to deprive any individual of employment opportunities, or would limit such employment opportunities or otherwise adversely affect his status as an employee or as an applicant for employment, because of such individual's race, color, religion, sex, or national origin; or

(3) to cause or attempt to cause an employer to discriminate against an individual in violation of this section.

(d) It shall be an unlawful employment practice for any employer, labor organization, or joint labor-management committee controlling apprenticeship or other training or retraining, including on-the-job training programs to discriminate against any individual because of his race, color, religion, sex, or national origin in admission to, or employment in, any program established to provide apprenticeship or other training.

(e) Notwithstanding any other provision of this subchapter, (1) it shall not be an unlawful employment practice for an employer to hire and employ employees, for an employment agency to classify, or refer for employment any individual, for a labor organization to classify its membership or to classify or refer for employment any individual, or for an employer, labor organization, or joint labor-management committee controlling apprenticeship or other training or retraining programs to admit or employ any individual in any such program, on the basis of his religion, sex, or national origin in those certain instances where religion, sex, or national origin is a bona fide occupational qualification reasonably necessary to the normal operation of that particular business or enterprise, and (2) it shall not be an unlawful employment practice for a school, college, university, or other educational institution or institution of learning to hire and employ employees of a particular religion if such school, college, university, or other educational institution or institution of learning is, in whole or in substantial part, owned, supported, controlled, or managed by a particular religion or by a particular religious corporation, association, or society, or if the curriculum of such school, college, university, or other educational institution or institution of learning is directed toward the propagation of a particular religion.

. . .

(h) Notwithstanding any other provision of this subchapter, it shall not be an unlawful employment practice for an employer to apply different standards of compensation, or different terms, conditions, or privileges of employment pursuant to a bona fide seniority or merit system, or a system which measures earnings by quantity or quality of production or to employees who work in different locations, provided that such differences are not the result of an intention to discriminate because of race, color, religion, sex, or national origin, nor shall it be an unlawful employment practice for an employer to give and to act upon the results of any professionally developed ability test provided that such test, its administration or action upon the results is not designed, intended or used to discriminate because of race, color, religion, sex or national origin. . . .

(i) Nothing contained in this subchapter shall apply to any business or enterprise on or near an Indian reservation with respect to any publicly announced employment practice of such business or enterprise under which a preferential treatment is given to any individual because he is an Indian living on or near a reservation.

(j) Nothing contained in this subchapter shall be interpreted to require any employer, employment agency, labor organization, or joint labor-management committee subject to this subchapter to grant preferential treatment to any individual or to any group because of the race, color, religion, sex, or national origin of such individual or group on account of an imbalance which may exist with respect to the total number or percentage of persons of any race, color, religion, sex, or national origin employed by any employer, referred or classified for employment by any employment agency or labor organization, admitted to membership or classified by any labor organization, or admitted to, or employed in, any apprenticeship or other training program, in comparison with the total number or percentage of persons of such race, color, religion, sex, or national origin in any community, State, section, or other area, or in the available work force in any community, State, section, or other area.

D. Workmen's Compensation Law (Idaho)
Idaho Code, Title 72

72-102. Definitions.—Words and terms used in the workmen's compensation law, unless the context otherwise requires, are defined in the subsections which follow.

. . .

(14) "Injury" and "accident."

(a) "Injury" means a personal injury caused by an accident arising out of and in the course of any employment covered by the workmen's compensation law.

(b) "Accident" means an unexpected, undesigned, and unlooked for mishap, or untoward event, connected with the industry in which it occurs, and which can be reasonably located as to time when and place where it occurred, causing an injury.

(c) "Injury" and "personal injury" shall be construed to include only an injury caused by an accident, which results in violence to the physical structure of the body. The terms shall in no case be construed to include an occupational disease and only such nonoccupational diseases as result directly from an injury.

(15) "Medical and related benefits" means payments provided for or made for medical, hospital, burial and other services as provided in this law other than income benefits.

(16) "Medical services" means medical, surgical, dental or other attendance or treatment, nurse and hospital service, medicines, apparatus, appliances, prostheses, and related services, facilities and supplies.

(17) "Occupational diseases."

(a) "Occupational disease" means a disease due to the nature of an employment in which the hazards of such disease actually exist, are characteristic of, and peculiar to the trade, occupation, process, or employment.

(b) "Contracted" and "incurred," when referring to an occupational disease, shall be deemed the equivalent of the term "arising out of and in the course of" employment.

. . .

72-208. Injuries not covered—Wilful intention—Intoxication.—(1) No compensation shall be allowed by the employee's wilful intention to injure himself or to injure another.

(2) If an injury is the proximate result of an employee's intoxication, all income benefits shall be reduced by fifty per cent (50%), provided that such reduction shall not apply where the intoxicants causing the employee's intoxication were furnished by the employer or where the employer permits the employee to remain at work with knowledge by the employer or his supervising agent that the employee is intoxicated.

72-209. Exclusiveness of liability of employer.—(1) . . . [T]he liability of the employer under this law shall be exclusive and in place of all other liability of the employer to the employee, his spouse, dependents, heirs, legal representatives or assigns.

. . .

(3) The exemption from liability given an employer by this section shall also extend to the employer's surety and to all officers, agents, servants and employees of the employer or surety, provided that such exemptions from liability shall not apply in any case where the injury or death is proximately caused by the wilful or unprovoked physical aggression of the employer, its officers, agents, servants or employees, the loss of such exemption applying only to the aggressor and shall not be imputable to the employer unless provoked or authorized by the employer, or the employer was a party thereto.

. . .

72-211. Exclusiveness of employee's remedy.— . . . [T]he rights and remedies herein granted to an employee on account of an injury or occupational disease for which he is entitled to compensation under this law shall exclude all other rights and remedies of the employee, his personal representatives, dependents or next of kin, at common law or otherwise, on account of such injury or disease.

72-212. Exemptions from coverage.—None of the provisions of this law shall apply to the following employments unless coverage thereof is elected [by the employer in writing.] . . .

(1) Household domestic service.

(2) Casual employment.

(3) Employment of outworkers.

(4) Employment of members of an employer's family dwelling in his household.

(5) Employment which is not carried on by the employer for the sake of pecuniary gain.

(6) Employment as the owner of a sole proprietorship; employment of a working member of a partnership; employment of an officer of a corporation who at all times during the period involved owns not less than ten per cent (10%) of all of the issued

and outstanding voting stock of the corporation and, if the corporation has directors, is also a director thereof.

. . .

(8) Agricultural pursuits. Agricultural pursuits, as used herein, shall include the raising or harvesting of any agricultural or horticultural commodity including the raising, pelting, shearing, feeding, caring for, training and management of livestock, bees, poultry and fur-bearing animals and wildlife raised in captivity, on inclosed lands and public ranges. Agricultural pursuits shall include the loading and transporting, by motor vehicle, of any agricultural or horticultural commodity to any storage, processing, distribution or manufacturing destination and the unloading of the commodity at such destination; provided, that the exemption for the transportation, loading or unloading of agricultural or horticultural commodities shall apply only to individuals, corporations, partnerships or other legal entities who are transporting, loading or unloading only those agricultural or horticultural commodites which the individual, corporation, partnership or other legal entity produced, raised or harvested. The return trip from a manufacturing, processing, storage or distribution destination is exempted if: the return trip to the original point of debarkation is by the safest and most direct route reasonably possible, the cargo transported on the return trip, if any, is to be used exclusively by the individual, corporation, partnership, or other legal entity which is transporting the cargo, and the cargo transported is to be used only in direct connection with the agricultural pursuit.

(9) Pilots of agricultural spraying or dusting planes. Employment as a pilot of an aircraft, used to apply fertilizers and pesticides to agricultural crops, when actually operating an aircraft, shall be exempt from the provisions of the workmen's compensation law, if: the employer files with, and has written approval by, the industrial commission, prior to employing a pilot for the purpose of engaging in the application of pesticides to agricultural crops by aircraft, proof of coverage of an insurance policy that will provide to the employed pilot of such aircraft while actually operating an aircraft, benefits in an amount of not less than: twenty-five thousand dollars ($25,000) accidental death and dismemberment, ten thousand dollars ($10,000) medical expense payments, and five hundred dollars ($500) per month disability income for a minimum of forty-eight (48) months.

(10) Associate real estate brokers and real estate salesmen. Service performed by an individual for a real estate broker as an associate real estate broker or as a real estate salesman, if all such service performed by such individual for such person is performed for remuneration solely by way of commission.

(11) Volunteer ski patrollers.

(12) Officials of athletic contests involving secondary schools . . .

. . .

72-428. Scheduled income benefits for loss or losses of use of bodily members.—
An employee who suffers a permanent disability less than total and permanent shall, in addition to the income benefits payable during the period of recovery, be paid income benefits for such permanent disability in an amount equal to fifty-five percent (55%) of the average weekly state wage stated against the following scheduled permanent impairments respectively:

	Weeks
(1) Amputations of Upper Extremities	
Forequarter amputation	350
Disarticulation at shoulder joint	300

Amputation of arm above deltoid insertion	300
Amputation of arm between deltoid insertion and elbow joint	285
Disarticulation at elbow joint	285
Amputation of forearm below elbow joint proximal to insertion of biceps tendon	285
Amputation of forearm below elbow joint distal to insertion of biceps tendon	270
Disarticulation at wrist joint	270
Midcarpal or mid-metacarpal amputation of hand	270
Amputation of all fingers except thumb at metacarpophalangeal joints	160
Amputation of thumb	
At metacarpophalangeal joint or with resection of carpometacarpal bone	110
At interphalangeal joint	80
Amputation of index finger	
At metacarpophalangeal joint or with resection of metacarpal bone	70
At proximal interphalangeal joint	55
At distal interphalangeal joint	30
Amputation of middle finger	
At metacarpophalangeal joint or with resection of metacarpal bone	55
At proximal interphalangeal joint	45
At distal interphalangeal joint	25
Amputation of ring finger	
At metacarpophalangeal joint or with resection of metacarpal bone	25
At proximal interphalangeal joint	20
At distal interphalangeal joint	12
Amputation of little finger	
At metacarpophalangeal joint or with resection of metacarpal bone	15
At proximal interphalangeal joint	10
At distal interphalangeal joint	5
(2) Amputations of Lower Extremities	
Hemipelvectomy	250
Disarticulation at hip joint	200
Amputation above knee joint with short thigh stump (3″ or less below tuberosity of ischium)	200
Amputation above knee joint with functional stump	180
Disarticulation at knee joint	180
Gritt-Stokes amputation	180
Amputation below knee joint with short stump (3″ or less below intercondylar notch)	180
Amputation below knee joint with functional stump	140
Amputation at ankle (Syme)	140
Partial amputation of foot (Chopart's)	105
Mid-metatarsal amputation	70
Amputation of all toes	
At metatarsophalangeal joints	42
Amputation of great toe	
With resection of metatarsal bone	42
At metatarsophalangeal joint	25
At interphalangeal joint	25
Amputation of lesser toe (2nd–5th)	
With resection of metatarsal bone	7
At metatarsophalangeal joint	4
At proximal interphalangeal joint	3
At distal interphalangeal joint	1

(3) Loss of Vision and Hearing

Total loss of vision of one eye	150
Loss of one eye by enucleation	175
Total loss of binaural hearing	175

. . .

72-432. Medical services, appliances and supplies—Reports.—(1) The employer shall provide for an injured employee such reasonable medical, surgical or other attendance or treatment, nurse and hospital service, medicines, crutches and apparatus, as may be required by the employee's physician or needed immediately after an injury or disability from an occupational disease, and for a reasonable time thereafter. If the employer fails to provide the same, the injured employee may do so at the expense of the employer.

(2) The employer shall also furnish necessary replacements or repairs of appliances and prostheses, unless the need therefor is due to lack of proper care by the employee. If the appliance or prosthesis is damaged or destroyed in an industrial accident, the employer, for whom the employee was working at the time of accident, will be liable for replacement or repair, but not for any subsequent replacement or repair not directly resulting from the accident.

(3) In addition to the income benefits otherwise payable, the employee who is entitled to income benefits shall be paid an additional sum in an amount as may be determined by the commission as by it deemed necessary, as a medical service, when the constant service of an attendant is necessary by reason of total blindness of the employee or the loss of both hands or both feet or the loss of use thereof, or by reason of being paralyzed and unable to walk, or by reason of other disability resulting from the injury or disease actually rendering him so helpless as to require constant attendance. The commission shall have authority to determine the necessity, character and sufficiency of any medical services furnished or to be furnished and shall have authority to order a change of physician, hospital or rehabilitation facility when in its judgment such change is desirable or necessary.

(6) Nothing in this chapter shall be construed to require a workman who in good faith relies on Christian Science treatment by a duly accredited Christian Science practitioner to undergo any medical or surgical treatment, providing that neither he nor his dependents shall be entitled to income benefits of any kind beyond those reasonably expected to have been paid had he undergone medical or surgical treatment, and the employer or insurance carrier may pay for such spiritual treatment.

. . .

72-437. Occupational diseases—Right to compensation.—When an employee of an employer suffers an occupational disease and is thereby disabled from performing his work in the last occupation in which he was injuriously exposed to the hazards of such disease, or dies as a result of such disease, and the disease was due to the nature of an occupation or process in which he was employed within the period previous to his disablement as hereinafter limited, the employee, or, in case of his death, his dependents shall be entitled to compensation.

72-438. Occupational Diseases.—Compensation shall be payable for disability or death of an employee resulting from the following occupational diseases:

(1) Poisoning by lead, mercury, arsenic, zinc, or manganese, their preparations or compounds in any occupation involving direct contact therewith, handling thereof, or exposure thereto.

(2) Carbon monoxide poisoning or chlorine poisoning in any process or occupa-

tion involving direct exposure to carbon monoxide or chlorine in buildings, sheds, or inclosed places.

(3) Poisoning by methanol, carbon bisulphide, hydrocarbon distillates (naphthas and others) or halogenated hydrocarbons, or any preparations containing these chemicals or any of them, in any occupation involving direct contact therewith, handling thereof, or exposure thereto.

(4) Poisoning by benzol or by nitro, amido, or amino-derivatives of benzol (dinitro-benzol, anilin and others) or their preparations or compounds in any occupation involving direct contact therewith, handling thereof, or exposure thereto.

(5) Glanders in the care or handling of any equine animal or the carcass of any such animal.

(6) Radium poisoning by or disability due to radioactive properties of substances or to Roentgenray (X-ray) in any occupation involving direct contact therewith, handling thereof, or exposure thereto.

(7) Poisoning by or ulceration from chromic acid or bichromate of ammonium, potassium, or sodium or their preparations, or phosphorus preparations or compounds, in any occupation involving direct contact therewith, handling thereof, or exposure thereto.

(8) Ulceration due to tar, pitch, bitumen, mineral oil, or paraffin, or any compound product, or residue of any of these substances, in any occupation involving direct contact therewith, handling thereof, or exposure thereto.

(9) Dermatitis venenata, that is, infection or inflammation of the skin, furunculosis excepted, due to oils, cutting compounds, lubricants, liquids, fumes, gases, or vapors in any occupation involving direct contact therewith, handling thereof or exposure thereto.

(10) Anthrax occurring in any occupation involving the handling of or exposure to wool, hair, bristles, hides, skins, or bodies of animals either alive or dead.

(11) Silicosis in any occupation involving direct contact with, handling of, or exposure to dust of silicon dioxide (SiO_2).

(12) Cardiovascular or pulmonary or respiratory diseases of a paid fireman, employed by a municipality, village or fire district as a regular member of a lawfully established fire department, caused by overexertion in times of stress or danger or by proximate exposure or by cumulative exposure over a period of four (4) years or more to heat, smoke, chemical fumes or other toxic gases arising directly out of, and in the course of, his employment. Recognizing that additional toxic or harmful substances or matter are continually being discovered and used or misused, the above enumerated occupational diseases are not intended to be exclusive, but such additional diseases shall not include hazards which are common to the public in general. . . .

E. Structural Pest Control Board Law (California)
(California Business and Professional Code)

§ 8505.2 Performance of fumigation under direction and supervision of licensee.
Fumigation shall be performed only under the direct and personal supervision of an individual who is licensed by the board as an operator or field representative in a

branch of pest control which includes fumigation or who is the qualified partner or responsible natural person of a partnership which is so licensed or the qualified officer or responsible natural person of a corporation or association which is so licensed.

. . .

§ 8520. Existence and authority of structural pest control board. There is in the Department of Consumer Affairs a Structural Pest Control Board, which consists of six members appointed by the Governor.
. . . [T]he board is vested with the power to and shall administer the provisions of this chapter.

§ 8521. Qualification of members. The board is composed of six members, four of whom shall be, and shall have been for a period of not less than five years preceding the date of their appointment, operators licensed under this chapter actively engaged in the business of pest control and who are residents of this state, and two public members who shall not be licentiates of the board.

. . .

§ 8525. Rules and regulations. The board . . . may . . . adopt, amend, repeal, and enforce reasonably necessary rules and regulations relating to the practice of pest control and its various branches. . . .

The board shall give notice of adoption of such rules and regulations to all persons licensed under this chapter at least 30 days prior to the effective date of the regulations.

. . .

§ 8550. Necessity of license. It is unlawful for any person to engage or offer to engage in the business of, act in the capacity of, or advertise himself as, or assume to act as, an operator or a field representative, or to engage or offer to engage in the practice of structural pest control, unless he is licensed under this chapter.

. . .

§ 8551. Fumigation in public structure. It is unlawful for any unlicensed person to perform fumigation with dangerous or lethal fumigating chemicals in any public structure, including rooming houses, or households when used as public structures, hotels, apartment houses, or any part thereof.

. . .

§ 8553. Violation as misdemeanor. Any person who violates any provision of this chapter, or who conspires with another person to violate any provision of this chapter, is guilty of a misdemeanor, and is punishable by a fine of not less than fifty dollars ($50) nor more than five hundred dollars ($500), or by imprisonment in the county jail for not more than six months, or by both such fine and imprisonment.

. . .

§ 8565. Examination; operators. The board shall ascertain by written examination that an applicant for a license as operator is qualified in the use and understanding of all of the following:

(a) The English language, including reading, writing and spelling.

(b) The building and safety laws of the State and any of its political subdivisions, if the branch or branches of pest control for which he is applying, require such knowledge.

(c) The labor laws of the State.

(d) The provisions of this chapter.

(e) Poisonous and other dangerous chemicals used in pest control, if the branch license or licenses for which he is applying, require such knowledge.

(f) The theory and practice of pest control in the branch or branches thereof for which the applicant desires to be licensed.

(g) Such other state laws, safety or health measures, or practices as are reasonably within the scope of structural pest control in the various branches.

. . .

§ 8568. Grounds for denial; powers and proceedings. After a hearing the board may deny a license unless the applicant makes a showing satisfactory to the board that the applicant, if an individual, has not, or if the applicant is a person other than an individual, that its manager and each of its officers, directors, employees, members and partners have not:

(a) Knowingly committed or aided and abetted the commission of any illegal act which, if committed by a licensee, would be ground for suspension or revocation of a license under this chapter.

(b) While unlicensed, knowingly committed or aided and abetted the commission of any act for which a license is required under this chapter.

(c) While acting as a partner, officer, or managing employee of a firm, partnership, or corporation, had guilty knowledge of and participated in the commission of any act resulting in the suspension or revocation of a license.

(d) Been convicted of a felony or a crime involving moral turpitude. The record of conviction, or a certified copy thereof, shall be conclusive evidence of such conviction.

(e) Knowingly committed or done an act involving dishonesty, fraud or deceit whereby the applicant has been benefited, or whereby some injury has been sustained by another.

(f) Misrepresented any material fact on his application for a license.

PART III.

Administrative Regulations

A. Food and Drug Administration Regulations

B. Equal Employment Opportunity Commission Regulations

C. Structural Pest Control Board Regulations (California)

A. Food and Drug Administration Regulations
Code of Federal Regulations, Title 21

§ 201.200 Disclosure of drug efficacy study evaluations in labeling and advertising.

(a) (1) The National Academy of Sciences—National Research Council, Drug Efficacy Study Group, has completed an exhaustive review of labeling claims made for drugs marketed under new-drug and antibiotic drug procedures between 1938 and 1962. The results are compiled in "Drug Efficacy Study, A Report to the Commissioner of Food and Drugs from the National Academy of Sciences (1969)." As the report notes, this review has made "an audit of the state of the art of drug usage that has been uniquely extensive in scope and uniquely intensive in time" and is applicable to more than 80 percent of the currently marketed drugs. The report further notes that the quality of the evidence of efficacy, as well as the quality of the labeling claims, is poor. Labeling and other promotional claims have been evaluated as "effective," "probably effective," "possibly effective," "ineffective," "ineffective as a fixed combination," and "effective but," and a report for each drug in the study has been submitted to the Commissioner.

(2) The Food and Drug Administration is processing the reports, seeking voluntary action on the part of the drug manufacturers and distributors in the elimination or modification of unsupported promotional claims, and initiating administrative actions as necessary to require product and labeling changes.

(3) Delays have been encountered in bringing to the attention of the prescribers of prescription items the conclusions of the expert panels that reviewed the promotional claims.

(b) The Commissioner of Food and Drugs concludes that:

(1) The failure to disclose in the labeling of a drug and in other promotional material the conclusions of the Academy experts that a claim is "ineffective," "possibly effective," "probably effective," or "ineffective as a fixed combination," while labeling and promotional material bearing any such claim are being used, is a failure to disclose facts that are material in light of the representations made and causes the drug to be misbranded.

(2) The Academy classification of a drug as other than "effective" for a claim for which such drug is recommended establishes that there is a material weight of opinion among qualified experts contrary to the representation made or suggested in the labeling, and failure to reveal this fact causes such labeling to be misleading.

(c) Therefore, after publication in the FEDERAL REGISTER of a Drug Efficacy Study Implementation notice on a prescription drug, unless exempted or otherwise provided for in the notice, all package labeling, . . . promotional labeling, and advertisements shall include, as part of the information for practitioners under which the drug can be safely and effectively used, an appropriate qualification of all claims evaluated as other than "effective" by a panel of the National Academy of Sciences—National Research Council, Drug Efficacy Study Group, if such claims continue to be included in either the labeling or advertisements. . . .

B. Equal Employment Opportunity Commission Regulations
Code of Federal Regulations, Title 29

§ 1604.2 Sex as a bona fide occupational qualification.

(a) The commission believes that the bona fide occupational qualification exception as to sex should be interpreted narrowly. Label—"Men's jobs" and "Women's jobs"—tend to deny employment opportunities unnecessarily to one sex or the other.

(1) The Commission will find that the following situations do not warrant the application of the bona fide occupational qualification exception;

(i) The refusal to hire a woman because of her sex based on assumptions of the comparative employment characteristics of women in general. For example, the assumption that the turnover rate among women is higher than among men.

(ii) The refusal to hire an individual based on stereotyped characterizations of the sexes. Such stereotypes include, for example, that men are less capable of assembling intricate equipment: that women are less capable of aggressive salesmanship. The principle of nondiscrimination requires that individuals be considered on the basis of individual capacities and not on the basis of any characteristics generally attributed to the group.

(iii) The refusal to hire an individual because of the preferences of coworkers, the employer, clients or customers except as covered specifically in paragraph (a)(2) of this section.

(2) Where it is necessary for the purpose of authenticity or genuineness, the Commission will consider sex to be a bona fide occupational qualification, e.g., an actor or actress.

(b) Effect of sex-oriented State employment legislation.

(1) Many States have enacted laws or promulgated administrative regulations with respect to the employment of females. Among these laws are those which prohibit or limit the employment of females, e.g., the employment of females in certain occupations, in jobs requiring the lifting or carrying of weights exceeding certain prescribed limits, during certain hours of the night, for more than a specified number of hours per day or per week, and for certain periods of time before and after childbirth. The Commission has found that such laws and regulations do not take into account

the capacities, preferences, and abilities of individual females and, therefore, discriminate on the basis of sex. The Commission has concluded that such laws and regulations conflict with and are superseded by title VII of the Civil Rights Act of 1964. Accordingly, such laws will not be considered a defense to an otherwise established unlawful employment practice or as a basis for the application of the bona fide occupational qualification exception.

(2) The Commission has concluded that State laws and regulations which discriminate on the basis of sex with regard to the employment of minors are in conflict with and are superseded by title VII to the extent that such laws are more restrictive for one sex. Accordingly, restrictions on the employment of minors of one sex over and above those imposed on minors of the other sex will not be considered a defense to an otherwise established unlawful employment practice or as a basis for the application of the bona fide occupational qualification exception.

. . .

(4) As to other kinds of sex-oriented State employment laws, such as those requiring special rest and meal periods or physical facilities for women, provision of these benefits to one sex only will be a violation of title VII. An employer will be deemed to have engaged in an unlawful employment practice if:

(i) It refuses to hire or otherwise adversely affects the employment opportunities of female applicants or employees in order to avoid the provision of such benefits; or

(ii) It does not provide the same benefits for male employees. If the employer can prove that business necessity precludes providing these benefits to both men and women, then the State law is in conflict with and superseded by title VII as to this employer. In this situation, the employer shall not provide such benefits to members of either sex.

(5) Some States require that separate restrooms be provided for employees of each sex. An employer will be deemed to have engaged in an unlawful employment practice if it refuses to hire or otherwise adversely affects the employment opportunities of applicants or employees in order to avoid the provision of such restrooms for persons of that sex.

§ 1604.3 Separate lines of progression and seniority systems.

(a) It is an unlawful employment practice to classify a job as "male" or "female" or to maintain separate lines of progression or separate seniority lists based on sex where this would adversely affect any employee unless sex is a bona fide occupational qualification for that job. Accordingly, employment practices are unlawful which arbitrarily classify jobs so that:

(1) A female is prohibited from applying for a job labeled "male," or for a job in a "male" line of progression; and vice versa.

(2) A male scheduled for layoff is prohibited from displacing a less senior female on a "female" seniority list; and vice versa.

(b) A Seniority system or line of progression which distinguishes between "light" and "heavy" jobs constitutes an unlawful employment practice if it operates as a disguised form of classification by sex, or creates unreasonable obstacles to the advancement by members of either sex into jobs which members of that sex would reasonably be expected to perform.

§ 1604.4 Discrimination against married women.

(a) The Commission has determined that an employer's rule which forbids or restricts the employment of married women and which is not applicable to married men is a discrimination based on sex prohibited by title VII of the Civil Rights Act. It does not seem to us relevant that the rule is not directed against all females, but only against married females, for so long as sex is a factor in the application of the rule, such application involves a discrimination based on sex.

§ 1604.5 Job opportunities advertising.

It is a violation of title VII for a help-wanted advertisement to indicate a preference, limitation, specification, or discrimination based on sex unless sex is a bona fide occupational qualification for the particular job involved. The placement of an advertisement in columns classified by publishers on the basis of sex, such as columns headed "Male" or "Female," will be considered an expression of a preference, limitation, specification, or discrimination based on sex.

. . .

§ 1604.7 Pre-employment inquiries as to sex.

A pre-employment inquiry may ask "Male........., Female........."; or "Mr. Mrs. Miss," provided that the inquiry is made in good faith for a nondiscriminatory purpose. Any pre-employment inquiry in connection with prospective employment which expresses directly or indirectly any limitation, specification, or discrimination as to sex shall be unlawful unless based upon a bona fide occupational qualification.

. . .

§ 1604.10 Employment policies relating to pregnancy and childbirth.

(a) A written or unwritten employment policy or practice which excludes from employment applicants or employees because of pregnancy, childbirth or related medical conditions is in prima facie violation of Title VII.

. . .

§ 1604.11 Sexual harassment.

(a) Harassment on the basis of sex is a violation of Sec. 703 of Title VII. Unwelcome sexual advances, requests for sexual favors, and other verbal or physical conduct of a sexual nature constitute sexual harassment when (1) submission to such conduct is made either explicitly or implicitly a term or condition of an individual's employment, (2) submission to or rejection of such conduct by an individual is used as the basis for employment decisions affecting such individual, or (3) such conduct has the purpose or effect of unreasonably interfering with an individual's work performance or creating an intimidating, hostile, or offensive working environment.

(b) In determining whether alleged conduct constitutes sexual harassment, the Commission will look at the record as a whole and at the totality of the circumstances, such as the nature of the sexual advances and the context in which the alleged incidents occurred. The determination of the legality of a particular action will be made from the facts, on a case by case basis.

(c) Applying general Title VII principles, an employer, employment agency, joint apprenticeship committee or labor organization (hereinafter collectively referred to as "employer") is responsible for its acts and those of its agents and supervisory employees with respect to sexual harassment regardless of whether the specific acts complained of were authorized or even forbidden by the employer and regardless of whether the employer knew or should have known of their occurrence. The Commission will examine the circumstances of the particular employment relationship and the job junctions performed by the individual in determining whether an individual acts in either a supervisory or agency capacity.

(d) With respect to conduct between fellow employees, an employer is responsible for acts of sexual harassment in the workplace where the employer (or its agents or supervisory employees) knows or should have known of the conduct, unless it can show that it took immediate and appropriate corrective action.

(e) An employer may also be responsible for the acts of non-employees, with respect to sexual harassment of employees in the workplace, where the employer (or its agents or supervisory employees) knows or should have known of the conduct and fails to take immediate and appropriate corrective action. In reviewing these cases the Commission will consider the extent of the employer's control and any other legal responsibility which the employer may have with respect to the conduct of such non-employees.

(f) Prevention is the best tool for the elimination of sexual harassment. An employer should take all steps necessary to prevent sexual harassment from occurring, such as affirmatively raising the subject, expressing strong disapproval, developing appropriate sanctions, informing employees of their right to raise and how to raise the issue of harassment under Title VII, and developing methods to sensitize all concerned.

(g) Other related practices: Where employment opportunities or benefits are granted because of an individual's submission to the employer's sexual advances or requests for sexual favors, the employer may be held liable for unlawful sex discrimination against other persons who were qualified for but denied that employment opportunity or benefit.

C. Structural Pest Control Board Regulations (California)
California Administrative Code, Title 16

ARTICLE 4. FUMIGATION AND PESTICIDE USE

1970. Standards and Record Requirements.

For the purpose of maintaining proper standards of safety and the establishment of responsibility in handling the dangerous gases used in fumigation and the pesticides used in other pest control operations, an operator shall compile and retain for a period of at least two years, a log or report for each fumigation job and for each pesticide control operation in which a pesticide is used by the operator or the operator's employee.

(a) The report or log for each fumigation job shall contain the following information:

Name and address of prime contractor.
Name and address of subcontractor, if any.
Address of property.
Name of owner or his agent.
Type of structure as to details of roofing and walls.
Cubic feet fumigated.
Target pest or pests controlled.
Kind of fumigant or fumigants used and amount.
Name of warning agent and amount used.

Type of sealing method used.
Weather conditions as to temperature and wind.
Time gas introduced (date and hour).
Name of licensee testing for leaks.
List of any extraordinary safety precautions taken.
Time gas released (date and hour).
Name of licensee making final test.
Names of crew at fumigation.
Names of crew at opening.
Time fire department was notified.
Time police department notified, where required by local ordinance.
Time ready for occupancy.
Signature of licensed operator or field representative in charge.

(b) The report for each pest control operation, other than fumigation, in which a pesticide is used shall contain the following information:
Date of treatment.
Name of owner or his agent.
Address of property.
Total area treated.
Target pests or pests controlled.
Pesticide and amount used.
Identity of person or persons who applied the pesticide.

. . .

1981. Rodenticides and Avicides.
Rodenticides and avicides shall be possessed and used in conformity with the following requirements:

(a) Where there is danger of food or drug contamination, poison bait or preparations thereof shall be placed in bait boxes that are adequate to contain the pesticide safely.

(b) No rodenticide or avicide shall be used in such manner as to be readily accessible to children or pets.

(c) All rodenticide and avicide shall be removed from readily accessible places upon termination of the particular service.

(d) All rodenticide and avicide shall be handled and stored in the manner prescribed by Section 1983.

(e) When a covered or uncovered bait station is used for any pesticide the bait station shall be adequately marked with the signal word or symbols required on the original pesticide label, the generic name of the pesticide, and the name, address and telephone number of the structural pest control company.

(f) Tracing powders shall be discolored and used only at floor level or in such places as warrant their safe use, and in no circumstances shall they be used in such manner as to contaminate foods or drugs or food or drug containers or preparation equipment thereof.

PART IV.

American Case Law

A. *Brown v. Board of Education of Topeka et al.* (1954)

B. *Dothard v. Rawlinson* (1977)

C. *Louie v. Bamboo Gardens et al.* (1947)

D. *Marvin v. Marvin* (1976)

Brown et al. v. Board of Education of Topeka et al.

347 U.S. 483, 74 S.Ct. 686, 98 L.Ed. 873 (1954)

MR. CHIEF JUSTICE WARREN delivered the opinion of the Court.

These cases come to us from the States of Kansas, South Carolina, Virginia, and Delaware. They are premised on different facts and different local conditions, but a common legal question justifies their consideration together in this consolidated opinion.

In each of the cases, minors of the Negro race, through their legal representatives, seek the aid of the courts in obtaining admission to the public schools of their community on a nonsegregated basis. In each instance, they had been denied admission to schools attended by white children under laws requiring or permitting segregation according to race. This segregation was alleged to deprive the plaintiffs of the equal protection of the laws under the Fourteenth Amendment. In each of the cases other than the Delaware case, a three-judge federal district court denied relief to the plaintiffs on the so-called "separate but equal" doctrine announced by this Court in *Plessy v. Ferguson,* 163 U.S. 537. Under that doctrine, equality of treatment is accorded when the races are provided substantially equal facilities, even though these facilities be separate. In the Delaware case, the Supreme Court of Delaware adhered to that doctrine, but ordered that the plaintiffs be admitted to the white schools because of their superiority to the Negro schools.

The plaintiffs contend that segregated public schools are not "equal" and cannot be made "equal," and that hence they are deprived of the equal protection of the laws. Because of the obvious importance of the question presented, the Court took jurisdiction. Argument was heard in the 1952 Term, and reargument was heard this Term on certain questions propounded by the Court.

Reargument was largely devoted to the circumstances surrounding the adoption of the Fourteenth Amendment in 1868. It covered exhaustively consideration of the Amendment in Congress, ratification by the states, then existing practices in racial segregation, and the views of proponents and opponents of the Amendment. This discussion and our own investigation convince us that, although these sources cast some light, it is not enough to resolve the problem with which we are faced. At best, they are inconclusive. The most avid proponents of the post-War Amendments undoubtedly intended them to remove all legal distinctions among "all persons born or naturalized in the United States." Their opponents, just as certainly, were antagonistic to both the letter and the spirit of the Amendments and wished them to have the most limited effect. What others in Congress and the state legislatures had in mind cannot be determined with any degree of certainty.

An additional reason for the inconclusive nature of the Amendment's history, with respect to segregated schools, is the status of public education at that time. In the South, the movement toward free common schools, supported by general taxation, had not yet taken hold. Education of white children was largely in the hands of private groups. Education of Negroes was almost nonexistent, and practically all of the race were illiterate. In fact, any education of Negroes was forbidden by law in some states. Today, in contrast, many Negroes have achieved outstanding success in the arts and sciences as well as in the business and professional world. It is true that public school education at the time of the Amendment had advanced further in the North, but the effect of the Amendment on Northern States was generally ignored in the congressional debates. Even in the North, the conditions of public education did not approximate those existing today. The curriculum was usually rudimentary; ungraded schools were common in rural areas; the school term was but three months a year in many states; and compulsory school attendance was virtually unknown. As a consequence, it is not surprising that there should be so little in the history of the Fourteenth Amendment relating to its intended effect on public education.

In the first cases in this Court construing the Fourteenth Amendment, decided shortly after its adoption, the Court interpreted it as proscribing all state-imposed discriminations against the Negro race. The doctrine of "separate but equal" did not make its appearance in this Court until 1896 in the case of *Plessy* v. *Ferguson, supra,* involving not education but transportation. American courts have since labored with the doctrine for over half a century. In this Court, there have been six cases involving the "separate but equal" doctrine in the field of public education. In *Cumming* v. *County Board of Education,* 175 U.S. 528, and *Gong Lum* v. *Rice,* 275 U.S. 78, the validity of the doctrine itself was not challenged. In more recent cases, all on the graduate school level, inequality was found in that specific benefits enjoyed by white students were denied to Negro students of the same educational qualifications. *Missouri ex rel. Gaines* v. *Canada,* 305 U.S. 337; *Sipuel* v. *Oklahoma,* 332 U.S. 631; *Sweatt* v. *Painter,* 339 U.S. 629; *McLaurin* v. *Oklahoma State Regents,* 339 U.S. 637. In none of these cases was it necessary to re-examine the doctrine to grant relief to the Negro plaintiff. And in *Sweatt* v. *Painter, supra,* the Court expressly reserved decision on the question whether *Plessy* v. *Ferguson* should be held inapplicable to public education.

In the instant cases, that question is directly presented. Here, unlike *Sweatt* v. *Painter,* there are findings below that the Negro and white schools involved have been equalized, or are being equalized, with respect to buildings, curricula, qualifications and salaries of teachers, and other "tangible" factors. Our decision, therefore, cannot turn on merely a comparison of these tangible factors in the Negro and white schools involved in each of the cases. We must look instead to the effect of segregation itself on public education.

In approaching this problem, we cannot turn the clock back to 1868 when the Amendment was adopted, or even to 1896 when *Plessy* v. *Ferguson* was written. We must consider public education in the light of its full development* and its present place in American life throughout the Nation. Only in this way can it be determined if segregation in public schools deprives these plaintiffs of the equal protection of the laws.

Today, education is perhaps the most important function of state and local governments. Compulsory school attendance laws and the great expenditures for education both demonstrate our recognition of the importance of education to our democratic society. It is required in the performance of our most basic public responsibilities, even service in the armed forces. It is the very foundation of good citizenship. Today it is a principal instrument in awakening the child to cultural values, in preparing him for later professional training, and in helping him to adjust normally to his environment. In these days, it is doubtful that any child may reasonably be expected to succeed in life if he is denied the opportunity of an education. Such an opportunity, where the state has undertaken to provide it, is a right which must be made available to all on equal terms.

We come then to the question presented: Does segregation of children in public schools solely on the basis of race, even though the physical facilities and other "tangible" factors may be equal, deprive the children of the minority group of equal educational opportunities? We believe that it does.

In *Sweatt* v. *Painter, supra,* in finding that a segregated law school for Negroes could not provide them equal educational opportunities, this Court relied in large part on "those qualities which are incapable of objective measurement but which make for greatness in a law school." In *McLaurin* v. *Oklahoma State Regents, supra,* the Court, in requiring that a Negro admitted to a white graduate school be treated like all other students, again resorted to intangible considerations: ". . . his ability to study, to engage in discussions and exchange views with other students, and, in general, to learn his profession." Such considerations apply with added force to children in grade and high schools. To separate them from others of similar age and qualifications solely because of their race generates a feeling of inferiority as to their status in the community that may affect their hearts and minds in a way unlikely ever to be undone. The effect of this separation on their educational opportunities was well stated by a finding in the Kansas case by a court which nevertheless felt compelled to rule against the Negro plaintiffs:

> "Segregation of white and colored children in public schools has a detrimental effect upon the colored children. The impact is greater when it has the sanction of the law; for the policy of separating the races is usually interpreted as denoting the inferiority of the negro group. A sense of inferiority affects the motivation of a child to learn. Segregation with the sanction of law, therefore, has a tendency to [retard] the educational and mental development of negro children and to deprive them of some of the benefits they would receive in a racial[ly] integrated school system."

Whatever may have been the extent of psychological knowledge at the time of *Plessy* v. *Ferguson,* this finding is amply supported by modern authority.* Any language in

*K. B. Clark, Effect of Prejudice and Discrimination on Personality Development (Midcentury White House Conference on Children and Youth, 1950); Witmer and Kotinsky, Personality in the Making (1952), c. VI; Deutscher and Chein, The Psychological Effects of Enforced Segregation: A Survey of Social Science Opinion, 26 J. Psychol. 259 (1948); Chein, What are the Psychological Effects of Segregation Under Conditions of Equal Facilities?, 3 Int. J. Opinion and Attitude Res. 229 (1949); Brameld, Educational Costs, in Discrimination and National Welfare (MacIver, ed., 1949), 44–48; Frazier, The Negro in the United States (1949), 674–681. And see

Plessy v. *Ferguson* contrary to this finding is rejected.

We conclude that in the field of public education the doctrine of "separate but equal" has no place. Separate educational facilities are inherently unequal. Therefore, we hold that the plaintiffs and others similarly situated for whom the actions have been brought are, by reason of the segregation complained of, deprived of the equal protection of the laws guaranteed by the Fourteenth Amendment. This disposition makes unnecessary any discussion whether such segregation also violates the Due Process Clause of the Fourteenth Amendment.

Because these are class actions, because of the wide applicability of this decision, and because of the great variety of local conditions, the formulation of decrees in these cases presents problems of considerable complexity. On reargument, the consideration of appropriate relief was necessarily subordinated to the primary question—the constitutionality of segregation in public education. We have now announced that such segregation is a denial of the equal protection of the laws. In order that we may have the full assistance of the parties in formulating decrees, the cases will be restored to the docket, and the parties are requested to present further argument on Questions 4 and 5 previously propounded by the Court for the reargument this Term.†
The Attorney General of the United States is again invited to participate. The Attorneys General of the states requiring or permitting segregation in public education will also be permitted to appear as *amici curiae* upon request to do so by September 15, 1954, and submission of briefs by October 1, 1954.

It is so ordered.

---

generally Myrdal, An American Dilemma (1944). [This original footnote, itself controversial, lists psychological studies which, it was claimed, support the Court's conclusion.—AUTHOR'S NOTE.]

†"4. Assuming it is decided that segregation in public schools violates the Fourteenth Amendment.

"(a) would a decree necessarily follow providing that, within the limits set by normal geographic school districting, Negro children should forthwith be admitted to schools of their choice, or

"(b) may this Court, in the exercise of its equity powers, permit an effective gradual adjustment to be brought about from existing segregated systems to a system not based on color distinctions?

"5. On the assumption on which questions 4 (a) and (b) are based, and assuming further that this Court will exercise its equity powers to the end described in question 4 (b),

"(a) should this Court formulate detailed decrees in these cases;

"(b) if so, what specific issues should the decrees reach;

"(c) should this Court appoint a special master to hear evidence with a view to recommending specific terms for such decrees;

"(d) should this Court remand to the courts of first instance with directions to frame decrees in these cases, and if so what general directions should the decrees of this Court include and what procedures should the courts of first instance follow in arriving at the specific terms of more detailed decrees?"

Dothard v. *Rawlinson*

433 U.S. 321, 97 S.Ct. 2720, 53 L.Ed. 2d 786 (1977)

MR. JUSTICE STEWART delivered the opinion of the Court.

Appellee Dianne Rawlinson sought employment with the Alabama Board of Corrections as a prison guard, called in Alabama a "correctional counselor." After her application was rejected, she brought this class suit under Title VII of the Civil Rights Act of 1964, 78 Stat. 253, as amended, 42 U. S. C. § 2000e *et seq.* (1970 ed. and Supp. V), and under 42 U. S. C. § 1983, alleging that she had been denied employment because of her sex in violation of federal law. A three-judge Federal District Court for the Middle District of Alabama decided in her favor. *Mieth* v. *Dothard*, 418 F. Supp. 1169. . . .

I

At the time she applied for a position as correctional counselor trainee, Rawlinson was a 22-year-old college graduate whose major course of study had been correctional psychology. She was refused employment because she failed to meet the minimum 120-pound weight requirement established by an Alabama statute. The statute also establishes a height minimum of 5 feet 2 inches.

After her application was rejected because of her weight, Rawlinson filed a charge with the Equal Employment Opportunity Commission, and ultimately received a right-to-sue letter. She then filed a complaint in the District Court on behalf of herself and other similarly situated women, challenging the statutory height and weight minima as violative of Title VII and the Equal Protection Clause of the Fourteenth Amendment. A three-judge court was convened. While the suit was pending, the Alabama Board of Corrections adopted Administrative Regulation 204, establishing gender criteria for assigning correctional counselors to maximum-security institutions for "contact positions," that is, positions requiring continual close physical proximity to inmates of the institution. Rawlinson amended her class-action complaint by adding a challenge to Regulation 204 as also violative of Title VII and the Fourteenth Amendment.

Like most correctional facilities in the United States, Alabama's prisons are segregated on the basis of sex. Currently the Alabama Board of Corrections operates four major all-male penitentiaries—Holman Prison, Kilby Corrections Facility, G. K. Fountain Correction Center, and Draper Correctional Center. The Board also operates the Julia Tutwiler Prison for Women, the Frank Lee Youth Center, the Number Four Honor Camp, the State Cattle Ranch, and nine Work Release Centers, one of which is for women. The Julia Tutwiler Prison for Women and the four male penitentiaries are maximum-security institutions. Their inmate living quarters are for the most part large dormitories, with communal showers and toilets that are open to the dormitories and hallways. The Draper and Fountain penitentiaries carry on extensive farming operations, making necessary a large number of strip searches for contraband when prisoners re-enter the prison buildings.

A correctional counselor's primary duty within these institutions is to maintain security and control of the inmates by continually supervising and observing their activities. To be eligible for consideration as a correctional counselor, an applicant must possess a valid Alabama driver's license, have a high school education or its equivalent, be free from physical defects, be between the ages of 20½ years and 45 years at the time of appointment, and fall between the minimum height and weight requirements of 5 feet 2 inches, and 120 pounds, and the maximum of 6 feet 10 inches, and 300 pounds. Appointment is by merit, with a grade assigned each applicant based on experience and education. No written examination is given.

At the time this litigation was in the District Court, the Board of Corrections employed a total of 435 people in various correctional counselor positions, 56 of whom were women. Of those 56 women, 21 were employed at the Julia Tutwiler Prison for Women, 13 were employed in noncontact positions at the four male maximum-security institutions, and the remaining 22 were employed at the other institutions operated by the Alabama Board of Corrections. Because most of Alabama's prisoners are held at the four maximum-security male penitentiaries, 336 of the 435 correctional counselor jobs were in those institutions, a majority of them concededly in the "contact" classification. Thus, even though meeting the statutory height and weight requirements, women applicants could under Regulation 204 compete equally with men for only about 25% of the correctional counselor jobs available in the Alabama prison system.

II

A

The gist of the claim that the statutory height and weight requirements discriminate against women does not involve an assertion of purposeful discriminatory motive. It is asserted, rather, that these facially neutral qualification standards work in fact disproportionately to exclude women from eligibility for employment by the Alabama Board of Corrections. We dealt in *Griggs* v. *Duke Power Co., supra,* and *Albemarle Paper Co.* v. *Moody,* 422 U.S. 405, with similar allegations that facially neutral employment standards disproportionately excluded Negroes from employment, and those cases guide our approach here.

Those cases make clear that to establish a prima facie case of discrimination, a plaintiff need only show that the facially neutral standards in question select applicants for hire in a significantly discriminatory pattern. Once it is thus shown that the employment standards are discriminatory in effect, the employer must meet "the burden of showing that any given requirement [has] . . . a manifest relationship to the employment in question." *Griggs* v. *Duke Power Co., supra,* at 432. If the employer proves that the challenged requirements are job related, the plaintiff may then show that other selection devices without a similar discriminatory effect would also "serve the employer's legitimate interest in 'efficient and trustworthy workmanship.' " *Albemarle Paper Co.* v. *Moody, supra,* at 425, quoting *McDonnell Douglas Corp.* v. *Green,* 411 U.S. 792, 801.

Although women 14 years of age or older compose 52.75% of the Alabama population and 36.89% of its total labor force, they hold only 12.9% of its correctional counselor positions. In considering the effect of the minimum height and weight standards on this disparity in rate of hiring between the sexes, the District Court found that the 5'2" requirement would operate to exclude 33.29% of the women in the United States between the ages of 18–79, while excluding only 1.28% of men between the same ages. The 120-pound weight restriction would exclude 22.29% of the women and 2.35% of the men in this age group. When the height and weight restrictions are combined, Alabama's statutory standards would exclude 41.13% of the female population while excluding less than 1% of the male population. Accordingly, the District Court found that Rawlinson had made out a prima facie case of unlawful sex discrimination. . . .

B

[Appellants argue] that they have rebutted the prima facie case of discrimination by showing that the height and weight requirements are job related. These require-

324   AMERICAN LAW

ments, they say, have a relationship to strength, a sufficient but unspecified amount of which is essential to effective job performance as a correctional counselor. In the District Court, however, the appellants produced no evidence correlating the height and weight requirements with the requisite amount of strength thought essential to good job performance. Indeed, they failed to offer evidence of any kind in specific justification of the statutory standards.

If the job-related quality that the appellants identify is bona fide, their purpose could be achieved by adopting and validating a test for applicants that measures strength directly. Such a test, fairly administered, would fully satisfy the standards of Title VII because it would be one that "measure[s] the person for the job and not the person in the abstract." *Griggs* v. *Duke Power Co.*, 401 U.S., at 436. But nothing in the present record even approaches such a measurement.

For the reasons we have discussed, the District Court was not in error in holding that Title VII of the Civil Rights Act of 1964, as amended, prohibits application of the statutory height and weight requirements to Rawlinson and the class she represents.

III

Unlike the statutory height and weight requirements, Regulation 204 explicitly discriminates against women on the basis of their sex. In defense of this overt discrimination, the appellants rely on § 703(e) of Title VII, 42 U.S.C. § 2000e–2(e), which permits sex-based discrimination "in those certain instances where . . . sex . . . is a bona fide occupational qualification reasonably necessary to the normal operation of that particular business or enterprise." . . .

We are persuaded—by the restrictive language of § 703(e), the relevant legislative history, and the consistent interpretation of the Equal Employment Opportunity Commission—that the bfoq exception was in fact meant to be an extremely narrow exception to the general prohibition of discrimination on the basis of sex. In the particular factual circumstances of this case, however, we conclude that the District Court erred in rejecting the State's contention that Regulation 204 falls within the narrow ambit of the bfoq exception.

The environment in Alabama's penitentiaries is a peculiarly inhospitable one for human beings of whatever sex. Indeed, a Federal District Court has held that the conditions of confinement in the prisons of the State, characterized by "rampant violence" and a "jungle atmosphere," are constitutionally intolerable. *Pugh* v. *Locke*, 406 F. Supp. 318, 325 (MD Ala.). The record in the present case shows that because of inadequate staff and facilities, no attempt is made in the four maximum-security male penitentiaries to classify or segregate inmates according to their offense or level of dangerousness—a procedure that, according to expert testimony, is essential to effective penological administration. Consequently, the estimated 20% of the male prisoners who are sex offenders are scattered throughout the penitentiaries' dormitory facilities.

In this environment of violence and disorganization, it would be an oversimplification to characterize Regulation 204 as an exercise in "romantic paternalism." Cf. *Frontiero* v. *Richardson*, 411 U.S. 677, 684. In the usual case, the argument that a particular job is too dangerous for women may appropriately be met by the rejoinder that it is the purpose of Title VII to allow the individual woman to make that choice for herself. More is at stake in this case, however, than an individual woman's decision to weigh and accept the risks of employment in a "contact" position in a maximum-security male prison.

The essence of a correctional counselor's job is to maintain prison security. A woman's relative ability to maintain order in a male, maximum-security, unclassified penitentiary of the type Alabama now runs could be directly reduced by her womanhood. There is a basis in fact for expecting that sex offenders who have criminally assaulted women in the past would be moved to do so again if access to women were established within the prison. There would also be a real risk that other inmates, deprived of a normal heterosexual environment, would assault women guards because they were women. In a prison system where violence is the order of the day, where inmate access to guards is facilitated by dormitory living arrangements, where every institution is understaffed, and where a substantial portion of the inmate population is composed of sex offenders mixed at random with other prisoners, there are few visible deterrents to inmate assaults on women custodians. . . .

There was substantial testimony from experts on both sides of this litigation that the use of women as guards in "contact" positions under the existing conditions in Alabama maximum-security male penitentiaries would pose a substantial security problem, directly linked to the sex of the prison guard. On the basis of that evidence, we conclude that the District Court was in error in ruling that being male is not a bona fide occupational qualification for the job of correctional counselor in a "contact" position in an Alabama male maximum-security penitentiary.

The judgment is accordingly affirmed in part and reversed in part, and the case is remanded to the District Court for further proceedings consistent with this opinion.

It is so ordered.

MR. JUSTICE MARSHALL, with whom MR. JUSTICE BRENNAN joins, concurring in part and dissenting in part.

I agree entirely with the Court's analysis of Alabama's height and weight requirements for prison guards, and with its finding that these restrictions discriminate on the basis of sex in violation of Title VII. . . . I must, however, respectfully disagree with the Court's application of the bfoq exception in this case.

. . .

It appears that the real disqualifying factor in the Court's view is "[t]he employee's very womanhood." *Ante*, at 336. The Court refers to the large number of sex offenders in Alabama prisons, and to "[t]he likelihood that inmates would assault a woman because she was a woman." *Ibid*. In short, the fundamental justification for the decision is that women as guards will generate sexual assaults. With all respect, this rationale regrettably perpetuates one of the most insidious of the old myths about women—that women, wittingly or not, are seductive sexual objects. The effect of the decision, made I am sure with the best of intentions, is to punish women because their very presence might provoke sexual assaults. It is women who are made to pay the price in lost job opportunities for the threat of depraved conduct by prison inmates. Once again, "[t]he pedestal upon which women have been placed has . . . , upon closer inspection, been revealed as a cage." *Sail'er Inn, Inc.* v. *Kirby*, 5 Cal.3d 1, 20, 485 P.2d 529, 541 (1971). It is particularly ironic that the cage is erected here in response to feared misbehavior by imprisoned criminals.

. . .

The proper response to inevitable attacks on both female and male guards is not to limit the employment opportunities of law-abiding women who wish to contribute to their community, but to take swift and sure punitive action against the inmate offenders. Presumably, one of the goals of the Alabama prison system is the eradication of inmates' antisocial behavior patterns so that prisoners will be able to live one day in free society. Sex offenders can begin this process by learning to relate to women guards in a socially acceptable manner. To deprive women of job opportunities because of the threatened behavior of convicted criminals is to turn our social priorities upside down.

Louie v. *Bamboo Gardens et al.*

67 Ida. 469, 185 P.2d 712 (1947)

MILLER, Justice.

This case was submitted to the Industrial Accident Board on a stipulation of the facts as agreed to between the parties, and from which, among other things, it is made to appear:

That Tom Louie, claimant and appellant, about 45 years of age, on the 18th day of October, 1946, and for more than three months prior thereto, was in the employ of the Bamboo Gardens, a restaurant in Boise, Idaho, as a dishwasher therein; that he was casually acquainted with one Fook Lee Hong, another Chinaman, but that said Hong was not a patron of the Bamboo Gardens, nor a customer thereof in that he had never taken his meals thereat and was in nowise interested therein. September 21, 1946, Fook Lee Hong and three other Chinese were arrested on a narcotic charge by officials of the United States; that during the latter part of September 1946, Hong was fined $50 by the U. S. District Judge, at Boise, Idaho, on account of his plea to said charge and thereupon discharged from further custody. Hong was a discharged veteran of World War II. After his discharge for the violation of the Narcotic Act, 26 U.S.C.A. Int. Rev. Code, §§ 2550 et seq., 3220 et seq., he seems to have labored under the delusion that it was thought that he had turned "State's evidence," and that someone was going to kill him. After his said discharge and prior to October 18, 1946, he stated to an Assistant United States District Attorney that members of a tong society to which Tom Louie belonged, and to which Hong did not belong were going to import "hatchet men" from Walla Walla, Washington to Boise, Idaho to kill him because members of such tong thought he had turned State's evidence against his former companions on the narcotic charge; that for several days before October 18, 1946, he was more or less in hiding at the American Legion Building in Boise, Idaho, asserting that someone was going to kill him. The Prosecuting Attorney of Ada County, Idaho, made an investigation and found there were no reasonable grounds for his suspicions that someone was going to kill him, but in his own mind he suffered the delusion that an attempt would be made upon his life.

October 18, 1946, at about 5:45 P.M., Tom Louie, claimant and appellant, received an injury, during his regular hours, and in the course of his employment, and while he was on duty performing the tasks for which he was employed at his employer's place of business, at 107 South 7th Street, Boise, Idaho, in that while taking water glasses from the kitchen to the serving table in the dining room, Fook Lee Hong entered the restaurant by the front door on 7th Street, carrying a loaded 38 caliber revolver, which he brandished in a threatening manner, and then shot the same within the restaurant three times, one of which shots struck Tom Louie, claimant and appellant, in the upper back region, piercing his chest cavity and his lungs. The employer was notified of such accident and injury sustained by said claimant and appellant, during the evening of October 18, 1946, and that a claim in writing, stating the name and address of the employer, the time, place, nature and cause of the injury, signed by claimant and appellant, was filed with the Industrial Accident Board on October 30, 1946; that as the result of the injury sustained, claimant and appellant was hospitalized at St. Luke's Hospital at Boise, Idaho, for a period commencing the evening of October 18, 1946, and until and including November 9, 1946, and that the hospital and medical charges in the sum of $475.55 were paid by claimant and appellant; that claimant and appellant was under medical care at the time of filing the stipulation of facts with the Industrial Accident Board and that at the time he was totally disabled for work and would continue to be so totally disabled for a period of time subsequently to be determined; that he was not then surgically healed and whether or not he will sustain a permanent injury is yet to be determined as well as the degree thereof, if permanent injury results therefrom.

On or about October 21, 1946, a criminal complaint was filed against Fook Lee Hong by the Prosecuting Attorney of Boise, Idaho, and on October 31, 1946, Hong was held by the Committing Magistrate to answer to the District Court for the crime of assaulting Tom Louie with a deadly weapon with intent to commit murder. An information was filed in said District Court, November 1, 1946, charging Hong with an assault to commit murder. A plea was interposed under I.C.A. Sec. 19-3202, that Fook Lee Hong was insane. The issue was tried to a jury, which returned a verdict of insanity and which was duly filed and entered in said District Court on November 18, 1946. November 20, 1946, the said District Court made and entered its commitment, committing Hong to the State Hospital South at Blackfoot, Idaho, by virtue of his having been found insane as aforesaid.

The Industrial Accident Board considered the stipulated facts and on January 6, 1947, made and entered its findings of fact, rules of law and order dismissing appellant's claim. The findings of fact follow very closely the stipulation. Finding No. 7, among other things, recites as follows: "The sole issue presented is one of law. It is conceded that the accidental injury to claimant Tom Louie arose in the course of his employment by the Bamboo Gardens. The precise issue is whether said accidental injury arose out of such employment." There is no dispute as to the facts.

. . .

We fail to find any evidence that would indicate that Fook Lee Hong, at the time he entered the restaurant at which Tom Louie was employed, or at the time he fired the shot resulting in the accidental injury of said Tom Louie, was looking for the appellant and had a real or imaginary grievance against him. There is no evidence to the effect that at the time Hong entered the restaurant that he knew that Tom Louie was employed there or that he would find him therein. In the conversation he had with various officials, no mention was ever made of Tom Louie and the only manner in which Tom Louie seems to have been connected with his delusion, is that Louie was a member of a tong that Hong asserted was going to bring in hatchet men from Walla Walla to kill him.

It may, however, be of no significance as to whether or not said Hong was looking for Tom Louie at the time he shot him and had either a real or imaginary grievance against him. The fact remains that it was an accidental injury and under the Workmen's Compensation Law, claimant and appellant is entitled to receive compensation as a result of said injury.

. . .

. . . The modern tendency of the decisions, in keeping with the spirit of the law, is to award compensation in all cases where a liberal construction of the statute would justify it. Even in view of this liberal construction, it is not enough for the applicant to say that the accident would not have happened if he had not been engaged in the particular employment or if he had not been at the particular place. He must go further and say that the accident arose because of something he was doing in the course of his employment and because he was exposed by the nature of his employment to some particular danger.

. . .

It would seem that the evidence in this case is such as justifies the conclusion that the injury was the result of a risk to which appellant was subjected in the course of his employment, and to which he would not have been subjected had he not been so employed. Appellant was injured not merely because he was a dishwasher in the Bamboo Gardens' restaurant, but because he was an employee within the Bamboo Gardens restaurant, and engaged in the performance of duties which his employment imposed upon him. It was his employment that placed him in the position and environment wherein he was assaulted and sustained the accidental injury. Appellant did not in any manner provoke the assault and attending accidental injury. At the precise time of the injury he was placed and engaged in the business of his employer. There is nothing to show that the brandishing of the pistol and the firing thereof was a deliberate intention to injure appellant. The intention of the assailant from the record may have been limited to "shooting up the place," and that it was a random shot that struck appellant.

. . .

The order of the board denying compensation constitutes a clear error of law. The order is, therefore, vacated and set aside, with directions to conduct such proceedings as may be necessary in a further consideration of appellant's claim and to make such findings and award as the evidence and law require consistent with the views herein expressed. Costs to appellant.

Marvin v. *Marvin*

18 Cal.3d 660, 557 P.2d 106, 134 Cal.R. 815 (1976)

TOBRINER, Justice.

. . .

Plaintiff avers that in October of 1964 she and defendant "entered into an oral agreement" that while "the parties lived together they would combine their efforts and earnings and would share equally any and all property accumulated as a result of their efforts whether individual or combined." Furthermore, they agreed to "hold themselves out to the general public as husband and wife" and that "plaintiff would further render her services as a companion, homemaker, housekeeper and cook to . . . defendant."

Shortly thereafter plaintiff agreed to "give up her lucrative career as an entertainer [and] singer" in order to "devote her full time to defendant . . . as a companion, homemaker, housekeeper and cook;" in return defendant agreed to "provide for all of plaintiff's financial support and needs for the rest of her life."

Plaintiff alleges that she lived with defendant from October of 1964 through May of 1970 and fulfilled her obligations under the agreement. During this period the parties as a result of their efforts and earnings acquired in defendant's name substantial real and personal property, including motion picture rights worth over $1 million. In May of 1970, however, defendant compelled plaintiff to leave his household. He continued to support plaintiff until November of 1971, but thereafter refused to provide further support.

On the basis of these allegations plaintiff asserts two causes of action. The first, for declaratory relief, asks the court to determine her contract and property rights; the second seeks to impose a constructive trust upon one half of the property acquired during the course of the relationship.

Defendant demurred unsuccessfully, and then answered the complaint. Following extensive discovery and pretrial proceedings, the case came to trial. Defendant renewed his attack on the complaint by a motion to dismiss. . . .

After hearing argument the court granted defendant's motion and entered judgment for defendant. . . . [Plaintiff] appealed from the judgment.

Defendant first and principally relies on the contention that the alleged contract is so closely related to the supposed "immoral" character of the relationship between plaintiff and himself that the enforcement of the contract would violate public policy. He points to cases asserting that a contract between nonmarital partners is unenforceable if it is "involved in" an illicit relationship . . . or made in "contemplation" of such a relationship. . . . A review of the numerous California decisions concerning contracts between nonmarital partners, however, reveals that the courts have not employed such broad and uncertain standards to strike down contracts. The decisions instead disclose a narrower and more precise standard: a contract between nonmarital partners is unenforceable only *to the extent* that it *explicitly* rests upon the immoral and illicit consideration of meretricious sexual services.

. . .

Although the past decisions hover over the issue in the somewhat wispy form of the figures of a Chagall painting, we can abstract from those decisions a clear and simple rule. The fact that a man and woman live together without marriage, and engage in a sexual relationship, does not in itself invalidate agreements between them relating to their earnings, property, or expenses. Neither is such an agreement invalid merely because the parties may have contemplated the creation or continuation of a nonmarital relationship when they entered into it. Agreements between nonmarital partners fail only to the extent that they rest upon a consideration of meretricious sexual services. Thus the rule asserted by defendant, that a contract fails if it is "involved in" or made "in contemplation" of a nonmarital relationship, cannot be reconciled with the decisions.

. . .

In summary, we base our opinion on the principle that adults who voluntarily live together and engage in sexual relations are nonetheless as competent as any other persons to contract respecting their earnings and property rights. Of course, they cannot lawfully contract to pay for the performance of sexual services, for such a contract is, in essence, an agreement for prostitution and unlawful for that reason. But they may agree to pool their earnings and to hold all property acquired during the relationship in accord with the law governing community property; conversely they may agree that each partner's earnings and the property acquired from those earnings remains the separate property of the earning partner. So long as the agreement does not rest upon illicit meretricious consideration, the parties may order their economic affairs as they choose, and no policy precludes the courts from enforcing such agreements.

In the present instance, plaintiff alleges that the parties agreed to pool their earnings, that they contracted to share equally in all property acquired, and that defendant agreed to support plaintiff. The terms of the contract as alleged do not rest upon any unlawful consideration. We therefore conclude that the complaint furnishes a suitable basis upon which the trial court can render declaratory relief. . . . The trial court consequently erred in granting defendant's motion for judgment on the pleadings.

. . .

. . . [W]e believe that the prevalence of nonmarital relationships in modern society and the social acceptance of them, marks this as a time when our courts should by no means apply the doctrine of the unlawfulness of the so-called meretricious relationship to the instant case. As we have explained, the nonenforceability of agreements expressly providing for meretricious conduct rested upon the fact that such conduct, as the word suggests, pertained to and encompassed prostitution. To equate the nonmarital relationship of today to such a subject matter is to do violence to an accepted and wholly different practice.

We are aware that many young couples live together without the solemnization of marriage, in order to make sure that they can successfully later undertake marriage. This trial period, preliminary to marriage, serves as some assurance that the marriage will not subsequently end in dissolution to the harm of both parties. We are aware, as we have stated, of the pervasiveness of nonmarital relationships in other situations.

The mores of the society have indeed changed so radically in regard to cohabitation that we cannot impose a standard based on alleged moral considerations that have apparently been so widely abandoned by so many. Lest we be misunderstood, however, we take this occasion to point out that the structure of society itself largely depends upon the institution of marriage, and nothing we have said in this opinion should be taken to derogate from that institution. The joining of the man and woman in marriage is at once the most socially productive and individually fulfilling relationship that one can enjoy in the course of a lifetime.

. . .

We conclude that the judicial barriers that may stand in the way of a policy based upon the fulfillment of the reasonable expectations of the parties to a nonmarital relationship should be removed. As we have explained, the courts now hold that express agreements will be enforced unless they rest on an unlawful meretricious consideration. We add that in the absence of an express agreement, the courts may look to a variety of other remedies in order to protect the parties' lawful expectations.

The courts may inquire into the conduct of the parties to determine whether that conduct demonstrates an implied contract or implied agreement of partnership or joint venture (see *Estate of Thornton* (1972) 81 Wash.2d 72, 499 P.2d 864), or some other tacit understanding between the parties. The courts may, when appropriate, employ principles of constructive trust (see *Omer v. Omer* (1974) 11 Wash. App. 386, 523 P.2d 957) or resulting trust (see *Hyman v. Hyman* (Tex. Civ. App. 1954)

275 S.W.2d 149). Finally, a nonmarital partner may recover in quantum meruit for the reasonable value of household services rendered less the reasonable value of support received if he can show that he rendered services with the expectation of monetary reward. (See *Hill v. Estate of Westbrook, supra,* 39 Cal.2d 458, 462, 247 P.2d 19.)

Since we have determined that plaintiff's complaint states a cause of action for breach of an express contract, and, as we have explained, can be amended to state a cause of action independent of allegations of express contract, we must conclude that the trial court erred in granting defendant a judgment on the pleadings.

The judgment is reversed and the cause remanded for further proceedings consistent with the views expressed herein.

WRIGHT, C. J., and McCOMB, MOSK, SULLIVAN and RICHARDSON, JJ., concur.

Notes

PREFACE

[1] John G. Wells, *Every Man His Own Lawyer and Business Form Book* (1867), pp. 3–5.

CHAPTER 1

[1] Donald Black, *The Behavior of Law* (1976), p. 2.
[2] H.L.A. Hart, *The Concept of Law* (1961), pp. 89–96.
[3] 408 U.S. 238 (1972). Legal citations, like this one, usually begin with a volume number (here 408). They then give the name of the collection of volumes of which the volume is a part. United States Supreme Court cases are collected in a series which is abbreviated "U.S." Lower federal cases are in series abbreviated "Fed." or "F.Supp." (See note 5.) The second number in the citation is the page number in the given volume (here, 238). Last comes the date.
[4] Richard L. Abel, "A Comparative Theory of Dispute Institutions in Society," *Law & Society Review* 8 : 217, 227 (1973).
[5] Blanks v. Richardson, 439 Fed.2d 1158 (5th Circuit, 1971).
[6] McIlvaine v. Pennsylvania State Police, 454 Pa. 129, 309 Atl.2d 801 (1973). See note 4. Note the abbreviation for the state ("Pa."), which identifies the series of volumes that set out the decisions of the highest court of Pennsylvania. "Atl." stands for "Atlantic"; the reference is to a series of volumes which groups case reports by region of the country. (Pennsylvania, Delaware, and New Jersey are among the states in the Atlantic region.) If there are many volumes in a series, the numbering sometimes starts over, with a second ("2d") or even third series. There are many other tricks and conventions of citation, but those listed in these footnotes are perhaps the most basic.
[7] 415 U.S. 968 (1976).
[8] John H. Merryman, *The Civil Law Tradition* (1969), p. 11.

CHAPTER 2

[1] Lon L. Fuller, *The Morality of Law* (1964), p. 106.

[2] Quoted in Stewart Macaulay, "Private Government," in Leon Lipson and Stanton Wheeler, eds. *Law and Social Science* (in presss).

[3] Frank Morn, *The Eye That Never Sleeps: A History Of The Pinkerton National Detective Agency* (1982).

[4] Goss v. Lopez, 419 U.S. 565 (1975).

[5] Leigh-Wai Doo, "Dispute Settlement in Chinese-American Communities," *American Journal of Comparative Law* 21 : 627, 647–48 (1973).

[6] *Wall Street Journal*, August 6, 1980.

[7] The term is from Robert H. Mnookin and Lewis Kornhauser, "Bargaining in the Shadow of the Law: The Case of Divorce," *Yale Law Journal* 88 : 950 (1979).

[8] Vice Commission of Chicago, *The Social Evil in Chicago* (1911), p. 329.

[9] Richard Maxwell Brown, *Strain of Violence: Historical Studies of American Violence and Vigilantism* (1974), chap. 4.

[10] Odie B. Faulk, *Dodge City: The Most Western Town of All* (1977), p. 152.

[11] Brown, *Strain of Violence*, p. 129.

[12] Ibid., pp. 150–51.

[13] John C. Schneider, *Detroit and the Problem of Order, 1830–1880* (1980) pp. 26–27.

[14] Pauline Maier, "Popular Uprisings and Civil Authority in Eighteenth-Century America," *William and Mary Quarterly*, 3rd ser. 27 : 3–35 (1970).

[15] See Allan G. Bogue, "The Iowa Claim Clubs: Symbol and Substance," *Mississippi Valley Historical Review* 45 : 231 (1958).

[16] Peter A. Munch, "Sociology of Tristan da Cunha," p. 305 in *Results of the Norwegian Scientific Expedition to Tristan da Cunha, 1937–1938*, Erling Christopherson, ed., vol. 1, Oslo, 1946.

[17] Breen v. Kahl, 419 Fed.2d 1034 (1969).

CHAPTER 3

[1] Douglas Greenberg, *Crime and Law Enforcement in the Colony of New York, 1691–1776* (1976), p. 43.

[2] Lawrence M. Friedman, *A History of American Law* (1973), p. 72; on the system in general, see Richard B. Morris, *Government and Labor in Early America* (1946).

[3] Julius Goebel, Jr., "King's Law and Local Custom in Seventeenth-Century New England," *Columbia Law Review* 31 : 416 (1931).

[4] Richard B. Morris, *Studies in the History of American Law*, 2nd ed. (1959), pp. 75–81.

[5] See Herbert A. Johnson, *Imported Eighteenth-Century Law Treatises in American Libraries, 1700–1799* (1978).

[6] See Benjamin H. Hibbard, *A History of the Public Land Policies* (1924; reprint ed. 1965), pp. 1–14.

[7] George Dargo, *Jefferson's Louisiana: Politics and the Clash of Legal Traditions* (1975), p. 156 ff.

[8] Leon Litwack, *North of Slavery: The Negro in the Free States, 1790–1860* (1961), p. 3.

[9] Latimer v. Alexander, 14 Ga. 259 (1853).

[10] See Jerome H. Skolnick, *House of Cards: The Legalization and Control of Casino Gambling* (1978).

[11] See Norma Basch, *In the Eyes of the Law: Women, Marriage and Property in Nineteenth-Century New York* (1982).

[12] Pete Daniel, *The Shadow of Slavery: Peonage in the South, 1901–1969* (1972).

[13] Hibbard, *Public Land Policies*, pp. 102–3.

[14] Ibid., p. 118.

[15] J. Willard Hurst, *Law and Social Process in United States Social History* (1960), p. 69.

[16] Proprietors of the Charles River Bridge v. Proprietors of the Warren Bridge, 11 Pet. 420 (1837).

[17] The case is fully discussed in Stanley I. Kutler, *Privilege and Creative Destruction: The Charles River Bridge Case* (1971).

[18] Oscar and Mary Handlin, *Commonwealth: A Study of the Role of Government in the American Economy, Massachusetts, 1774–1861* (1969), p. 62.

[19] Stuart Bruchey, *The Roots of American Economic Growth, 1607–1861* (1968), p. 132.

CHAPTER 4

[1] Maureen Mileski, "Courtroom Encounters: An Observation Study of a Lower Criminal Court," *Law & Society Review* 5 : 473 (1971).

[2] Beatrice Moulton, "The Persecution and Intimidation of the Low-Income Litigant as Performed by the Small-Claims Court in California," *Stanford Law Review* 21 : 1657, 1662 (1969).

[3] See, generally, John C. Rohnka and Steven Weller, *Small-Claims Courts: A National Examination*, National Center for State Courts (1978).

[4] Judicial Council of California, 1982 Report, pp. 74–79.

[5] Cal. Const., Art. 6, Sec. 11.

[6] Ohio Rev. Code, Sec. 2505.29.

[7] See John A. Stookey, "Creating an Intermediate Court of Appeals: Workload and Policymaking Consequences," in Philip L. Dubois, ed., *The Analysis of Judicial Reform* (1982), p. 153.

[8] Administrative Office of the Illinois Courts, 1978 Annual Report, pp. 104, 106.

[9] Gerhard Casper and Richard A. Posner, *The Workload of the Supreme Court*, American Bar Foundation (1976), pp. 3, 59.

[10] Const., Art. III, Sec. 2 (2).

[11] Arizona v. California, 373 U.S. 546 (1963).

[12] Neb. Rev. Stats., Sec. 24–204.

[13] Karen M. Knab, ed., *Courts of Limited Jurisdiction: A National Survey*, National Institute of Law Enforcement and Criminal Justice (1977), is the source of much of this material.

[14] John H. Merryman, *The Civil Law Tradition* (1969), p. 111.

[15] Sheldon Goldman, "Judicial Appointments to the United States Courts of Appeals," *Wisconsin Law Review* 1967 : 186.

[16] Const., Art. II, Sec. 2 (2).

[17] Cynthia O. Philip, Paul Nejelski, and Aric Press, *Where Do Judges Come From?*, Institute of Judicial Administration (1976), introduction, pp. i, ii.

[18] Harry Kalven, Jr., and Hans Zeisel, *The American Jury* (1966).

[19] See Theodore F. T. Plucknett, *A Concise History of the Common Law*, 5th ed. (1956), pp. 673–707.

[20] Herbert Jacob, *Justice in America: Courts, Lawyers, and the Judicial Process*, 3rd ed. (1978), p. 200.

[21] Richard E. Miller and Austin Sarat, "Grievances, Claims, and Disputes: Assessing the Adversary Culture," *Law & Society Review* 15 : 525, 544 (1981).

[22] See H. Laurence Ross, *Settled Out of Court* (1970), pp. 20–21.

[23] Robert H. Mnookin and Lewis Kornhauser, "Bargaining in the Shadow of the Law: The Case of Divorce," *Yale Law Journal* 88 : 950 (1979).

[24]National Center for State Courts, *State Court Case Load Statistics: Annual Report, 1975* (1979), p. 194.

[25]Judicial Council of California, 1978 Report, p. 100.

[26]Wayne McIntosh, "150 Years of Litigation and Dispute Settlement: A Court Tale," *Law & Society Review* 15 : 823, 838–40, (1980–81).

[27]Packing Company Cases, 105 U.S. 566 (1881).

[28]Robert A. Kagan et al., "The Business of State Supreme Courts, 1870–1970," *Stanford Law Review* 30 : 121 (1977).

[29]See Rita J. Simon, *The Jury: Its Role in American Society* (1980).

[30]Kalven and Zeisel, *The American Jury*, pp. 286–97.

[31]Lawrence M. Friedman et al, "State Supreme Courts: A Century of Style and Citation," *Stanford Law Review* 33 : 773, 785–92 (1981).

[32]S. Sidney Ulmer, "The Political Party Variable in the Michigan Supreme Court," *Journal of Public Law* 11 : 352 (1962).

[33]See, generally, Joel B. Grossman, "Social Backgrounds and Judicial Decision-Making," *Harvard Law Review* 79 : 1551 (1966).

[34]James L. Gibson, "From Simplicity to Complexity: The Development of Theory in the Study of Judicial Behavior," *Political Behavior* 5 : 7 (1983).

[35]John Hagan, "Extra-Legal Attributes and Criminal Sentencing: An Assessment of a Sociological Viewpoint," *Law & Society Review* 8 : 357 (1974).

[36]Ilene H. Nagel, "The Legal/Extra-Legal Controversy: Judicial Decisions in Pretrial Release," *Law & Society Review* 17 : 481 (1983).

[37]See Walter F. Murphy, *Elements of Judicial Strategy* (1964).

[38]Henry R. Glick, *State Courts in State Politics: An Investigation of the Judicial Role* (1971).

[39]See Friedman et al., "State Supreme Courts: A Century of Style and Citation," *Stanford Law Review* 33 : 773 (1981); and John H. Merryman, "Toward a Theory of Citations: An Empirical Study of the Citation Practice of the California Supreme Court in 1950, 1960, and 1970," *Southern California Law Review* 50 : 381 (1977).

CHAPTER 5

[1]George S. Blair and Houston I. Flournoy, *Legislative Bodies in California* (1967), p. 62.

[2]369 U.S. 186 (1962).

[3]James Bryce, *The American Commonwealth*, 2nd ed. (1891), vol. 1, p. 190.

[4]James Driscoll, *California's Legislature* (1976), p. 171.

[5]On this development, see Lawrence M. Friedman and Jack Ladinsky, "Social Change and the Law of Industrial Accidents," *Columbia Law Review*, 67 : 50 (1950).

[6]Quoted in Charles M. Cook, *The American Codification Movement: A Study of Antebellum Legal Reform* (1981), p. 75.

[7]91 Stats. 1647, 1656–57; acts of June 27, 1977, November 14, 1977, November 15, 1977.

[8]Ala. Laws, 1849–50, Act No. 335.

[9]Ala. Laws, 1849–50, Act No. 392.

[10]Ill. Const. 1870, Art. IV, Sec. 22.

[11]For the background of the Sherman Act, see William Letwin, *Law and Economic Policy in America: The Evolution of the Sherman Antitrust Act* (1965).

[12]Ohio Code, Sec. 3715.59.

[13]443 U.S. 193 (1979).

[14]McBoyle v. United States, 283 U.S. 25 (1931).

[15]59 Stat. 536, act of September 24, 1945.

[16]Ohio Code, Sec. 3763.01(A).

[17] Karl Llewellyn, "Remarks on the Theory of Appellate Decision and the Rules or Canons about How Statutes Are To Be Construed," *Vanderbilt Law Review* 3 : 395 (1950).

[18] "The Re-evaluation of the Use of Legislative History in the Federal Courts," *Columbia Law Review* 52 : 125 (1952).

[19] Quoted in Harry W. Jones, John M. Kernochan, and Arthur W. Murphy, *Legal Method: Cases and Text Materials* (1980), p. 432.

[20] Robert A. Dahl, *Pluralist Democracy in the United States: Conflict and Consent* (1967), p. 24.

[21] U.S.C.A., Tit. 2, Sec. 267.

[22] John A. Ferejohn, *Pork Barrel Politics: Rivers and Harbors Legislation, 1947–1968* (1974), p. 2.

[23] See, in general, James Buchanan and Gordon Tullock, *The Calculus of Consent* (1962).

CHAPTER 6

[1] Tenn. Code, Sec. 63-1803(1).

[2] 46 Fed. Reg. 38,285; 56,043 (1981).

[3] J. Willard Hurst, *Law and Markets in United States History* (1982), p. 107.

[4] Leonard D. White, *The Federalists: A Study in Administrative History* (1948), p. 177.

[5] Quoted in Leonard D. White, *The Jacksonians: A Study in Administrative History, 1829–61* (1956), p. 550.

[6] Conn. Stats. 1854, p. 240.

[7] Spencer L. Kimball, *Insurance and Public Policy* (1960).

[8] Conn. Stats. 1866, p. 182.

[9] Ill. Laws, 1871–72, pp. 618, 635, 769.

[10] 94 U.S. 113 (1876).

[11] 24 Stats. 379, act of February 4, 1887.

[12] N.J. Laws, 1851, p. 37.

[13] N.H. Laws, 1858, Chap. 1777.

[14] Gabriel Kolko, *Railroads and Regulation, 1877–1916* (1965).

[15] 78 Stats. 241, Tit. VII, 253, 258, act of July 2, 1964.

[16] Eugene Bardach and Robert A. Kagan, *Going by the Book: The Problem of Regulatory Unreasonableness* (1982), pp. 11–12.

[17] Texas Nat. Resources Code, Sec. 85.046(10).

[18] Cal. Bus. and Prof. Code, Sec.'s 3010, 3011.

[19] Marver Bernstein, *Regulating Business by Independent Commission* (1955).

[20] David Serber, "Resolution or Rhetoric: Managing Complaints in the California Department of Insurance," in Laura Nader, ed., *No Access to Law: Alternatives to the American Judicial System* (1980), pp. 317, 339.

[21] 12 U.S.C.A., Sec. 45.

[22] *New York Times*, October 31, 1981, p. 10.

[23] 92 Stats. 1101 (1978).

[24] 38 U.S.C.A., Sec. 211a.

[25] On the development of rules of standing, see Richard B. Stewart, "The Reformation of American Administrative Law," *Harvard Law Review* 88 : 1669, 1723–1747 (1978).

[26] 295 U.S. 495 (1935).

[27] William H. Allen, quoted in Walter Gellhorn, Clark Byse, and Peter L. Strauss, *Administrative Law: Cases and Comments*, 7th ed. (1979), p. 343.

CHAPTER 7

[1] Leonard D. White, *The Federalists: A Study in Administrative History* (1948), p. 123.

[2] James S. Young, *The Washington Community, 1800–28* (1966), pp. 28, 31.

[3] Mary K. Bonsteel Tachau, *Federal Courts in the Early Republic: Kentucky, 1789–1816* (1978).

[4] Thomas W. Church, Jr., et al., *Justice Delayed: The Pace of Litigation in Urban Trial Courts*, National Center for State Courts (1978).

[5] Ibid., p. 83.

[6] See Jack W. Peltason, *Fifty-Eight Lonely Men: Southern Federal Judges and School Desegregation* (1961).

[7] Edwards v. California, 314 U.S. 160 (1941).

[8] Const., Art. IV, Sec. 2.

[9] Const., Art. IV, Sec. 2.

[10] See Paul Finkelman, *An Imperfect Union: Slavery, Federalism, and Comity* (1981).

[11] Paul v. Virginia, 75 U.S. 168 (1868).

[12] See in general, Gilman M. Ostrander, *Nevada: The Great Rotten Borough* (1966).

[13] Lawrence M. Friedman, *A History of American Law* (1973), p. 439.

[14] See Jerome H. Skolnick, *House of Cards: The Legalization and Control of Casino Gambling* (1978).

[15] 247 U.S. 251 (1918).

[16] 156 U.S. 1 (1895).

[17] 379 U.S. 294 (1964).

[18] Bibb v. Navajo Freight Lines, Inc., 359 U.S. 520 (1959); Southern Pacific Co. v. Arizona, 325 U.S. 761 (1945).

[19] Dean Milk Co. v. Madison, 340 U.S. 349 (1951).

[20] Philadelphia v. New Jersey, 437 U.S. 617 (1978).

[21] Baldwin v. Montana Fish & Game Commission, 436 U.S. 471 (1978).

[22] 64 Stat. 1100, act of September 30, 1950.

[23] 79 Stat. 27, act of April 11, 1965.

[24] 82 Stat. 197, act of June 19, 1968.

CHAPTER 8

[1] See Craft v. Elder & Johnston Co., 34 Ohio Abs. 603, 38 N.E.2d 416 (1941).

[2] Stewart Macaulay, "Non-Contractual Relations in Business: A Preliminary Study," *American Sociological Review* 28 : 55 (1963).

[3] Farwell v. Boston & Worcester Rr. Corp, 45 Mass. 49 (1842).

[4] See Lawrence M. Friedman and Jack Ladinsky, "Social Change and the Law of Industrial Accidents," *Columbia Law Review* 64 : 50 (1964).

[5] Mark A. Peterson and George L. Priest, *The Civil Jury: Trends in Trials and Verdicts, Cook County, Illinois, 1960–1979* (1982), p. 13.

[6] Marvin B. Sussman, Judith N. Cates, and David T. Smith, *The Family and Inheritance* (1970), p. 63.

[7] See generally Nelson Blake, *The Road to Reno: A History of Divorce in the United States* (1962).

CHAPTER 9

[1] Ga. Code, Sec. 16-11-61.

[2] E. Adamson Hoebel, *The Law of Primitive Man: A Study in Comparative Legal Dynamics* (1954), p. 28.

[3] Eric H. Monkkonen, "A Disorderly People? Urban Order in the Nineteenth and Twentieth Centuries," *Journal of American History* 68:539 (1981).

[4] Rhode Isl. Stats., Sec. 20-7-10.

[5] Fla. Stats. Ann., Sec. 370.12.

[6] U.S. Department of Justice, Bureau of Justice Statistics, *Criminal Victimization of California Residents* (1981), p. 45.

[7] Essex Institute, *Records and Files of the Quarterly Court of Essex County, Massachusetts, vol. 1, 1636–56* (1911), p. 380.

[8] Mark T. Connelly, *The Response to Prostitution in the Progressive Era* (1980), p. 3.

[9] Ark. Laws, 1907, no. 380.

[10] 36 Stats. 825, act of June 25, 1910.

[11] 38 Stats. 785, act of December 17, 1914.

[12] On the upsurge of interest in victimless crime, see Lawrence M. Friedman, "History, Social Policy, and Criminal Justice," in David J. Rothman and Stanton Wheeler, eds., *Social History and Social Policy* (1981), p. 203.

[13] See John Kaplan and Jerome H. Skolnick, *Criminal Justice: Introductory Cases and Materials* (1982), pp. 105–9.

[14] Vera Institute of Justice, *Felony Arrests*, rev. ed. (1981), p. 3.

[15] Tex. Code Crim. Proc., Art. 19.06.

[16] Minn. Rules Crim. Proc., Rule 26.02(6).

[17] See Laurence J. Severance and Elizabeth F. Loftus, "Improving the Ability of Jurors to Comprehend and Apply Criminal Jury Instructions," *Law & Society Review* 17 : 153 (1982).

[18] Harry Kalven, Jr., and Hans Zeisel, *The American Jury* (1966), p. 56.

[19] Rita J. Simon, *The Jury: Its Role in American Society* (1980), p. 70.

[20] Michael O. Finkelstein, "A Statistical Study of Guilty Plea Practices in the Federal Courts," *Harvard Law Review* 89 : 293 (1975).

[21] Herbert Jacob, *Urban Justice: Law and Order in American Cities* (1973), p. 103.

[22] See Anne M. Heinz and Wayne A. Kerstetter, "Pretrial Settlement Conference: Evaluation of a Reform in Plea Bargaining," *Law & Society Review* 13 : 349 (1979).

[23] Milton Heumann and Colin Loftin, "Mandatory Sentencing and the Abolition of Plea Bargaining: The Michigan Felony Firearm Statute," *Law & Society Review* 13 : 392, 424–26 (1979).

[24] John H. Langbein, "The Criminal Trial Before the Lawyers," *University of Chicago Law Review*, 45 : 263 (1978); Lawrence M. Friedman and Robert V. Percival, *The Roots of Justice: Crime and Punishment in Alameda County, California, 1870–1910* (1981), p. 194.

[25] Friedman and Percival, *Roots of Justice*, pp. 176–78.

[26] Raymond Moley, *Politics and Criminal Prosecution* (1930), pp. 159–64.

[27] Wilbur R. Miller, *Cops and Bobbies: Police Authority in New York and London, 1830–1870* (1977), p. 16.

[28] See Robert M. Fogelson, *Big City Police* (1977).

[29] Vera Institute, *Felony Arrests*, p. 8.

[30] See David J. Rothman, *The Discovery of the Asylum: Social Order and Disorder in the New Republic* (1971).

[31] Friedman, "History, Social Policy, and Criminal Justice," pp. 203, 209.

[32] Ibid., p. 207.

[33] See Austin Turk, *Criminality and Legal Order* (1969), p. 165.

[34] Alfred Blumstein et al., *Research on Sentencing: The Search for Reform*, vol. I (1983), pp. 88 ff.

[35] 384 U.S. 436 (1966).

[36] 372 U.S. 335 (1963).

[37] Kaplan and Skolnick, *Criminal Justice*, pp. 351–58.

[38] See Ronald Berkman, *Opening the Gates: The Rise of the Prisoners' Movement* (1979).

[39] Malcolm Feeley, *Court Reform on Trial: Why Simple Solutions Fail*, Twentieth Century Fund (1983), p. 208.

[40] Ibid., p. 128.

[41] See H. Laurence Ross, *Deterring the Drinking Driver* (1981), for American and foreign examples.

[42] Friedman and Percival, *Roots of Justice*, p. 325.

CHAPTER 10

[1] 249 U.S. 45 (1919).

[2] 1 Cranch 137 (1803).

[3] 118 U.S. 356 (1886).

[4] 372 U.S. 335 (1963).

[5] 337 U.S. 1 (1949).

[6] Laurence H. Tribe, *American Constitutional Law* (1978), p. 13.

[7] Fletcher M. Green, *Constitutional Development in the South Atlantic States, 1776–1860* (1966), pp. 285–86.

[8] See, for example, Indiana Const. 1851, Art. IV, Sec. 21.

[9] Lawrence M. Friedman, *A History of American Law* (1973), p. 312.

[10] Cal. Const., Art. 2, Sec. 8.

[11] Cal. Const., Art. 13A, approved by the voters June 6, 1978.

[12] 1 Cranch 137 (1803).

[13] 60 U.S. 383 (1857).

[14] A masterful and exhaustive treatment of the case is Don E. Fehrenbacher, *The Dred Scott Case: Its Significance in American Law and Politics* (1978).

[15] 6 Cranch 87 (1810).

[16] 4 Wheat. 518 (1819).

[17] Charles Fairman, *Mr. Justice Miller and the Supreme Court, 1862–1890* (1939), p. 62.

[18] 198 U.S. 45 (1905).

[19] William Swindler, *Court and Constitution in the 20th Century: The Old Legality* (1969), pp. 344–45.

[20] 295 U.S. 495 (1935).

[21] 348 U.S. 483 (1955).

[22] Griswold v. Connecticut, 381 U.S. 479 (1965); Roe v. Wade, 410 U.S. 113 (1973).

[23] 408 U.S. 238 (1972).

[24] *New York Times*, October 30, 1981, p. 10, col. 1.

[25] 290 U.S. 398 (1934).

[26] 1 Stat. 596, act of July 14, 1798.

[27] Va. Code, 1849, Tit. 54, Chap. 198, Sec. 22; Russel B. Nye, *Fettered Freedom* (1963), p. 156.

[28] Civil Rights Cases, 109 U.S. 3 (1883).

[29] 98 U.S. 145 (1878).

[30] See Stanley I. Kutler, *The American Inquisition: Justice and Injustice in the Cold War* (1982).

[31] See Peter Irons, *Justice at War: The Story of the Japanese-American Internment Cases* (1983).

[32] 7 Pet. 243 (1833).

[33] 302 U.S. 319 (1937).

[34] 110 U.S. 516 (1884).

[35] Okla. Stats., Sec. 1040.23.

[36] 354 U.S. 476 (1957).

[37] William Cohen and John Kaplan, *The Bill of Rights* (1976), p. 94.

[38] Paul S. Boyer, *Purity in Print: Book Censorship in America* (1968), p. 136.

[39] See, for example, A Book Named "John Cleland's Memoirs of a Woman of Pleasure" v. Attorney General of Massachusetts, 383 U.S. 413 (1966).

[40] Jenkins v. Georgia, 418 U.S. 153 (1974).

[41] 422 U.S. 205 (1975).

[42] 219 U.S. 219 (1911).

[43] William Cohen, "Negro Involuntary Servitude in the South, 1865–1940: A Preliminary Analysis," *Journal of Southern History* 42 : 31 (1976).

[44] 347 U.S. 483 (1954).

[45] David S. Clark, "Judicial Protection of the Constitution in Latin America," *Hastings Constitutional Law Quarterly* 2 : 405 (1975).

[46] An English translation of this decision can be found in *John Marshall Journal of Practice and Procedure* 9 : 605 (1976).

[47] Mauro Cappelletti, *Judicial Review in the Contemporary World* (1971), pp. 64–65.

CHAPTER 11

[1] On the effectiveness of Prohibition, contrast Andrew Sinclair's *Prohibition: The Era of Excess* (1962), with J. C. Burnham, "New Perspectives on the Prohibition 'Experiment' of the 1920s," *Journal of Social History* 2 : 51 (1968).

[2] John Kaplan, *Marijuana: The New Prohibition* (1970), p. 25.

[3] Marvin B. Sussman, Judith N. Cates, and David T. Smith, *The Family and Inheritance* (1970), p. 64.

[4] Uniform Commercial Code, Sec. 2-302.

[5] "Legal Knowledge of Michigan Citizens," *Michigan Law Review* 71 : 1463 (1973).

[6] Martha Williams and Jay Hall, "Knowledge of the Law in Texas: Socioeconomic and Ethnic Differences," *Law & Society Review* 7 : 99 (1972).

[7] June Tapp and Lawrence Kohlberg, "Developing Senses of Law and Legal Justice," *Journal of Social Issues* 27 : 65 (1971).

[8] William J. Chambliss, "Types of Deviance and the Effectiveness of Legal Sanctions," *Wisconsin Law Review* 1967 : 703.

[9] 408 U.S. 238 (1972).

[10] See Gordon Tullock, "Does Punishment Deter Crime?" *Public Interest* 36 : 103 (Summer 1974).

[11] Herbert L. Packer, *The Limits of the Criminal Sanction* (1968), p. 39.

[12] See, for example, George Antunes and A. Lee Hunt, "The Impact of Certainty and Severity of Punishment on Levels of Crime in American States: An Extended Analysis," *Journal of Criminal Law & Criminology* 64 : 487 (1973).

[13] J. Chaiken, M. Lawless, K. Stevenson, *The Impact of Police Activity on Crime: Robberies on the New York City Subway System*, Rand Institute, New York (1974), p. 23.

[14] See H. Laurence Ross, "Law, Science and Accidents: The British Road Safety Act of 1967," *Journal of Legal Studies* 2 : 1, 76 (1973).

[15] Malcolm Feeley, *The Process Is the Punishment* (1979), p. 199.

[16] Ted R. Gurr, *Rogues, Rebels, and Reformers: A Political History of Urban Crime and Conflict* (1976).

[17] H. Laurence Ross, "The Neutralization of Severe Penalties: Some Traffic Law

Studies," *Law & Society Review* 10 : 403–4 (1976); see also Ross's book, *Deterring the Drinking Driver* (1981).

[18] See Tom Wicker, "Making Things Better," *New York Times*, July 13, 1982, p. 27, col. 8.

[19] Roger Lane, *Violent Death in the City: Suicide, Accident and Murder in Nineteenth-Century Philadelphia* (1979), p. 79.

[20] *Statistical Abstract of the United States, 1981*, p. 177.

[21] Jack K. Williams, *Vogues in Villainy: Crime and Retribution in Ante-Bellum South Carolina* (1959), p. 100.

[22] Michael S. Hindus, *Prison and Plantation: Crime, Justice, and Authority in Massachusetts and South Carolina, 1767–1878* (1980), pp. 156–58.

[23] 408 U.S. 238 (1972).

[24] 428 U.S. 153 (1976).

CHAPTER 12

[1] Victor Eisner, *The Delinquency Label: The Epidemiology of Juvenile Delinquency* (1969), p. 105.

[2] Johannes Feest, "Compliance with Legal Regulations: Observation of Stop Sign Behavior," *Law & Society Review* 2 : 447 (1968).

[3] Lionel I. Dannick, "Influence of an Anonymous Stranger on a Routine Decision to Act or Not to Act: An Experiment in Conformity," *Sociological Quarterly* 14 : 127 (1973).

[4] See C. W. Kohfeld and T. W. Likens, "Mass Compliance and Social Interaction: A Dynamic Formulation," *Law and Policy Quarterly* 4 : 353 (1982).

[5] Alan Hyde, "The Concept of Legitimation in the Sociology of Law," *Wisconsin Law Review* 1983 : 380.

[6] Arthur H. Miller, "Political Issues and Trust in Government: 1964–1970," *American Political Science Review* 68 : 951 (1974).

[7] See Austin Sarat, "Support for the Legal System: An Analysis of Knowledge, Attitudes, and Behavior," *American Politics Quarterly* 3 : 3 (1975).

[8] Harry V. Ball, "Social Structure and Rent-Control Violations," *American Journal of Sociology* 65 : 598 (1960).

[9] Charles R. Tittle and Alan R. Rowe, "Moral Appeal, Sanction Threat, and Deviance: An Experimental Test," *Social Problems* 20 : 488 (1973).

[10] See, for example, H.L.A. Hart, "Positivism and the Separation of Law and Morals," *Harvard Law Review* 71 : 593 (1958).

[11] 410 U.S. 113 (1973).

[12] 36 Stats. 825, act of June 25, 1910.

CHAPTER 13

[1] Anton-Hermann Chroust, *The Rise of the Legal Profession in America*, vol. 1 (1965), p. 72.

[2] Gerard W. Gawalt, *The Promise of Power: The Emergence of the Legal Profession in Massachusetts, 1760–1840* (1979), p. 14.

[3] B. Peter Pashigian, "The Number and Earnings of Lawyers: Some Recent Findings," *American Bar Foundation Research Journal* 1978 : 51.

[4] Murray L. Schwartz, "The Reorganization of the Legal Profession," *Texas Law Review* 58 : 1269–70 (1980).

[5] Ibid., p. 1275.

[6] *New York Times*, April 2, 1982, p. 31, col. 3.

[7] Lawrence M. Friedman, *A History of American Law* (1973), p. 270.

[8] Claude M. Fuess, *Daniel Webster* (1930), vol. 1, p. 232.

[9] Merle Curti, *The Making of an American Community* (1959), p. 23.

[10] On the practice relating to marine insurance, see Julius Goebel, Jr., ed., *The Law Practice of Alexander Hamilton: Documents and Commentary*, vol. 2 (1969), pp. 391 ff.

[11] Quintin Johnstone and Dan Hopson, Jr., *Lawyers and Their Work: An Analysis of the Legal Profession in the United States and England* (1967), p. 35.

[12] James B. Stewart, Jr., "Inside the World's Largest Law Firm," *American Lawyer*, January 1980, p. 21.

[13] Erwin O. Smigel's book, *The Wall Street Lawyer: Professional Organization Man?* (1964), is one exception.

[14] Marc Galanter, "Mega-law and Mega-lawyering in the Contemporary United States," in R. Dingwall and P. Lewis, *The Sociology of the Professions: Lawyers, Doctors and Others* (1983), p. 152.

[15] John P. Heinz and Edward O. Laumann, *Chicago Lawyers: The Social Structure of the Bar* (1982), pp. 43–44.

[16] *New York Times*, November 3, 1979, p. 23, col. 1.

[17] Bradwell v. State, 83 U.S. 130 (1873).

[18] Donna Fossum, *Women in the Legal Profession: A Study of Social Change*, Ph.D. thesis, State University of New York at Buffalo (1981), pp. 51, 77.

[19] Maxwell Bloomfield, *American Lawyers in a Changing Society, 1776–1876* (1976), pp. 302–39.

[20] Allan P. Sindler, *Bakke, DeFunis, and Minority Admissions: The Quest for Equal Opportunity* (1978), p. 141.

[21] Heinz and Laumann, *Chicago Lawyers*, pp. 186, 190.

[22] For a description of apprenticeship, see Chroust, *Rise of the Legal Profession*, vol. 2 (1965), pp. 174–75.

[23] J. W. Shuckers, *The Life and Public Services of Salmon Portland Chase* (1874), pp. 30–31.

[24] Edward S. Martin, *The Life of Joseph Hodges Choate*, vol. 1 (1920), p. 81.

[25] See, in general, Robert B. Stevens, "Two Cheers for 1870: The American Law School," in Donald Fleming and Bernard Bailyn, eds., *Law in American History* (1971), p. 405.

[26] Arthur E. Sutherland, *The Law at Harvard: A History of Ideas and Men, 1817–1967* (1967), pp. 149–50.

[27] On legal education in general, see Robert B. Stevens, *Law School: Legal Education in America from the 1850s to the 1980s* (1983).

[28] Frances K. Zemans and Victor G. Rosenblum; *The Making of a Public Profession* (1981), p. 101.

[29] Jerold S. Auerbach, *Unequal Justice: Lawyers and Social Change in Modern America* (1976), pp. 65–66, 239.

[30] Ibid., p. 287.

[31] Goldfarb v. Virginia State Bar, 421 U.S. 579 (1976).

[32] 433 U.S. 350 (1977).

[33] Johnstone and Hopson, *Lawyers and Their Work*, p. 72.

[34] Deborah L. Rhode, "Why the ABA Bothers: A Functional Perspective on Professional Codes," *Texas Law Review* 59 : 689, 718 (1981).

[35] Douglas Rosenthal, *Lawyers and Clients: Who's In Charge?* (1974), p. 100.

[36] Chroust, *Rise of the Legal Profession*, vol. 2, p. 127.

[37] Stephen Barlas, "Where Have All the Lawyers Gone?" *National Law Journal*, January 19, 1981, p. 13.

[38] Heinz Eulau and John D. Sprague, *Lawyers in Politics: A Study in Professional Convergence* (1964); Green, Schmidhauser, Berg, and Brady, "Lawyers in Congress:

A New Look-at Some Old Assumptions," *Western Political Quarterly* 26 : 440 (1973).

[39]O'Connor, Engstrom, Green, and Kim, "The Political Behavior of Lawyers in the Louisiana House of Representatives," *Louisiana Law Review* 39 : 45 (1978).

[40]Richard W. Rabinowitz, "Law and the Social Process in Japan," *Transactions of the Asiatic Society of Japan*, 3rd ser., vol. 10, 1968, pp. 5, 49–50.

[41]*Wall Street Journal*, February 9, 1981, p. 14.

[42]Kevin Tierney, *Darrow: A Biography* (1979).

[43]372 U.S. 335 (1963).

[44]John M. Maguire, *The Lance of Justice* (1928), pp. 3, 240.

[45]Joel F. Handler, Ellen J. Hollingsworth, and Howard S. Erlanger, *Lawyers and the Pursuit of Legal Rights* (1978), p. 70.

[46]*New York Times*, July 20, 1982, p. 30, col. 1.

CHAPTER 14

[1]J. Willard Hurst, *Law and Economic Growth: The Legal History of the Lumber Industry in Wisconsin, 1836–1915* (1964).

[2]Ibid., p. 190.

[3]Ibid., p. 607.

[4]Herbert S. Klein, *Slavery in the Americas: A Comparative Study of Virginia and Cuba* (1967), p. 43.

[5]Va. Laws, 1662, Act XII.

[6]Va. Laws, 1667, Act III.

[7]Ira Berlin, *Slaves Without Masters: The Free Negro in the Antebellum South* (1975), pp. 372–74.

[8]See Pete Daniel, *The Shadow of Slavery: Peonage in the South 1901–69* (1972); Daniel A. Novak, *The Wheel of Servitude, Black Forced Labor After Slavery* (1978).

[9]109 U.S. 3 (1883).

[10]See, in general, C. Vann Woodward, *The Strange Career of Jim Crow*, 2nd ed. (1966).

[11]163 U.S. 537 (1896).

[12]Ark. Stats. 1903, Sec. 5901.

[13]238 U.S. 347 (1915).

[14]*Voting: 1961 Commission on Civil Rights Report*, p. 143.

[15]347 U.S. 483 (1954); on the background of the case, see Richard Kluger, *Simple Justice* (1976).

[16]J. Harvie Wilkinson III, *From Brown to Bakke: The Supreme Court and School Integration, 1954–1978* (1979), p. 65.

[17]Swann v. Charlotte-Mecklenburg Board of Education, 402 U.S. 1 (1971).

[18]Heart of Atlanta Motel, Inc. v. U.S., 379 U.S. 241 (1964); Katzenbach v. McClung, 379 U.S. 294 (1964).

[19]Regents of the University of California v. Bakke, 438 U.S. 267 (1978).

[20]Wis. Const., Art. 1, Sec. 18.

[21]Quoted in Leonard J. Arrington and Davis Bitton, *The Mormon Experience* (1979), ch. 9.

[22]12 Stats. 501, act of July 1, 1862.

[23]98 U.S. 145 (1878).

[24]406 U.S. 205 (1975).

[25]Katz v. Superior Court of San Francisco, 73 Cal.App.3d 952, 141 Cal. R. 234 (1977).

[26]Joseph Gusfield, *Symbolic Crusade: Status Politics and the American Temperance Movement* (1963).

[27]California Penal Code, sec. 307 (1881).

²⁸ David F. Musto, *The American Disease: Origins of Narcotic Control* (1973), pp. 219–20.

²⁹ See John Kaplan, *The Hardest Drug: Heroin and Public Policy* (1983).

³⁰ 18 Cal.3d 660, 557 P.2d 106, 134 Cal. R. 815 (1976).

³¹ Bureau of the Census, *Marital Status and Living Arrangements:* March 1978, Current Population Reports, Series P-20, no. 338, May 1979, p. 3, Table D.

³² *National Law Journal*, April 16, 1979, p. 14.

CHAPTER 15

¹ *U.S. News & World Report*, December 20, 1982, p. 58.

² Bayless Manning, "Hyperlexis: Our National Disease," *Northwestern University Law Review* 71:767 (1977).

³ *U.S. News & World Report*, December 20, 1982, p. 58.

⁴ Joel Grossman and Austin Sarat, "Litigation in the Federal Courts: A Comparative Perspective," *Law & Society Review* 9 : 321 (1975).

⁵ David S. Clark, "Adjudication to Administration: A Statistical Analysis of Federal District Courts in the Twentieth Century," *Southern California Law Review* 55 : 65, 86–88 (1981).

⁶ Wayne McIntosh, "150 Years of Litigation and Dispute Settlement: A Court Tale," *Law & Society Review* 15 : 823 (1981); Lawrence M. Friedman and Robert V. Percival, "A Tale of Two Courts: Litigation in Alameda and San Benito Counties," *Law & Society Review* 10 : 267 (1976).

⁷ 22 Stats. 209, act of July 2, 1890.

⁸ See Lawrence M. Friedman, "The Six Million Dollar Man: Litigation and Rights Consciousness in Modern America," *Maryland Law Review* 39 : 661, 672 (1980).

⁹ Laura Nader, ed., *No Access to Law: Alternatives to the American Judicial System* (1980), p. 5.

¹⁰ See Janice A. Roehl and Royer F. Cook, "The Neighborhood Justice Centers Field Test," in Roman Tomasic and Malcolm M. Feeley, eds. *Neighborhood Justice: Assessment of an Emerging Idea* (1982), p. 91.

¹¹ *Washington Post*, August 18, 1980, p. 1, col. 2; *New York Times*, June 16, 1980, p. 16, col. 2; *New York Times*, November 3, 1979, p. 44, col. 4.

¹² *US News & World Report*, December 20, 1982, p. 58.

¹³ Friedman, "Six Million Dollar Man," p. 667.

¹⁴ Nader, *No Access to Law*, p. 5.

Index

California Supreme Court, and cohabitation,
276–68
Canada, 123, 131
  law of, 15
canon law, 70
canons of construction, 100–102
capital punishment, *see* death penalty
Cardozo, Benjamin, 192
Carnal Knowledge, 195
Carter, Hughes and Dwight, 235
case-law, 16
case-method, in legal education, 242
Castro, Fidel, 251
chancellor, and development of equity, 70
charitable foundations, 150
Charles River Bridge case, 52
charters, of corporations, 151
Chase, Salmon P., admission to bar, 241
Chessman, Caryl, 216
Chicago, Illinois, 145, 235
  regulation of vice, 26
  survey of lawyers, 240
Chicanos, *see* Mexican-Americans
child labor laws, 133
children, knowledge of law, 205
Chinese-Americans, 33, 273
  and drug laws in California, 262
  rights of, 56
Chinese Benevolent Associations, 23, 24
Choate, Joseph Hodges, 242
Church of Jesus Christ of the Latter-Day
  Saints, *see* Mormons
civic-mindedness, 222
Civil Aeronautics Board, 107, 280
civil disobedience, 227–28
civil law, 15–17, 140
  judiciary, 64
  procedures, 69–70
  survivals in Western states, 44
civil liberties, in 19th century, 191
  see also Bill of Rights
Civil Rights Act of 1875, 262
Civil Rights Act of 1964, 99, 103, 266, 291–
  92, 302–4
  and commerce clause, 134–35
  and litigation rate, 284–85
civil rights,
  impact of laws, 220
  in 19th century, 191
  in post-Civil War South, 260–61
  struggle for, 265
civil rights, *see also* race
Civil Rights Cases, 262

civil rights movement, 197
Civil War, 45, 54, 260
  and constitutional change, 186
claim clubs, on frontier, 30
claims of right, 13–14
Cleland, John, 194
Code Napoleon, 16
Code of Civil Procedure (Field Code), 92
codification, in civil law, 16
cohabitation, legal status of, 275–78
Coke, Lord, 40–41
Colombia, judicial review in, 197
colonial period, 36–42
  strong ties with England in 18th Century,
    41
  and victimless crime, 161
Commentaries on American Law, 141
Commentaries on the Laws of England, 42,
    140, 141, 146, 242
commerce clause, 134–36
  in 20th century, 134–35
commercial law, 143
  in 18th century, 41
common-law, characteristics of, 16
  core of American law, 47
  contrasted with equity, 70–71
  doctrines of "estates" in land, 147
  lack of uniformity, 92
  procedures, 68–70
  spread of, 16–17
community, and informality of law, 31–32
community property system, 44, 150
Comstock law, 162
conscience, as factor in legal behavior, 221
  strength of, 226
  see also legitimacy; morality
Confederate States, law of, 29
Conference of Commissioners on Uniform
  State Laws, 93
conflict resolution, 9–10
Congress, control over administrative agencies, 118
  creates new rights, 285
  delegation by, 96–97
  as institution, 105–6
  and judicial review of agencies, 118–19
  private legislation, 94, 183
  quality of legislators, 90
  and victimless crime, 162
Connecticut, 111
  bank regulation, 111
  railroad regulation, 111–12
conservation, and criminal justice, 159

Massachusetts, 93, 194, 240
  budget in late 18th century, 53
  death penalty in, 214
  lacks courts of equity, 41
  Land Court, 64
  lawyers in, 232
  selection of judges, 65
Massachusetts Bay,
  criminal justice in, 31–32
  inheritance rules, 40
  law as deviating from English patterns, 38–39
  punishment of victimless crimes, 161
McCarthy, Joseph, 191
medical malpractice, 279, 284
Memoirs of a Woman of Pleasure, see Fanny Hill
Mexico, 44, 131
Mexican-Americans, and laws against marijuana, 272
Michigan,
  court of claims, 64
  decision-making in high court, 81–82
  high dissent rate, 80
  legal knowledge in, 203–4
  plea bargaining in, 167–68
Mileski, Maureen, 58
Minnesota, 165, 278
  moratorium law, 190
Miranda v. Arizona, 175
misdemeanors, 156
Mississippi, 65, 260
  married women's rights, 48
Missouri, 64
Missouri Compromise, 260
Missouri plan, 66
Montana, 92, 127, 136
  vigilantes, 27
morality,
  impact on legal behavior, 220–21, 222
  relationship to law, 228–30, 271–73
  strength of, 274
Mormons, and the law, 29, 56, 227, 273
  persecuted because of polygamy, 269–70
  Supreme Court ruling, 191
Morrill Act, 49, 269–70
Morton, Thomas, 231
Mountain States Legal Foundation, 253
Munn v. Illinois, 112
murder, 155
  frequency in United States, 213

Nader, Laura, 286
Nagel, Ilene H., 82–83

Napoleonic Code, 44
National Association for the Advancement of Colored People, 264
National Industrial Recovery Act, 120, 188
National Labor Relations Board, 109, 114
National Motor Vehicle Theft Act, 100
National Rifle Association, 105
native Americans, rights of, 56
Natural Resources Defense Council, 253
Nebraska, 139
  Supreme Court, 63
negligence, concept of, 145
negotiable instruments, 143
Negotiable Instruments Law, 93
Nehru, Jawaharlal, 251
Neighborhood Justice Centers, 286
"neovigilantes," 27
Nevada,
  gambling in, 47, 132
  legalization of prostitution, 26
  and "market" for laws, 131–32
New Deal, 55
  and administrative regulation, 113–14
  and child labor laws, 133
  and Constitutional change, 188–89
  effect on government, 136
New Hampshire, railroad charters, 112–13
New Jersey, 47, 240, 278
  amount of "law" in, 281
  attitude of judges, 85
  citation patterns, 86
  court reform, 63
  railroad charters, 112–13
  regulation of landfill companies, 135
New Orleans, 162
New York, 65, 240
  divorce laws of, 132–33
  Dutch influence on, 36–37
  election of judges, 67
  harsh drug laws, 177
  and indeterminate sentencing, 171
  marine insurance law, 46
  married women's rights, 48
  merges law and equity, 64
  property qualification in, 146
  rejects codes, 92
  small claims courts, 59
  slavery in, 38
  strict divorce laws, 150
  trial courts, 59
New York City,
  bail decisions, 82–83
  behavior of lawyers, 247
  corruption at the bar, 245